D1541997

Rebel against Injustice

Missouri Biography Series
William E. Foley, Editor

Rebel against Injustice

The Life of Frank P. O'Hare

Peter H. Buckingham

University of Missouri Press
Columbia and London

Library of Congress Cataloging-in-Publication Data

Buckingham, Peter H., 1948–
    Rebel against injustice : the life of Frank P. O'Hare / Peter H.
Buckingham.
        p.   cm.
    Includes bibliographical references and index.
    ISBN 0-8262-1055-4 (alk. paper)
    1. O'Hare, Frank P., d. 1960.   2. Socialists—United States—
Biography.   I. Title.
HX84.039B83   1996
335'.0092—dc20
    [B]   95-53146
                                                                              CIP

Designer: Stephanie Foley
Typesetter: BOOKCOMP
Printer and binder: Thomson-Shore, Inc.
Typefaces: Palatino and Sabon

To the memory of H. A. (Gene) Peciulis,
who learned much from Frank O'Hare and
was more than willing to share it.

Contents

Acknowledgments

At the outset, I must confess that this biography of Frank P. O'Hare began as
a life study of his first wife, Kate Richards O'Hare. By the time I discovered
that at least two scholars had a long head start on me, I had learned enough
about Frank to become fascinated with him as a person in his own right,
one equally worthy of a full-fledged biography. Consequently, I would like
to thank Neil K. Basen for indirectly discouraging me away from Kate
O'Hare and his subsequent countenancing of my interest in her singular
first husband. A more straightforward thanks is due to Sally M. Miller, Kate
O'Hare's published biographer, for her insights and encouragement. I hope
that my life of Frank is a worthy companion to hers of Kate.

Thanks to everyone at the University of Missouri Press for making publi-
cation of this book possible, especially Director and Editor-in-Chief Beverly
Jarrett, Missouri Biography Series Editor William E. Foley, Managing Editor
Jane Lago, Acquisitions Editor Clair Willcox, Marketing Manager Karen D.
Caplinger, and my editor John Brenner.

Piecing together Frank O'Hare's life has put me in contact with a host
of dedicated archivists and librarians who deserve a published thank-you.
I am especially grateful to Martha Clevenger of the Missouri Historical
Society in St. Louis, a peerless professional, for her many kindnesses.
Her associate, Deborah Brown, tracked down many of the photographs
in this book. Janie C. Morris at Duke University found other great old
photographs for me in the Socialist Party Papers. Special thanks go to Gene
DeGruson of Axe Library at Pittsburg State University, Michael Stevens
of the State Historical Society of Wisconsin, and Raymond Teichman of
the Franklin D. Roosevelt Library. I appreciated the efforts of the staff of
the Western Manuscript Collection at the University of Missouri–St. Louis;
James Bantin of Ellis Library, University of Missouri–Columbia; Marilyn
Burlingame of University Archives, University of Missouri–Kansas City;
and Marie Concannon and Fae Sotham of the State Historical Society of

Missouri. I am indebted to Stephen L. Recken of the Public History Program at the University of Arkansas–Little Rock and Michael J. Dabrishus and Andrea E. Cantrell of Special Collections at the University of Arkansas Library, Fayetteville. I would also like to thank the staffs of the Library of Congress, the National Archives in Washington and Kansas City, the New York Public Library, the Tamiment Institute at New York University, the Barker Center and the main library at the University of Texas–Austin, and the Oklahoma Historical Society. Professionals from scores of other repositories helped me to obtain microfilms on interlibrary loan. Thanks to Connie Carter of the *St. Louis Post-Dispatch* for helping me to track down Frank O'Hare's writings in the newspaper he both loved and loved to hate.

I am grateful to Alice Swanter for providing access to her father's files on Frank O'Hare. The late H. L. Mitchell gave me suggestions and support early in this project. I thank Frank's friend, Irving Dilliard of the *Post-Dispatch*, for sharing his memories and for suggesting the title to this work. I am also indebted to Meredith Tax for lending me her taped interviews with Kathleen O'Hare.

When relations between Frank O'Hare and his children became strained, his daughter-in-law, Barbara O'Hare, was there to smooth things over. A half-century later, her generous spirit is still manifest in her willingness to share her memories and her letters with me. Many thanks to her and also to her daughter Kate O'Hare Henderson and her daughter Debra.

Closer to home, I would like to acknowledge the contributions of my colleagues and my students at Linfield College in McMinnville, Oregon. I owe a great debt to the staff of Northrup Library, especially Lynn Chmelir, Frances Rasmussen, and Susan Whyte. Thanks to the Instruction Committee for providing funds for my research trips and to my faculty colleagues, especially John Fincher, Vince Jacobs, Barbara Seidman, and Dean Marv Henberg. My student assistants in the History Department helped me in many ways and, hopefully, learned a few things about research in the process. They are Barbara Anderson, Ryan Donihue, Jennifer Gabrielli, Robyn Halvorsen, Eric Huson, Nancy Karnosh, Lisa Scanlon, and Melissa Smith.

My parents, Henry and Jean Buckingham, my wife, Ann, and my children, Will and Katie, have my special gratitude for their love, patience, and support from start to finish.

With deep appreciation, this book is dedicated to the late Professor Gene Peciulis, Frank O'Hare's pupil and soul mate, for the many hours he spent teaching me about his mentor. Gene was also very generous in sharing his collection of O'Hare material with me.

Rebel against Injustice

Introduction

On October 30, 1960, three and one-half months after his death, friends of Frank P. O'Hare gathered for a memorial service in St. Louis. Twelve cohorts presented tributes to "FPO," with only twice that many in the audience, in spite of advance publicity, at the Sheldon Memorial Hall. Seemingly, it was one last disappointment in the life of a man whose efforts had, more often than not, fallen short of success. Still, one of the organizers of the event, Caroline Nations, did not see it that way. Frank's friend of fifty years, Roger Baldwin, founder of the American Civil Liberties Union, had set the record straight in his remarks, she thought. "I was glad he corrected the general view that F. P. O. was simply a magnificent failure. He was a mover and a shaker in his day." Years later, Baldwin (at age ninety-seven) would pay tribute to his friend again, concluding: "The strength of our democracy lies largely with its dissenters, its rebels, its optimists and prophets. Frank O'Hare was all of these."[1]

Often forgotten even in the annals of American radicalism, except as the husband of the better-known Kate Richards O'Hare, he was indeed "a mover and a shaker" in Socialist circles at a time early in the century when an Americanized Marxism threatened mainstream politics by electing some one thousand candidates to public office. Frank O'Hare became a premier organizer for the Socialist party, specializing in creating locals in areas where other agitators had come up empty. In the Southwest, O'Hare perfected the Socialist version of the venerable camp meeting as a vehicle for preaching Marx to the mass of poor farmers and miners who felt trampled by both the local elites and the national trusts. He built the *National Rip-Saw* into one of the largest Socialist monthly magazines in American history. His wife and Eugene V. Debs, the two most popular figures in the movement, depended on Frank O'Hare to orchestrate their many public appearances and to edit their copy. After World War I, he organized publicity "crusades" that contributed to the freeing of American political prisoners and to the

1

end of contract prison labor. In his later years, he was a businessman, a salesman, an inventor, a national and community organizer, a student of higher mathematics, a newspaper columnist, and, above all, an inveterate letter writer.

O'Hare's relative present-day obscurity was partly his own doing. In 1925, he burned most of his personal papers in a basement furnace, including hundreds of letters to and from his estranged wife, a priceless record of the lives of the most famous soapboxing couple in the Socialist movement. A few years earlier, he had lost the scrapbooks containing the newspaper and magazine clippings of their activities. In 1950, O'Hare tried to write his autobiography, acknowledging at the outset that "Personal biographies are rather fictitious. Those I have read, of men I know certainly are in large part. Fiction is more factual." Two years earlier, he wrote to a friend: "How little I care for history and biography, knowing how it is written. Those who know cannot write it; Those who write it cannot know." Given this pessimism, it is not surprising that O'Hare abandoned the effort, half-finished.[2]

Yet Frank O'Hare often expressed the hope that somehow the story of his life might be told. As early as 1942, he observed that he was writing letters and saving carbon copies because "Some day I hope some hard boiled person will winnow the trash out, and if there is anything left, it will be snap shots of the prerevolutionary day." Years later, in the midst of a twenty-six-page missive to a professor of education at the University of Wisconsin, who had produced a film on mathematics he admired, O'Hare explained that he was writing to a perfect stranger in appreciation for her work and keeping a copy of the letter:

> And some day, someone will go over the letters I have written—and cull out the materials for the "memoir" my friends ask me to write. For they think that my stories of life among the Cherokee Indians, my adventures in the coal strikes of the 1900s, the many mobs I have met, and the battles for free speech over a period of some sixty years have a certain interest.

By that time, O'Hare had already forwarded several thousand pages of letters, essays, and clippings to the Missouri Historical Society in St. Louis, but he was intent on casting a wider net for some future "hard boiled person." Knowing that his friend Roger Baldwin had already made arrangements for the collection of his papers, O'Hare wrote him a letter explaining in detail how "anybody who wants to reconstruct the life of one of the pioneer USA Socialists" could do it with enough time and effort.[3]

Frank O'Hare's basement blaze of 1925 proved to be a serious deterrent to scholarly works on either him or his more famous wife, but it has not been an insurmountable obstacle. Kate O'Hare's biography was published in 1993, and a more comprehensive version of her life and times may yet see the light of day. The Frank O'Hare Papers furnish a good starting point for research on the man behind Kate O'Hare, as he liked to think of himself. The discovery of letters Kate and Frank wrote to Gertrude Petzold, Frank's half sister, helps to fill in the lacuna from the early years. The forty-four boxes of O'Hare material in the collection constitute the core of what O'Hare wanted scholars to know about him. Although the Missouri Historical Society has done yeoman service in arranging the dated correspondence, there are boxes of undated letters and scattered fragments that make sense only after years of studying other sources. Access to the letters and essays that Frank left in his second wife's care rather than to the Missouri archive, most of them very personal and familial, has helped to round out the O'Hare papers. Several other archives across the country contain significant material on Frank O'Hare as well. By tracking the O'Hares' movements as publicized in the Socialist press and then checking microfilms of local newspapers, it has been possible to recreate a fair cross section of Frank's long-lost clippings file. The insights of a few surviving close friends proved to be invaluable.

Finally, following the advice of a modern master of biography, Stephen Oates, to visit "the landmarks where one's subject lived and died" in order to "radiate a sense of intimacy and familiarity," Frank O'Hare's steps have also been retraced. The directions given on an old handbill as to how to reach the site outside of Grand Saline in East Texas where O'Hare spoke at the first modest Socialist encampment still produce greetings by wary, toothless tenants and their beautiful, ragged children playing amidst broken glass, old bedsprings, and countless half-starved cats. It is possible to imagine what Frank might have seen and felt by walking the streets of his beloved St. Louis, along the Mississippi waterfront he prowled as a boy, downtown past the former locale of the old *Rip-Saw* on Olive Street, in the working-class neighborhoods where O'Hare lived most of his life, and the magnificent city parks he loved so. Only after examining all of these sources, archival and the more intangible mileposts, does a more complete picture begin to emerge of what Henry James's biographer, Leon Edel, has called "the figure under the carpet . . . the life-myth of a given mask."[4]

The life of Frank P. O'Hare is worthy of examination for the light it sheds on everyday existence in the Middle Border over an extended period of time. O'Hare's story reflects the ordinary in the sense that like America, he was born in the country and raised in the city. Brought up on the Bible, the example of P. T. Barnum, and the fantasies of dime novels, he fought his way out of Kerry Patch slum into the world of business. At the turn of the century, O'Hare, like so many others, began to sense that a terrible evil had come with the good in the rise of industrial capitalism—and he labored most of his life to change the system for the better.

O'Hare opposed American participation in World War I, as did the majority of his fellow Missourians (at least at the outset), and when the war was over, he joined in the craving for "a return to normalcy." In the 1920s, his life continued to reflect the larger culture in that he turned away from politics, got divorced, and lost all of his money. O'Hare suffered the terrible privations wrought by the Great Depression, along with most everyone else. He was an isolationist and, after Pearl Harbor, a strong supporter of the war effort. Like many older Americans, he did not share in the Truman-Eisenhower prosperity of the postwar period, scraping by on Social Security and handouts until his death from cancer in 1960.

This man, ordinary in so many ways, lived an extraordinary life. In 1900 he joined the Socialist movement, becoming a part of what he called "an entrancing world of intellectual adventure. Everybody brought what he had and threw it in the pot. It was the greatest 'adult education' movement this continent has ever seen." For the next sixty years, his faith in democratic socialism defined his life, a *weltanschauung* he described to historian Ira Kipnis as "that something that bound so many humble members into a brotherhood that it seems to me must have been something like that of the other revolutionary movement, 1900 years ago, now so distorted by 'history.'" He was, as Kate O'Hare scholar Neil Basen observed, "a resourceful, behind-the-scenes organizational wheelhorse" for the party. His beloved friends and hated enemies included Eugene Debs, Max Eastman, Morris Hillquit, Floyd Dell, "Big Bill" Haywood, Elizabeth Gurley Flynn, Jane Addams, Art Young, Scott Nearing, Henry Ford, and Victor Berger, as well as nameless cow punchers, sharecroppers, lumberjacks, miners, prostitutes, preachers, capitalists, actors, and criminals. O'Hare made a thousand speeches before a total of a million people and reached millions more through hundreds of newspaper and magazine articles. So, he helped to define American socialism just as American socialism defined him. Through the first six decades of the twentieth century, his life rose and fell with the Socialist movement. In that sense, at least, if a failure, he was "a magnificent failure."[5]

"I think that you are nuts," the novelist Irving Stone wrote to O'Hare, "but in as amusing a fashion as I could have encountered in many a moon. If you hadn't fallen for the wiles of Socialism you would have been a humorist in the George Ade, Will Rogers tradition." That was the way many people saw Frank O'Hare, a clever and stubborn fellow who might have made something more of himself except for his stubborn faith in an ideological abstraction. His closest friends saw an idealist with a sustained, clear-eyed vision of a more perfect society and a burning sense of outrage against present wrongs.[6]

Frank O'Hare's life was full of mistakes and miscalculations suggestive perhaps of the limits of the Americanized socialism he preached with such missionary zeal. This does not deprecate the lifelong, altruistic calling he felt to share his sublime dream of an America liberated from war, racism, poverty, and unspoken class conflict. O'Hare never wavered from this vista and refused to bow to convenient, momentary realism. In the end, his militant recalcitrance made him a lifelong rebel against injustice.

1

The Making of a Socialist,
1877–1902

Then twenty-four years old, Frank O'Hare was ready for a change in his life when Walter Thomas Mills vaulted over a fence in Tower Grove park, St. Louis, to see him in the summer of 1901. Startled members of the informal Clarion Club heard Mills insist that O'Hare come to Girard, Kansas, where he planned to open a training school for Socialist organizers. A recent graduate of "Little Professor" Mills's correspondence school, "The International School of Social Economy," O'Hare accepted the invitation on the spot. In the next few months, he would leave behind his hard-won middle-class life to embark on a new career dedicated to bringing about the "Cooperative Commonwealth." Frank O'Hare's snap decision to become a full-time Socialist organizer was the result of a growing conviction of the evils of capitalism and his own part in it, as well as personal unhappiness. Like his father before him, he decided to flee as a means of gaining control over his life.[1]

Early Years

Frank's father, Peter Paul O'Hare, spent much of his life on the run. Born in Belfast, Ireland, he was apprenticed at the age of sixteen to an uncle, a dealer in linens. O'Hare soon ran off to join the British Navy, where he picked up some carpentry skills before jumping ship. He tried prospecting in Canada, but involvement in radical politics forced him across the American border. Pausing in St. Paul, Minnesota, Peter became attracted to Elizabeth Petzold, a widowed storekeeper and mother of two

6

children, George and Gertrude. Shortly after their marriage, they moved to New Hampton, Iowa, where Francis Peter O'Hare was born on April 23, 1877. Another son, Will, followed two years later.[2]

Unable to make ends meet through his work as a day laborer in New Hampton, Peter O'Hare abandoned his family to seek his fortune in Gunnison County, Colorado. O'Hare opened a silver mine, naming it "Little Gertrude" after his stepdaughter. "I am just beginning to reap the benefit of a hard two years work," he wrote to his wife on May 27, 1882, "and I have every confidence that this summer will see me well on my feet." Occasionally, a one-hundred-dollar bill accompanied his letters to Elizabeth, although the money stopped after she refused his pleas to bring the family to Denver. Losing financial control of the silver mine, Peter O'Hare moved on to Oklahoma, then Mexico, South America, and South Africa. At the age of sixty, he joined Kronje's commandos, volunteering to ride dynamite-filled boxcars into British camps, leaping off just before they exploded. He lived out his last years in poverty at the edge of Fruita, Colorado; even on his deathbed in 1905, he was too proud to contact his family because he had not made good on his promises of riches. Ironically, the year before Peter O'Hare died, Frank attended the Louisiana Purchase Exposition at St. Louis, where, for twenty-five cents, spectators could witness General Kronje and a cast of hundreds recreate the shot and shell of the Boer War twice daily, after the fashion of Buffalo Bill's Wild West Circus. Both father and son, each for his own reasons, chose to avoid the exhibition.[3]

Throughout his long life, Frank O'Hare felt deeply ambivalent about a father he barely remembered. He never spoke ill of the man he referred to as "this Colorado pioneer mining engineer." In the last half of his life, Frank usually referred to himself as an engineer, yet it was only one of his many trades. He thought of Peter O'Hare as "An inveterate socialist," although the evidence for this view was scant. Like his father, he spent much of his life on the move for various causes, living his last years in poverty in St. Louis, the scene of his greatest happiness. But Peter O'Hare's abandonment hurt Frank deeply. Years later he remembered the shame that came over him yearly when his new teachers asked about his father's whereabouts. "Every other playmate had two parents," he wrote, "instead of one and a secret."[4]

Elizabeth O'Hare was left in rural Iowa to raise four children by herself. Born Elizabeth Weijers in Holland, she had arrived in Iowa at the age of four with her family, crossing the Atlantic to keep her father out of debtors prison. Following the death of her parents in a cholera epidemic in 1850, Elizabeth moved to St. Louis to become part of her married sister's comfortable middle-class household. In 1862 she married Major Hugo

Petzold, who died ten years later in St. Paul while serving as adjutant general of Minnesota. The widowed Mrs. Petzold opened a small variety store in partnership with one of her sisters until she met the footloose Peter O'Hare. After the family moved to Iowa, his wanderlust put the family in a difficult position in small-town New Hampton, where Elizabeth made ends meet by taking in the sewing of sympathetic neighbors. Her eldest son, George, left school to take odd jobs, including one on the *New Hampton Courier.* Sometimes he brought his little half brother Frank along to the newspaper office with him, setting the four-year-old in a corner with a box of wooden poster types to play with as blocks. It can be said to have marked the beginning of Frank O'Hare's lifelong fascination with words and publishing. He attended school in New Hampton briefly, making an average grade of 90 percent in orthography, reading, writing, and arithmetic.[5]

Impoverished and unhappy, Elizabeth O'Hare moved the family to St. Louis in 1881, where she had spent her teen years. They took a train from New Hampton to Dubuque and from there embarked on the steamboat *Mary Morton* for the journey downriver to St. Louis. A thriving industrial and commercial hub for the trans–Mississippi West and Southwest, St. Louis had a population of 350,000. The city was in a state of transition at the time of the O'Hares' arrival, spreading westward rapidly into the rolling Missouri countryside from the waterfront, a reflection of the growing importance of railroads and the concomitant decline of river traffic. Once the *Mary Morton* had docked at the levee near the seven-year-old Eads Bridge, Elizabeth shepherded the four children to a large warehouse at 208 Walnut Street, site of her brother-in-law Gerard Bensberg's wholesale whiskey business. Frank O'Hare's first memory of St. Louis was an odoriferous mixture of aged bourbon and rye, coffee, tobacco, chemicals, glue, hides, and spices that pervaded Uncle Gerard's premises.[6]

After a sumptuous welcome, the prosperity of the Bensberg clan did not rub off much on the O'Hares except in odd doles of caviar, preserves, used clothing, and a newspaper route purchased for George. Elizabeth and her four children settled in a three-room house near the corner of Franklin Avenue and Twenty-third Street in Kerry Patch, a notorious slum composed primarily of Irish immigrants with pockets of Germans, British, and internal American migrants, although by 1890 Jewish, Polish, and Italian ethnic groups were also beginning to populate the area on the near north side of St. Louis. Frank O'Hare described "The Patch" as "[a] crazy-quilt of 'neighborhoods' each stanchly self-contained; melange of kindly and brutal, prim and riotous; pious and profane; where drunken husbands beat their slattern wives, and patient mothers wore their fingers to the bone scrubbing, sewing, patching, knitting, cooking, breast-nursing."[7]

NEW HAMPTON CHICKASAW CO. IOWA.

New Hampton, Iowa, at about the time of Frank O'Hare's birth (courtesy New Hampton Public Library).

Ashamed of her poor circumstances, Elizabeth avoided her old acquaintances, venturing from her tiny house only for early Sunday mass and an occasional visit to her sister's home on fashionable Washington Avenue. A devout Roman Catholic, she spent much of her time acting as "a one woman Hull House," counseling and consoling the troubled women of the neighborhood who found their way to her back door. "Underneath her 'bourgeois culture,'" Frank wrote, years later, paying her the ultimate compliment, "there was a great DEBS soul in Elizabeth."[8]

Too young to attend public school in St. Louis, Frank O'Hare spent his first years in Kerry Patch running errands for his reclusive mother and keeping her company. While Elizabeth stitched and sewed, Frank recited from the only book his mother ever read, the Catholic Priny Douay version of the Bible, building his vocabulary and asking questions about the verses. He also read and reread a life of the popular showman P. T. Barnum and browsed *Chase's Medical Compendium.* Like millions of other young boys, he loved dime novels, short stories that glorified the westward movement and reinforced the mythology of rags to riches.[9]

Elizabeth was determined that her offspring would not become "street arabs," wild, neglected children who roamed Kerry Patch, often gravitating toward lives of crime. She clung to Frank until he could attend the

Frank O'Hare, his half sister Gertie Petzold, and his brother Willie, taken shortly after their arrival in St. Louis (courtesy Missouri Historical Society).

Carr Lane public school beginning in the fall of 1885. When he was ten, his half brother George set him up with a paper route for the *St. Louis Chronicle*. After school, he rushed to the office, folding the single-sheet, four-page papers by hand before delivery to his two hundred subscribers. His young ears endured the foul talk overheard while he gulped down nickel slabs of pie at the cafe next to the *Chronicle*. He saw the seamier side of Gilded Age St. Louis as his regular customers included houses of prostitution and saloons surrounding infamous Clabber Alley. His route crossing the boundaries of several tough Kerry Patch gangs necessitated careful daily planning. For this he earned one dollar a day, the same wage received by many unskilled adult workers. O'Hare ranged through the *Chronicle*'s offices, watching legendary publisher E. W. Scripps from a distance and learning about the newspaper business. In spite of being raised in a poor, one-parent home, Frank looked back on his childhood as a happy one; he revered his mother for her simple Christian kindness and for teaching him to give more than he received, and also his half brother for talking to him about the newspaper business and national politics.[10]

Working

After Elizabeth O'Hare's death in 1891, the three boys moved into a rented room together while their heartbroken sister Gertie went to Minnesota to live with relatives. Frank spent most of his time that year at the Polytechnic Building at Seventh and Chestnut Streets, where he attended freshman high school and buried himself in books on electricity at the library on the ground floor until it was time to deliver his newspapers. Two years later, at age sixteen, Frank O'Hare dropped out of high school to seek full-time work. He could not have chosen a worse time, for St. Louis was mired in a deepening national depression. After three months, he finally landed a job with the Union Switch and Signal Company, part of the Westinghouse trust, contracted to build an electro-pneumatic interlocking system at Union Station. He later described his job as "timekeeper, toolkeeper, stockman, assistant to the engineers, and general nuisance." Work on the great railroad station continued during the Pullman strike of 1894, when Frank saw terminal switchmen fired for walking off the job in sympathy with Eugene Debs's American Railway Union. While he felt a certain sympathy for his fellow workers, he accepted management's view that strikers were troublemakers.[11]

Frank, chafing under his half brother's paternalism, began to quarrel with George. "Finally," Frank explained to his sister, "he told me to get.

I did so and am not one bit dissatisfied." Once the job at Union Station was completed, O'Hare decided to finish high school. He lasted only a week, finding the confines of the classroom to be unbearable after a year of work among men. On the fiftieth anniversary of the building of Union Station, he told readers of the *St. Louis Star-Times* that "I was surrounded by working-class heroes—engineers, switchmen; by men who loved their work and were grateful of their accomplishments." He was proud "that this monument exists, that as a boy I helped a little and that I was accepted into that fine horny-handed fellowship." O'Hare never bothered to complete high school, although he took his textbooks home to read, thereby beginning a lifelong process of self-education.[12]

Out on his own, Frank O'Hare decided that he wanted a career in business. His job on the railroad had brought him into contact with the Simmons Hardware Company, a large wholesaler with more than two thousand employees. In 1894, after pestering his contacts there for a month, Frank was assigned to the pricing department headed by Thomas Meston, an ambitious graduate of Notre Dame and a nephew of Alexander Meston, who had pioneered conveyor production lines at the Michigan Car and Foundry Company. Tom Meston took a liking to the bright and eager young O'Hare, instructing him in marketing, business theory, and labor management.[13]

Meston also lent Frank a copy of Herbert Spencer's *First Principles*, a book that caused O'Hare to question his mother's religious teachings for the first time. "The whole Catholic fabrication fell away," he later wrote, "like an iceberg shattering in the gulf stream." From Spencer, O'Hare turned to John Stuart Mill, then John Fiske, John Ruskin, Ralph Waldo Emerson, Edward Bellamy, and, finally, Karl Marx, always discussing and arguing about what he had learned with the man who had become his intellectual mentor. Day after day, the two men sat on either side of a double desk pricing hardware orders and calculating discounts while carrying on a running conversation about ideas and the world. Meston protected Frank's place in the company when Frank fell ill for several weeks with diphtheria. "Tom Meston was the man I had been looking for all my life," O'Hare later wrote, adding, "I guess I was the kid he had been looking for all his life." Determined to escape the drudgery of wholesale pricing and win plaudits for themselves, together, Meston and O'Hare applied the scientific management ideas of Frederick W. Taylor and others to the hardware business, working nights to standardize pricing procedures. Thus "Taylored," unskilled low-wage women clerks replaced relatively high-salaried "hardwaremen," providing Simmons with significant savings in labor costs. In 1897, when Meston left Simmons to join his brother Charles and Herbert L. Parker at the fledgling Emerson Electric Company, Frank O'Hare followed loyally. Rising quickly

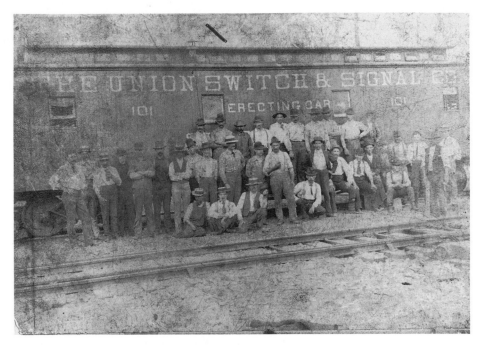

Timekeeper and toolkeeper Frank O'Hare (third from right) poses with the crew of the Union Switch and Signal Company that helped to build Union Station in St. Louis in 1893 (courtesy Missouri Historical Society).

through the ranks, he became the head of the switch and switchboard manufacturing department.[14]

As if following a dime novel plot, O'Hare, through a combination of good fortune and hard work, had made a fair beginning at a career in business at a time when the United States was suffering from the most severe economic depression of the nineteenth century. The depression occurred in the midst of a period of social, ideological, and political upheaval that went far beyond a mere downturn in the business cycle. While some observers expected a revolution to follow, the actual result, as Martin Sklar has observed, was nothing less than a corporate reconstruction of American society as the country accommodated a new corporate-capitalist order dominated by large-scale business enterprises that managed the market and enlarged federal and state governments that regulated the companies. While the transition was relatively peaceful and most came to endorse the new world of corporate liberalism, a significant minority, including Frank O'Hare, began to question the basic tenets of capitalism itself.[15]

At Emerson Electric, his relationship with Tom Meston soured as the discussions about ideas turned into bitter arguments over "the amoral system of free enterprise . . . the double standard of morality, the scorn for the 'lumpy jawed' as he [Meston] put it, wage workers." After work, O'Hare began to seek out other businessmen, as well as writers, newspaper reporters, preachers, and his old father confessor to talk about the new world of ideas coursing through his mind. He read works on socialism and economics at the St. Louis Public Library, enrolled in a course in economics offered by the Young Men's Christian Association, and attended lectures of the Social Science Club on contemporary issues.[16]

The writings of George D. Herron made a profound impression on young O'Hare. A Congregationalist minister and professor of Applied Christianity at Iowa College (later Grinnell), Herron came into prominence as a leader of the Social Gospel movement, which sought to synthesize Christian ethics with social justice and political equality to bring about a new social order. Denying that limits ought to be placed on social change short of the overthrow of capitalism, Herron resigned from Iowa in 1899 to devote more time to lecturing and to work openly for the new Social Democratic party. "Socialism is the only living religion," he wrote, "the only program of faith that is offered at the present time. . . . I have no expectation that the present system can be mended—it can only be ended." Frank O'Hare made his own final break with organized religion in 1899, resigning from the St. Bridget's Lyceum when another young man was given a part in a church-sponsored play that he thought was rightfully his. He had little use for organized religion ever after. "Finally," O'Hare later wrote, "I discovered that I was a Socialist. When I told Meston this he flew into a blind rage. But he got over it." Intelligent, hard-working, optimistic, and ripe for conversion, Frank O'Hare had found a demanding new faith in socialism that advanced a new way of looking at the world. By 1901, when Emerson Electric sold off the switchboard department to the Frank Adam Electric Company, O'Hare was no longer enjoying his business career. While Meston offered to keep him on in another capacity, Frank felt betrayed by his mentor and left Emerson Electric feeling bitter.[17]

Socialist Neophyte

O'Hare joined the fledgling Social Democratic party (SDP) in 1900 at the time of a strike by St. Louis Transit Company workers for union recognition and the ten-hour day. Class lines in St. Louis had hardened to the point where a federal judge had sanctioned the formation of a *posse comitatus*, which subsequently ambushed a peaceful parade of strikers at Eads Bridge, killing three and wounding fourteen. The strike would collapse after six months of bitter confrontation. The next year, hearing that the Machinists' Union had begun a recruiting drive in St. Louis, O'Hare suggested to some of the mechanics at Frank Adam Electric that they might want to sign on. When his new boss demanded to know what he was doing, O'Hare replied blithely that he wanted "to see the boys in the shop get some of the gravy." Needless to say, O'Hare later wrote, "a brilliant young executive was bounced out on his ear."[18]

A few days later, he went to work for Gerard Swope, a resourceful sales manager with Western Electric, which was in the midst of setting up a wholesale distribution company. O'Hare's job was to act as a kind of "goodwill missionary" to the electrical trades on behalf of Western Electric, a task that put him in day-to-day contact with the working class for the first time since his railroad apprenticeship. Calling on hundreds of factories and other businesses in South St. Louis, he became enraged by what he saw of working conditions, from the overheated boiler room of a luxury hotel to a brass works where workers inhaled dust and gas that would disable them in a matter of a few years. Frank's camaraderie with Gerard Swope made the job bearable for a time. A philosophical anarchist, Swope not only tolerated O'Hare's socialism, but invited him along on several impromptu investigative forays into working-class neighborhoods at night.[19]

O'Hare conversed with other young men equally disgruntled with the deleterious effects of monopoly capitalism. A drugstore clerk at Russel Riley's recommended that Frank attend programs at the Ethical Society, a forum for traveling lecturers. There he met Eugene De Prez, a French tailor who invited O'Hare to join lunchtime meetings at his shop on Locust Street, where a handful of Socialists, anarchists, Christian Scientists, and freethinkers discussed common readings well into the afternoon, including what O'Hare called "my extremely vague Socialism." Whenever he made a sale or bought materials from another wholesaler for the company, Frank would try to sell a year's subscription to what had become his favorite newspaper, J. A. Wayland's *Appeal to Reason*.[20]

Appeal to Reason of Girard, Kansas, was one of the largest weekly political publications in the United States. The folksy "One-Hoss Philosophy" of publisher Julius A. Wayland that dominated the paper mixed a basic faith in American democracy with Midwestern populism and socialist ideas derived from Laurence Gronlund, Edward Bellamy, and John Ruskin. The paper prospered because it struck a responsive chord among the discontented and because Wayland was a clever businessman. To educate the public about socialism as a practical scheme for making the country over into the Cooperative Commonwealth, even as he made a handsome profit for himself, Wayland sold advertising space in the paper and expanded circulation by offering premiums to readers selling the most subscriptions. He created the *Appeal* Army column to recognize his subscription hustlers in print and to make them feel like part of the paper. One of these volunteer salesmen of socialism talked Frank O'Hare's half brother George into a subscription and he, in turn, sold Frank on the paper. Frank O'Hare became a part of what Wayland would call "the greatest Army in the nation."[21]

In some ways, O'Hare was a typical recruit to the *Appeal* Army—and to the Socialist movement. Like most of Wayland's newspaper hustlers examined in James R. Green's study of the 495 top "salesmen-soldiers" of 1914, he was a native-born white male. He was from the Southwest, a six-state area that had the highest percentage of *Appeal* agitators. His conversion to socialism was also typical; for, as with the overwhelming majority in the 1914 survey, O'Hare became interested in the movement through a combination of bitter personal experience and reading leftist literature. Frank later wrote that his business mentors had trained him in socialism quite inadvertently; for Marx "described the capitalist order as I independently had observed it." In other ways, O'Hare was not typical. Sixty-nine percent of the salesmen in the *Appeal* Army were middle-aged whereas O'Hare was only twenty-four in 1901. He was also in the minority in that he lived in a large city. Finally, his status as middle class and white collar was less common than the working-class majority (57 percent) of Wayland's volunteer salesmen. Given his middle-class status and his youth, O'Hare might have been drawn to the reformist Progressive movement then coalescing as a concomitant of the new liberal corporate capitalism, but the idealism imparted by his mother, his working-class origins, the tutelage of his freethinking bosses Tom Meston and Gerard Swope, and his corporate experience all help to explain his growing interest in socialism.[22]

Nights, O'Hare began to learn more about socialism through Mills's correspondence school. An ordained minister, Mills had embraced a variety of reform causes including Prohibition, Populism, and communalism before finding his calling as a Socialist educator. In the widely circulated pamphlet "How to Work for Socialism," Mills urged his readers to keep detailed records of their activities in a pocket notebook. Make a list of "jurors," he suggested, who might be persuaded to socialism: wage earners, salesmen, corporate employees, teachers, mail carriers, farmers ("No one will be more benefited [*sic*] by Socialism than farmers"), women ("Socialism means more for women than it does for men"), and children over the age of eleven. Interview them, write to those at a distance, raise money for the cause, give away pamphlets, loan books, sell subscriptions to Socialist papers, organize public meetings, support strikes, and publicize your efforts. Above all, Mills emphasized education. "You must," he wrote, "know the points of controversy between the Economists and the Socialists, and must be able to meet them on their own ground and with their own weapons." By 1900 he claimed that study groups in sixty-three cities and towns were using his materials and more than 10 percent of all Socialists were taking his lessons by correspondence.[23]

In return for three dollars, O'Hare received a set of twenty lessons with exam questions to be returned to the school in Chicago. Lesson one endeavored to prove, in twelve steps, that the people had a natural and an inherent right to all of the earth. Subsequent lessons covered "primitive industry"; the evolution of slavery, serfdom, and the wage system; industrial capitalism; political economy; socialism as a way out of wage slavery; and labor unions. Mills's course—and his subsequent text *The Struggle for Existence*—presented in simple form world history, culture, and religion in a context that owed more to Spencer and Darwin than to Marx, who was credited by Mills with little more than developing a scientific defense of Socialist principles. The writings of Mills were popular because they fulfilled a craving on the part of Socialist converts for an acquaintance with a higher learning that they could then use in organizing for the party. Mills made the history of modern radicalism accessible and understandable. Like his pamphlet on Socialist organizing, the correspondence course and the text prepared eager students such as Frank O'Hare to help build a movement.[24]

The Social Democratic party that O'Hare joined in 1900 had been formed two years earlier out of the political actionist wing of the Social Democracy of America movement, including followers of labor leader Eugene V. Debs and Milwaukee Socialist Victor Berger. An avowedly Marxist political party, the founding platform argued that "The trades union movement and independent political action are the chief emancipating factors of the working class, the one representing its economic, the other its political wing, and both must co-operate to abolish the capitalist system of production and distribution." While the SDP emphasized activism among the working class, most of the membership was middle class and much of its program smacked of Populism and Progressive reformism. The idea was to build a genuinely revolutionary movement through the demand for multiple reforms, thus dramatizing the contradictions of capitalism while amassing an ever-increasing power base in politics and trade unions until the inevitable triumph of socialism. The St. Louis chapter adopted a municipal platform calling for initiative, referendum, and proportional representation; public ownership of streetcars, subways, bridges, and gas and electric companies; free hospitals, orphanages, and insane asylums as well as facilities for abandoned women, the aged, and the homeless. The SDP local also demanded a new public library; an end to the contracting out of public works and child labor; classified civil service; compulsory education; health and safety inspections of factories, dairies, and food processing facilities; and the inauguration of public works projects to provide a decent living for the unemployed.[25]

Divisions over ideology and strategy, the comrades' angry denunciations of one another, calls for merger with other revolutionary and reform groups, and factional infighting created an atmosphere of near chaos that belied the notion of inevitable victory over capitalism. By 1900 the party had split in two—with rival headquarters in Springfield, Massachusetts (supported by the Missouri SDP), and Chicago—over the merits of unifying with a breakaway faction of the Socialist Labor party (SLP) dubbed "the Kangaroos" by SLP boss Daniel DeLeon. Still, the Springfield and Chicago SDP factions and the former SLP Kangaroos closed ranks behind the presidential candidacy of Eugene Debs and his running mate, Job Harriman, who received endorsements from several national, regional, and local labor organizations, including the St. Louis Trades.[26]

Frank O'Hare loved the weekly sessions of the St. Louis local of the Social Democratic party. Meeting in a drab, dirty storefront near Twelfth and Olive Streets, some forty regular participants raced through the routine business so that they could get to the pure debate, which is what most of them had really come for, including O'Hare. At one of his first meetings, he rose to denounce his comrades for using unnecessarily technical terminology in their arguments such as "class struggle," "Proletarian revolution," and "class consciousness," phrases he obviously did not fully grasp. Years later, he liked to joke about a mythical Irishman who echoed his sentiments, saying "I know many organizations—the Clan na Gael, the Ancient Order of Hibernians, but bejasus this is the vorst time I ever heard of the Prowling Terriers." Louis Kober, an elderly cigarmaker proud of his Marxian scholarship, responded to young O'Hare by reminding his comrades that this was not a soapbox propaganda meeting; properly run, a party debate ought to be the study of scientific socialism in all its aspects including history, economics, and politics. Frank took this to be a confirmation of what his mentor, Tom Meston, had taught him: never confuse selling the merchandise, which is the art of propaganda, with the cold, hard science of business management, where sentiment had no place. From that point on, O'Hare, who had first read Marx at Meston's behest, took it upon himself to put complex Marxian ideas (at least as he understood them) into an American idiom for his comrades. And they were his comrades, for as he wrote more than a half century later: "There I found my people."[27]

By 1900, O'Hare had found a new faith, a new political party, and for the first time in his young life, he had fallen deeply in love. The object of his affection was Marie E. Beimdick, a schoolteacher who had grown up within two blocks of the O'Hare home in Kerry Patch. They renewed their childhood acquaintance at a party given by a mutual friend, Thais Magrane. In the custom of the time, Marie asked Frank to call at her mother's home. Near the end of a pleasant evening of conversation, O'Hare asked Marie why she had invited him over. She told him that after hearing of his reputation as arrogant and conceited she had had the urge to demolish his large, immature ego. "For the first time," O'Hare wrote to Thais Magrane much later, "I had found someone who could listen to me until I had gotten the thought out. And, of course then I was a 'different' person." Frank and Marie saw a lot of one another after that; only with her could he "unfold without reservation."[28]

For the SDP and many members of the St. Louis working class, the high point in the 1900 presidential campaign came on October 9 with the appearance of their candidate, Eugene V. Debs. The six thousand people who packed Lemp's Park hall heard Debs call for the abolition of "the private control of opportunity" and use the bitter St. Louis street railway strike as a prime example "of the evil of monopoly." He ended his rousing address with an appeal to support Socialist principles in order to better the condition of the laboring class. Meanwhile, a dramatic torchlight procession of party officials and workers led by a band and a drum corps had marched from the old French Market to a pavilion adjacent to the hall, where Debs repeated his remarks to the enthusiastic crowd. Frank O'Hare took his sweetheart Marie to hear Debs and later remembered that "We were both carried away." After the speech, they rushed forward through the throng to press Debs's hand. A moment of eye contact and a brief exchange of words made them feel "blessed." Debs had that effect on many people, who regarded him as a priestly (even Christlike) leader prepared to do battle against the murderous consequences of industrial capitalism. That night, Debs became Frank O'Hare's hero and savior. Having been abandoned by Peter Paul O'Hare and rejected by Tom Meston, O'Hare would take the messianic figure of Debs to be his true father figure, fighting by his side against all comers both outside and inside of the Socialist movement for years to come. "All I am," he explained almost fifty years later, "I owe to Eugene Debs."[29]

Debs received fewer than one hundred thousand votes in the 1900 election, against 7.2 million for William McKinley and 6.5 million for William Jennings Bryan, while swamping the Prohibitionists, the Populists, and the SLP. In Missouri, the Debs ticket garnered more than six thousand votes (2,775 in St. Louis), trailing only New York, Illinois, California, and Wisconsin in Socialist strength. The results encouraged SDP partisans to think that they had made a splendid beginning. "At last," J. A. Wayland wrote, "the decks are cleared for action."[30]

O'Hare's enthusiasm for the cause impressed his SDP comrades. The official state party organ, *Missouri Socialist,* commended him for selling almost all of the thirty-five subscription cards to the paper that he had taken out. A few weeks later the paper observed that he "never allows the guilty to escape" without buying a sub card. The comrades thought enough of O'Hare to elect him treasurer of the state committee ("[a] high-sounding but nearly empty office," he later said) and as a representative of the twenty-fifth ward in the House of Delegates. In the summer of 1901 he joined the board of directors of the *Missouri Socialist.*[31]

Meanwhile, senior party members traveled to Indianapolis to attend a unity convention. The result was a loose-knit federation renamed the Socialist Party of America. More a coalition of regional groups than a modern political party at its birth, the SP included a right wing centered around the Austrian-born Victor Berger, the Milwaukee Socialist committed to building a constructive, stable political structure allied with trade unions. Morris Hillquit of New York anchored the Center along with several of his former SLP Kangaroo comrades including Californian Job Harriman, J. Mahlon Barnes of Pennsylvania, and Cleveland labor leader Max Hayes. Highly intelligent and steeped in Marxist theory (at least by American standards), Hillquit had developed a successful law practice within a decade of arriving in the United States from Latvia, and with it a taste for expensive clothing, fine art, and high culture. Distrusted by many as too bourgeois and too intellectual, Hillquit made himself indispensable through his flexibility on political and economic issues, his shrewd party politics, and his talent for mediating divisive issues. The most charismatic figure in the early SP, Eugene V. Debs, was regarded as the leader of the left wing, not so much for any real ideological differences with Berger and Hillquit as for his identification with the emotional radicalism and contradictory Marxism of the rural Western Socialists. Soon, the militant socialism and anarcho-syndicalism of William D. Haywood of the Western Federation of Miners and his followers would add yet another dimension to the contending array of voices in the SP amalgam.[32]

Yet paradoxically, the very multiformity of Socialist convictions and a common faith in the inevitability of socialism held the implicit promise of a party with strength enough to grow as it exercised a real influence in American politics. Years of futile wrangling and the limited success of Debs's presidential run combined to create a unified party with autonomous state organizations and a weak center. Gottlieb (Gus) A. Hoehn, a St. Louis delegate widely admired for having once challenged Daniel DeLeon for leadership of the SLP, engineered a key compromise that kept immediate reformist demands, except those aimed at farmers, in the party platform. The convention chose St. Louis as the new national headquarters because, as Leonard Abbott of New York put it, Chicago "has been the very center of the dissensions that have been splitting the party in the past year." For good measure, he praised the St. Louis local as "most progressive and American in spirit." Leon Greenbaum of St. Louis, who had joined the movement only recently (and thus had offended no one) became national secretary while five other St. Louis comrades, as a Local Quorum, made up the National Executive Committee (NEC). As treasurer of the state committee, Frank O'Hare became the SP's first national treasurer, although the position was a token one as he did not serve on the NEC.[33]

On the side, O'Hare and his friend Eugene De Prez tried to establish a working model of the British Fabian Society in St. Louis. Hiring a lodge hall on Easton Avenue, they invited their acquaintances and had what they thought was a fruitful meeting. The next week, not one member of the audience returned. A tandem appearance before a captive audience of Columbian Knights on behalf of the Socialist party proved more successful. Thus encouraged, O'Hare emulated the example of some Cincinnati comrades interested in the "Clarion Fellowship" of British Socialists by founding the Clarion Club of St. Louis with some twenty members, all middle-class professionals, who met Sunday mornings to discuss Socialist literature, the *Communist Manifesto,* and material from Walter Thomas Mills's correspondence course.[34]

By all accounts, Frank O'Hare was reasonably happy, although he later described himself during this period as "conceited, annoying, exhibitionary, and with a terrific inferiority complex." He continued to work for Gerard Swope, a decent man accepting of Frank's radical activism, and he spent much of his free time organizing for the Cooperative Commonwealth to come through the Socialist party, the Public Fund and Welfare Association, and the Rochdale Cooperative. O'Hare might have gone on living his compartmentalized life as a businessman/Socialist indefinitely except that in the summer of 1901 Marie Beimdick, after pledging her eternal love, turned down Frank's proposal of marriage inexplicably. Devastated, he decided that he could no longer bear to live in St. Louis. Less than a year later, his first love would die of spinal tuberculosis.[35]

When Walter Thomas Mills appeared at the Clarion Club on the morning of August 18, 1901, to invite O'Hare to join him in Girard, Kansas, where he was opening a training school for Socialist party organizers, Frank did not have to give the matter much consideration. He quit his job, resigned his party posts, gave his furniture to his half sister Gertrude, and accepted De Prez's parting gift of a fine suit of clothes as well as a modest purse Swope raised from among O'Hare's friends. "While the local movement will miss his services and local comrades will suffer the loss of his pleasant companionship," the *Missouri Socialist* observed after O'Hare's departure, "they know that the general movement will acquire a good worker and wish him all success in his new field." His half sister cried, but Peter Paul O'Hare would have understood the impulse for a fresh start.[36]

Girard—and Kate Richards

Frank O'Hare's haste to leave St. Louis was such that he set out for the Mills school several weeks before classes began. Knowing that only "suckers" paid full train fare, he settled for a student rate when the ticket agent refused to be talked into a free "drag." With fifty dollars in his pocket, a trunk containing his remaining possessions, and wearing his fine new suit, the "Dude Socialist" (as his friends called him) boarded a train for Girard from Union Station. During the trip he made the acquaintance of Henry Mulford (Harry) Tichenor, a Springfield, Missouri, Socialist editor, who jumped on the train to avoid a mob fired by a rumor that he had played a part in the recent assassination of President William McKinley. The incident was the first practical lesson in O'Hare's training as an agitator. As he would discover at first hand on at least a dozen occasions in the future, the radical organizer had to be prepared to stand and fight—or flee for life as the situation demanded, a far cry from the safe, if lively, debates in St. Louis that had won his heart to the movement.[37]

"This is a nice town," O'Hare wrote upon his arrival in Girard, "shady and well laid out—nice little houses—quiet as a church." J. A. Wayland had thought so too when he moved the *Appeal to Reason* there in 1897. Cheaper labor costs did not hurt either. The local elite came to admire Wayland as a successful businessman even if his politics caused some uneasiness. Wayland had lured Mills into relocating his International School of Social Economy from Chicago to Girard. In return, the *Appeal* publisher pledged to subsidize the school with all profits from the paper above his fixed salary. The training school for Socialist party activists offered a twelve-week course that covered the same material Mills had compiled for correspondence study plus voice, public speaking, grammar, speech preparation, party organizing, and parliamentary drill. Successful graduates could expect to be employed full-time by the *Appeal* as SP organizers. Mills targeted young single men and women who were willing to commit four or five years to the cause. In an extension of Wayland's "soldier-salesman" idea the *Appeal* mused: "This will be a good substitute for the military service which capitalism exacts from the young men in most countries, and will exact in increasing numbers in our own country." Tuition was five dollars, free for those like O'Hare who had completed the correspondence course.

Male students were to be housed in a co-operative boarding house with costs not to exceed two dollars per week.[38]

O'Hare made himself useful around the *Appeal*'s offices as he waited for the school to open. When Mills decided to invite the townspeople to a reception at the local opera house, Frank delivered hundreds of invitations door-to-door. The *Girard Press* took the occasion to remind its readers that Mills had appeared in their environs before: in 1888 to campaign for the Prohibitionist candidate for president, in 1896 to stump for William Jennings Bryan, and four years later as a supporter of Debs. After the gathering, the paper repeated an old soldier's suggestion that Mills "would make an excellent circus clown, but a mighty poor leader for the people of the United States to follow." "While a certain element are [sic] opposed to the Appeal and Socialism," O'Hare wrote to his half sister Gertie, "I think that a large number of most desirable citizens are with us." As the students began to drift in to the Mills school, Frank helped to get them settled, the men in quarters above the Odd Fellows lodge, the women in private homes. He had been disappointed that the three women students he had checked in were older or married. When word reached him that a young single female had arrived, he rushed down from the *Appeal* office to greet her. "My heart sank," he remembered years later, "Tall, narrow as a lath, and without, I thought, the least pulchritude." Hardly a word passed between them as he dropped the new student at the home of M. V. and Lillian Tubbs. She had introduced herself to O'Hare as Kate Richards.[39]

Carrie Katherine Richards was born on March 26, 1876, to Andrew and Lucy Sullivan Richards on a rural Kansas homestead. The drought of 1887 pushed the family into Kansas City, Missouri, where her father, left partially disabled from his service with the Union army during the Civil War, found work as a laborer and then with Richards and Conover Hardware, jointly owned by a distant relation and his old commanding officer. For a time, the shock of the poverty and suffering Kate Richards witnessed in the West Bottom slums reinforced her Disciples of Christ (Campbellite) faith and fired her desire to aid the disadvantaged. With women barred from the pulpit and the missionary field in her church, she chose education as a career, receiving a teacher's certificate from Pawnee City Academy in Nebraska. She quit the teaching field after less than a year in a one-room schoolhouse and eventually took a job with her father at a machine shop. Perseverance and hard work led to a punishing four-year machinist's apprenticeship and pioneering entry into the International Association of Machinists. At the same time, she worked at the Florence Crittenton mission in Kansas City to help rehabilitate prostitutes through the inculcation of middle-class values. Richards also continued her church-based missionary activities among the poor till she could no longer stand what she saw as the hypocrisy of wealthy parishioners, especially lumber baron R. A. Long, pious philanthropist and brutal exploiter of timber workers.[40]

One night in 1895 a Socialist street speaker aroused her curiosity about Marxism as an alternative path to social justice. Shortly thereafter, an impromptu speech at a Cigarmaker's Union ball by the legendary union organizer "Mother" Mary Harris Jones on the Socialist cause transfixed her. Mother Jones introduced Kate to some local Socialists eager to load her down with leftist classics. She returned them some weeks later, frustrated and confused because she could not readily grasp the theoretical works. At that point, J. A. Wayland, who had recently started up his *Appeal to Reason* in Kansas City, took an interest in the eager young woman, starting her off with a few simple booklets and working up to Marx and Engels. "Recreated," she later wrote, "I lived again with new aims, new hopes, new aspirations and the dazzling view of the new and wonderful work to do." Richards joined the Socialist Labor party in 1899, switched to the Social Democratic party the next year, and to the Socialist Party of America with its founding in mid-1901. Like Frank O'Hare, she was ready for a change in her life when Wayland recruited her for the Mills school; stiff competition from larger firms threatened her father's small operation and, as a tall, plain, and outspoken woman, her prospects for marriage seemed increasingly remote. Both Kate and Frank came to Girard because they had found their life's work: helping to create a democratic Socialist commonwealth they were sure would follow. Having come that far, all they lacked was each other.[41]

Although Frank had fled in disappointment from plain Kate and Kate undoubtedly had a bad first impression of arrogant, immature Frank, a mutual attraction developed quickly. A few days after their first meeting, O'Hare stumbled across Kate reading the palm of Ed Backus, a fellow student who had been expelled from the University of Missouri for striking one of his professors. When she examined Frank's hand, she floored him by cataloguing accurately all of his personal failings. He later remembered: "I was dazed. So I had to go back for more—that night. And then she read on, and saw 'possibilities' and 'purpose.'" Like his first love, Marie, Kate Richards had charmed O'Hare by demolishing his ego and then stroking it. He was not the only one thus smitten. In addition to Backus, Wilbur C. Benton, a young lawyer from Kentucky, also fell for Kate. After the three had all proposed, Kate chose Frank O'Hare to be her husband and her partner in the great work to come.[42]

Walter Thomas Mills made his school an intensive learning experience, filling his students' days with classes on political economy, socialism as philosophy and as politics, trade unionism, cooperative movements, speech writing, voice, library research, and, on one occasion, a field trip to the state party convention. Nights he took some, including Benton and Backus, out to the Opera House to practice their oratory. The students received a practical lesson in the politics of rural Kansas when one of them remarked to a crowd consisting of several members of the Grand Army of the Republic that "This government is rotten to the core." Mills added fuel to the fire by addressing the angry old soldiers as his "comrades" and was subsequently shoved off his soapbox. The mayor asked the students not to speak again until tempers in town had time to cool. O'Hare and Richards preferred to spend their free time together at her rooming house in order to, as Kate told Gertie Petzold, "study and plan and work on what we have mapped out as our life work." They planned to be married as soon as the term was over and embark immediately on a lecture tour. The couple's management of the commissary quickly drew criticism when they assessed students far in excess of the two dollars per week that Wayland had advertised as the boarding fee, an incident that turned out to be a preview of their marriage as neither of them ever mastered the art of family budgeting. Seeing that the school could do with some music, Kate had her parents ship the family piano to Girard. They also arranged the parties where young women from town were invited to dance with Mills's students. Final examinations came at the end of December, with Kate and Frank's answers to such questions as "Trace the class struggle from prehistoric times" and "Why is Socialism the only platform upon which all workers, including farmers, can be united?" considered good enough to be reprinted in *Appeal to Reason*.[43]

On January 1, 1902, Reverend Walter Thomas Mills married Kate Richards and Frank O'Hare at Wayland's home. In announcing their wedding plans two weeks earlier, the *St. Louis Republic* reported that "Both the young people had been followers of Professor Herron for several years." In keeping with the unorthodox nuptial vows of Herron and his bride Carrie Rand the previous spring, Kate and Frank had decided on "a Socialist wedding," with Mills declaring: "I pronounce you man and wife as long as life or love shall last." After the reception—and borrowing one hundred dollars from members of the wedding party—the couple went to nearby Pittsburg, Kansas, where Kate's railroad friends had prepared a social gathering in their honor. Next it was on to Liberal, Missouri, the first stop on their two-week honeymoon lecture tour. Before the happy couple left Girard, Wayland called Frank aside to tell him solemnly that he would face many hardships ahead as a Socialist organizer. He might even have to sleep in a haystack, but if that ever happened . . . (O'Hare expected him to say next "Wire me at my expense") then he should sleep on "the wind side of the stack" so as not to be smothered if the hay blew over. At the time, the insecure O'Hare viewed this as another example of Wayland's hostility toward him for not marrying his love-smitten daughter Olive. Only in later years did he come to appreciate Wayland for "His sublime dedication." As his star pupils, Wayland expected as much from the O'Hares as he did from himself; he assumed that Kate and Frank would give their all for the cause. In reporting the wedding to its vast readership, the *Appeal* (probably Wayland himself) observed: "Both are excellent speakers, and will thus be able to join hands as well as hearts in a cause both have dedicated their lives to." Indeed, their marriage and their commitment to socialism were bound up inextricably together. Joined in matrimony only months after the birth of the Socialist Party of America, their marriage would endure as long as the party did—but not much longer.[44]

2

Missionary Career,
1902–1911

Frank and Kate Richards O'Hare had planned their lives together with care during their courtship at the Mills School. Kate promised her future sister-in-law that she would take care of Frank: "in all his wanderings up and down the earth for the uplifting of humanity . . . there will ever be by his side a loving sensible helpful woman to share every joy and sorrow every success and reverse." In the traditional mores of the day he was to be the star, she the helpmate, even though it meant aiding him to overthrow the existing order. They were to be a team. It worked that way for a time, but Kate's growing fame as an orator and a writer, financial problems, plus the birth of four children combined to alter their dreamy plans. Like the Socialist movement, which enjoyed its "Golden Age" in the years before World War I, the O'Hares' marriage would be a combination of missionary zeal, sacrifice, reward, and internecine strife.[1]

Socialist Honeymoon

The newlyweds made their debut as husband-wife Socialist orators on January 4, 1902, at the opera house in Liberal, Missouri. Frank delivered the main address to an audience filled mostly with farmers on the topic of socialism and agriculture. Following her brief remarks to the women, eager comrades surrounded Kate to shake her hand, perhaps because most had never heard a woman speaker before. Many in the crowd followed the couple to their hotel for a reception. "The party broke up in the we sma' hours in the morning," a comrade reported, "all feeling that it was good to be a Socialist." Next came Nevada, Missouri, where the crowd found Frank "persuasive" and Kate "earnest." They followed Mills's advice in arranging their tour, arriving in each town a day early to conduct a business meeting with local party members and arrange for publicity. At one stop they were asked to stay over to speak for another night. Not wanting to admit that he had only one set speech, Frank accepted, distributing pencils and paper to the audience so that they could ask the couple questions about socialism. Having been drilled by Mills in delivering three-minute answers to questions most likely to be asked, the evening went well. In the midst of the three-week tour Frank wrote that "the interest and enthusiasm of the comrades is the most encouraging thing in the world."[2]

With their engagements fulfilled, the O'Hares stayed for several days in St. Louis, where Frank introduced his wife to friends and family, including half sister Gertie Petzold, who had become a disagreeable and disappointed unmarried woman, and was prepared to dislike Kate. Back on the hustings, they continued to learn how to be Socialist missionaries as they went along. To find out more about their audiences, Frank discovered that he could drop by the local hardware store to find someone he had done business with in the past while Kate would look up the town's Campbellites. At first, Frank gave the main address and Kate would follow with a few minutes of offhand remarks aimed at the women, but as it became apparent that she often went over better than he did, they became tandem orators. Frank also paid his respects at the local newspaper office so that he might garner a little free publicity, favorable or not, leading the *Appeal to Reason* to comment: "Not only do the O'Hares make the right kind of speeches, but they also succeed in getting them before the 'breakfast table audience' through the capitalist press."[3]

When the newlyweds came down with tonsillitis, they headed straight for the home of Kate's parents in Kansas City, canceling a series of speeches in little towns along the Wabash rail line. Frank's initial efforts impressed a Kansas City reporter, who wrote: "He is a pleasing speaker, has all the socialist arguments at his tongue's end, and possesses the happy faculty of telling unpalatable truths without antagonizing anyone." O'Hare explained that the honeymoon tour had gone well "and even those who disagreed with us did not throw any hen fruit, possibly because eggs are 35 cents a dozen." When Kate recovered her health, they spoke together on the subject of "Women and Socialism." After Kate's rousing appeal for feminine activism from the secure base of the home, Frank urged the married women "to make it mighty unpleasant for your husband if he is not a Socialist." Single women should get married and raise children rather than engage in "work that ought to be done by a man." Marriage under socialism, he promised, would be happier because poverty, rents, child labor, and kitchen drudgery would be eliminated and then "women can choose their own vocations and their husbands [sic] if they want to." While the audience, composed largely of women drawn by the novelty of a female orator, appreciated the speechmaking, they may have come away confused by a host of contradictions presented by the dynamic young newlyweds.[4]

The O'Hares made Kansas City their home and base of operations in early 1902. The Socialist vote there had dropped from 499 in 1900 to 382 the next year due to bickering over political methodology. Hired as an organizer for the Jackson County chapter of the Socialist party (which included Kansas City), Frank wasted little time in organizing new locals and implementing new ideas. He kicked off the first meeting of the Eighth Ward with an address on the abolition of poverty under socialism. At a party meeting he spoke of his St. Louis experiences, emphasizing the value of neighborhood organizing. Then he asked each of the comrades to explain how he had converted his friends and neighbors to socialism. Those declining to speak were fined ten cents apiece with the proceeds going to equip a Junior Socialists drum corps. His mother-in-law, Lucy Richards, and other members of the women's auxiliary volunteered to make bright red zouave-style uniforms. Marching four abreast down city streets followed by a furniture van draped with Socialist signs, the procession halted every few blocks so that Frank could make "short but spicy speeches to large crowds which assembled rapidly." O'Hare devised a notebook for workers so that they might budget their time and money more efficiently for the party. He also spent many weeks across the river in neighboring Kansas helping fellow Mills graduate Wilbur Benton to organize the Jayhawk state. On one trip, he teamed up with "Comrade Dr. Ray's medicine show," making fifteen-minute speeches for socialism once a curious crowd had gathered. He would try anything so long as it furthered the movement, although as he told the *Kansas City Star*, reformist schemes such as municipal ownership, Populism, and even cooperative colonies were not ends in themselves because "they cannot give the workers the benefit of a complete industrial democracy."[5]

Kate decided to run for a seat on the Kansas City school board, explaining to the *Kansas City World:* "I would much prefer to be at home, but a sense of duty forces me to do something to improve the condition of women in the industrial struggle for existence." Only the Socialist party, she added, promised women the voting franchise. Speaking with her husband at the Eighth Ward meeting, she urged the women to work for socialism because it would elevate them to their "highest sphere." In March, she and Frank signed on to write for the *Coming Nation*, a Socialist weekly founded by J. A. Wayland, taken over by the Ruskin Cooperative Association, and restarted by former *Appeal* assistant editor Fred Warren, who felt that

Traveling lecturers and writers for *Coming Nation*, 1902 (courtesy Missouri Historical Society).

Wayland had strayed from his original publishing ideals. The first regular woman columnist in a Socialist paper, Kate continued to insist that party women ought to be companions and helpers to their husbands above all else because "Home is as good a 'sphere' as any other for a woman." Her work with the short-lived *Coming Nation* marked the beginning of her national reputation and, ironically, a voice independent from her husband. For his part, Frank contributed a few short stories on the evils of the competitive system, including a fanciful tale of a comrade who circumnavigates the earth in a flying machine, and columns of observations on the contemporary scene patterned after the musings of J. A. Wayland. Clearly he preferred to concentrate on speechmaking and organizing whereas Kate put her writing ahead of party fieldwork.[6]

Kate and Frank continued their work together during this period as well. To demonstrate the party's solidarity with striking Kansas City bakers, they organized an evening of recitations and music, with proceeds amounting to $118.75 going to the bakers' union. Frank learned the hard way that local authorities were not always tolerant of his activities. In May while speaking to a crowd out-of-doors, he was arrested, roughed up, and charged with blocking the street. He welcomed the opportunity to "solidify and clarify the Socialist movement," arguing that the party would stagnate if it confined its activities to speaking with neighbors in hushed tones and meeting in musty halls. So, Frank made a point of insisting on his right to speak in public without a permit, as he would many times in the future. The O'Hares took organizing trips into rural Kansas, with Kate providing advice on how to talk to Kansans, who responded more enthusiastically to talks sprinkled with biblical references than to lectures on Socialist political economy. She also helped him to overcome a bout of mental depression following the death of his first sweetheart, Marie Beimdick. "Kate, as you know was 'psychic,'" he wrote to a friend years later, "and in our honeymoon days, or nights, she would *see* Marie's loving face gazing on us and blessing us, and tell me, skeptic, what she saw." Frank and Kate played an active part in hammering out strategy for the fall election campaign at the state convention in Springfield, Missouri. The party platform called on farmers to ally themselves with the working class under the party banner and demanded that the state militia be disbanded, while the delegates ignored the mayor of Springfield's request to address the convention. The party chose Frank O'Hare to reorganize the Springfield chapter, which had been disbanded for alienating local Socialists. He was also nominated to run for the state supreme court. The convention ended with the O'Hares among the speakers at large rallies held in the opera house and the local baseball park.[7]

Six months after their graduation from the Mills school, the O'Hares had become leaders of the Socialist party in Missouri. Like many of their comrades, they were not hard-core Marxists. Daniel Bell's observation that many Socialists were driven by "the moral indignation at poverty and the evangelical promise of a better world" describes the O'Hares' animus quite aptly. Kate wrote late in her life that "my Socialist activities [were] merely the effort to solve, at least, the economic causes of crime." They felt the need to get at the roots of injustice by studying America at first hand rather than Marxist ideology. "We were not 'literary' or 'book' Socialists," Frank observed. "We wanted to know everything about industrial and rural America. Let the doctrinaire Socialists go their way. What in Hell could Karl Marx know about the USA! . . . He was of positively no use to us at all, in the American Socialist movement, which was so largely rural." They were effective precisely because they understood rural Americans, their wants and needs, and could communicate what socialism would do for them. Frank gained the admiration of a reporter from the *Beloit Daily Call* for explaining the tenets of socialism "in a dignified, eloquent and convincing manner. There was no harshness or bitterness in his expressions and, while laying bare the class antagonisms now existing, and demanding that the working class organize to take political control . . . he never descended to abuse or villification." Rather, he appealed to his listeners' basic decency and invoked the ideals of Christianity and the Founding Fathers. "While young in years," the account continued, "he is a master of the socialist arguments and holds even the prejudiced while he explains its demands and aims." The final proof of his effectiveness, the reporter concluded, lay in the large audiences that turned out to hear and to applaud what he had to say. But the prospect of living in Kansas City and making forays into the surrounding countryside for the rest of their lives did not even begin to fulfill the O'Hares' missionary impulses. When the call came for volunteers to support striking anthracite coal miners in Pennsylvania, they could hardly resist.[8]

A Different America

The Socialist party's national office, still located in St. Louis, supported the Pennsylvania state committee's plea for money and organizers when the miners went out in May of 1902. Two months later the Local Quorum reversed itself on the ground that the party should aid the strikers solely with relief, but Frank and Kate went anyway. Working under state party secretary J. Mahlon Barnes, the O'Hares traveled from mining camp to mining camp, boosting morale and urging patience as the strike wore on. At one point, Kate divided a bouquet of dahlias among a dozen young girls on their way to the night shift at a local lumberyard, leading Frank to write in the *Coming Nation*: "Poor, disinherited babies! We want you to get your freedom, little ones. And your freedom comes when your parents get all the coal your father digs and that will come when the people own the mines." This was a new America for the midwestern O'Hares. In one of his first expeditions, Frank, who prided himself on interacting with his audience, could not get the miners to respond at all, only to find out later that they spoke no English. After that, when necessary, he and Kate went out accompanied by interpreters. The *Hazleton Plain Speaker* found Frank to be "a trained and forcible speaker whose earnestness carries conviction to his audience. He is master of his subject and ridicule will not suffice to down men of his class." As a former hardware clerk, Frank was familiar with mining equipment; in passing the hours with strikers, he learned at first hand how it was used. Kate divided her time among filing her columns for the *Coming Nation,* speaking two and three times a day, and tending to her husband.[9]

In Wilkes-Barre, Frank stood on a chair to speak to several hundred miners, only to be pulled down in midsentence by a policeman on the orders of a local politician. O'Hare avoided an ugly confrontation by suggesting that anyone who wanted to hear more could follow him to a nearby park on the riverfront. Some burly coal miners hustled him back into his chair and carried him three blocks, where, according to a sympathetic report, "the story, and a number of others, was recited, each carrying home some truth of Socialism with trip-hammer force, and each of them was cheered to the echo." With speakers in short supply, Frank decided that the couple would have to split up. The contrast between the miners' miserable shanty towns and the natural beauty of the Allegheny Mountains moved Kate deeply. She confessed to her *Coming Nation* readers that she had tried and failed to describe accurately the appalling human sights she had witnessed in the mining camps. "Draw on your imagination, paint the blackest scene you can," she wrote, "then if it was intensified a hundred-fold, you would have some idea of conditions as they really exist."[10]

Stranded in Philadelphia without enough money to return home when the strike ended in October, Frank contacted William Butscher, a Brooklyn party official, who promised them work in New York City. They began the next day as organizers on the East Side, living with a fellow soapboxer and his family in a cramped railroad tenement until they could find their own apartment. The O'Hares lectured to a "heartily approving audience" (according to the *Brooklyn Standard-Eagle*) at the New York Philosophical Club. Afterward they were invited for tea at the home of Morris Hillquit, leader of the New York Socialists. Years later, what O'Hare chose to remember about his speech was that "Hillquit sat in the front seat, as a bishop, to judge of my fitness, at times he sneered, because I spoke in USA, and not in Marxian lingo." In terms of culture and ethnicity, Hillquit could not have been more different from Frank and Kate O'Hare and still have belonged to the same political movement.[11]

Morris Hillquit quickly took a dislike to the O'Hares. A group of Jewish teenagers asked Frank to tutor them in socialism, a move that Hillquit approved, provided that the boys kept him informed about this potential spy from the hinterland who admired Debs more than Marx. O'Hare taught them public speaking skills, including breathing techniques, enunciation, and proper grammar, before attempting to render Marx into an American idiom. To demonstrate how to put on a program, he had his class hire a hall and organize a lecture. While their first two choices, Debs and Mother Jones, could not come, Walter Thomas Mills accepted eagerly, which outraged Hillquit, who regarded Mills, and, for that matter, J. A. Wayland, as "fakirs," a standard epithet directed at other party factions. Hillquit may have been behind an incident at a fund-raising event to establish a New York Socialist daily newspaper (which became the *New York Call*) when Frank Hill (Hillquit's brother) urged O'Hare to take money out of the proceeds to compensate for having his gold watch stolen. O'Hare declined and then watched in horror when another party member was disgraced in a kangaroo court by the charge of stealing funds from the same event.[12]

Kate spent her time working for *Wilshire's Magazine* and speechmaking to party and union groups. Intrigued by New York as "the city that perhaps offers a greater field for sociological study than any other city in the world," she took a series of working-class jobs "to get information by actual experience" for her stories, first published in Bernarr Macfadden's *Fair Play* and later widely reprinted. Wearing a shabby suit and calling herself "Katie Kelly," she labored in an artificial flower factory on lower Broadway. She made pearl buttons on the East Side with immigrant girls. Working in a candy factory, Kate swore off taffy after seeing trays of the sweets dropped on dirty floors and returned to the batches that workers sat on to keep the candy warm before packaging. She had a similar impulse not to buy ready-made clothes ever again after a stint in a garment factory, observing that many women took extra work back to their tenements after a long day in front of a sewing machine. Following the finished goods into the store, Kate became a sales clerk during the Easter rush. Although they were recruited from the fringes of the middle class, O'Hare came to perceive her fellow employees to be particularly pathetic because they seemed to accept their exploitation as the natural order of things. At the urging of a friend, she became a waitress, finding the work easier, the pay better, and the conditions more sanitary than her other jobs, but hating the work because of the way male customers treated her. Women workers, as she saw it, faced bleak futures whether they continued their toil, succumbed to the temptations of vice, or entered into impoverished marriage and motherhood. "Did God intend," she concluded, "that nine-tenths of the race should be denied the right to life and happiness and become machines to supply one-tenth not with the means of life but of vicious luxury?" Clearly not, if socialism could provide basic social and economic justice.[13]

While Kate investigated the plight of New York's working class, Frank took leave for six weeks to fulfill several speaking engagements as a "Special Traveling Agent" for the *Coming Nation* in Pennsylvania, Ohio, Illinois, Kansas City, St. Louis, West Virginia, and other points, "making things happen as usual" as the *Iowa Socialist* reported. Borrowing the money for a return ticket from his old boss, Gerard Swope, he found that his wife too was broke. They each brought a story to Bernarr MacFadden, who wrote them out checks large enough to make it through the week. The International Association of Machinists hired Frank part-time to start a program of formal labor education. As he would do several times in the coming years when they could not make ends meet as professional Socialists, he resumed his "double life" in business. He covered most of the wholesale hardware houses in New York, finally accepting a position at ten dollars a week at Dunham, Carrigan and Hayden proffered by a fellow alumnus of Simmons Hardware. "I had the pleasing task," he later wrote, "of perfecting the business machinery so that he [the boss] could change his six important and high-priced men into cringing clerks." The repeat exercise in "Tayloring" hardware clerks did not offer much incentive to stay, for as Frank wrote to his brother George, "we can get better board and more fun on the road."[14]

Word had reached the O'Hares of Mills's plan for a new School of Social Economy on a large tract of land outside of Kansas City. Mills was to build a one-story structure with one thousand rooms spread over seven acres complete with a power plant, central kitchen and dining room, and auditorium, plus a gymnasium, a playground, and a park. For two hundred dollars, Socialists and their families would receive a fifty-year lease on their own living quarters. According to a report in the *Kansas Agitator,* Frank O'Hare had already engaged space for his family. But while the O'Hares found the prospect of "a home for life" attractive, they did not have the money. Even if they did, Frank explained to his half sister, they would have sent it to Kate's parents "for boarding us when there was 'nothing doing.'" Following the demise of his machine shop, Andrew Richards had grown restless working in the hardware business again, dreaming that he and his wife Lucy Richards would someday escape to Oklahoma to start life anew on a farm. By the spring of 1903, with Kate's investigative forays completed and Frank (like Andrew Richards) stuck in a dull, low-paying hardware job and his Socialist organizing confined to Brooklyn by Hillquit, it was time to move on. More importantly, Kate had become pregnant with their first child. They had learned a great deal about industrial America and the hostility of the eastern wing of the party toward their brand of hinterland socialism, lessons that would continue to shape their attitudes for years to come. They were not at all discouraged, though, for as Frank later wrote, they had become part of "a truly *religious movement*—for which men would give their all."[15]

They toured the country for several months in mid-1903, barnstorming through New York State and Ohio before hitting Michigan, a state the party had not had much luck in organizing previously. Charles J. Lamb, the state party secretary, simply provided the O'Hares with a list of likely towns, a rail schedule, and the names of local comrades. They soon found out why Michigan had not been well organized. Only a local bully kept Frank from being mobbed in Bad Axe after a boy threw a large firecracker at his feet during a soapbox oration. He showed up unannounced in Dryden, where he had hardly begun to speak when a constable informed him that he was blocking the street. "The idea," he later wrote, "of obstructing traffic in Dryden, Michigan at 8 p.m. seemed so funny to the soapboxer that he laughed and the crowd laughed too." When the burly cop tried to remove O'Hare from his perch, the two men fell to the ground, "the 'law' underneath, clutching the Socialist firmly around the torso while the latter beat a tatoo on the bearded face with clenched fists." After the crowd separated the combatants, Frank was allowed to finish his speech "and Socialism became a matter of interest in Dryden." Subsequently, O'Hare worked a large crowd in Card City that had gathered to commemorate the Battle of the Boyne (when William of Orange defeated James II in 1690), explaining that today the Socialists were engaged in a similar battle against the new economic kings. In Pine River, he delivered a Fourth of July oration "and though the audience was hostile at first," the *Coming Nation* reported, "[he] completely won it."[16]

Calling him "a brainy, level-headed, logical speaker," the *Brown City Banner* gave him a fair hearing as no Socialist had ever spoken in that town before. O'Hare explained that the Industrial Revolution had brought immense power to the trusts and squeezed workers, farmers, and small businessmen. Socialism stood for producer ownership and control; the alternative would be peonage for the many. "The stars and stripes must be run up," he concluded, "and the black flag of private piracy forever hauled down from the industries which all of the people depend on for their life." Only then would peace, progress, and prosperity prevail in America. Owing to her pregnancy, Kate hit upon the idea of concentrating on church groups, speaking "clear-cut Socialism, minus only the name." Her addresses went over so well that she had many more invitations than she could fill. The O'Hares' tour of Michigan played at least a small part in the doubling of votes for the party there between 1902 and 1904.[17]

In West Virginia, site of a series of violent labor disputes, Frank found organizing to be even more difficult. In one of the few positive press reports, the *Parkersburg News* observed: "There is no question about the much-talked-of Socialist's ability as an orator whose words carry considerable conviction to his hearers." Speaking was especially dangerous in the mining districts where company-hired thugs ruled by gunplay. He stood alone in the open at Glenjean to address miners hidden in the brush, turning his back on a gunman dispatched to intimidate him. At other locales mobs disrupted his speeches. On August 17, Kate and Frank spoke at a rally supporting striking machinists replaced by nonunion men in a three-month-old dispute at a plant in Benwood. A few days earlier, more than one thousand shots had been fired in a four-hour riot that local newspapers blamed on the strikers. Arguing that the ruling class had a monopoly on force, Kate said "the boys," meaning the unionists, did not take part in the melee. Frank made what the *Wheeling Register* called "a rattling Socialistic address, with an occasional reference to the strike just to keep his audience interested. . . . His tone was decidedly unfriendly to the press."[18]

In McMechen, following a speech that angered some local residents, Frank was arrested for blocking the street. After the mayor dropped the charge the next day, Frank spoke in Kate's place. About twenty minutes into his address, according to the *Register*, "he made the statement that 'no laboring man of McMechen was fit to have a wife' or words to that effect." Immediately, "some choice fruit long past its prime came from a dozen different sources and found lodgement on his immaculate shirt front and classic countenance." Wiping his face, O'Hare tried stubbornly to continue before being hustled onto a streetcar back to Wheeling. In nearby Moundsville, O'Hare attended the trial of two men charged with assaulting him, addressing the court at length to the cheers of more than two hundred cigarmakers who took part of the day off as a gesture of solidarity. "O'Hare's petty hobby," the *Register* commented, "seems to be that he is making a martyr of himself, and in doing so he is being pretty thoroughly advertised." Evenhandedly, the mayor found the fruit throwers and Frank all guilty of disturbing the peace and fined them each five dollars and court costs. Returning to Wheeling, O'Hare defied a local ordinance prohibiting political speaking on the Sabbath by delivering a Socialist sermon based on the book of Nehemiah. When he attempted to preach again the following Sunday, he was arrested. On Labor Day, he spoke along with two politicians at a gathering under the auspices of the West Virginia Trades Assembly. While carrying the main speaker's remarks verbatim, the hostile *Register* observed curtly that O'Hare "made one of his characteristic speeches." Subsequently, Frank got out his own version of the day's events. In copy that he probably spoon-fed to a friendly editor, the *Cleveland Citizen* reported that "it is said that the arguments of the two politicians fell upon barren ground in comparison to arguments of the Socialist speaker."[19]

While Frank O'Hare had been busy chancing his neck organizing for the Socialist party during his *Coming Nation* tour, party officials monitored his activities with growing concern. By 1903, the loose-knit organization of the party had led to a number of state and local battles between various factions in the Midwest and West. Fearing that hinterland, right-wing Socialists under the leadership of Walter Thomas Mills were maneuvering for control of the party, the largely eastern Center-Left, led by Morris Hillquit, plotted a counterattack. First, at a National Committee meeting in St. Louis early in the year, Hillquit helped to depose the St. Louis Local Quorum and National Secretary Leon Greenbaum. Next, the Center-Left succeeded in electing Hillquit's ally, William Mailly of Massachusetts, as national secretary, although the easterners could not prevent the new party headquarters from being moved even further west to Omaha, Nebraska.

In a letter to his wife, Hillquit expressed pleasure at having clashed several times with "the soul and master mind of the gang," Walter Thomas Mills, adding that "if they represent the spirit of the new growth in the movement, there will be lots of trouble ahead." Job Harriman warned Hillquit that with a seat on the new Local Quorum, "scoundrel" Mills was capable of trouble because "He is an excellent speaker and both he and Debs have many followers of the worshipping type." Reading this, Hillquit may well have thought of Frank O'Hare, the brash young Mills graduate and Debs partisan who had dared to bring the heretical "Little Professor" to New York City.[20]

Mailly soon reported that Mills had given up his School for Socialists, a sure sign "that he's out for the presidential nomination for fair." By mid-July, the national secretary claimed to have evidence linking Wayland's *Appeal to Reason* to the anti–Eastern plot. Ten days later, Mailly fired off an angry letter to the state secretary of West Virginia, demanding to know why the tour of George H. Goebel, one of the few authorized SP speakers in the field, had been canceled abruptly "so as to have the Comrades O'Hare" in his place. In October, Mailly urged Hillquit to take a more active role in heading off the westerners, writing from Omaha that "I have had to sit here and watch Mills and his cursed scheme and engineer to get control of the party." Mills and his allies were openly predicting a split, he continued, "[and] Utah, Ohio, Kansas, North and South Dakota and now West Virginia (through the work of O'Hare) are being prepared for the outbreak." Mills's ouster from the Local Quorum brought an end to his intrigues and he turned his attention back to education. Frank O'Hare's role as a foot soldier in the Mills conspiracy was, at most, tangential. After all, he worked for the *Coming Nation,* not the scheming Little Professor. But the very fact that he was Mills's star pupil made him guilty by association and more or less permanently suspect in the eyes of the new National Office and Morris Hillquit. So far as the O'Hares were concerned, the mistrust was mutual.[21]

Years later, Frank told Upton Sinclair that an angry Mother Jones had cursed him for risking his life several times in West Virginia with a pregnant wife back in a Wheeling hotel room worrying about his safety. Frank spurned the criticism as arrangements for the birth and postnatal care had already been made locally. The work in West Virginia, he told the *Ohio Socialist,* had been a great success in that he had held numerous meetings, organized seven new locals, arranged for eleven county committees "to push the work," and collected a daily average of $4.50 in donations while spending only $1.95 per day. But with Kate "nervous and homesick," the O'Hares headed for Ohio in the first week of October, where Frank spent a month campaigning for the party and organizing locals. The couple returned to the home of Andrew and Lucy Richards in Kansas City, where

Francis Richard "Dick" O'Hare was born on November 24, 1903. O'Hare later referred to this incident as "The first *false move* on our part. Going| | home to mama to have the baby." Like Peter Paul O'Hare, Frank could have stayed on the road forever. Of course, Peter had not been married to Kate Richards O'Hare.[22]

Barnstorming the Southwest

The O'Hares resumed their work for socialism shortly after arriving back in Kansas City. Kate published *What Happened to Dan,* a Socialist examination of sexual purity. To publicize the plight of the "girls of pack-ingtown," she worked as a scab at the Armour meatpacking plant. The stench that clung to her from the "veritable inferno" was so bad that, at her family's request, she took her meals on the porch and slept in a tent. She described the replacement workers as "for the most part coarse, stolid travesties on womanhood who worked liked machines in work hours and quarreled and cursed each other like demons between times." Kate and Frank both taught at the new International School for Social Economy for a time, but Mills had no money to pay them, much less the financing necessary to build his thousand-room house for Socialist comrades. Frank and fellow teacher George Kirkpatrick helped Mills to prepare *The Struggle for Existence,* a textbook based on his correspondence course and school lectures. To induce Frank to resign rather than paying his and Kate's back salaries, Mills suggested that he was not interesting enough as a teacher. Angry at the Little Professor's perfidy and convinced that he had done a good job teaching, Frank gave notice immediately that he planned to return to full-time organizing.[23]

On the road, with an itinerary provided by state party chairmen, Frank fell into a regular routine again that began with a trip to the local newspaper office, where he could sometimes talk his way into getting free publicity in the paper or help to shape a news story about his visit. He might ingratiate himself with a harried editor by tagging and sorting while the advertising handbills were run off. When a newspaper reported a speech favorably, he would obtain several copies, clip the story, and send it to comrades on *Appeal to Reason* mailing lists. Even the most hostile of reports might contain a line or two that could be excerpted for later use. He would dine at his hotel, get a barbershop shave, and make his meeting. After that, he might visit the office of the morning newspaper, read for an hour, and then go to bed. Before his train left the next day he called on party comrades, collected his fee (five dollars plus expenses when he could get it), wrote a letter home, and made a report to the state secretary. If invited, he would speak at factories, schools, churches, or even the local Chamber of Commerce before leaving for the next date.[24]

Frank had developed a number of themes that he could use in speech-making, depending on the composition of the crowd. Knowing that most of his audience had voted for either Republicans or Democrats, he hammered away at the old parties as controlled from the top down by the wealthy. Then he would explain what made the Socialist party different. He spoke in practical terms, seldom making theoretical arguments or even mentioning Marx. In Neodesha, Kansas, he found that E. W. Hoch, Republican candidate for governor, was scheduled to make an address at the same time in a different hall. O'Hare could not resist writing Hoch an open letter, which the local paper printed on the editorial page, challenging him to devote a portion of his speech to explaining how the common people could use the Republican party to protect themselves against "incorporate greed" and fight against "Trust rule." Frank pledged to explain how this could only be accomplished by his party. "You sir," he thundered, "propose peace, progress and prosperity for the people. The Socialists claim such ideals cannot be realized until labor, united, brings into existence the co-operative commonwealth." While Hoch refused to reply, O'Hare had guaranteed himself an audience that night curious to know more.[25]

The O'Hares' travels, the many speeches, and Kate's writings were making them famous among the party's rank and file and to thousands more who read Socialist and mainstream newspapers and magazines. They continued to work on improving their communications skills. When one spoke, the other would sit in the audience and afterward would provide a critique. A perfectionist, Frank O'Hare pushed his wife hard to polish her speaking. The high, shrill sound of her voice on a recording made at the 1904 World's Fair in St. Louis so shocked her that she insisted the machine must have been broken. After that she managed to lower her register significantly. "It used to drive me nuts," he wrote, "to hear her build up to a climax, and then fail to cap it—to deliver the punch line," so Frank also worked with her on timing and delivery. They each developed their own style, with Kate striving to move her audience emotionally while Frank preferred to teach his listeners. A few years later, in 1907, when their itineraries crossed, Frank watched his wife speak without her knowledge, a performance "which showed me that it was better for me to open the way for her." As a spellbinder, the helpmate had already left the husband far behind.[26]

In the spring of 1904, Frank toured for the party under the aegis of *Appeal to Reason* in Texas and in the Twin Territories, Oklahoma and Indian Territory. He reported to the *Appeal*'s readers that he was selling about fifty copies a day of "Finnegan Stories," the folksy collected columns of

E. N. Richardson about a group of small-town characters who gathered at a cigar store to talk politics, especially socialism. *Appeal* Army editor Richardson wrote that in Indian Territory Frank O'Hare and fellow organizer R. O. Dearer "are doing pioneer work and sending applications for charters at the rate of two a week." Concentrating their efforts on miners, ranchers, and farmers working marginal lands, the party attracted voters through promises of political and agrarian reform that sounded as much like populism as they did socialism. In April, with Frank's help, Socialists "won one more skirmish with capitalism" by electing the mayor, the recorder, and three of six alderman positions in the mining town of Coalgate, described by O'Hare at the time as "unlighted, unwatered, unpaved, uncouth—a great sprawling village of toilers: no mansions; just little cottages and shacks—no saloons and few churches." Hoping to build on this victory, he returned to Coalgate the next month to preside over a conference to map out strategy for the systematic dissemination of Socialist propaganda. As originally planned, Kate was to join him and take over the operation while he continued the fieldwork, but at the last minute the local comrades decided that they would run the office themselves.[27]

After the parley, he stopped off at Chandler, a pleasant little town where he had lectured earlier in the tour. He told the *Daily Publicist* that he had found the people "cordial and open-minded," although some "irresponsible individuals" had disrupted his efforts. "I am surprised at the poverty of the producing classes here," he said. "Their condition seems to be far inferior to the eastern workers in spite of the great natural wealth of the locality and the immense shipments of products." This was not mere hyperbole; he would later remember the most moving moment in his entire career as an organizer coming at the end of a very long day when he shared with an Oklahoma mining family a stomach-turning meal consisting of corn bread, grease, molasses, coffee from reboiled grounds, and "the dirt that goes with the most abject poverty." There was not enough to go around, but the family wanted to share what they had. After that experience, if he truly believed in what he was doing, how could he not stay and fight on their behalf?[28]

Later that summer, two Texans, Lee and Jake Rhodes, invited Frank O'Hare to speak at what was billed as "the first annual encampment" of Texas Socialists at a grove located a mile west of Grand Saline in Van Zandt County. A decade earlier, Populists had brought their message to the rural poor of Texas and the Twin Territories with encampments that in their organization resembled old-time American religious revivals and in content resembled the political carnivals of Europe. Veteran Populists, the Rhodes brothers brought the idea back to further the Socialist cause. From all over northeast Texas came poor farmers and their families in covered wagons to hear two "Speakers of National prominence," Frank O'Hare and Benjamin Franklin Wilson, as well as Texas Socialists Stanley J. Clark, W. D. Simpson Jr., John Kerrigan, and the Rhodes brothers. While local newspapers claimed that the encampment drew between four and six thousand people, O'Hare remembered that heavy rains limited attendance to only a few hundred for most of the encampment. Three times a day, the speakers preached the gospel of working-class emancipation. O'Hare marveled at his audience's interest and intensity. The Grand Saline experiment convinced him that with better planning and better luck the encampment could become the perfect vehicle for organizing the countryside for socialism.[29]

After a brief recuperation from the summer's labors, Frank set out on another round of organizing in the Midwest. In Red Oak, Iowa, he paused long enough to dash off an article for a local Socialist newspaper designed to inspire and instruct the Hawkeye state comrades. "The people are HUNGRY for a way out," he assured his readers, urging them "to mount the hurricane deck of a soapbox and answer the questions from those around them" on the aims of socialism and the SP. In keeping with his philosophy that a good soapboxer educated rather than harangued, O'Hare advised would-be speakers to be serene and smiling. Let the losers in the old parties get violent, snarling, and angry; for "Our power to control America depends upon our power to control ourselves, our feelings—our tongues. Our quietly spoken words pierce ignorance and reach the mark like radium rays pierce rocks." Once the losers had tried all of their dirty tricks, "then their short program is over [and] we take charge of the work."[30]

This was advice from a young veteran with a solid faith in himself and his movement, a reflection of the view held in common by hundreds and thousands like him of the close inevitability of a Socialist America. This romantic historical determinism revealed a basic flaw in Socialist thinking: the gross underestimation of the capitalist enemy as a sluggish, stationary target incapable of enduring against seemingly inherent economic contradictions. By the early 1900s, though, corporate capitalism was well on the way toward a major adjustment that made it a formidable moving target for advocates of radical change, more overwhelming, it turned out, than the Socialists ever dreamed, through the reorganization of property ownership and the market economy undertaken in concert with conservative Progressive reformers.[31]

Kate O'Hare was growing restless at their home in Rosedale, outside of Kansas City. Frank's second visit to Chandler had led to an offer to work at the *Daily Publicist*, whose publisher, Mrs. W. H. French, was impressed with Frank's speaking ability and knowledge of the newspaper business and with Kate's writing. But in Oklahoma, little "Dick" O'Hare would no longer be able to go over to Grandma Richards's house when Kate and

Frank were both at work or on the road. In late 1904 a woman identifying herself as Mrs. Baker approached Frank at the Rosedale post office soliciting funds for the "Joseph'd Home" in Joplin, Missouri, a shelter for widows and unmarried mothers with children. Authorities, she explained, routinely seized children from fatherless families because of possible neglect. Frank declined to give a donation but introduced her to Kate, who grasped the possibility of hiring the right single mother as a housekeeper. Leaving Dick with Lucy Richards, Kate and Frank went to Joplin to verify Mrs. Baker's story. Deeply moved by the plight of the women and children she met at the shelter, Kate agreed to be the manager there temporarily. Disaster struck when a typhoid epidemic swept through the crowded house, with the money earmarked for Kate's salary going for medicine and nurses. As the weeks passed, the couple pined for their own son—and the open road. Frank, Kate told her sister-in-law, "is worse than a fish out of water when he is not working too. He seems never happy unless he is working day and night."[32]

Oklahoma

In early January 1905, with the typhoid crisis passed, the O'Hares moved to Chandler accompanied by their new housekeeper Anna, a Swedish immigrant with a child about Dick's age. Mrs. French rolled out the welcome mat for the "very pleasantly remembered" Frank and "his gifted wife who is one of the most convincing writers of the day." With the child care problem apparently solved, equality restored to the marriage, jobs in hand, and the Twin Territories ripe for organizing, they settled in Chandler. Kate joined the *Publicist*, becoming the associate editor while Frank wrote editorials and did odd jobs for the paper when he was in town. The *Publicist* ran her "Kitty Kelly" exposé of life among New York's working class through January and February. In "What Do Women Want?" she explained how capitalism oppressed all women. In Millsian fashion, "Barometer of the Race" covered the history of the world from the dawn of humankind to the near future when, as the present system crumbled, women would finally emerge as equals. The paper ran her report on life in a Kansas City meatpacking house and commentaries on politics, racism, health care, hunger, and the trusts.[33]

Frank managed to book Eugene V. Debs for Chandler in March. Both of the O'Hares had already met Debs briefly. Ten years earlier, following his release from Woodstock Prison and his conversion to socialism, Debs ate supper with the Richards family one night in Kansas City; in 1900 he "blessed" Frank and his sweetheart Marie Beimdick during a memorable campaign swing through St. Louis. Debs was at the heart of the Socialist movement, a folk hero to party members and millions more in the working class. Foreign-born party leaders such as Morris Hillquit and Victor Berger may have sneered at his vulgar, Americanized Marxism, but Debs understood the heartland in ways that they never could. Berger and Hillquit controlled their own enclaves and the national party machinery; Debs was the only national Socialist leader. He enjoyed the Oklahoma tour, writing his mother a few days before the Chandler appearance that "everything is beautiful in this former paradise of the Red Man." To make certain that the opera house would be filled, Frank O'Hare devised a contest offering five dollars to the child who sold the most reserved (25 cents) and general admission (15 cents) tickets. Frank reported the enthusiastic responses of several prominent citizens to Debs's "Progress of Civilization" address in which he predicted that the "fierce death grapple" of capitalism would soon be replaced by cooperative ownership. "His peroration was matchless," O'Hare enthused in the *Publicist,* "and during many of his vivid descriptions hardly a breath stirred." The power of Debs's appearance was such that it made Kate and Frank feel truly welcome in Chandler.[34]

The O'Hares spent much of their time barnstorming through the Twin Territories in the spring and summer of 1905. Kate's schedule was so tight that she had to disappoint her audience in Chandler when a rain shower made open-air speaking impossible, leaving her no alternative but to board a train for another speech the next day in Shawnee. She made it up to her adopted hometown a month later, giving two addresses that drew a connection between the rise of large trust companies and poverty and how public ownership of land, the means of production and transportation under socialism would bring about a new equality.[35]

In reporting his wife's speeches, Frank wrote that they "greatly enlarged the circle of her friends among all classes of people in Chandler," a comment that, when considered alongside what he had said about the Debs lecture, would seem to indicate a continued longing for acceptance into the small town's social network. Living in an area where socialism enjoyed strong grassroots support, the O'Hares remained controversial for their feminism. Shortly after Kate spoke in Oklahoma City, an editorial in the *Times-Journal* accused her of trying to draw attention to herself by daring to discuss the institution of marriage in public, hissing: "If the fake be a female, while she tells all about marriage, wifehood, and motherhood, it can be put down that she has no children and hates brats." In a published reply, Kate wrote that she was married to the man with the most "brains, ability, and character" in the territory and her son made her glory in motherhood. "If you want to find the happiest marriages, the cleanest home lives, the most loved and welcomed children," she observed, "just look for them in the homes of socialists." When Kate spoke in Oklahoma City again, state party secretary-treasurer J. E. Snyder reported that her lecture had been followed by a large picnic where Socialist women had gotten together to become acquainted under party auspices for the first time. In Guthrie, she spoke before a huge throng, including several newspaper editors in town for a convention, using the occasion, as she told the *Appeal to Reason*, to hand them "larger chunks of pisin, unvarnished facts than they were used to getting."[36]

Following his philosophy of teaching people rather than carrying them away emotionally in his public appearances, Frank O'Hare gave an address on "practical patriotism" in Chandler on the Fourth of July. He began with a history of the origins of the American Revolution. Today, he said, we "celebrate the day reform ceased and revolution began." The Founding Fathers provided Americans with the power to establish democracy, but true freedom would come only with the end of class rule. In the search for ever-increasing profits, monopolists starved industrious farmers and artisans. Labor-saving devices had actually eroded the standard of living for the many. Did this mean smashing the machinery that created trusts? "No! No! Rather let the toilers unite in trade unions, and discuss and learn how to use machinery as a blessing and prevent its acting as a curse." O'Hare urged his audience to enjoy the holiday and then get busy tomorrow organizing themselves so that farmers could control the marketplace and workers could run the factories. The people would then own the monopolies instead of the other way around. Teddy Roosevelt Republicans, Bryan Democrats, Populists, and Socialists all agreed that trust rule had to change. In that sense, they were all revolutionaries. When the peaceful transformation came, Americans could celebrate another independence day, "the independence of the people from plutocracy." Control of the many by the greedy, gold-seeking, and violent few must end, he concluded, for "The republic of the workers, the brotherhood of man is at hand."[37]

Frank concentrated his efforts for much of the summer on Indian Territory, an area where the "American Dream" of a hard-working farmer climbing up the agricultural ladder from the low rung of landless toiler to the middle position of proud yeoman had become an ordeal of relentless drudgery, exploitative tenancy, and increasing indebtedness to (in the memorable words of Frank's friend Patrick Nagle) the "interlocked parasites in the electric light towns." O'Hare started up locals and spoke at Socialist picnics of farmers and miners, sometimes in tandem with Mother Jones. Organizing the primitive, poor hamlets of the Indian Territory was difficult work, even in Muskogee, where Frank found a handful of enthusiastic converts including his old friend, Henri Beraud, a Socialist and former St. Louis chef, whose restaurant at the 1904 World's Fair had gone broke. O'Hare was arrested for blocking the street during one of his first speeches.

"When he was taken to court and fined $5 and costs," the *Muskogee Times* reported, "he cast some aspersions on the court and stated his opinion as to the unsocialistic manners of the officers and judge. These little remarks cost him just $10 more." Having learned the hard way that there was no place in town suitable for speaking, Frank suggested that the local comrades build one. Volunteer crews of teamsters, carpenters, electricians, and masons took apart a large lumber shed that the party bought with merchants' contributions and reassembled it on donated land from a set of Frank's hastily drawn blueprints. Having set this plan in motion, O'Hare moved on to other engagements and was astonished some years later to find an even more elaborate structure in place than the one he had designed. For a time, the Muskogee Labor Temple became the talk of the Twin Territories, an example of the possibilities of Socialist-led community cooperation.[38]

In the summer of 1905 the O'Hares moved to Miles in northeast Indian Territory where, after careful scouting, Andrew Richards had located a site suitable for farming, allotted Cherokee land that could eventually be purchased. Frank later wrote that they had left Chandler because Kate became ill and he had grown bored with small-town newspaper work. The *Publicist*'s ongoing financial problems may have played a part in the decision as well. A few years earlier, while still living in New York, Frank had told his brother "you couldn't hire me to *stay* on a farm for keeps," and he had no intention of doing so now. Rather, he hoped to use the place as a base for his family while he continued his organizational work, leaving Andrew to do most of the farming. While Kate was happy to be living with her parents again, she wanted to resume her speaking career, not stay at home for several years until Dick reached school age as Frank wished. Their second child, born July 9, 1906, remembered her mother saying years later: "I really wanted Dick. Then your father wanted me to stay home. I just had you for spite." Nor could Kate and Frank agree on what to name this girl. Kate called her Wilberta; to Frank she was (and subsequently became) Kathleen.[39]

So long as he had the freedom to hit the road periodically, Frank enjoyed life on the farm. There were comic moments, such as the first time he and housekeeper Anna tried to milk a cow and his many failures in horsemanship. He admired his father-in-law greatly, both for his farming skills and his socialism. Paying him the ultimate compliment, Frank wrote that "he was as great souled as I picture my mother as being." Together, they plowed and planted, raised livestock, dug wells, and built fences and dwellings. But Frank's most important priority was party organization. "Frank is on the road now," Kate wrote on August 5, capturing his enthusiasm, "and says the day of our opportunity has come, the day that we have long looked forward to and we have only to be strong enough to meet the opportunity to light a flame for protest that will stop short of nothing but the abolition of capitalism."[40]

In 1906 the Twin Territories Socialist party escalated the campaign to create a grassroots movement capable of winning elections. At Frank's urging, local Socialist picnics gave way to regional encampments similar to the one that he had attended at Grand Saline two years earlier. During July, August, and September, the party sponsored small Socialist encampments throughout the region. Typically, several locals would sponsor meetings together lasting from one day to a week. Careful planning included securing a suitable place with a source of water, plenty of shade, and enough space for thousands of people to camp out. The local comrades could not afford to absorb the large losses the Rhodes brothers incurred, so they raised funds through donations from party members and local merchants (who stood to make money from the affairs) and by selling space to food vendors in advance for cash. Thousands of handbills plus posters, newspaper advertisements, and press notices promoting the appearance of prominent Socialist speakers, camping facilities, music, and the promise of a good time proved irresistible to isolated farmers with not much to do in the sweltering weeks just before or after harvest (depending on the crop), to miners eager for a little diversion, and to other working-class Sooners.[41]

Frank spoke at as many encampments as he could, along with such Socialist luminaries as Mother Jones and Eugene Debs. In early September, Kate left the farm to speak with Frank at nearby Black Jack Grove. Then he moved on alone to southeast Indian Territory, organizing a club of fifty-six in Wilburton and another at Red Oak. "The coal mining region of Indian Territory," he reported to the *Appeal*, "is aflame with Socialism, and the farmers of the region are not far behind in their endorsement of the movement." Aflame or not, the party had made great strides in mining and rural districts where O'Hare found "a true proletarian class—landless farmers and toilless laborers" eager to hear his message. The camp meeting format was effective as an organizing tool and perfectly appropriate for a people who remained devoutly religious. Indeed, the confluence of two strains of millenarianism, one Christian, the other Socialist, made the movement much more than just another political party. The encampments offered the converted the implicit promise of a culture all their own as well as political empowerment.[42]

After the encampment season ended, Frank O'Hare went to Colorado, where the state Socialist party had nominated William D. Haywood for governor. Secretary-treasurer of the Western Federation of Miners and a co-founder of the Industrial Workers of the World, Haywood, WFM President Charles Moyer, and Denver businessman George Pettibone had been kidnapped to Idaho and charged with the bombing death of former governor Frank Steunenberg. In perhaps the most revolutionary pronouncement of his political career, Eugene Debs issued a call to arms for Socialists and all working people to mobilize behind the defendants. Before leaving

Oklahoma, Frank had joined the IWW "as a gesture" so that he could campaign more effectively among the miners. Critical of the party's state committee for not routing Eugene Debs effectively, O'Hare took the liberty of booking the Socialist Hero on an open date—a big mistake, it turned out, because the exhausted Debs drank too much at lunch and performed poorly that night. Frank moved up his own speech to a miners' local the following day in order to be with Debs on a train bound for his next engagement. "That day we became comrades indeed," Frank wrote, years later, "and the warm personal love that welled up then never failed to throb in my heart for him." Knowing that Debs was still in no shape to speak, O'Hare hustled him away to his hotel for a nap, leaving instructions for the local comrades to wake him at 8 P.M., feed him a quick meal of soup and coffee, and escort him to the hall by 8:30. O'Hare stalled the packed house with an introduction to the speaker and, much to his relief, Debs strode on stage at the appointed time to give a captivating speech. Haywood lost the election (while polling some sixteen thousand votes) and eventually won acquittal of the murder charge, thus handing the party, especially the *Appeal to Reason*, an enormous propaganda victory.[43]

Frank did not return home to Miles until after the election and planned to be on the road again by mid-January. In a letter to the *Appeal*, he wrote that as he and Kate approached the fifth anniversary of their first speeches in Liberal, he felt like a veteran campaigner. "But," he continued, "I have the same old enthusiasm except when I am on the fagend of a trip, full of malaria, which is thrust upon you down here, but have no thought of leaving the road." When Kate took the children and her mother on an extended family visit to Kansas that stretched into February, he grew impatient. He struggled with his feelings in a letter to his half sister, explaining that while he should have been content with the comforts of home, good meals, pleasantly diverting farm work, and a loving wife and children, "I cannot be content, except to deprive myself of these blessings, and put up with cheap hotels and the discomforts of travel, for the sake of raising as much hell as I can." He had to raise hell through his party work because "Capitalism invades whatever retreat I seek, and my only relief from it is to fight it." There was more to it than that, for he so identified with the Socialist cause that he could not bear life away from it. As a Colorado comrade put it: "People who come in contact with him soon discover that the one thing that he is particularly proud of is that he is a Socialist."[44]

A letter of Kate's to Gertie Petzold written during this time made scant reference to Frank, except to say that he would be gone for several months and that little Dick "has many of Frank's traits but will be more tractable." She seemed much more concerned that longtime housekeeper Anna had left to get married. The burden of housework, child care, and sewing was such that she spent one whole day riding fifteen miles on horseback in a futile search for another woman helper. Under the circumstances, professional work was out of the question. A few weeks later the hiring of "a nice little nurse girl" seemed to have eased Kate's burdens considerably and put her in a better frame of mind toward her husband. She loved him enough, she told Gertie, to support his need for the excitement of the road. In the years since their marriage, he had "improved wonderfully." He was more thoughtful, more mature, "and hard experience has rubbed off the rough edges of his nature and left the better more prominent." Proud of his work for the cause, she would remain content to manage their home and their children—until she could find an opportunity to get away.[45]

Socialist possibilities in Arkansas excited Frank O'Hare's thoughts in 1907. He toured there under the auspices of state secretary Dan Hogan from March to early June, visiting fifty-five towns, only a fraction of which had active chapters. The *Appeal* reported that he organized more than a dozen locals and signed up several members at large in other locations while making the tour "practically self-supporting." Hogan warned O'Hare that other outsiders had not done well because they did not know how to talk to Arkansans. To publicize the tour and introduce him to the locals, O'Hare and Hogan asked the *Appeal* to make special mention of the campaign in its Central States edition. He had a brochure printed up containing his picture, a brief biography, favorable press notices, and testimonials from his comrades. The back page featured an endorsement that opened many doors to him in the coming years:

> The successful meetings of Comrade Frank O'Hare in almost every part of the country bear convincing testimony of his exceptional ability as a speaker and organizer. Having been brought into close touch with him in the recent Colorado campaign, I am in [a] position to know how well equipped he is for platform work and what tremendous energy he brings into play in organizing his meetings, enthusing his audiences and firing the local comrades with fresh zeal, renewed courage and unconquerable determination. O'Hare is a versatile genius, and as a lecturer, propagandist and organizer he has had such varied and practical experience that his equipment is complete for the best kind of work, and that he is equal to every demand is borne out by the uniform expressions of hearty approval wherever he has been seen and heard. EUGENE V. DEBS

With the Haywood trial now making news almost daily, O'Hare ran into some hostile local officials; in other places such as Hope the reception was warm. The lone Socialist in Benton gave O'Hare a week's wages of five

The "Dude Socialist" has his picture taken at Batesville, Arkansas, about 1907 (courtesy Missouri Historical Society).

dollars for the cause. Being the good stump speaker that he was, Frank chose his themes to fit the audience. Pious Fayetteville heard him speak on the theme "The Sermon on the Mount: Is It Practical?" He skewered the two old parties, especially Senator Jeff Davis, at Newport. In the hillbilly town of Yellville, he discovered that he could make himself understood by speaking simple Elizabethan English, which had developed as a local dialect. Dan Hogan came to appreciate his work as "beautiful. . . . pleasing, logical, and effective. As a propagandist he has no superior in my judgment."[46]

In the midst of his Arkansas tour, O'Hare crossed the Mississippi into Memphis, where he spoke on the Moyer–Haywood–Pettibone case. The kidnapping of the three by "Pinkerton thugs" working for the smelter trust, he told his audience, was a crime so great that if they got away with it working people would soon have no Constitutional rights at all. Moyer, Haywood, and Pettibone had not even been in Idaho during the time of the murder. Furthermore, state judges and the Supreme Court refused to review the illegal extradition. "Cheap executive" Teddy Roosevelt delighted in promoting his Square Deal program, but he did not favor a square deal for the accused, as he had already pronounced them unfit to be Americans. There were two sets of laws in this country, O'Hare declared, one for enemies of the trusts and another for the ruling class. His denunciations of John D. Rockefeller led to calls from the crowd for the oil baron's lynching. If the court in Boise found the three guilty and sentenced them to die, he warned, "it would simply mean that capital would be signing its own death warrant." The outrage and the excitement of the case had pushed O'Hare, Debs, and other Socialists away from their evolutionary strategy and toward calls for a defensive class war. Given their stance, if Moyer, Haywood, and Pettibone had been found guilty, the quest for socialism might have ended on the streets in 1907, or, had they failed to act in the face of their fiery rhetoric, there would not have been a "Golden Age" of socialism at all.[47]

One night, sometime after his return to Oklahoma for the encampment season, O'Hare arrived very late at a picnic where he heard a roughly dressed man speaking with a German accent. The stranger later introduced himself as Oscar Ameringer. Unlike most other Socialist immigrants who brought Marxism with them from the Old World, the Bavarian-born Ameringer was radicalized in the United States by American writers and his own experiences as an itinerant musician, painter, hobo, and union organizer. The poverty of the farmers he spoke to as a party organizer shocked him. He became a full-time "world saver" because, as he put it in his *Autobiography*, "This thing was too terrible to be tolerated." Ameringer and O'Hare became fast friends. Frank drilled him in English grammar and commented on his speechmaking while Oscar critiqued Frank's performances and tutored him in the Bible. Both liked to tell the story of how they encountered a group of drunken Choctaws who wanted to accompany them to a schoolhouse meeting for socialism. Ameringer thought himself clever for talking the natives into coming instead to a subsequent meeting in the mountains when he would be addressing Indian problems specifically. O'Hare, who knew the Choctaws, told Oscar that they would be there— and they were, in force and intoxicated, along with a group of equally drunken lumber cutters. The speeches, punctuated by frequent rebel yells and Indian war cries, went well after all. Oscar Ameringer became one of the most effective organizers in the Midwest, beloved for his humorous, accented speeches and his penetrating analysis of farmers' problems. At the many encampments where they appeared together, Frank loved setting Ameringer up with a comic introduction, such as the time he told an audience that he knew Oscar would make a great speech because O'Hare had made the same one last week. Deadpan, Oscar replied: "Ven I become a spitch schtealer, I vill schteal spitches from der same place Frank O'Hare schteals his: FROM HIS VIFE'S BOOK!"[48]

That fall, entrusting their two children to the care of Lucy Richards, Kate and Frank both hit the road again to fill separate itineraries. Although the *Newport Daily Independent* found Kate to be "a thoroughly feminine woman, an ardent lover of home life," it was in that Arkansas town that Frank realized how great she had become when, their paths crossing, he watched his wife speak ("perfect in form and perfect in treatment") on socialism and the trusts. Accompanying her in a taxi to the edge of town, he watched mournfully as she and a male comrade stepped into a small boat and poled off into a swamp so she could make her next meeting in an Arkansas lumber camp. Frank rationalized that the pilot would defend her with his life as necessary, but he also gained insight into how she must have felt on countless occasions as he went off to face the thrill of danger for the cause. His second Arkansas tour of the year satisfied nonetheless because the Panic of 1907, sweeping through the country in October and November, gave him the opportunity to explain "the money question" to attentive, angry audiences. In one cotton center, where merchants held the debts of farmers and sharecroppers, banks and wholesalers held the debts of the merchants, and no one was buying cotton, O'Hare spoke from the back of a wagon parked in front of the biggest bank in town to teach the crowd how socialism would cure the evils of the present system. He also spoke to mill hands, railroad workers, and miners. One gathering was made up almost entirely of African Americans, so, in keeping with the mores of Jim Crow, he had to "watch my step, and not be too polite to them" or risk facing a white lynch mob. Before leaving, he made a gift of John M. Work's Socialist classic *What's So and What Isn't* to a black preacher with its promises of justice, brotherhood, equality, and love in the cooperative commonwealth.[49]

A National Reputation

In his history of the American Socialist movement, Ira Kipnis refers to the period 1907–1908 as "the stagnant years." With the rate of growth in the party's membership declining and those who joined apt to drop out quickly, he found that the old militancy was gone. This seemed true enough at least in regard to socialism as an urban movement. The SP's most popular figure and only real national leader, Eugene Debs, remained popular among all sectors of the rank and file, but he paid scant attention to the inner workings of the party. His followers on the Left, including Christian Socialists, western radicals, and anarcho-syndicalists, remained far from the levers of party power as well. Hillquit, the linchpin of the Center, never identified with what he regarded as untutored and wild-eyed westerners in the movement, and he had detested anarcho-syndicalism ever since his clashes with Daniel DeLeon in the 1890s. Proud of his role in wooing thousands of middle-class Americans into the movement, Hillquit envisioned a party patterned after the French and German Social Democrats. As early as 1903, when they had worked together to scotch the ambitions of Walter Thomas Mills, Hillquit and Victor Berger had begun to reconcile their ideological differences to forge a Center-Right alliance of urban Socialists (New York, Milwaukee, and Chicago) and bourgeois intellectuals that came by default to dominate the SP's increasingly powerful National Executive Council. Not that they liked one another personally, for Hillquit continued to distrust the Milwaukee Socialist's bossism and "yellow" (reformist) tendencies, while Berger's idea of a good joke was to tell the New Yorker that he regarded Hillquit as "an opportunistic impossibilist and an impossible opportunist," but they needed one another badly to check the combative industrial unionism and vigorous agitation of "Big Bill" Haywood, Debs, and westerners like the O'Hares on the Left.[50]

So while the SP may have become "stagnant" at the top, many comrades saw great possibilities in the upcoming 1908 elections. The party had more than three thousand locals. Between them, *Appeal to Reason* and *Wilshire's Magazine* had a circulation of five hundred thousand. Millions more were reading such brilliant Socialist propaganda as Upton Sinclair's *The Jungle* and the works of Jack London. Hundreds of Socialist newspapers dotted the country from New York City to the Pacific Northwest. Furthermore, the mood for change was such among the electorate that the two old parties had become dominated by Progressives, conservatives by Socialist standards, to be sure, but reformers calling attention to the need for antitrust laws, expansion of democracy, increased support for education, and laws protecting workers.[51]

Certainly, stagnation did not reign in Oklahoma. Almost 13 percent of ballots cast in the 1906 elections had been for Socialists. Shut out of the new state's constitutional convention the next year, the comrades voted to oppose the resulting document. Ironically, the constitution they opposed contained most of the immediate demands in the party's platform. But the Oklahoma Constitution also legitimized the Boomer capitalist mentality, and opposition to that mindset is what had made the Socialists different from the other parties. The Oklahoma SP ran a full slate of candidates in the fall election. While voters approved the new constitution and swept the Democrats into office, the results also showed significant Socialist strength in western and southeastern counties. Most of the Socialist votes came from rural areas, indicating that farmers were the party's main supporters, although they were not numerous enough to have elected a single state or federal official. Yet there were more Socialists in Oklahoma per capita than

Friends and enemies: The National Executive Council of the Socialist Party of America in 1911 (top, left to right, Victor Berger, George H. Goebel, and Robert Hunter; bottom, left to right, Morris Hillquit, John Spargo, Lena Morrow Lewis, Carl Thompson, and J. Mahlon Barnes). Courtesy Perkins Library, Duke University.

in any other state. O'Hare told the *Chicago Daily Socialist* that the party had 350 locals, a remarkable total he attributed "to our excellent choice of state and county secretaries." Sooner Reds could also boast that their circulation of *Appeal to Reason* was second only to California. Eager to capitalize on the growing farm vote in general and Oklahoma in particular, Victor Berger recruited several organizers, including Oscar Ameringer and Otto Branstetter, to build a successful political machine roughly along the lines of the Milwaukee model. By 1908, state party secretary-treasurer Branstetter and Ameringer had become leaders of the Oklahoma movement. So had the peripatetic Frank O'Hare, who was elected as a delegate to the national party convention in Chicago.[52]

Frank O'Hare's actions at the party convention proved him to be both a strong supporter of Debs and an advocate of the farmer as a wage earner (as opposed to the farmer as a small-time capitalist), a position he held in common with the Center-Right, including Algie M. Simons, the party's leading expert on "the farm question." During one debate, O'Hare, speaking "both as a farmer and a Socialist agitator," supported the idea of a committee consisting exclusively of farmers that would bring recommendations before the convention because "we want to have our Socialist farmers get together and pronounce 'revolution' so the other farmers will know what they are talking about." When the report of the Farmer's Committee (chaired by Berger lieutenant the Reverend Carl D. Thompson) came under attack as being too Populistic for pledging to fight against monopolies while leaving private farmland untouched, O'Hare tried to paper over the majority's concern. He explained that in Oklahoma "the revolutionary, class-conscious Socialists" were fighting for private ownership rather than renting from the state. Until farming became cooperative, the party ought to make it clear that "the man who is doing a piece of work shall have a place to put his feet while he is working." Unmoved, the convention accepted the minority report written by a lone Oregon farmer pledging relief "through the socialization of the national industries, in the production for use and not for profit."[53]

The convention's main business came with nominations for the presidential ticket. A disastrous speaking tour muted enthusiasm for Haywood, who yielded the Left to Debs. Frank O'Hare heard rumors that Berger, Hillquit, and National Secretary J. Mahlon Barnes would block Debs's candidacy because he had become too close to the industrial unionism of the IWW. Following Debs's nomination and John Spargo's lukewarm seconding, Seymour Stedman of Chicago proposed the name of Algie M. Simons, recently sacked as editor of the *International Socialist Review* for his increasingly "yellow" or rightist views (by publisher Charles Kerr who was moving in the opposite direction), citing the precarious state of Debs's health. Frank O'Hare rose to present another seconding speech for Debs. Calling him "my elder brother in this movement," O'Hare insisted that "the American embodiment of the proletarian movement" was perfectly fit physically. New York's Ben Hanford followed by reading a letter from Debs saying that he had recovered completely from a throat operation. Victor Berger then nominated his trusted Wisconsin ally, Reverend Thompson. Hoping to siphon off enough votes from Debs and Simons to deliver the nomination to Thompson, the Right arranged (despite his protests) to nominate James F. Carey of Massachusetts. But in the ensuing stampede for Debs, Hillquit could not even control his own delegation. The seconding speeches for Debs, including Frank O'Hare's, had proven effective. For the third time in six years, young O'Hare had incurred the anger of the party's powerful eastern Center-Right, although he still had more in common with it ideologically than any of them would have cared to admit.[54]

Back in Oklahoma, with Kate pregnant again and Frank frequently on the road, the couple, their children, and the latest in a long string of housekeepers left the family farm for the comforts of a cottage on the abandoned campus of an Indian college in nearby Vinita. Kate was sick for most of the summer and prepared herself mentally for the possibility of miscarriage. Frank had hoped to be home for the birth, but the encampment season and his new position as a member of the state party leadership made that unlikely. On the night of October 16, when he telephoned the family, he learned that she had given birth to twin boys. Jokingly, he wrote to the *Appeal* "that if every Socialist in the United States would do as well, we could have Socialism in twenty-one years without any further agitation." Kate had named the boys Eugene Robert and Victor Edwin, after Eugene Debs, Robert Hunter (a social settlement pioneer and Socialist writer), and Edwin Markham (the California poet who wrote "The Man with the Hoe"). This time there would be no argument over names. "If ever you saw a proud papa," Kate wrote Gertie Petzold, "it's Francis Peter, to see him swell up and strut and boast about his boys you would think he did the whole job by himself. He has been in twice for a few hours since they came but will not be home again until after election."[55]

The Oklahoma organization worked at a fevered pitch through the summer, making special appeals to landless tenant farmers with Populist-style platform land planks. In early July, Eugene Debs swung through Oklahoma to speak at several Socialist encampments. The next month, twenty full-time organizers sponsored some 165 major meetings. In the south-central Oklahoma town of Konawa, a crowd of more than ten thousand heard Frank O'Hare, Oscar Ameringer, and Kansas organizer W. T. Banks urge voters to mark the Socialist ballot. Democratic nominee William Jennings Bryan carried the state (122,363 votes) while William Howard Taft finished second (110,474 votes) and Debs third (21,425). Debs had garnered more than twice as many votes as were cast for the Socialist gubernatorial candidate the previous year; one congressional candidate received 13.2 percent of votes while three counties ran close to the 25 percent mark. The party had done best again in the west and southeast, with more than 90 percent of the Socialist votes coming in rural counties. The vote in the country as a whole did not match the encouraging results in Oklahoma. In spite of Debs's exhausting and expensive whistle-stop tour aboard the "Red Special" for the stretch run, his candidacy yielded 420,973 votes, only 18,000 more than four years earlier. The SP had expected between one and two million. Some blamed Samuel Gompers, president of the American Federation of Labor, for abandoning his longtime political neutrality and endorsing Bryan; others blamed the economic depression; while still more thought that Progressive reformism in both old parties had cut into the

Socialist appeal. The disappointing national figures made the rapid strides in Oklahoma all the more remarkable.[56]

Frank O'Hare had big plans for 1909. While he did not run the party in Oklahoma, his voice carried considerable weight with secretary-treasurer Branstetter, who had admired O'Hare ever since he heard him speak in Norman at the University of Oklahoma years earlier, and with Ameringer, a friend since the time when they "took on" the Choctaws together and coached one another in speaking. Frank now had a national reputation. And he was the husband of Kate Richards O'Hare, who had a national following. Working out of offices in Oklahoma City, O'Hare, Branstetter, and J. O. Watkins organized a retreat for potential fieldworkers with lectures on history, race, the land question, women, politics, and economics. Frank also further refined the experiment he had helped to launch at Grand Saline, Texas, by arranging for ten "monster encampments" that covered all of the Sooner state. He bought a large circus tent, contracted for carnival shows, and booked "high grade Socialist orators" such as Mother Jones, Bill Haywood, Walter Thomas Mills, and, of course, Kate O'Hare. Luring Eugene Debs, the greatest Socialist drawing card of all, proved more difficult since Debs charged one thousand *Appeal to Reason* subscription cards per appearance. Rather than selling all the subscriptions before booking Debs, sponsoring locals bought the "subs" in advance in the hope of selling them later, a hard lesson for the cash-strapped Oklahoma organization. Ameringer scouted the locations, using charm, humor, and a businesslike approach to solicit underwriting from local businessmen through Chambers of Commerce. Local comrades tacked up posters in every town and crossroads for many miles around. Crews would set up the Big Top, smaller tents for sleeping, speakers' stands, food concessions, and the amusements. Some purists complained about the circus atmosphere, but it drew big crowds and paid the bills.[57]

Breakdown

Although he had not felt well for weeks, O'Hare supervised the first encampment, saw that everything was set up for the second, and then collapsed. He went home to the cottage in Vinita, where the family doctor diagnosed him as having malaria. When he did not bounce back, Kate took him and the household over rutted roads in a borrowed lumber wagon to the O'Hare farm. Eventually told to get away from the Oklahoma climate, Frank left his wife, four children, more than one thousand dollars in debts, and a movement he had helped to build for a boardinghouse room in Kansas City. He remembered feeling "scared and desperate" after being told that on top of the malaria he had suffered a nervous breakdown. A loss of nerve meant that he had let Kate and the party down. It is now known that malaria is responsible for a wide range of mental disorders, so in all probability, the disease and not some sudden loss of what was then regarded as "masculine nerve" brought on his frightening condition.[58]

O'Hare languished at the boardinghouse for some time before taking up Kate's suggestion to see one of her cousins about a job in real estate. His chief responsibility turned out to be looking after Kate's cousin John, an alcoholic alternating between benders and delirium tremens. Caring for someone worse off than himself gave him the confidence to look for more satisfying work. He landed a job with Richards and Conover Hardware Company, where Andrew Richards had clerked some years before. While working in business again turned out to be "a severe wrench" after the freedom of the road, he enjoyed the challenge of rewriting and redesigning the outdated mail-order catalogue. Slowly, his double life returned in the form of "the quiet activities of the Socialist Club" and "lunch daily with the City Club," an establishment catering to local businessmen. Remembering how the Oklahoma comrades had taken a financial bath under the *Appeal* subscription plan in their eagerness to book Eugene Debs for the encampment season, O'Hare chaired a special committee that put on a subscription drive to bring Debs to Kansas City. In early 1910, when Kate moved back along with the children and her parents, they took out a mortgage on a cottage in the Chelsea neighborhood of Kansas City, Kansas.[59]

Kate had no intention of settling into a bourgeois lifestyle. By this time, as Oscar Ameringer observed, "Kate Richards O'Hare was a close second to Debs as a riler-up of the people." In May, Frank asked his half sister Gertie to come to Kansas City so that Kate could go on the road and her now-retired parents could take their leave. "I hate to think of your worrying about four kids," he wrote, "but they are awful good kiddies, and you will only have to whistle to get anything needed to work with." In return, he promised expense money, "a good girl to help," and the opportunity to meet new friends. Kate lit out for her first engagement in Coffeyville before the reluctant Gertie Petzold arrived, advising her sister-in-law by mail to be firm with the children, patient with the housekeeper, and to "just take things easy."[60]

She returned home in time to accept the party's nomination for the second congressional district seat. Posed on the front porch of the O'Hare's "comfortable cottage" with the four children, Kate told a reporter that as soon as she was sworn in she would introduce a bill for the government takeover of all the trusts, and then work to end white slavery and create programs to rehabilitate prostitutes. "Since our first child came," she explained, somewhat defensively, "I have contented myself with a three

An advertisement for the Rip-Saw Lecture Bureau, offering the services of Kate O'Hare, H. G. Creel, and Frank P. O'Hare in return for selling Rip-Saw subscriptions (courtesy State Historical Society of Missouri).

months lecture tour each year, but during my absence the children have never been neglected." When asked how he felt, Frank was quoted as saying: "Let less clever women bake bread and sweep," a comment that probably did not offend his wife, who agreed that a woman's natural place was in the home. With that said, Kate left for a summer tour of the Texas and Oklahoma encampments and a five-day "Workers' Chautauqua" in Oklahoma City, forming "a unique combination" with Ameringer. In September she returned along with Ameringer to campaign for her seat in Congress. On the eve of the election, Frank, himself a candidate for attorney general of Wyandotte County on the Socialist ticket, admitted, "From the first we have not hoped for her election, but we are repaid for the work of the campaign by the interest we have awakened." Garnering 5 percent of the vote in a state where women did not yet hold the franchise, she at least had the distinction of being the first woman congressional candidate in Kansas history.[61]

That summer, Jim Phillips, a conductor on the Rock Island line and a faithful Socialist, asked Frank to make a Labor Day speech at Eldon, Missouri, a chore O'Hare gladly accepted. Phillips never missed an opportunity to sell his passengers subscriptions to his favorite Socialist magazine, the *National Rip-Saw* of St. Louis. Frank mentioned that he had been looking for someone to reprint and circulate Kate's *The Sorrows of Cupid*, a revised version of her popular booklet on male-female relationships from a socialistic perspective, previously titled *What Happened to Dan*. When *Rip-Saw* chief Phil Wagner heard about the O'Hares' situation from Phillips, he asked to see Kate about publishing all of her writings. Busying herself in St. Louis in early 1911 with speaking engagements and ghostwriting for the ailing Colonel Dick Maple, the *Rip-Saw*'s resident sage, she showed little interest in returning home. In a letter to Gertie Petzold, Kate expressed worry over Frank because he had stopped writing to her, but added: "I am getting along so well with my work that [I] should hate to be disturbed." Curious about his wife's newly found attachment to his old hometown, Frank called on Wagner and made an efficiency survey of the *Rip-Saw*'s office procedures. On his next visit, Wagner offered both Kate and Frank permanent positions at the *Rip-Saw*. "I said no and Kate said yes," he later recalled, "But in our family, Kate is very frequently the majority, as she was in this case." Tired (again) of life as a full-time businessman and part-time agitator, Frank warmed quickly to the idea of plunging back into the mainstream of Socialist activism.[62]

Frank O'Hare had come full circle geographically in ten years. In 1901, he had left St. Louis to become a Socialist agitator. The movement had bonded him and Kate from the beginning. Together and apart they barnstormed through much of the country, giving more than a thousand speeches in great cities, towns, hamlets, and the middle of nowhere. They had helped to build the strongest grassroots Socialist organization in American history. Frank had been harassed, threatened, mobbed, jailed, admired, and even loved; Kate had done as much and given birth to four children too. They spent almost half of their married lives away from one another for a higher cause, yet they still loved one another, as they loved the movement. In every sense of the word, they had been missionaries. Now Frank was coming home to a new challenge. Nearly ten years earlier, in announcing their marriage, *Appeal to Reason* had wished them well: "May they live to see the fruits of their labor realized in the establishment of the Co-operative Commonwealth." However far-fetched that may have seemed at the time, in 1911 that dream appeared to be a little closer at hand.[63]

3

Editorial Career,
1911–1917

The *National Rip-Saw* was not much when Frank and Kate joined the staff in 1911. Together with a group of talented writers and the unique appeal of Eugene Debs, they made the *Rip-Saw* over into one of the most popular Socialist monthly magazines in American history. The O'Hares' marriage and the fortunes of their cause continued to parallel one another in the period from 1911 to 1917, for just as Kate and Frank enjoyed the most productive and harmonious period of their relationship during their stint with the *Rip-Saw,* so the Socialist party reached the zenith of its popularity. Everything began to change in 1917 when the United States declared war on Germany. Leading the fight against American involvement in what was once called the Great War, the O'Hares fell victim to a reign of terror unleashed in the name of saving democracy. The wartime campaign against the American Left put a terrible strain on the movement that the O'Hares had devoted themselves to building and sowed the seeds that would ultimately destroy their lives together.

Building the Rip-Saw

Upon acceptance of Phil Wagner's offer to join the *Rip-Saw,* Frank moved quickly to disengage from his bourgeois life in Kansas City. Out of gratitude for taking him in when he was down and out two years earlier, O'Hare gave George Richards ninety days' notice of leaving so that he could finish writing the latest hardware catalogue. When he went to sell their home in the Chelsea section of Kansas City, Kansas, he rediscovered the truth of what he had told Gertie Petzold back in Oklahoma, that "Capitalism invades whatever retreat I seek." At the behest of the meatpacking interests, the rail line linking Chelsea with Kansas City had been rerouted through the reeking stockyards, making his home difficult to market. Almost cheerfully, the O'Hares simply abandoned their dwelling in favor of a rented house on Cook Avenue on the edge of downtown St. Louis. Within a short time, they moved to a larger rental adjacent to Tower Grove Park, where Frank's Clarion Club had met a decade earlier.[1]

The Socialist movement in St. Louis had continued to grow in the decade since the "Dude Socialist" had lit out for Girard as an itinerant agitator. Closely paralleling Victor Berger's Milwaukee movement, which had parlayed a close alliance between the party and local trade unions into electoral victories, the St. Louis SP worked closely on an informal basis with the Central Trades and Labor Union and the Missouri Federation of Labor. Both of these central labor bodies, as amalgams of largely skilled workers organized by crafts, were sanctioned by the American Federation of Labor, whose longtime national leader, Samuel Gompers, detested socialism, a situation that led to periodic friction between the St. Louis activists and the supposedly nonpartisan AFL. Many unionists supported the party at the polls and served as stockholders in *St. Louis Labor* and *Arbeiter Zeitung,* local Socialist newspapers. In turn, the party included labor leaders on the SP slate and continued to support political reforms as part of the immediate demands strategy, designed to improve the lives of workers even as the Socialist millennium approached.[2]

Gus Hoehn, a close friend of both Victor Berger and Eugene Debs, editor of both Socialist papers, and an able champion of labor activism, remained the leader of the St. Louis local of the SP, assisted by William (Billy) M. Brandt, secretary of both the SP and the Central Trades and Labor Union. As firm supporters of the SP's Center-Right, Hoehn and Brandt stood for a constructive socialism, pledged both to trade unionism and political action. While welcoming the O'Hares into the local as ardent Socialists and comrades with national reputations, the St. Louis leadership regarded the couple as outsiders, perhaps because they perceived them as infected with Western radicalism and as allies of the syndicalist Industrial Workers of the World, founded as a revolutionary industrial unionist alternative to the AFL by Debs, Bill Haywood, and Daniel DeLeon. After all, Frank carried an IWW card and had campaigned hard for Haywood in Colorado, while Kate had spoken from the same platform as "Big Bill" on the encampment circuit and was widely admired among the IWW rank and file. By 1911, though, following the lead of their hero Debs, the O'Hares' flirtation with the IWW had passed. All three had come to see the Wobblies as too violent and anarchistic, although they continued to insist that industrial unionism remained essential to the prospects of Socialist democracy. During their St. Louis years, Frank would play an active, if minor, role in local party affairs, while Kate limited herself to public appearances on behalf of the St. Louis SP.[3]

Phil Wagner had hired the O'Hares in desperation. The magazine had been started seven years earlier as a money-making venture with Seth McCallen, who, writing under the name of Colonel Dick Maple, provided most of the copy. As Frank described it, "Seth would loll back in his chair, chaw tobacco, and dictate copy that would keep the hillbillies in stitches. . . . It was very low-brow indeed." The mail-order advertisements for quack medicines and get-rich-quick schemes that became the paper's financial mainstay made Maple's vulgarities seem profound by comparison. When Wagner and McCallen became Socialists, they entered the market as a rival to *Appeal to Reason*. Following McCallen's incapacitating stroke in 1910, Wagner hired W. S. Morgan to imitate the Maple style. By the time Kate and Frank joined the staff, circulation had dropped to the point where Wagner was reduced to filling long-expired subscriptions and mailing copies to addresses from street directories to keep up advertising rates.[4]

Under the terms of their agreement with the *Rip-Saw*, Kate would be a salaried associate editor, paid by the word for her writings plus royalties on her books and pamphlets. Frank received a straight salary for his work as circulation manager. Wagner would phase him in as de facto editor, yielding control over what went into the magazine as the contracts of the current contributors expired. Meantime, O'Hare was free to hire new writers "more authentic in their Socialist theories." Immediately, he recruited Harry Tichenor, whom he had met ten years earlier on the train bound for the Mills school. Frank also lured former police reporter Herrlee Glessner Creel away from the *Appeal to Reason*. W. S. Morgan would be retained to write under his own byline. Later in the year, Oscar Ameringer joined the *Rip-Saw* staff. The magazine's greatest coup came in 1914 when Debs hired on to write editorials and deliver speeches. Kate remembered:

> It was a marvelous combination. Phil a canny publisher, O'Hare a whooper-upper, Morgan a shepherd of the hungry farmers, Harry the brilliant iconoclast, Gene to the American underdogs of the turn of the Century what Jesus of Nazareth was to the Jews of his day, Oscar the profound philosopher and supreme humorist, and Kate O'Hare—well just Kate O'Hare.[5]

Years later, Frank O'Hare told his son Victor: "I was the actual editor, listed as 'circulation manager.' That was MY mistake. Wagner had suggested my name on the mast-head as 'editor' but I was of the opinion that it would be better business to let Kate have the honor." When one of his secretaries asked why he had told a *Rip-Saw* visitor that his job was "just this and that," Frank replied that he had to be modest because his job, including editorial work, was to sell the magazine and its writers (especially Kate) to the public. Harry Tichenor went a step further, telling Frank he was a "damn fool" for not writing more himself.[6]

At the time it suited O'Hare to downplay his own role. He assigned the stories and left the copy alone, except for Kate and, later, Debs, for they both sometimes got carried away with fiery phrases that sounded better on the hustings than they read in print. As he came to see it, "Kate was the perfect instrument for bringing to the world my dynamic contribution. She was SO perfect in every way." He never doubted that she was the better writer. Under the routine they developed, when Kate was on the road, Frank simply edited her reports for print. At home he often gave her an idea or a lead for a story and she would return with copy. He would work on it, then she would make the final revisions. It was a partnership not unlike the one that Wayland had with Fred Warren at the *Appeal* or that Debs had with his brother Theodore.[7]

The *Rip-Saw* editorial staff, 1914 (courtesy Missouri Historical Society).

As she explained a decade after his death, Kathleen O'Hare thought her father "had an absolutely first-class brain. My mother had a very good second-class brain . . . he had a tremendous imagination. My mother never would have, never, never would have achieved what she did without my father. He was the one who stage managed the whole thing." As long as they worked together in this fashion, their arrangement produced great reporting and contributed to the increasing popularity of the Socialist party, especially in the South and Southwest.[8]

Frank O'Hare's demands on Kate as a wife, a mother, a writer, and a touring lecturer put a strain on their marriage. In an article for *Reedy's Mirror*, written as a rejoinder to the complaints of a wealthy young man at loose ends with himself, Kate described her life with Frank, in terms meant to be humorous, but with a subtext of candor:

> I have not lived in any ideal Arcadia. My husband never sprouted wings. He smokes a pipe, scatters cigar ashes on the parlor rug, eats spring onions and limburger cheese, puts his feet on the best chairs. Sometimes he prefers sitting with a bunch of cronies over a glass of beer, spouting philosophy, to reading Emerson, Wilde, Nietzsche, and Shaw with me. He has even been guilty of the heinous crime of expressing admiration for small, plump blonde women. (I am very tall, dark and thin). There have been times when he neglected to tell me three times a day that he loved me, *and yet*—I have not been supremely happy, but I have proved that I am not a weakling, I have laid hold on life and taken its bitter along with the sweet.

Counting her blessings, she noted that she lived in order to love, to serve, and to create. "As long as I can give my life to the work of teaching the whole race this lesson of life," she concluded, "I shall be happy." Now that their positions within the family had become reversed from a few years earlier, perhaps Kate had at least come to appreciate Frank's old feeling of being "a fish out of water" at home.[9]

As circulation manager, O'Hare enlarged on an idea Fred Warren had used to route Debs's speaking engagements through the *Appeal*. He set up the *Rip-Saw* Lecture Bureau, arranging for Kate to give a lecture in towns east of the ~~Rocky~~ Mountains upon receipt of a minimum of two hundred twenty-five-cent yearly subscriptions (west of the Rockies, the price was three hundred subscriptions). The more subscriptions a local could sell, the longer she would stay. The magazine paid for traveling expenses, hotels, and advertising matter. The scheme proved so popular that within two years, the price for Kate's lectures had risen to five hundred subscriptions, although for three hundred "subs" a local could get Frank or H. G. Creel. In 1914 Frank began routing Debs for eight hundred subscriptions per lecture while the rate for Kate's speeches dropped to four hundred. The lecture bureau scheme and the dynamic contents of the magazine boosted subscriptions to 180,000, making the *Rip-Saw* second only to *Appeal to Reason* in popularity among Socialist readers.[10]

During their first months at the *Rip-Saw*, while Kate wrote features on women's issues, including the Triangle Shirtwaist Fire, property rights, and white slavery, Frank contributed an article on how the Socialist party is managed ("It is organized on the lodge basis. We call the 'lodges' 'locals.'") He also began a monthly "Circulation Chat" patterned after E. N. Richardson's "*Appeal* Army" column. In his first offering, he felt compelled to explain that Phil Wagner played a vital part in the management of the magazine, although "Phil is no great shakes when it comes to writing." As for himself, Frank explained that he would be dashing off "some stuff" but "the comrades don't hanker after my stuff like they do after my better half's, and I certainly admire their taste." He also used the column to introduce readers to the office secretaries, boost Socialist pamphlets published by the *Rip-Saw,* and recognize "subgetters" and locals that qualified for Kate's lectures. He printed pages of testimonials to Kate's power as a public speaker to sell ever more subscription cards. "Recalling the sweet sacredness of the Sermon on the Mount," wrote one enthralled comrade, "was the Sunday morning meeting on the little hill just across the railroad tracks." Another correspondent from Yellville, Arkansas (where Frank had communicated in Elizabethan English four years earlier) observed of Kate's visit that "we were all so happy and excited that we didn't know whether we were down here or up yonder. It was simply wonderful the way she captured that crowd. Many a man and woman went away regenerated, sanctified and baptised with the Holy Ghost and speaking in new tongues." Given such superlatives, it is not surprising that by the end of 1911, Kate's schedule had already been filled for much of the next year. Having accepted his role as her manager, Frank pushed his wife to the limits of her endurance.[11]

"I am feeling fine and having a great time," Kate wrote to her sister-in-law from Wilcox, Arizona, in February 1912. "[I] have enjoyed every moment of my trip." Her only complaints were that she missed the children and that Frank wrote "might unsatisfactory letters." A week later in San Francisco, she suffered a severe ankle sprain, but elected to continue the tour in a cast rather than accepting an invitation to recuperate in a Socialist doctor's hospital in Sacramento. On February 23, exhaustion and agonizing pain from the poorly set ankle led to her "nervous collapse" (as reported by the *Chicago Daily Socialist)* in Portland, Oregon, where local doctors shipped her to the Sacramento comrade's facility. According to Frank, after several incoherent letters from his wife, he was finally able to win her release. Back at home in St. Louis, while the ankle healed, "her mind did not. She was like a dead woman. No love for anyone—she said so." That summer (as Frank later remembered it), when she went back on the circuit again, a friendly doctor diagnosed her as suffering from the aftermath of cocaine addiction, a common enough occurrence at a time when cocaine was still dispensed as a pain-killing prescription and sold legally as a component in patent medicines. On that same tour, the *Rip-Saw* and at least one St. Louis newspaper reported that the mayor of Tallapoosa, Georgia, had sprayed her with a fire hose, although, Frank soon discovered, the mayor succeeded only in drenching himself. More seriously, in the fall, after refusing treatment for injuries sustained in an automobile accident, Kate nearly bled to death when an abscess burst inside her nose. Frank

Frank O'Hare at work routing his *Rip-Saw* "stars," about 1914 (courtesy Missouri Historical Society).

demanded extraordinary efforts from the *"Rip-Saw* Army" too, telling his volunteer salesmen that the magazine could have a circulation of one-half million if only they would work harder. "You have started to double the circulation of the Rip," he wrote, "now rip in and do it."[12]

He pushed himself just as hard. The system for increasing circulation through Kate's lecturing kept her away from home much of the time, which meant that he had to preside over the home front more than he ever had to in previous years. "Now," he later wrote of the situation that he had created, "being a mother to children—even when there are maids and maiden aunts to assist—is a job a father should really not take over." Housekeepers continued to come and go, but half sister Gertie Petzold became a fixture in the household. Kathleen O'Hare, for one, grew to hate her Aunt Gertie, believing that "between the housekeeper and my father, we'd have been better off than with this horrid creature who made our life a misery and who my mother detested." Frank was the parent Kathleen remembered with fondness, observing that "He was very difficult to get along with in some ways, but that basically he had

great, great love for us and that
my mother actually didn't have
that much for us, that we were
very secondary in her scheme of
things."[13]

With Gertie Petzold anchor-
ing the O'Hare home the best
that she could, Frank felt free to
resume his travels, even when
Kate was on the road. He made a
lecture swing through Missouri
and Arkansas in April 1912. The
next month, he attended the
party's national convention in
Indianapolis, more as the husband of Kate Richards O'Hare,
who sat on the National Executive Committee, and representative of the *Rip-Saw* than as an
active participant, in keeping
with the magazine's policy of
staying out of party battles.
"One absolute rule on the front
page of the *Rip-Saw*," Frank
later explained, "was that the
story must sit well with the
casual reader. It was NOT written to please Morris Hillquit,

The O'Hare family poses outside of their
residence on 3955 Castleman Avenue,
St. Louis, about 1915 (left to right, Dick,
Kathleen, Eugene, Kate, Kathleen, Victor,
and Frank O'Hare). Courtesy Missouri
Historical Society.

John Spargo, or Max Eastman. But to help Henry J. Dubb nab new subscriptions."[14]

Frank's report on the party convention glossed over the ongoing and
increasingly bitter division between the Center-Right, which supported
evolutionary reforms inching toward socialism, and the Left, which envisioned revolutionary class struggle through propaganda and industrial
unionism. O'Hare portrayed the delegates as a fair cross section of the
party membership when, in fact, the many unskilled workers attracted by
Haywood and other leftists in recent years were very underrepresented.
The report of the Committee on Labor Organization, Frank wrote, "was
greeted with the most spontaneous enthusiasm and adopted by unanimous
vote." This was true enough in that the compromise resolution neither

Frank O'Hare in his backyard, about 1915 (courtesy Missouri Historical Society).

endorsed nor condemned industrial unionism, but Frank said nothing about a subsequent resolution amending the rules for party membership in Article II, Section 6, of the SP Constitution (engineered by Berger and Hillquit) that called for the expulsion of any party member opposing political action or endorsing industrial sabotage, a provision the Center-Right would use to purge Haywood from the National Executive Committee through a membership referendum after the fall election. O'Hare put the best possible face on the contest for the presidential nomination featuring three candidates "well qualified to have been named as standard bearer." With Hillquit and Berger supporting their own candidates, Debs received only 60 percent of the votes.[15]

The most controversial action of the convention, which Frank did not even mention, came at the eleventh hour when Hillquit pushed through what he later claimed was the National Executive Committee's unanimous recommendation of J. Mahlon Barnes as Debs's campaign manager. Barnes had scandalized the party by refusing to acknowledge a child he had allegedly fathered with a party employee. Since Hillquit's statement clearly implied support from Bill Haywood and Kate (who both opposed Barnes), the resolution passed. Rather than reporting this, O'Hare chose to pay tribute to Hillquit for his "magnificent address" that opened the convention as well as the work of Berger, Haywood, and John Spargo. He ended by predicting that the time had come "to shove the Socialist vote well up into the millions." Like O'Hare, Debs said nothing in public during the campaign about the Center-Right, "the machine that is now throttling the party," as he put it privately. Rather than risking an open confrontation with the party bosses over the Barnes affair, which had the potential to be, as Hillquit put it to Berger, "a trial of strength between the Reds and us," Debs acceded to a national referendum that led to Barnes's retention as campaign manager and helped to solidify the Center-Right's control of the party. In November, Debs received 897,000 votes, a great improvement over his showing four years earlier, but well shy of O'Hare's hoped-for millions.[16]

Frank O'Hare used the national convention to float a new subscription scheme: the *Rip-Saw* Illustrated Lecture. In return for several hundred subscription cards, the magazine would donate a Victor Stereopticon and a set of slides to a local. Qualified lecturers could then tour with the machine under state party auspices, charging one hundred sub cards for each presentation. The idea sounded good enough to Fred Warren of the financially strapped *Appeal* that he offered to match O'Hare's offer. In the summer of 1912, Frank began signing up state organizations. The illustrated lecture was to be divided into five parts dealing with the evils of present-day capitalism, the evolution of society (à la Professor Mills), the struggle of the working class, the Socialist movement (this part "will knock the nonsocialists off the Christmas tree"), and organizing for the future. After viewing these lectures, O'Hare promised, "the working man who can refuse to sign an application card needs a surgical operation rather than an argument."[17]

Frank gave the slide lecture idea a thorough tryout in the working-class neighborhoods and branch libraries of St. Louis, pronouncing it "the greatest thing for metropolitan agitation yet devised." In October, with Kate recuperating at home from her near fatal abscess, Frank took the opportunity to fill her dates. The Amus-U Theatre in Birmingham was packed in anticipation of hearing Mrs. O'Hare but, as a local Democratic paper reported, Mr. O'Hare "lectured in her place to the satisfaction of everyone present." The Birmingham *Labor Advocate* observed that the audience was particularly responsive to O'Hare's references to "the magnificent prospects" for Socialist gains in the upcoming election "and his destructive criticism of the three capitalistic parties was also relished by his hearers." In Winston-Salem, North Carolina, the *Journal* expressed surprise that O'Hare's "entertaining and profound" illustrated lecture could pack the courthouse on a night when the largest crowd of the year was seen across town at the theater. The contrast between the two gatherings did not go unnoticed; "The dress suit and evening gown was the badge of distinction at one meeting; the overall and the cotton checks shirt was the prevailing apparel at the other."[18]

O'Hare took his Stereopticon show along to fill Kate's dates in Florida, using slides of St. Louis slums to illustrate the plight of poor children in a city where the Democrats had long reigned supreme. His message was that only socialism offered the poor the promise of equal opportunity. "Socialism not only seeks to emancipate the laboring class," he said in

Tampa, soft-pedaling the class struggle, "but to make things better even for the capitalists and make this world more beautiful and joyful for all men." While Frank found the meeting in Tampa to be "grand," the audience at the next stop in DeLand was small and chilly and he consoled himself afterward with a long letter to his wife. He was glad to be able to fall back on the slide show. "O, lord but I would have been worn out if I had to make a straight lecture," he wrote. Still, the effort pleased him: "I made a pippin. Cool, deliberate, half speed, poised, I handed the stuff over the footlights with no chance for the critical to find a loop hole in statement of fact or conclusion." He never forgot that he was filling in for Kate, telling her that women "come in great numbers to the meetings, expecting you. I wonder how they feel at being gold-bricked." The great longing Frank felt for her was evident too. "I am eager to get back to you, dear," he concluded, "for I need your kisses and caresses, I am so lonely for you." Meanwhile, recovering rapidly from what she described as an illness that put her "down near death's door, so near the great eternal rest that its langour [sic] touched me and I had lost all interest in the world's struggle," Kate Richards O'Hare itched to fill her own dates.[19]

The period after the 1912 election was a let-down for the party and the *Rip-Saw*. The suicide of J. A. Wayland on November 10 stunned the movement. Much has been made of a cryptic note he left behind expressing his discouragement with the political struggle, but this must be weighed against his prolonged feelings of depression as a widower and the government's persecution of the *Appeal* as factors that brought about his tragic end. "We shed no tears of grief;" Kate wrote to Wayland's son, "grief is for the naked lives of those who have made the world no better." Frank attended the funeral as the *Rip-Saw*'s personal representative. He draped over Wayland's casket a silk red flag with gold thread that the magazine's employees had stitched together—and he wept.[20]

Returning to St. Louis, O'Hare laid plans for another Stereopticon tour as he worked to find a way to book all of the requests for Kate. While locals continued to send in subscription bundles that qualified them for free lectures by the O'Hares, the magazine's circulation rose only slowly. Like the Socialist party, which continued to suffer from a high turnover rate, the *Rip-Saw* failed to hold its audience. Beginning in November 1912, in spite of many new subscribers, circulation began to drop from a peak of nearly 180,000. Four months later O'Hare told his "hustlers" that the average increase for the time he had been managing the paper of one thousand per month was not good enough. The comrades, he scolded, "have not done their level best for the *Rip-Saw*, because they did not know how necessary it is that they put in every lick they can." In the spring of 1913, he alternately blamed the "after clap" of the presidential election and "a good number of the boys . . . 'laying down' on the job" for further drops in renewals. O'Hare made no mention of the impact of the recall of Haywood from the NEC in early 1913 (which the O'Hares sanctioned tacitly by their public silence) and the subsequent exodus from the party of thousands of his followers, many of them *Rip-Saw* subscribers. By July the magazine had lost twenty thousand readers before leveling off through the rest of the year.[21]

Faced with a steady erosion in the *Rip-Saw*'s circulation, O'Hare struggled to keep the magazine afloat with increased advertising revenues. While some comrades groused about the quack cures and get-rich-quick schemes that bordered the hard-hitting interviews and exposés of capitalist outrages, Frank rationalized, as had Wayland (and O'Hare's boyhood hero P. T. Barnum) before him, that the *Rip-Saw* needed the money and the readership had sense enough to decide what was and was not fraudulent. The *Industrial Worker* of Spokane, Washington, combined their complaints about the *Rip-Saw*'s ads with a protest against the anti-IWW writings of columnist Harry Tichenor and "the delicate little stabs of Mrs. O'Hare" by reprinting the comments of a pro-Haywood local of the SP in Rosepine, Louisiana. The comrades claimed to be "more vitally interested in the Class Struggle than you people, because we have no clientele of quack medicine advertisers and other grafters to contribute to our support." The Spokane paper went a step further when it commented in July: "The Rip Saw may oppose 'direct action' but their skirts will never be clean unless they use that method in cleaning up the rotten advertisements that take up more space than the reading matter." Ridiculing an ad that beckoned the *Rip-Saw* readership to "Be a Detective" through a correspondence course (and, by implication, a spy on the working class), the *Industrial Worker* taunted that O'Hare's magazine had "Better purge yourselves with some of the fake medicine you advertise; it may cure the 'yellows,' you Rip Saw bunch." The O'Hares were hardly in a position to rebut these broadsides because, like Debs, they had become increasingly disenchanted with Haywood's anarchist rhetoric, even if they disapproved of the Center-Right's use of Article II, Section 6, to cast their one-time ally on the Left out of the party.[22]

In regard to the *Rip-Saw*'s advertisements, Frank did attempt to distinguish between what he regarded as harmless frauds and those with potential political overtones. When George McKay Miller approached the magazine with an offer to place full-page advertisements soliciting land sales at his Ruskin colony in Florida, the staff was leery as Miller had been struggling to keep the communal experiment solvent for six years after moving Ruskin from Illinois and, prior to that, Missouri. O'Hare, who had turned down "Professor" Miller's offer to join "Ruskin Commongood Company" before he enrolled at the Mills school in 1901, felt obliged to inspect the site near Tampa Bay, Florida, personally. In a cautiously worded story, Frank reported that most of the Socialists recruited to the scheme "seem to be of a high type." He advised city mechanics without farming experience not to come to Ruskin, although he opined "that reasonably industrious workers who are willing to follow the methods of farming in vogue here, are practically sure of a good living." Anyone thinking about relocating to Ruskin, he wrote in conclusion, ought to investigate the colony carefully first, preferably in person. Apparently satisfied that Ruskin was not another of the proliferating Florida land swindles, the *Rip-Saw* began running Miller's advertisements proclaiming "Not Socialist Communities, But Communities of Socialists." When the periodic O'Hare wanderlust hit a few years later, Frank would come to believe his own copy about Ruskin.[23]

Kate O'Hare continued to push herself hard in 1913, fulfilling the many speaking engagements that Frank arranged for her and writing columns and features for the *Rip-Saw*. She and Frank were especially proud of the magazine's "Hookworm Special" featuring stories publicizing the crusade to eliminate the debilitating hookworm from southern life. While Kate argued that Socialists should cooperate with the work of the Rockefeller Hookworm Commission and various state health agencies, she blamed the parasitic disease on capitalism for keeping southern working people too poor to afford sanitary privies and shoes. Rockefeller and other business-men ("the Big Hookworms") wanted to eradicate little hookworms to bring about more efficient employees and a better sales territory; Socialists want to deliver the South from the big and the little hookworms to strengthen the working class. In later years, Frank liked to say "that a just god will forgive my many crimes" because of his part in the antihookworm campaign.[24]

The O'Hares enjoyed a moment of triumph over the Hillquit-Berger faction in 1913. By virtue of her election as international secretary and a subsequent party vote not to send an additional delegate to the Inter-national Socialist Bureau, twin slaps at Hillquit by the Left, Kate became the party's sole representative to the ISB's convention in London. Berger sniffed to Hillquit that "As for your friend, Kate Richards O'Hare making the American Socialist Party ridiculous at the sessions of the International Bureau—why of course she will make it ridiculous. But by doing so she will just represent the exact state of our American movement." To Berger, the "ridiculous . . . exact state" of the SP lay in the fact that the largely rural West and Southwest, with its heretical mixture of vulgar Marxism and Populism, was still so powerful. Algie Martin Simons put it another way the next year when he lamented to Hillquit that "The three most influential papers in the Socialist movement in America, measured by circulation, are the Appeal, the Ripsaw and the [Hallettsville, Texas] Rebel. Is it not a beautiful trinity?"[25]

Plainly enjoying her celebrity, Kate Richards O'Hare paid a "pleasant call" on the National Office in Chicago, explaining that she was on her way to Calumet, Michigan, to cover the big copper strike for the *Rip-Saw*. She told the *Party Builder* that she had spoken to more than one hundred thousand people during a recent summer tour of the Oklahoma encampments, helping to defeat "a vicious mining law" passed by the legislature, but turned down by the voters in a subsequent SP–sponsored referendum. Before leaving for the International's meeting in London, the *Builder* noted, Kate was to speak under the National Party's auspices in the East to defray her expenses. She would be glad that Eugene Debs had scraped together some cash for her out of his own pocket so that she could "make the trip in comfort and dignity" as he was correct in his assumption that the bitter eastern clique would not come through as promised. As for Berger's comment to Hillquit about her making the party look "ridiculous," Kate later wrote: "I was something of a sensation." The first woman to sit on the International Bureau, she impressed such European Socialist leaders as Jean Jaurès and Karl Kautsky. She spoke to strikers in Dublin and antimilitarists in London. In an article for the *Rip-Saw*, she detailed the splendor and the decay she had seen, coming away from her experience convinced that "the struggle and the suffering of the people are but the birth pangs, the travail that must be the accompaniment of the ushering in of a new social order."[26]

As his wife's stature grew as a Socialist leader, Frank O'Hare labored to carve out his own niche in the movement. He promoted his Stereopticon lectures in the January 1914 *Rip-Saw* with a testimonial from Socialist author James Oneal, who called his presentations "the best and most impressive propaganda . . . witnessed in years." Frank contrasted his first trip through Indiana ten years earlier "going into town after town to greet small but heroic groups of Socialist comrades battling against almost overwhelming odds of local prejudice and ridicule" with his latest efforts that saw "Immense audiences of laughing and cheering men, women, and children, fine enthusiasm, multitudes of new faces, and eager interest." He announced that he would limit his tours to ten days in a different state each month so as not to interfere with his work at the *Rip-Saw*. In January he gave several illustrated talks in Ohio, including Conneaut, which had elected a Socialist city government a few years earlier. The *Hamilton Evening Journal* found it ominous that "Although, Mr. O'Hara's [sic] speech was socialistic throughout, there were possibly as many non-socialists in the crowd that heard him as there were socialists." The Hamilton meeting was his last illustrated lecture. Abruptly the self-promotion ended and the *Rip-Saw* put up the Stereopticon machines and slides for sale due to increasing competition from the SP National Office and locals in Milwaukee, New

York, Ohio, and Los Angeles, all of which had followed his lead in using slide shows as propaganda. Instead, except to accompany Kate on the Southwest encampment circuit, Frank stayed in St. Louis to manage his wife's career and the magazine's newest contributor, Eugene Debs. His real niche, he had come to realize, was as a Socialist impresario.[27]

Debs joined the *Rip-Saw* in early 1914 after parting from *Appeal to Reason* and editor Fred Warren on bad terms. In return for a salary of five thousand dollars per year, he was to write monthly articles and deliver one hundred lectures. With Debs as the new "dean of the bunch," O'Hare told the *Rip-Saw* Army, "I tackle my job with renewed enthusiasm." As with Kate, Debs was listed on the masthead as an editor, but Frank moved quickly, when, as he put it, "Debs DID try to use the *Rip-Saw* as a sewer" in his battle against Samuel Gompers, president of the American Federation of Labor and a staunch enemy of socialism. To keep the magazine out of the controversy between Debs and what he called "rotten craft unionism," O'Hare excised a paragraph from Debs's first contribution and wrote a letter to him explaining why. The Socialist Hero accepted Frank's decision with good grace. O'Hare soon discovered that once he had established the precedent of blue-penciling Debs, Kate was more accepting of his editing of her work as well. When the O'Hares could not agree on a final piece of copy, Phil Wagner acted as a referee.[28]

If Debs acquiesced in Frank's editing, he soon rebelled against the punishing speaking calendar that O'Hare inflicted on him. "Whatever possessed you to put Tooelle [*sic*] into this schedule?" he asked in early 1915. Debs had climbed into an open horse-drawn buggy "steaming hot" from a speech in remote Tooele, Utah, to make a trip through snow and mud—only to miss the train connection to his next stop, Burley, Idaho. "Must I have such a damned killing dose as [this] administered to me on every trip?" Debs insisted that he was not angry with Frank, but heartsick for having to cancel his speech in Burley. In July, during a swing through the East, he threatened to quit the *Rip-Saw*. This time the complaints went beyond "the eternal riding and jolting on cars all day long and the crazy rush to get from one place to another." Comrades had been grousing about "the rotten advertising" in the magazine too. One woman told Debs that ads "of a sex nature appealing to 'sporty socialists' " so offended her that she had urged a boycott of the *Rip-Saw*. Debs did not resign, but instead drove himself to exhaustion through the summer heat of the Southwest encampments. Theodore Debs felt compelled to write Phil Wagner, canceling a speech in West Virginia and demanding that his brother's next trip to the West Coast be done away with altogether. O'Hare soothed the Debs brothers with an apology and then booked the western tour anyway. Furious, the Socialist standard bearer wrote that the subscription lecturing made him feel like "a cog in a wheel, a fixture" at a time when he should be out inspiring striking workers. While he had never been associated "with a whiter, lot of comrades," Debs concluded, he was determined to quit. This time, O'Hare papered over Debs's concerns by sending out letters to local arrangements committees giving detailed instructions ("First appoint a couple of *big husky comrades* . . .") on how to conserve his energy. After working out his one hundred engagements with greater care for the next year, Debs agreed to continue.[29]

Responding to criticisms by Debs and others, Frank issued a press release in September 1914 announcing that the *Rip-Saw* was now in a financial position to refuse advertisements deemed offensive to good Socialists. "It was pretty tough," the release admitted, "to have to run Kate O'Hare's and Debs' and Tichenor's articles on a page flanked by display ads that, to say the least, were unpalatable." Frank estimated that the move cost the magazine at least twenty thousand dollars in lost revenues, which made the subscription lecture scheme more important than ever. He regarded the plan as not only vital to the *Rip-Saw*'s financial well-being but also as "the method by which we unite in one powerful whole the combined work of the press, the platform and the Socialist local."[30]

In a series of articles published in the *Rip-Saw* in early 1914, O'Hare outlined his vision of what the party ought to be. United by the dream of a world without classes, poverty, and exploitation, local comrades came together to form a self-governing "baby local." Once it became strong enough to field a slate of candidates for election, the local matured into a political club. As membership grew, committees (not bosses like Berger and Hillquit), democratically elected by the rank and file, handled specialized tasks. With persistent education and community organizing, Socialists would be elected to office. Elected comrades should be accountable to local party legislative committees, for "the individual who is 'too big a man' to be 'dictated' to by a Socialist local is too big for the Socialist party." The rank and file had to pay close attention to their state organizations in anticipation of the time in the near future when the party became strong enough to elect statewide officials. To fight the "Repo-Democratic Punch and Judy show," he urged comrades to pay their dues and participate in the election of local, state, and national committees to keep the party clean. "Only by the building of a competent organization which can secure the support of the masses and thereby the control of the government," he wrote, "can the radical change be brought about." In a pamphlet designed to help party workers sell *Rip-Saw* subscriptions for the lectures of Debs and Kate as well as a new idea, "the *Rip-Saw* movie," O'Hare argued that subscription canvasing not only helped to spread propaganda but could teach comrades how to work together and bring out managerial and executive ability.[31]

Nowhere in his explanations did O'Hare discuss the role of labor unions or the ideas of Marx. He advocated "common sense" socialism not unlike that of the Socialist bosses Hillquit and Berger, whom he continued to detest personally. Frank put his faith in the party and the *Rip-Saw* as agents for bringing about class solidarity, which, in turn, would bring about public control over the trusts and other necessary means of production through the democratic process.[32]

After fifteen years in the movement, Frank never doubted that the Cooperative Commonwealth would soon come about. He also knew that it would not be as easy as many comrades had once thought. The struggle to keep up the *Rip-Saw*'s circulation during the period between 1912 and 1916 mirrored the fortunes of the party, which had ceased to register steady growth. The graduated income tax, direct election of senators, child labor laws, the Federal Trade Commission Act, the Clayton Anti-Trust Act, and a host of laws aimed at helping farmers and workers, tuned up the capitalist system without bringing about basic changes in the lives of working people. Yet Progressive social reforms, especially the "New Freedom" of President Woodrow Wilson, and the appeal of the Gompers brand of conservative trade unionism cut into Socialist strength. The 1916 Socialist presidential nominee, Allan L. Benson, drew only 590,000 votes, 68 percent of what Debs garnered four year earlier. Even this news was not all bad, for Benson, a man Debs had called "an inflated jackass" in 1915, conducted a poor campaign and ran well behind local candidates in many areas. Socialists improved on their vote totals in many legislative and local elections in 1916 in spite of Progressive municipal reforms (which often eliminated minor party representation) and tacit alliances of business groups and urban reformers.[33]

Having reached the logical limits of improving the status quo by combing out the grosser abuses of industrial capitalism, the Progressive movement itself went into rapid eclipse after 1916. So Frank O'Hare's continuing optimism about the future of American socialism was not necessarily misplaced. Furthermore, the country's growing preoccupation with the war in Europe offered the Socialist party a dynamic issue that could help to bring about a new class consciousness. Therein lay a great opportunity and a greater danger.

Fighting Preparedness

When war broke out in Europe in the summer of 1914, President Wilson asked his countrymen to "remain neutral in thought as well as in deed." Few Americans, including the pro-British and anti-German Wilson, succeeded.

Most American Socialists opposed the war, a stance that helps to explain a drop in membership from 103,000 in 1914 to 79,000 a year later. Just as quickly, though, the party's opposition to the Wilson administration's pro-war Preparedness Campaign caused membership to begin climbing again. Within the party, feelings against possible American participation in the war were strong enough in 1916 that when Debs declined to run, the nomination (by referendum) went to Allan Benson, based largely on his antipreparedness writings in *Appeal to Reason*. The referendum offered party members a choice between two antiwar activists for vice president, with Rand School professor George R. Kirkpatrick getting the nod. The losing candidate was Kate Richards O'Hare.[34]

Kate's crusade against the conflict in Europe began with a heartfelt tribute to Jean Jaurès, the French Socialist leader assassinated by a nationalist fanatic on July 31, 1914. She remembered standing before the first meeting of the International Bureau in London the previous December tongue-tied and "blushing like a school girl" until Jaurès tottered forward to encourage her. There was also the moment when Kate, who had played a tacit role in evicting the Haywood faction from the American movement, asked the Socialist Congress to put the matter of sabotage and direct action on the agenda for the next convention. Jaurès, she recalled, had chided her gently for trying to start a fight within the ranks of the working class at a time when Europe was on the brink of a disastrous war. He had expressed great interest in the O'Hares' "Kodak pictures" of the Socialist encampments, promising that he would accompany her to the Southwest in 1916. To encourage him to come, Kate wrote, Frank had already taken a new series of photographs as a Christmas greeting. Now, "the earth he loved is soaked with human blood; the working class for whom he gave his life writhes in the cursed hell of war, but Jaures lived and taught not in vain." The war, she hoped, echoing the sentiments of Lenin (a gratis subscriber of the *Rip-Saw*) would bring about working-class democracy in place of rule by monarchs and exploiters.[35]

The O'Hares did not waver in their opposition to the war. When the conflict in Europe caused a breakdown in American cotton exports, Frank took the opportunity to blast the Wilson administration for rejecting a federal cotton valorization scheme in favor of a privately funded bankers pool "that will absolutely strip the poor devil who produced the cotton!" The only solution left was for the comrades to buy "a bale of RIP-SAWS, and shove it under the noses of the poor dupes that voted for Wilson and the Democratic plunderbund." In an "Open Letter to President Wilson," Kate took aim at the Chief Executive for preaching neutrality while allowing the export of armaments. Instead of working for peace, she continued, the president asked Americans to pray, "a pious cloak behind which you

[Wilson] tried to screen your service to the profit mongers who demand their pound of flesh all wet with human blood." In a subsequent article, she blamed Congress and the president directly for doing nothing to check the war-induced recession at home and fueling the conflict in Europe with the sale of American goods. Month after month through 1915, Kate urged *Rip-Saw* readers, especially the women, to protest against the administration's tilted neutrality before war engulfed the United States. The O'Hares wrote a play entitled *World Peace* (with Frank "skeletonizing" the plot while Kate wrote the dialogue), performed throughout the country on the Socialist lecture circuit, contrasting the suffering in Europe with the greed of American munitions makers. By the end of the year, though, the Wilson administration became fully committed to gearing up the country for war through military preparedness. Ominously, the president had also begun to think aloud about the necessity of dealing severely with the disloyal, should war come.[36]

Members of the Socialist party and assorted independent radicals advocated genuine neutrality, but were by no means alone as millions of farmers, workers, pacifists, and progressives who supported the old parties espoused similar beliefs. The O'Hares did not hold purist misgivings about building bridges to nonsocialists on issues that mattered to them. As feminists, they had worked in the past with many middle- and upper-class groups advocating women's suffrage. Kate served on committees appointed by St. Louis Mayor Henry Kiel to examine the problems of the poor. Frank had joined the City Club of St. Louis, a luncheon group founded by social worker and Harvard renegade Roger Baldwin to discuss civic reform and other public questions. Along with other civic-minded residents of his hometown, O'Hare had lobbied the city council on behalf of public improvements. Kate and Frank used their extensive social and political networks in St. Louis and around the country in the fight against preparedness and continued to seek out new allies wherever they could find them.[37]

In early 1916, this search spawned one of their most unusual investigative reports in which the *Rip-Saw* asked the question, "Has Henry Ford Made Good?" Two years earlier, Ford had launched his famed five-dollar wage for an eight-hour day scheme for select workers at his moving belt assembly line plant at Highland Park, Michigan, in order to combat high labor turnover and the Industrial Workers of the World. This ingenious attempt to coax laborers into adjusting to higher standards of productivity through the payment of a "family wage" stabilized his workforce. After a two-day investigation of the plant in November 1915, Kate wrote the first of three articles. In his preface, Frank wrote that Kate's words had been "toned down for fear that many readers would not believe the whole truth." He felt compelled to remind *Rip-Saw* readership that "The markets of the world never can absorb the SURPLUS values created by the workers, as long as the wage system exists." Having said that, the article concluded that while the five-dollar day was certainly not socialism, "Henry Ford has brought the joy of living to thousands of sordid, dreary work worn lives and made labor in one little corner of the economic world a boon and not a curse." Introducing Part II, written after the O'Hares' second visit in January, Frank theorized that should "foxy" Henry Ford's "benevolent capitalism" be copied by other employers, "the effect would be to simply clear the way for a Socialist movement that would concentrate itself on one or two essential points," private versus co-operative ownership and true democracy versus industrial monarchy, rather than immediate demands that had come to dominate the Socialist party's platforms in recent years. If anything, Kate's second installment, which contrasted the plight of several men and women she had known in the past with those who lived decently thanks to the five-dollar day, was even more laudatory of Ford than the first.[38]

The third installment related what happened when Kate cornered Ford in his glass-walled office for a rare interview. As Frank later described it: "The duel was on. Henry was a machinist. Kate was a machinist. Henry was a farmer, Kate was a farmer. Henry was an individualist. Kate was an individualist. Henry had [a] positive idea. Kate had positive ideas. . . . The hell of it [was] that Henry was so often right." There was no duel of wits over the relative merits of industrial capitalism and socialism; perhaps by prior arrangement, neither subject came up. Instead, Ford and Kate discovered that they had much in common on the peace issue. Having met with almost universal derision for sailing to Europe with a shipload of pacifists in a futile attempt to bring about peace, Ford was eager to tell his side of the story, even to Kate O'Hare and the *Rip-Saw*. He said that in an atmosphere of growing war hysteria in the United States, he simply wanted people to think and dream about peace. When Kate tried to get him to make a connection between capitalism and war, he politely sidestepped the question. She tried another tack: did he blame bankers and munitions makers for the war? No, he blamed people as a whole for allowing themselves to be exploited. Ford did not hesitate to denounce Wilson's military preparedness program. Praising the automaker for braving the criticism of his five-dollar day from other capitalists "in order to do partial justice to his employees," Kate compared her work and his, saying, "We are both getting just what every man or woman from the days of Jesus on down to the last strike has received; it is the experience of all who help to blaze the trail of social justice." Pacing the tiny office, Ford said that he could only agree. He ended the conversation with a tirade against "the organized power of a greedy, unscrupulous, gold maddened group of ammunition makers." The American people can have peace and social justice, he said, only if they tell Wilson what they think of preparedness.[39]

The seeming lack of support for preparedness in the countryside encouraged the Socialists to believe that American entry into the war might be averted. Debs had written from North Dakota to Frank O'Hare in the summer of 1915: "If you could only be here and see this demonstration! . . . The farmers and their families have come from a hundred miles around— and they are red to the core." The next year, Kate wrote that the crowds who came to the Oklahoma encampments were the largest ever. In Ada, local Democrats did their best to sabotage the meetings by forcing the cancellation of a permit obtained to use the local park and then plowing up the road leading to a pasture where the encampment had been relocated. The people came anyway, although the heat and the dust caused Kate to collapse in the middle of her lecture. Of her audience, she wrote: "The smoldering spark that gleams in their eyes was just a little deeper and more burning and they said: 'Never mind Comrade O'Hare, election day is coming and then we will avenge the thousands of wrongs that have been heaped upon us by the blood-sucking parasites.' " As it turned out, most midwestern farmers were not "red to the core," and while the Oklahoma Socialist party led the nation with 15.6 percent of votes cast, Woodrow Wilson's New Freedom reform program and his campaign slogan "He kept us out of war" led to mass defections from the Socialist column in many locales. Running for the U.S. Senate in Missouri, the first woman ever to do so in any state, Kate Richards O'Hare polled 2 percent.[40]

Fighting War

"When the stress and hurry of the 1916 campaign was over," Kate told her readers, "every one at the RIP-SAW office was worn out, nerves were frayed to the quick and tempers poised on a hair trigger." The O'Hares took a pleasant two-week vacation in Kentucky, where Frank gave an audience consisting of a Methodist and a Baptist congregation "the message of Socialism . . . expressed in the symbols that mean most to them, the language and symbols of the Bible. They feasted on it and pronounced it good." Upon returning to St. Louis, Frank O'Hare tendered his resignation from the *Rip-Saw*, although Kate agreed to stay on—and fill the many lectures to which she was already committed. In an article summarizing his wife's career in *The Call Magazine*, he wrote of his decision: "I swore an oath that I would again return to the job of establishing a suitable home for the children out of the crowded city."[41]

This explanation seems quite incomplete, even disingenuous considering the circumstances. Given his penchant for driving himself and those around him to the limit, it can be surmised that Frank was among those whose "nerves were frayed to the quick and tempers poised on a hair trigger" at the *Rip-Saw*. In 1918, Kate told Phil Wagner that he had developed a "personal prejudice" against her husband, but this may have had more to do with the terrible events of that year than with Frank leaving the magazine. For his part, Frank never had anything bad to say about Wagner, so he might have felt simply that six years at the *Rip-Saw* was enough. He also may have experienced the pull of utopianism. With the party in evident decline and American involvement in the European war on the horizon, several Socialist editors and writers, including Fred Warren, Eli Richardson, and Lincoln Phifer of the *Appeal*, and Kansans Ben Wilson and H. H. Stallard, who had worked with Frank for years in the Oklahoma encampments, associated themselves with the Nevada Cooperative Colony near Fallon in late 1916. A few months after Frank left the *Rip-Saw*, Wagner visited the Nevada cooperative and eventually became the colony's publicity director. Perhaps acting on a similar impulse, Frank O'Hare found himself drawn not to the Nevada mountains but to another potential Socialist haven in sunny Florida.[42]

O'Hare had walked away from friends and work he loved before (St. Louis, 1901; Chandler, 1905; Kansas City, 1911) to take on a new position, always within the confines of the Socialist movement. Now he was quitting the *Rip-Saw* to live socialism in Ruskin Colony on Tampa Bay. Under the arrangement with Ruskin founder George McKay Miller, Frank would split his time between promoting Ruskin through the sale of land and teaching at Ruskin College. Meanwhile, the front page of the March 1917 edition of the St. Louis Socialist monthly contained two important announcements. The first explained that the old name *Rip-Saw* had outlived its usefulness. Henceforth, the magazine would be called *Social Revolution* as "more suggestive of its larger mission . . . the greatest revolution in human history." The name change underscored the sense of urgency the staff felt with the approach of war.[43]

Also, the magazine trumpeted a new subscription contest. The comrade who sold the most "subs" in the next six months would win "10 acres of fertile Florida land in Ruskin colony" (worth three hundred dollars it was said) and enough money for a one-way railway ticket to get there. Town lots in Ruskin Colony served as second, third, and fourth prizes. The agreement with Miller, whom Frank had admired for years, appealed for several reasons. He liked the Ruskin scheme whereby teachers at the Christian Socialist Guild School spent half of their time in the classroom and half laboring for the colony. Because Miller would pay him in land for the promotional work, he had the opportunity to own a home within a Socialist community while working for the common good. And it gave him a new start far from the frayed atmosphere of the *Social Revolution* at a time when the country was sliding into involvement with Europe—a Socialist haven in a war-torn world. The fact that he was lending his (and Kate's) good name to a venture teetering on the edge of financial disaster seems not to have occurred to one optimistic enough to have devoted his adult life to the higher cause of socialism.[44]

Woodrow Wilson's policy of pursuing closer economic relations with the Entente powers and Germany's resort to unrestricted submarine warfare in the European war zone combined to make American involvement in the war almost certain by early 1917. While a minority of party members led by John Spargo, Upton Sinclair, and Charles Russell inched toward support of the Wilson administration, the overwhelming majority of the comrades remained adamant in their opposition to war. Kate O'Hare spoke for them when she thundered: "I am a Socialist, a labor unionist and a follower of the Prince of Peace, FIRST; and an American, second. I will serve my class, before I will serve the country that is owned by my industrial masters." The situation was dangerous enough that in March the National Committee called an emergency convention in St. Louis for April 7 to discuss, after two years of indecision, a specific program of action. As a veteran organizer with time on his hands before the move to Ruskin, Frank O'Hare was chosen as convention manager. With only two weeks notice, he booked the Planter Hotel, made arrangements for the entertainment of the comrades, and attended to the many other details necessary to accommodate 193 delegates from 44 states.[45]

The formal declaration of war on April 6 brought the party face to face with the gravest crisis in its history. Not surprisingly, as Morris Hillquit later wrote, the atmosphere made for "a tense and nervous gathering," perhaps because, as he noted in his opening address, the party remained as "the only considerable organized force which has still retained a clear vision." Personally, Hillquit may have been "tense and nervous" because he had spent much of the past two and a half years trying to keep the party together and, in the process, drifted to the left politically while suffering the continued slings and arrows of his former antagonists. A special Committee on War and Militarism was charged with hammering out the party's position on the war. Kate received the most votes of the delegates running for the committee, narrowly defeating Hillquit for the chairmanship. Others elected to the committee of fifteen included John Spargo, the only prominent pro-war Socialist to serve, who came in tenth, and Victor Berger, who barely beat out the obscure Wilbur C. Benton, Kate's former suitor. After several days of hearings, Hillquit, Algernon Lee, and Charles E. Ruthenberg wrote a report for the majority that declared the party's "unalterable opposition to the war just declared." The only war of concern to workers should be the struggle against capitalist exploitation and political oppression. Rather than heed the call for workers to suspend the fight for better conditions, "the acute situation created by war calls for an even more vigorous prosecution of the class struggle." Specifically, the committee pledged that the party would oppose the war by all means, fight against military conscription, resist "all reactionary measures" limiting constitutional freedoms, propagandize against militarism, and educate workers about the war.[46]

Frank and Kate O'Hare always maintained that the party's militant stance against the war had been right. Morris Hillquit was not so certain; in his *Autobiography*, he wrote that the statement that he had largely crafted merely reiterated the party's long-held feelings about war and did not offend against the law. But, he wrote, "the tone of the proclamation was extraordinarily aggressive, defiant, and provocative. Had it been written in normal circumstances, it would undoubtedly have been couched in more moderate and less irritating language." Clearly, in order to retain control of the issue and his share of power within the party, Hillquit, who had become a quintessential evolutionary Socialist (with Victor Berger by his side), allowed the party's resurgent left wing to push him into taking an uncompromising, revolutionary position. In the past, he had sneered at the O'Hares and Debs because they were not thoroughly steeped in scientific socialism and, hence, unreliable and irresponsible. Now he had joined them, as well as the detested Industrial Workers of the World, in opposing the war on principle. Not to have done so would have meant preserving the party by joining the war effort while denying its voice and its long-held mission.[47]

The war had forced the Socialists to make a choice: to continue as they had since 1912 as an increasingly reform-minded and middle-class organization, purged of the most militant without having broadened its appeal significantly, or using the dangerous opportunity offered by a terrible war to find their way again as a revolutionary organization. Most, including the O'Hares, chose the latter course. In an editorial entitled "You Are Playing with Fire, Gentlemen!" Kate declared that for years those in the movement "have ceaselessly held up the ideal of socialized life" to be brought about through education and the ballot box. "We wanted it to come by the paths of peace," she concluded, "but if that is not to be, then we will snatch it from the bloody jaws of war." Having upped the stakes at a time of national emergency, the party would have to prepare itself for repression. It was a task that the SP had no idea how to accomplish.[48]

Meanwhile, the federal government grappled with ways to repress those perceived as disloyal, presumably German-Americans, but also the Socialist party, whose St. Louis Manifesto Woodrow Wilson had branded as "almost treasonable." In April, Congress began considering a series of bills drawn up by the Department of Justice that were rolled together into the

Espionage Act. This legislation consisted of far more than the outlawing of spies. One provision, which provoked howls of protest from leading newspaper publishers, would have given the president the right to censor the press. While Congress balked at this, Title XII of the bill gave the postmaster general the power to refuse to allow the mailing of material "advocating or urging treason, insurrection, or forcible resistance to any law of the United States." Another provision, hardly questioned by Congress because it seemed so trivial, made it a crime to make false statements or reports for the purpose of interfering with a military operation or that might incite disloyalty in the armed forces "or shall wilfully obstruct the recruiting or enlistment service of the United States." Those found guilty could be fined and imprisoned for up to twenty years. The May issue of the *Social Revolution* reprinted on page one a cartoon from the *Milwaukee Leader* in which a large snake labeled "Espionage Bill" constricted Lady Liberty; the caption read "A Possible Result." The Espionage Bill passed Congress on June 15, 1917. Also that spring, President Wilson issued an executive order creating the Committee on Public Information (CPI), charged with publicizing the administration's version of the truth to inform Americans about the war; in other words, it was to be an agency of propaganda. Armed with the Espionage Act and applauded by the CPI's manufactured consent, the government moved quickly against its critics. As the Socialists soon discovered, in opposing American involvement in the war, they too were "playing with fire."[49]

Kate O'Hare resumed her lecturing for *Social Revolution* shortly after the party's Emergency Convention. The Department of Justice's Bureau of Investigation did not wait for passage of the Espionage Act to begin tailing her. Reporting Kate's "thoughts and expressions" in Atlanta on April 17, an agent remembered her as asking if the munitions makers and the trusts wanted the United States in the war, "why should we not insist that they should fill the trenches with the mutilated carcasses of their own sons?" She returned to St. Louis in time to attend an antiwar rally on April 29 that Frank had organized on behalf of the party. Speaking before a crowd of four thousand "principally of German birth or lineage," as the *Post-Dispatch* was careful to observe, Frank asked for a show of hands to see who would give a dollar for the cause. On this cue, collectors appeared with baskets to collect the crumpled bills. Kate then spoke, predicting that the press would "weep great tears because this is not a patriotic demonstration." After explaining that she did not have to prove her patriotism to anyone, she told her listeners not to believe anything they read in pro-war St. Louis newspapers.[50]

A few days later, Kate and Frank left St. Louis for their new home in Ruskin, Florida. She wrote to her younger children (still in school in St. Louis) that she wished they could be with them because they would enjoy "the trees and flowers and water and everything." Kate described Ruskin as an agricultural paradise, a place they would enjoy every minute of their stay. Once school was out, she promised, "then we will arrange things so you can have a nice change while I do my summer's work." The O'Hares befriended a young visitor to Ruskin, William Edward Zeuch, who had just received his master's degree in sociology from Clark University. The three shared their common dream of establishing a Socialist college for workers free from the interference of capitalist trustees. They agreed that Ruskin had great potential, although Miller's college had existed heretofore only "in skeleton form."[51]

After a brief respite at her new home, Kate traveled to the West Coast, working her way from Los Angeles to the Pacific Northwest before heading east. July began ominously with the news that the postmaster general had declared several Socialist newspapers and magazines, including the *Social Revolution*, unmailable as second-class matter under terms of the Espionage Act. When Phil Wagner printed another edition, minus the material that he guessed postal authorities had found objectionable, the bundles were again refused. With the *Social Revolution*'s second-class mailing privilege revoked for political reasons, Wagner could only send the magazine through the post as third-class mail by placing a one-cent stamp on every copy. The added costs of postage and labor, combined with a disastrous drop in advertising revenues, slowly bled the magazine financially.[52]

In mid-1917, President Wilson seemed uncertain about the implications of the post office's high-handed actions. When Max Eastman, Amos Pinchot, and John Reed (all of whom had supported the president in 1916) wrote to him protesting the suppression of *The Masses*, Wilson told Postmaster General Albert S. Burleson that "These are very sincere men and I should like to please them." A few days later, Wilson refused Victor Berger's request for a brief interview on the subject of press censorship, commenting, "I have seen very many evidences of late that the bulk of the Socialists in this country have genuine American feeling and in no case represent the revolutionary temper such as Mr. Berger has shown." The drop-off in votes for Socialists the previous year and the defection of a handful of eastern party activists may have led Wilson to the conclusion that the antiwar forces could be safely isolated with little fuss. Then again, Wilson was not inclined to stand up to Burleson, contenting himself with a few polite questions and evasive bureaucratic answers, even after his adviser, Colonel Edward M. House, urged him to "take the matter largely into your own hands for he [Burleson] could never have a proper understanding of it." Nor did the president protest when other executive departments harassed "revolutionary" critics of the war, including Kate O'Hare. At the behest of the American Protective League (APL), a superpatriot organization granted quasi-governmental status by the Wilson administration, the Justice Department made certain to report on Kate's activities in Idaho as "certain alleged I. W. W. members would incite trouble with the aid of Mrs. O'Hares [sic] talks."[53]

On July 17, 1917, Kate Richards O'Hare spoke to 143 people at the Cozy Theater in tiny Bowman, North Dakota, where the town's lone Socialist sold tickets for twenty-five cents each to his friends and neighbors. Her lecture, substantially the same one she had delivered at least seventy times before, explained the party's position against the war. The next day, one M. S. Byrne, visiting Bowman while on furlough from the U.S. Navy, fired off telegrams to the U.S. district attorney for North Dakota, Melvin A. Hildreth, and to his superior officer in Minneapolis, complaining about Kate's remarks. Byrne also wrote a more detailed account to Senator Porter J. McCumber of North Dakota, who, on July 23, had the letter read into the *Congressional Record.* "Her entire speech, I was informed, as I was not myself present, was of an anarchistic variety," the senator's source said, "tending in its entirety toward the discouraging of enlistment and resistance of draft." On July 29, as Kate O'Hare bought a newspaper at her hotel in Devil's Lake, North Dakota, a federal marshal told her that she was under arrest. The next day, she was arraigned in Fargo on a grand jury indictment charging her with violating the Espionage Act. Specifically, according to the government, during the Bowman speech she stated

> in substance that any person who enlisted in the army of the United States of America for service in France would be used for fertilizer, and that is all that he was good for, and that the women of the United States were nothing more or less than brood sows to raise children to get into the army and be made into fertilizer.

Therefore, she had obstructed the enlistment and recruitment of American military personnel. After posting a one-thousand-dollar bond to guarantee her appearance at U.S. District Court in Bismarck in December, she was released.[54]

Laughing off the indictment, Kate resumed her work, but the incident marked a great divide not only in her life and those of her husband Frank and their children but also for the Socialist party. The war provided the machinery and the rationale for the government and its vigilante allies to persecute the party. In turn, the party became less an organization dedicated to fighting for socialism than a group defending its right to exist and assisting jailed comrades. No longer would Frank and Kate O'Hare enjoy the freedom to organize and write for an ideal that had defined their world. It was the beginning of the end of their lives together and of their involvement in the Socialist movement.

4

Family Martyrdom,
1917–1920

America's entry into the war tugged Frank and Kate Richards O'Hare in opposite directions in 1917. Frank later wrote that he had expressed the hope that his wife "should retire for the duration, for the country had definitely gone to town on the war. It was all right for Debs to do whatever he wanted to. He had no children." The country had indeed "gone to town," self-righteously persecuting political opponents of the war, especially the Socialists and the IWW, as well as all things German. Frank's instincts led him to Ruskin, Florida, where the family could ride out the storm of ultranationalism while building a future for themselves based on Socialist principles. But Kate had no intention of forsaking her sincere commitment to fighting against the war. At the same time, she may have felt more comfortable out on the road taking on the government than becoming a part-time teacher *and* full-time mother and housewife; for, as Kathleen O'Hare observed bitterly: "The simple truth is that she was, for some reason, not happy in her home and quite happy being the great goddess KRO."[1]

Chair of the Committee on War and Militarism and a high-profile antiwar activist, Kate became the first important Socialist leader to be indicted. The O'Hares' lives did not change all at once, but the pressures of mounting a defense, the trial, the fund-raising for an appeal, Frank's failing business interests, and Kate's prison sentence all put tremendous strains on their marriage. While they enjoyed a second honeymoon following her release, their relationship was never the same. In retrospect, both dated the beginning of the end of their marriage from the time of the family's martyrdom. Again, their partnership mirrored the fortunes of the Socialist party, which held together in the face of government persecution only to limp along as a result of increasingly irreconcilable differences in the postwar era.

Trial

Their lives did not change all at once because the O'Hares had a hard time believing that Kate would be convicted. "We lived under the illusion," Frank remembered, "that the Bill of Rights 'protected' something." While admitting that she faced the prospect of imprisonment, Kate told her readers in the September 1917 issue of *Social Revolution* that the terms of the Espionage Act were so outrageous that no jury would find her guilty. Instead of raising money for her defense, she simply asked her supporters to subscribe to the magazine, which would take care of legal costs. Awaiting trial, she continued to lecture under the auspices of *Social Revolution.* For the first time in years she did not speak before vast audiences of the Socialist faithful at the Oklahoma encampments that she and Frank had helped to foster. What was once the most promising Socialist movement in American history had been wiped out in the aftermath of the Green Corn Rebellion, an ill-fated rising of poor farmers in eastern Oklahoma against "Big Slick" Wilson's conscription. Meanwhile, Frank O'Hare, president of the Ruskin Plaza Company, beckoned readers through half-page advertisements to "Join Us in Florida," promising "No Pioneering," meaning that the company provided everything for would-be owners including livestock, farm equipment, fencing, irrigation, comfortable homes, electricity, roads, and schools.[2]

In reality, life was not easy for any of the O'Hares. Frank wrote to his half sister Gertie that the Ruskin venture had little operating capital and, in the face of conscription, a lack of young men. He had only been able to invest a few hundred dollars of his own, not surprising considering that he still had a mountain of debts from St. Louis to pay. He reported that Kate, in spite of her public optimism, "is of course worried and uneasy, and I have to use every skill to write her as cheering a letter as possible." The O'Hares' housekeeper Kitty painted an even gloomier picture in her own way, telling "Aunt Gearty" that "This is shure some place that you shure can be glad that you did not come down . . . the kids shure do wish that thay ware back in St. Louis. . . . I think Mrs. OHare had one of hear pipe dreams . . . you cant git every thing you want and cant never get any meat." Toward the end of the year, Frank began to downplay the Socialist side of Ruskin in his advertisements, telling *Social Revolution* subscribers that "Co-operative features are carried out to just the extent that conservative and successful farmers can approve of, as being practical under present-day conditions."

Little wonder that Frank wished that he was out organizing instead of Kate. But the freedom of the road that he imagined Kate still had was a thing of the past. The exhilaration of building socialism had been replaced by the American Protective League, the Secret Service, and the Department of Justice shadowing her everywhere, opening her mail, searching her hotel rooms, and holding up her baggage. "Every sort of trap that ingenuity could fashion has been laid for me," she wrote, not the least of which included taking down her every public utterance for possible future use.[3]

In spite of government and superpatriot harassment of antiwar Socialists, the party grew in popularity through 1917. On the eve of the war declaration, Socialists elected two aldermen in Chicago and won a few races in other Illinois towns. In August the party prevailed in nine of Dayton, Ohio's twelve wards. "I have reason to believe that we have grown more in Wisconsin than we did in the East," Victor Berger wrote, "and according to the primary elections held in Buffalo, Toledo, Dayton, Reading, etc. we have gained from 700 to 1800 per cent in the East since the last presidential election." These victories presaged an impressive showing in the November municipal elections, which *American Socialist* editor J. Louis Engdahl called at the time "Socialism's greatest triumph in America." Making opposition to the war the centerpiece of his campaign for mayor of New York, Morris Hillquit received 21.7 percent of ballots cast in a four-way race, more votes than any Socialist had ever received in a local or statewide contest. New York Socialists elected ten assemblymen, seven aldermen, and a municipal court justice. To the ecstatic Hillquit, the results "signify a veritable political revolution. . . . I feel that our party and our movement have now been definitely established." More than a third of all votes cast in Chicago went to Socialists while the party got between 20 and more than 50 percent of the ballots in many large cities in Ohio, Pennsylvania, Indiana, and New York. Some liberals and intellectuals, including John Dewey, cast Socialist ballots to protest against the exclusion of radical publications from the mails. The bulk of the votes came from working-class districts, native-born workers in smaller cities and towns in the Midwest, and immigrants in New York, Buffalo, Rochester, Chicago, and Cleveland. The Socialist party, Eugene Debs wrote, "is growing more rapidly at this hour than ever in its history, and this notwithstanding the suppression of its press and its speakers." The Bolshevik Revolution in Russia, which created the world's first Socialist state the day after the American election, gave the party further cause for celebration—at least for the moment.[4]

The good news did not last for long. Two weeks after the party's triumph at the polls, Attorney General Thomas Gregory warned those who opposed the war: "May God have mercy on them for they need expect none from an outraged people and an avenging Government." This was a clear signal that in the wake of the elections and the Bolshevik Revolution, the administration had worked out its "war party line" and dissenters could expect to be silenced by a variety of legal and extralegal means already previewed in the suppression of newspapers and magazines, the arrest of Kate O'Hare, and a series of raids on IWW offices and the Socialist Party headquarters in Chicago. The initial government/superpatriot campaign against war protesters had already undermined the party's antiwar position. Never comfortable with the St. Louis platform, Morris Hillquit maintained during his New York campaign that the party neither advocated an immediate retreat from the war effort nor the breaking of any laws. The Bolshevik seizure of power further softened the position of Hillquit and other New York comrades who were coming to see the war as one for democracy. President Wilson's support of the Socialist ideal of a peace without annexations or indemnities won over other leftists to the administration's side, including Emanuel Haldeman-Julius's *New Appeal,* the former *Appeal to Reason.* Furious that the *Appeal* had become "a capitalist war organ," Debs canceled his free subscription. For the many Socialists like Debs who continued to oppose the war in absolute terms, the most ominous news yet for their movement came in mid-December from Bismarck, North Dakota, where Kate O'Hare's case had come to trial.[5]

⌋ When Kate Richards O'Hare agreed to give a lecture in Bowman, North Dakota, she walked unknowingly into the middle of an intense local political feud. On one side was James E. Phelan, president of four North Dakota banks and the Western Lumber and Grain Company, and the former political boss of Bowman County. His self-serving rule had come under withering criticism from a local newspaper owned by two brothers with liberal-progressive reputations, George (a Congregationalist minister) and Edward P. Totten (a state's attorney). While Phelan managed to bankrupt the Tottens' paper, the election of Woodrow Wilson gave E. P. Totten political power over federal patronage and the means to retaliate against the Phelan faction. The Tottens allied themselves with the Nonpartisan League, an organization of farmers bent on curbing the greed of bankers and grain elevator operators such as Phelan. In 1916, the coveted job of the postmaster of Bowman went to E. P. Totten's wife, Lillian, rather than to Phelan crony James E. James. Phelan seized on the visit of Kate O'Hare as an opportunity to strike back at the Tottens. In his remarks to the Senate on July 23, Senator Porter McCumber quoted an unnamed source (M. S. Byrne) as saying that "the post-mistress and her husband both attended the speech and enthusiastically applauded the seditious utterances of the speaker." With the groundwork thus laid, Phelan attempted to persuade federal authorities in Fargo to indict Lillian Totten. While this stratagem failed, U.S. Attorney Melvin A. Hildreth arranged for Phelan and four of his associates to testify before a grand jury, which indicted Kate O'Hare on charges of "willfully obstructing the enlistment [and recruiting] service of the United States."[ ] If a jury found her guilty, Phelan might yet succeed in having Mrs. Totten removed. Of course, the petty Phelan-Totten feud did not interest the U.S. government, but the opportunity to silence a leading critic of the war was too good to pass up.[6]

The flimsiness of the government's case may have lulled Kate into a false sense of security. After all, of the five witnesses examined before the grand jury, only the disappointed office seeker, James E. James, had actually been present during her lecture. Ironically, in light of the government's extensive surveillance of her activities, no notes of the Bowman lecture had been taken. Kate could not produce a copy of her speech because it was her habit to base her addresses on simple outlines. Not until 1919 did she publish what she claimed was "the absolute and exact reproduction of my lecture at Bowman." Working from "her copy of the speech," the O'Hares' friend William E. Zeuch published a slightly different version of the two offending passages, a clear indication that no verbatim copy existed, only fragmentary notes. Verner R. Lovell, a prominent Fargo attorney and Democrat retained for her defense, located several people who supported her contention that she had been misquoted in the indictment. By the time her case went to trial, District Attorney Hildreth had shuffled his prosecution witnesses, replacing the four original complainants who had not been present (while retaining James E. James) with a local doctor and a grain buyer who had attended the lecture and two people who had overheard the lecture from outside. This made the government's case only marginally stronger. Then the prosecution got a lucky break. Another defendant scheduled to stand trial in the December term of the federal district court in Fargo on an obscenity charge, the editor of a local sheet called *Jim Jam Jems*, obtained a writ of prejudice against Judge Charles F. Amidon, widely admired for his cultured background and civil libertarianism. Consequently, Judge Martin J. Wade of the Southern District of Iowa took his place. By the time O'Hare and her attorney discovered this development, it was too late for her to file a petition against a judge with a ferocious bias against leftists.[7]

Beginning with his two lead-off witnesses, James and Dr. A. A. Whittimore, Prosecutor Hildreth followed the simple strategy of endeavoring to convince the jury that Kate did indeed "state in substance that any person who enlisted in the army of the United States of America for service in France would be used for fertilizer, and that is all he was good for, and that the women of the United States were nothing more nor less than brood sows to raise children to get into the army and be made into fertilizer" and that young men of draft age were in the audience. Lovell got James and Whittimore to admit that they could not remember O'Hare's rhetoric

Kate O'Hare, before (left) and after (right) her ordeal of arrest, conviction, and imprisonment under the Espionage Act (photos courtesy Perkins Library, Duke University).

exactly, but they insisted the indictment had quoted her correctly in substance. Judge Wade would not allow Kate's counsel to question James or the other witnesses about the Phelan-Totten feud except to say that the town had two political factions.[8]

In her testimony, Kate stated that she had not opposed American entry into the war and while she was against conscription, she had not fought against it. She denied having obstructed the administration's war plans during her Bowman lecture, which she described as "carefully prepared," not extemporaneous. When Lovell asked if she had made the statements quoted in the indictment, she explained that she had said that she was not against enlistment:

> "If any young man feels it is his duty to enlist in the army of the United States then he should enlist, and God bless him." I said, "His blood may enrich or possibly fertilize," speaking to farmers,—"His blood may enrich the soil of France." Then I stopped and questioned,—"Perhaps that may be the best use for it?" But that was a question.

What of the other alleged remark about American women as brood sows?

> The Statement that in my judgment has been distorted into the allegation was this: When the governments and churches of the European

countries demanded of the women of Europe that they should give themselves to the soldiers going away to war, in marriage or out, in order that those soldiers might breed before they died,—that when the church and government demanded that of women, they reduced them to the status of breeding animals, or brood sows on a stock farm.[9]

During cross-examination, the U.S. attorney tried to get O'Hare to admit that young men had been present, a crucial point because the charge under the Espionage Act was obstructing enlistment and recruiting. She would only say that the crowd was largely middle-aged. Lovell asked if she had been in communication with German Socialists. No, she said, not since 1914. The two spent several minutes sparring over what she had said about American soldiers as fertilizer and women as brood sows, but she merely reiterated that her words had been garbled.[10]

Kate's attorney called to the stand a series of witnesses to corroborate her version of the lecture and one to say that he had been outside the hall and heard little of the lecture due to the noise of a passing freight train. During Edward P. Totten's testimony, Lovell tried once again to ask questions about the local political feud, with Hildreth objecting each time the issue was raised, until Judge Wade remarked that "it does not make any difference what kind of squabbles they have in a neighborhood, it does not affect the trial of a lawsuit that is not connected with it." After that, Lovell did not press the issue again until he asked the final defense witness, George Totten, if the government witnesses belonged to a different political faction than he and his brother. When Totten replied that the Phelan ring was against President Wilson, Wade ordered the answer stricken out, but allowed the answer "they belong to the other faction" to remain on the record.[11]

In his charge to the jury, Judge Wade said that the case "has not anything to do with the Tottens." Nor did it matter what others thought of the Espionage Act, although he added: "Let us all hope that all persons who have violated this law, or any other law, will receive proper punishment ultimately." Mrs. O'Hare was not charged with intent to violate the law, but "She is charged with doing things with an intent to have a certain effect, which the law says shall be punished." She spoke in a county where young men had enlisted, therefore the government had a right to protect itself "against the few who might assume that they knew more than the other ninety millions of people, and who might assume to obstruct so far as they might this duty." If she said, in substance, the words as charged in the indictment "with the intent as I have instructed you," he continued, then she was guilty. While Lovell took exception to many of the judge's remarks, Wade took nothing back. Judge Wade having cleared the way for a guilty verdict based on possible intent, the jury took only thirty-five minutes to find for the government.[12]

Kate later wrote that Judge Wade put off sentencing her for a week "to break my spirit and bring me before him for sentence, a nervous wreck, willing to plead mercy at his hands." But the judge had another reason for the postponement. Immediately after the verdict, he asked the Bureau of Investigation and Postmaster Burleson for information that would help him in passing the sentence. The BI's agent in charge of the St. Louis office, Edward J. Brennan, wired back that Kate and Frank O'Hare had associated themselves with "anything and everything that would give aid and comfort to the enemy." While the Bureau did not have any evidence that Kate had violated federal laws in St. Louis, his office had "placed her in a class that we are morally certain whose hearts and souls are for Germany and against our Country." For good measure, he added that "Nothing would please this office more than to hear that she got life." A postal solicitor wired the judge that "Party appears to be of the extreme type who have [sic] attempted to handicap the Government in every way in the conduct of the present war."[13]

On December 14, 1917, Kate Richards O'Hare took the opportunity to speak to the court before Wade passed sentence. Reading from a carefully prepared manuscript, she asserted that she had delivered her lecture many times before the watchful eyes of federal authorities and she had not become "suddenly smitten with the hydrophobia of sedition" in Bowman. Rather, "the real thing in this case . . . was the contest over the postoffice." In an atmosphere of hysteria the real crime that she stood convicted of was stirring up the people. If that was a crime, then she pled guilty. She scorned the notion of asking for clemency or mercy. "It may be," she said, anticipating the coming years, "that down in the dark, noisome, loathsome hells we call prisons, under our modern prison system, there may be a bigger work for me to do than out on the lecture platform." She was ready to accept any sentence "serene and calm and unafraid" knowing that her ideals would triumph in the end.[14]

Judge Wade then made one of the most remarkable speeches ever to come from a federal bench. He explained that he had conducted his own investigation into O'Hare's background to guide him in determining an appropriate sentence. He read to the court the telegrams he had received from federal authorities. The judge quoted from an article written by Debs in the April issue of the *Rip-Saw,* pronouncing it to be "the foundation of the entire gospel of hate which she and her associates are preaching." Next, he moved on to Kate's denunciation of conscription and the SP's St. Louis platform. On *World Peace,* the play Kate and Frank had written in 1915, Wade said: "Blasphemy! I wonder if that is the sort of stuff the Christian people of North Dakota want their children to be fed . . . it has not any place on the American soil either in times of war or times of peace." Turning to the present, the judge remarked that at no time during the trial had Kate "said anything about this good, old United States; that she ever expressed pride in its power, in its justice, or its right; that she ever paid a tribute to the American flag." He went on to pay his own homage to "the greatest empire God had ever made," a land that welcomed impoverished immigrants and allowed a poor boy such as himself to prosper through hard work. The American people would not allow themselves to be insulted by remarks likening mothers to brood sows and soldiers to fertilizer. Kate O'Hare, he concluded, "is the apostle of despair and carries only a message of hate and defiance. . . . Why, every day she is at liberty she is a menace to the government." He then sentenced her to five years in the Missouri State Penitentiary at Jefferson City, Missouri.[15]

Appeal

The trial left Kate stunned. Writing in the February issue of *Social Revolution*, she observed that "we cannot bring ourselves to feel that it is real." Only her sense of humor had kept her going through an ordeal in which she had been convicted of an intent to commit a crime. She paid tribute in passing to her family and her Socialist comrades for their support, but most of all she was grateful to her lawyer, V. R. Lovell, for defending her ably even though he was not a Socialist. Kate may have felt compelled to defend him because he was the only one she had permitted to help her directly. Turning her back on friends and family and accepting money only from Phil Wagner on his terms, which included keeping Frank away from the magazine, Kate had taken on the government and lost. The trial had indeed been "grotesque and fantastic," as she called it, but Kate, her attorney, and Wagner had made a number of crucial errors that led to her conviction. Had she convinced Wagner to rehire Frank to coordinate publicity and raise funds in St. Louis, Kate believed in hindsight, she would have had more money and better legal advice. She might have been in a stronger position to counter the atmosphere of hostility engendered by conservative North Dakota newspapers that accused the Nonpartisan League of being behind her appearance. In a state where 80 percent of the residents farmed for a living, Lovell and O'Hare accepted a jury composed of several bankers, men who not only despised the Nonpartisan League but must have been well acquainted with the president of the State Bankers' Association, James Phelan—and his intimate connection with the case. Furthermore, Phelan should have been subpoenaed by the defense. The connection between Senator McCumber's remarks in the Senate and the indictment should have been explored. A different lawyer might have recognized the perils of allowing Martin Wade to try the case before it was too late to secure a writ of prejudice. She had not sought martyrdom, but by her conduct in the case she had not done nearly enough to avoid it either.[16]

The verdict infuriated Frank O'Hare for the simple injustice of it all, but also because Phil Wagner had not asked for his help and his role had been confined to minding the children and tending to his own business. As he waited through Christmas for her to come home, Frank vented months of frustration on the man he admired the most in the world, Eugene Debs. O'Hare charged that, with the exception of Phil Wagner, the staff of *Social Revolution* and "the star chamber bunch" (the party's National Executive Committee) had done nothing to assist Kate. "She will be home tomorrow—," he wrote, "I cannot keep her here—it is true—but it will break the fearful three months since she started away." He was proud of her courage in the face of terrible adversity, which made all of Debs's experiences "sink to the level of a petty pleasure picnic." In closing, Frank issued the most respected man in the Socialist movement an order: "I want you to find out from the so-called leaders of the party just what the hell they are going to do and report to me." He would not sit idly by again the way he had for six months while the government crucified his family.[17]

"Why did you write me such a letter?" Debs asked a week later in a lengthy rebuke written at a time when he was suffering "a physical and nervous breakdown." He urged Frank "to get it out of your head that Kate is the only martyr in the revolutionary movement." She had not been whipped, tarred, and feathered like a group of Oklahoma Wobblies or hosed down in the middle of a Chicago winter like other IWWs or jailed without a word of publicity like hundreds of accused radicals. While he favored giving Kate's case publicity, he wrote, slipping into sarcasm, "I don't propose that . . . it shall be degraded into an advertising campaign, and this reminds [me] of what they used to tell me at the Rip-Saw office about your proneness along that line." Regarding the National Office, Debs reminded his old friend that Berger, Hillquit, and Spargo had worked against *him* for years. If Frank really believed that Kate had suffered more in the past few months than he had in thirty-seven years of labor and party activism, "you need to have something done to restore your mental balance." As to Frank's peremptory order to find out what the party was going to do about Kate, Debs wrote, "whatever else may ail you there is nothing the matter with your gall." A few days later, O'Hare wrote a letter of apology and a much relieved Debs accepted it in full, closing a note of January 12 with an offer to do anything he could and assurances of his continued love and loyalty.[18]

Kate O'Hare had come home to Ruskin in time to celebrate New Year's Day. "What a wonderful day that was!" she wrote two years later, "I had just undergone the hell of the trial and horrors of the bitter cold of

Following Kate's conviction, an all-too-brief family reunion at Ruskin, Florida, December 31, 1917, just before supper (courtesy Perkins Library, Duke University).

North Dakota; and Florida, home and loved ones meant so much to me." Frank reintroduced her to William Ernest Zeuch, a young academic who shared their abiding interest in labor education and communal living. They went for a long walk with their children through piney woods, fields, and down to a homesite Frank had picked out on an inlet of Tampa Bay. Returning to the settlement, several neighbors extended "words of love and comradeship" and contributed vegetables from their gardens for a New Year's feast. Before preparing the meal, Frank set up his camera, tripped a timer, and joined the family for a reunion photograph, an all-too-brief moment of respite from the troubles that lay ahead.[19]

Kate's brief return home and the bitter exchange of letters between two men who had grown very close over the years galvanized Frank back into action. He found his wife "floating on a sea of illusion," still convinced that she would not go to prison because she was innocent. With Kate "in absolutely no condition to think," Frank convinced her to stay at Ruskin for a few weeks while he organized a network of "Kate O'Hare Clubs" and a defense committee to raise money on her behalf. Frank hired Zeuch to go to North Dakota and Iowa to make his own investigation of the case. When news of his campaign reached the NEC, Executive Secretary Adolph Germer wrote to Phil Wagner, demanding to know if

Frank's movement had his approval and complaining about the O'Hares' criticisms of the party leadership. In New York, Morris Hillquit refused to meet with Frank for several days before granting him a brief interview, during which he declined to take part in the work of the defense committee. Neatly summarizing his attitude toward O'Hare's work of the past fifteen years, Hillquit told Germer that "I think these free-lance, self-advertising movements are an unmitigated nuisance, and I shall try my best to put my foot down on O'Hare's movement here." Hillquit urged Germer to tell O'Hare "to desist from his activities" and, if he failed to take the hint, to issue a public statement denouncing his campaign as counterproductive to the NEC's efforts on behalf of all imprisoned comrades.[20]

Revising his plans, Frank worked through February with other Socialists and liberals to create the Liberty Defense Union (LDU) with an executive board composed of *New York Call* managing editor Charles W. Ervin as well as Amos Pinchot and Roger Baldwin (cofounders of the National Civil Liberties Union), Helen Phelps Stokes, Theresa Malkiel, and Scott Nearing. Frank also hoped to establish LDU branches in one hundred cities throughout the country. While Ervin was able to secure Hillquit's reluctant cooperation, Adolph Germer still regarded the LDU as an infringement on the party's own Liberty Defense Fund. O'Hare did have the blessing of Debs, who wrote: "You are the comrade for the job. I know that you have the ability for that sort of thing amounting to genius." With Charlie Ervin on board, the *Call* published a page one account of Kate's side of the trial and a long biographical piece by Frank in its Sunday magazine. Monies from the LDU, *Social Revolution,* and the Socialist party were funneled into the Kate Richards O'Hare Appeal Fund for her legal expenses.[21]

Frank kept in close contact with Phil Wagner, requesting that *Social Revolution* publish LDU appeals while making it plain that he was now in charge of Kate's schedule. Wagner told Kate that he found her husband's demands to be unfair because the magazine had already booked her for many speaking engagements. "I am convinced," he wrote, "that had his Florida proposition been a success he would not have thought to go into this proposition." Furious with Wagner's "very masculine attitude," Kate replied that she had given him years of loyalty and allegiance in spite of having been "the hardest worked and most poorly paid employee on your trained staff and that my judgement and ideas never received any particular attention." His lack of vision and his personal prejudice against Frank, she charged, had contributed to her conviction, although she did appreciate what had been done for her. She would fulfill her contract with *Social Revolution,* but only on her own terms. "Buck up . . . ," she concluded, "and let me do the bossing now for a while. You have had a long turn and I have suffered much when I knew that you were not doing as well as I could." Frank papered over the dispute, for both Kate and Phil had more on their minds than quarreling over tactics. Fast running out of money, Wagner had to watch every word that went into *Social Revolution* lest the magazine be held up by postal authorities again.[22]

In mid-February Kate opened a new lecture tour in New York City, where a member of the "Neutrality Squad" of the U.S. Army Corps of Intelligence Police reported that she had made "a 'stock' lecture, which is just about within the law" similar to an article she had written in the current issue of *Social Revolution.* She ran afoul of local authorities at subsequent stops. At Buffalo, the police commissioner would not permit her to

KATE O'HARE IN HER HOME CIRCLE.

SHALL THIS FAMILY BE BROKEN UP?

The O'Hare family on page one of Social Revolution, February 1918 (courtesy State Historical Society of Missouri).

speak in a local music hall after the Socialist party there failed to submit her remarks in advance; in Erie, the city council passed an ordinance against her public appearance; and in McKeesport, Pennsylvania, a few words from the Justice Department caused the mayor to cancel her talk. In places where she did speak, government agents or "special employees" who knew stenography made detailed reports.[23]

Having set the wheels in motion for the Liberty Defense Union and with Kate once again on the road, Frank decided to stay in New York to recruit farmers and college students for Ruskin, explaining that "it is too lusty an infant to let die." He borrowed money against his life insurance policy for living expenses rather than ask the LDU for a job that "would bring on it all the opposition and hatred that has been directed my way for many years by certain influential comrades." He was astonished when the New York Socialist party offered him a position as a fund-raiser. He confided to Debs that he did not know whether he should take the job because "I have a hell of a prickly personality and do not know how I would work in the collar here." Furthermore, he still had no idea what to do about Ruskin. He had plunged his and Kate's life savings into what he thought was a "gilt edged" proposition, but the war and his wife's case made success impossible. He had lost faith in the president of Ruskin, his old friend George McKay Miller, calling him "a man who is impossible for me to work with." Without having the money, O'Hare and Zeuch offered to buy thirty-seven hundred acres of land in the heart of the colony, including the college. If Miller and his investors did not accept the proposition, Frank told fellow colonist R. W. Earlywine, in a bid to move the sale along, "it will be necessary for us to find some other location for our colony and our school; but, believe me, Zeuch has the thing lined up. I have met a number of university people here, and they are wild over the idea." From his sickbed in Terre Haute, Debs wrote that he hoped the O'Hares were not overwhelming themselves with work. "Let me warn you," he said, "especially Kate, to keep your eye on the speedometer often enough to avoid the inevitable disaster." O'Hare wrote back that "I have been near the breaking point a couple of times, and I am sure that at times Kate was so tensed that I thought every moment something would snap." He spent every waking moment working, he explained, so he would not brood about his children, who had been farmed out to friends and relatives.[24]

For the sake of his family—and his shattered nerves—Frank O'Hare returned to live in his old hometown of St. Louis. To make ends meet, he sold vacuum cleaners for the J. L. Kretz Company. An article he wrote on the LDU appeared without a byline in the May issue of *Social Builder,* "a militant constructive magazine" Phil Wagner had started as a successor to *Social Revolution.* On May 17, citing "the heavy burden I was under," Wagner decided to suspend publication after just one issue. The O'Hares had little time to lament for Wagner as Kate's appeal was scheduled for the twenty-fourth of the month. Back in February, Seymour Stedman, a Chicago attorney and founding member of the Socialist party, had volunteered his services on Kate's behalf. Frank wrote to Verner Lovell, telling him that Kate preferred to retain him, not Stedman, for personal reasons. Among other things, Kate and Frank had not forgotten Stedman's role in trying to sabotage Debs's nomination in 1912, although Debs himself had long since forgiven his old pal "Stedy." At the behest of the party, the O'Hares relented. Unfortunately, under the pressure of defending several party comrades simultaneously, Stedman confessed to Frank two days before Kate's court date that he "forgot" about her case. Frank then scrambled to hire St. Louis lawyer Chester R. Crum to file a brief. Again, circumstances had weakened Kate's defense. Judge Martin Wade was worried enough about the case being overturned that he wrote to the Justice Department that "The truth is, that the indictment . . . is somewhat defective . . . [in] that it did not charge an offense." He urged Washington to examine the arguments carefully to provide prosecutor Hildreth with suggestions should Mrs. O'Hare's attorneys raise the matter. He wanted no mistakes and no delays, Wade wrote, because "She [Kate] is doing more harm now than she ever did before" because of her denunciations of the American system of justice.[25]

The O'Hares spent much of the next four months in St. Louis together, with Kate hitting the road in September for a lecture tour as she awaited the results of her appeal. At Akron, Ohio, on October 3, she spoke on psychology, a subject that had become of intense interest to her. A few weeks later, she put her studies to the test in New York while visiting Roger Baldwin, who, days away from entering prison for defying his draft board, was poring over papers at the Federal Building confiscated from the National Civil Liberties Bureau. According to the Justice Department agent assigned to watch them, Kate had written a letter to Baldwin accusing him of being a spy "in order to secure his reply [and] to note his 'reactions' as she claims to be a student of psychology and says she can determine in her own mind just where Baldwin stands by his reply." O'Hare also stated flatly that she would not go to prison. But on October 28, the Eighth Circuit Court of Appeals upheld her conviction. As Wade had anticipated, her attorneys contended that the indictment had not actually charged her with an offense under the Espionage Act, to which the court replied that the two counts, coupled together, were equivalent to the charge of willful obstruction. On the matter of excluding the evidence on Bowman's bitter political feud, the court found that this only remotely affected the credibility of witnesses. Objections to Wade's charge to the jury were also dismissed.[26]

Under different circumstances, the Armistice of November 11, 1918, might have ended the atmosphere of hysteria and intolerance that was sweeping Kate O'Hare toward prison. Brighter days seemed to lie ahead; in spite of the persecution, Socialist party membership had actually increased during the war and the party had held its own in the fall elections. But as the guns fell silent in Europe, the war against those perceived as subversive proceeded unabated as "Reds" replaced Germans and the antiwar movement as the antithesis of Americanism. The demand for loyalty had become a habit, a craving for the continued gratification of fighting a crusade. The war quickened long-term trends toward ever greater industrialization and urbanization, leaving some Americans with a need to compel submission from groups (both political and ethnic) demanding further change. Yet the causes of the postwar "Red Scare" cannot simply be dismissed as irrational superchauvinism. The Bolshevik Revolution was, for many, a frightening reality promising to turn a war-weary world topsy-turvy. The American

Running for president from prison in 1920, Eugene V. Debs (left) shakes hands with his running mate, Seymour Stedman, a Chicago attorney and founding member of the Socialist party who agreed and then "forgot" to file Kate O'Hare's appeal two years earlier (courtesy Perkins Library, Duke University).

Left, which the Wilson administration and its cohorts had hounded for opposing the war in Europe, drew fresh inspiration from the Bolsheviks—or what it knew of them. Furthermore, the composition of the Socialist party had changed during the war: foreign-language federations that accounted for about a third of the party's membership in 1917 topped 50 percent by 1919, breathing new life into the hoary myth of radicals as "unAmericans." At the very time when Woodrow Wilson's peace plan seemed to be exculpating the party's brave stance against a murderous war, forces from within and without were poised to wreck the Socialist movement as the O'Hares knew it.[27]

After recovering from the shock of losing their appeal, the O'Hares left St. Louis, Kate to campaign for her freedom and Frank to salvage what he could of the Ruskin project, as their lawyers presented a petition for certiorari to the Supreme Court. In Des Moines, when several superpatriot groups threatened to block Kate from speaking, Frank rushed north by train from St. Louis in time to fill in for her. According to the *Iowa Unionist*, he claimed not to know of his wife's whereabouts, "but thought that she was in good hands all right." In a lengthy address, Frank explained why his wife had neither violated the law nor defied the government. O'Hare used his appearance in Judge Wade's home state to go on the offensive against the government, revealing a nugget of information uncovered by his friend Zeuch's investigation regarding the jurist's prejudices. "Frank said," the *Unionist* reported, "he believed Judge Wade was honest—that he was a great jurist, but had, previous to the trial, before the state bar association expressed his opinion that a socialist was no better than a criminal and a traitor." A few nights later in Omaha, he vowed that if the Supreme Court denied his wife's appeal, he would bring her case to the American people "through the medium of moving pictures."[28]

In March, Kate returned to Des Moines determined to be heard. A Justice Department agent branded her speech "bitter and bolsheviki and dangerous," adding for good measure that "her talk was made to long haired men and short haired women." On March 12, 1919, she was notified that the High Court had declined the petition for certiorari. In thirty days she would have to surrender to U.S. marshals in Fargo, who would escort her to the Missouri State Prison to begin serving her five-year sentence.[29]

Still not ready to give up, Frank arranged a "final farewell tour" for his wife to thirteen cities in the East and Midwest. Her subject was "Americanism and Bolshevism," in which she detailed the crushing out of freedom of speech in the United States during the war and contrasted it with fragmentary reports received from Russia about the successful implementation of socialism. Frank published hastily cut and pasted stenographic notes of the speech for sale during Kate's last days of freedom. On April 2, a Justice Department agent paid a call on Frank O'Hare, who expressed disappointment that the new pamphlet would not be ready in time for Kate's meeting and farewell reception that night in St. Louis. The agent reported that he had learned confidentially that the pamphlet was ready for distribution along with what purported to be Kate's Bowman speech and Zeuch's investigation, *The Truth about the Kate Richards O'Hare Case*, "but owing to some stronger statements contained therein, it was decided not to place them on sale at this meeting."[30]

Frank believed that they still had to be cautious. There was reason to think that Kate could receive a pardon at the last minute—if she requested it. While she would not beg the government for clemency, the Wilson administration might grant it anyway, to avoid the embarrassment of sending the mother of four children to prison. Failing that, she hoped to serve her sentence in North Dakota, a state controlled by the Nonpartisan League, where sympathetic authorities could make her confinement as comfortable as possible while allowing her to carry out a systematic sociological investigation of life in prison. Shortly after the St. Louis farewell, North Dakota Governor Lynn J. Frazier wrote Frank, explaining "that you do not understand the situation here . . . and how bitter the opposition has been." He urged the O'Hares, even at the cost of "some humiliation," to apply for a pardon.[31]

But the O'Hares had had enough of humiliation, at the hands of the government and, as they saw it, at the hands of the NEC. After weeks of indecision, Kate allowed herself to become a candidate in opposition to Morris Hillquit for the post of international secretary. Stopping off at the National Office to say her goodbyes, she was asked by Adolph Germer (who thought he had talked her out of running twice before) if she was sure that she did not wish to withdraw. "She said," he told Hillquit, "that it was not her desire to be a candidate but that Frank insisted on it and to avoid any quarrel with him, she accepted." Her reluctant candidacy had been designed by Frank as a kind of obscene gesture aimed at the unindicted Hillquit. Even if she won, of course, Kate was going nowhere except to prison.[32]

Following her final speech at Minneapolis, Kate and Frank arrived a few days early in Fargo. Amidst rumors that they and their supporters were planning some last-minute demonstration, Frank decided to return to St. Louis on April 11, having assured himself that his wife would be well cared for on the trip to Jefferson City by her longtime friend, Grace Brewer. On April 14, prison doors clanged shut behind her. The previous day, her friend and mentor, Eugene Debs, had begun serving his ten-year sentence for violating the Espionage Act. When Frank showed up that first day of her sentence to see her, he was turned away. After making the rounds of several state offices, authorities allowed him a few minutes' visit. In frustration, he wrote to Attorney General A. Mitchell Palmer that "I am anxious to secure from you information regarding the next move to make." It should be obvious in light of other federal espionage cases that Judge Wade had been prejudiced against his wife. "Will it be necessary," he asked, "for me to secure a million seconds to my request for your attention?"[33]

Kate's conviction had already begun to receive close attention at the Department of Justice. Back on March 6, Alfred Bettman, chief assistant in the department's War Emergency Division, had written to his boss, John Lord O'Brian, that "All together you will see not a strong case under the original act." The charges against her had been made only a month after the passage of the Espionage Act, before the new law had been interpreted authoritatively. Based on "the slightness of the facts" and the character of the defendant, Bettman concluded, she may deserve "considerable reduction of sentence." Prompted by an inquiry about the case from the White House on the eve of her imprisonment, Attorney General Palmer asked O'Brian for an opinion. Bettman took the opportunity to write: "I feel very skeptical as to the justifiability of sending her to the penitentiary." He also requested a summary from the Bureau of Investigation of what Kate had said about the case during her speaking tours. The Bureau's report, which contained more information on "F. P. O'Hara" than his wife, did not impress Bettman as disqualifying her from executive clemency. As far as he could determine, she had said only that her conviction arose from perjured testimony springing from a local feud and that Judge Wade had been prejudiced against her, allegations that may well have been true. The chief assistant then asked Solicitor General Alexander King for his advice, suggesting that a sentence of eight months to a year would be more just. King concurred, linking Kate with her friend Rose Pastor Stokes (who had received a ten-year prison term) as "two ill-advised brilliant women, with highly emotional natures and a great lack of the saving grace of common sense (wouldn't they be mad to hear this?)" On May 27, O'Brian recommended to Palmer that O'Hare's sentence be commuted to eight months. When the Attorney General observed that he would prefer to cut it to six months or less, O'Brian replied that "elements of aggravation," including "the character of the attacks which this woman and her husband have repeatedly made upon Judge Wade" made a reduction to less than six months unwise. Subsequently, a document commuting Kate's term to six months was typed for President Wilson's signature.[34]

Responding to rumors that Kate's sentence was about to be reduced, Judge Wade wrote to Palmer that "she is more dangerous than Debs, because she is more subtle." Kate O'Hare had to be kept in prison because she had the power to convince people that there was no justice and no hope of appeal "and when a person becomes convinced of these things he is ready to use bombs." During her appeal process, she "did more harm than she could pay for in a hundred years imprisonment." In conclusion, Wade predicted that any reduction in sentence "would raise Cain" all over the Midwest. Palmer later claimed that timely receipt of a petition from "American War Mothers" opposing commutation proved even more damaging to the O'Hares' cause, although the only such petition in the files of the pardon attorney dates from February 1920, months after the attorney general reversed himself on clemency. "Strong protests," he later told President Wilson, combined with "indiscreet utterances in behalf of Mrs. O'Hare" led him to the conclusion "that an extension of executive clemency at that time would be misunderstood by those who were demanding and urging the pardon, and also by many loyal citizens who opposed any extension of clemency." In other words, what Palmer and his advisers saw initially as a matter of simple justice, was not expedient politically—and it would remain inexpedient well into the next year. In March of 1920, when *St. Louis Post-Dispatch* editor George S. Johns appealed to Woodrow Wilson's secretary, Joseph Tumulty, to take up the O'Hare case with the president, he was told "that there was a block in the Department of Justice where she was regarded as a dangerous woman."[35]

Prison: Within and Without

Frank O'Hare, as Eugene Debs once remarked, had an ability for publicizing and fund raising amounting to genius. He was determined to use those talents to keep Kate's case before the public so she might be released as quickly as possible through the granting of either a new trial or a presidential pardon. He told historian Ray Ginger that "It was not until KRO was safely in M[iss]o[uri] Pen[itentiary] that a real program could be developed. Then she could not monkey with the machinery." To this end, he hit upon the scheme of publishing her letters from prison along with *Frank O'Hare's Bulletin,* a mimeographed newsletter. As Frank explained in a cover letter to "new friends": "Gradually the facts about the Kate O'Hare matter will come out. All we need to do is to keep on keeping on until the stain of Kate O'Hare's incarceration is wiped from the escutcheon of the Republic." He used the contributions he received to pay for the printing and mailing of the letters to a list of people and organizations that grew over twenty-two months from ten to more than twenty-three hundred, to coordinate the activities of various local Kate O'Hare defense committees, and to help other women prisoners whom Kate befriended.[36]

Prison authorities censored some portions of her letters that reflected badly on the justice system, but a sympathetic Catholic chaplain smuggled out others to the family exactly as she had written them. In her very first letter, Kate wrote: "I have either much more poise, courage and strength of character than I dreamed of possessing or I am psychologically stunned." As much as he still loved her, Frank was convinced that she was both courageous and stunned. She had not been stable emotionally since the indictment, he later told *Unity* magazine. "Every one of her 'letters,'" he added, "had to be carefully edited and reedited before I could release them, or she never would have gotten out of Jefferson City. Wilson would have cut off his hand before letting her out if her letters had been unexpurgated." At the time when he published her early prison letters in booklet form, O'Hare swore to his readers that he could have edited every sentence so that excerpts would not be misused but "This I do not wish to do." Considering that the original letters no longer exist, it is impossible to determine how much editing Frank did, although in all probability he began publishing them as they were written and resorted to a certain amount of judicious bowdlerizing during Kate's subsequent bouts of anger and depression.[37]

The O'Hare letters paint a vivid picture of life under an archaic system of confinement. While Kate used pictures and personal mementos to make her cell "cheerful and pretty," the forced nine-hour shifts in front of a sewing machine and the unclean toilet facilities enraged her. As a "political," she considered herself, along with the famed anarchist Emma Goldman and eighteen-year-old Gabriella Antolini (caught transporting explosives), to be the elite of the prisoners, most of whom were poor and African American. Carrying out her own informal study of prison life, she distanced herself from the others, pitying them and freely sharing the food sent from the outside but in a rather patronizing manner. She got along famously with "the tender, cosmic mother, the wise, understanding woman, the faithful sister, the loyal comrade," Goldman. For her part, Goldman "discovered a very warm heart beneath Kate's outer coldness." Goldman also observed that Kate "was greatly sustained by Frank" through his faithful visits and the publication of her letters.[38]

The summer heat of 1919 sapped Kate's strength to the point where Frank found their visit of June 29 to be "the most melancholy and solemn" half hour of his life. When he tried to get medical help for her, Acting Warden William R. Painter complained angrily about the publication of Kate's letters, threatening to cut them off entirely instead of merely censoring the most outspoken parts. The O'Hares grew to respect Painter, who acted on many of their complaints about bathing facilities, hot food, and the library. Some of these reforms were in place by the time federal prison inspector J. F. Fishman arrived in response to the outcry raised by readers of *O'Hare's Bulletin*. Fishman rejected most of the protests, dismissing Kate as "a dominating woman." When she raised the matter of transferring to North Dakota so that she might conduct a scientific prison survey, the inspector cited it "as an illustration of Mrs. O'Hara's [sic] desire to 'run things' no matter where she may be located." He and Painter chuckled condescendingly over what they saw as her tendency to demand credit for the institutional improvements, but there is little doubt that the O'Hares' publicity had forced them to act.[39]

From her prison cell, Kate could only read about what she called "the volcano that has broken forth in the Socialist movement." The Bolshevik Revolution and the Foreign Language Federations further radicalized the party in 1919, to the point that in the spring elections for the National Executive Committee, the Left won twelve of fifteen seats and four of the five positions for international delegates, one of which went to the imprisoned Kate Richards O'Hare, widely assumed to be in sympathy with the radical insurgents. To keep control of the party, the outgoing committee (which included Center-Right denizens Hillquit, Berger, Germer, Stedman, and John Work) suspended several Foreign Language Federations and the state organization of Michigan and then declared the recent elections null and void. Frustrated that the work of twenty years was going to waste and that she could be at the National Convention only in spirit, Kate wondered "whether the Socialist movement will go forward and fulfil the destiny we have had faith it would fulfil, or whether it will crumble under the strain and leave the big work of reconstruction to other forces." But the Center-Right had already decided to hold the party machinery even at the cost of two-thirds of its membership.[40]

During the week of August 30, 1919, not one but three conventions met in Chicago as the SP split into the Socialist, Communist, and Communist Labor parties. The O'Hares decided to stay with the Socialist party, perhaps because they chose to believe what they read in the *New York Call* and the *Milwaukee Leader,* newspapers controlled by Hillquit and Berger respectively. Or perhaps they saw hope in the SP's resolutions denouncing British policy in Ireland and pogroms against the Jews as well as freedom for political prisoner Tom Mooney, industrial unionism, and solidarity with the Soviets. Kate admitted that she had no real grasp of the left wing because "all I have had concerning it comes from the enemy," meaning Hillquit and Berger, but the idea "that order will come out of chaos" clearly appealed. Her new nickname of "Red Kate" (hung on her by the mainstream press) and her authorship of a pamphlet on Bolshevism belied her position as a member of the SP's radical left.[41]

The cultural differences that for almost twenty years had separated those who looked to the rural heartland for their inspiration rather than urban America and Western Europe did not seem so great by comparison with the hardcore Reds who advocated a Bolshevik-style vanguard. So, despite the deep-seated personal animosity the O'Hares (and their great friend Eugene Debs) had felt toward the SP's Old Guard through the years, their theoretical views had often corresponded with the Center-Right—and still did.[42]

While the O'Hares chose to remain affiliated with the truncated SP, their enthusiasm for the party as a vehicle for social change began to cool. Frank became involved in the founding convention of the Committee of Forty-Eight, an organization of Democratic and Republican liberals disillusioned with the Progressive movement, and single taxers, laborites, and a few Socialists like the O'Hares disenchanted with the party's Old Guard, all hoping to build bridges to trade unionists and the Nonpartisan League for the purpose of creating an effective third political party. From her cell, Kate cheered Frank on, writing: "Ever since my visit to England I have hoped for some such coalition of radical forces in this country. . . . Perhaps the time is ripe for it." Meeting in St. Louis in December 1919, the committee hammered out a program calling for public ownership of transportation, public utilities, and natural resources; a high tax on unused private land; and a return to civil liberties under the Bill of Rights. Here were proposals, Frank wrote in the *Bulletin*, "broad enough to enlist the support of all opponents of reaction and privilege. . . . It was a joy to attend the sessions." Kate too regarded the movement as a sign that radicals and Progressives were finally uniting. Any Socialist who would not join hands with the Nonpartisan League was nothing but "a narrow egotist." "I don't think any one can question my loyalty to the Socialist movement," she wrote, "yet I am ready to join hands with all forces that are willing to help remove the political barnacles from the ship of state."[43]

Frank's activities did not go unnoticed among Socialist party officials. In March 1920, Billy Brandt, longtime secretary of the St. Louis local, reported to Otto Branstetter at the National Office that, curious about a notice advertising young Dick O'Hare as a speaker at a noon meeting of the Committee of Forty-Eight, he had attended "and found our own Frank P. O'Hare speaking." Brandt wrote that in his discussion of politics, Frank had "made no distinction between us and the old capitalist parties" and stated that the aim of the committee was nothing less than the creation of a new movement. While Frank would drop out of the Committee of Forty-Eight shortly thereafter, when it became obvious that the majority had more in common with Robert La Follette than Eugene Debs, his flirtation with the fusion movement would not be forgotten by the Socialist Old Guard, even those who harbored similar thoughts themselves.[44]

"I 'lived' prison . . . ," Frank later wrote, "It was tougher on me to be on the *outside.*" He pushed himself to the limit, publishing the *Bulletin* and Kate's letters, coordinating publicity for her case and, to pay the bills, offering freelance professional advice on factory and merchandising problems, including "Tayloring" workforces for business. As for his four teenagers, O'Hare told his readers that "in order not to rob the kids of the possession of a daddy I have them come down to the office after school and 'help.'" He did not feel ostracized socially as he was still welcome at the "Nuts' Table" of radicals at the City Club of St. Louis. As busy as he was, Frank still jumped at the invitation to edit a special edition on political prisoners for the *New Appeal.* Thus began a stormy relationship between the O'Hares and Emanuel Haldeman-Julius, who, along with Louis Kopelin, had purchased the paper from the Wayland family in 1918. That same year, Haldeman-Julius bought from Phil Wagner the mailing list of the *Social Builder* (successor to the old *Rip-Saw*), so Frank may have been attracted to the job out of nostalgia as much as the chance for a wider outlet of publicity for Kate's case. The stint as guest editor almost blew up in Frank's "much embarrassed" face when his *Bulletin* readers stopped sending in donations, thinking that he had defected to the "capitalist war organ," as Debs had called the *New Appeal.* "I am in no way and never have been an employee of a weekly paper published at Girard, Kansas," he wrote on January 31, 1920, adding that he would have to suspend publication of the letters and the *Bulletin* within two weeks because of a growing deficit. While his readers came through with enough cash for him to keep going, by the end of the year O'Hare would indeed move to Girard to work with Haldeman-Julius.[45]

Prison life wore Kate down both physically and psychologically. She put up photographs of Ruskin in her cell that Frank had sent, but took them down when she became depressed. She continued to "firmly believe that Ruskin will be our home after the dark days have passed." Naturally, she worried about her family, especially Frank. She asked him at one point to "please put the 'lid' on our precocious daughter as much as possible and confiscate the lip stick and rouge pot and see that she wears her hair in a civilized manner," adding that this was a difficult problem even when the government was not putting mothers in prison in order to make the world safe for democracy. Frank's subsequent observation that Kathleen had become "rather disturbingly flapperish" did not assuage her fears. Kate missed the comradeship of Emma Goldman terribly following the anarchist's release in late September 1919, but was cheered by reports of a Kate Richards O'Hare testimonial dinner in New York six weeks later. In her remarks, Goldman revealed that Kate not only encouraged and sustained her fellow prisoners, but upon their release she would "send them to poor Frank O'Hare, who is worked to death (Laughter) in his own position, and in the amnesty work and with the children" so that he could help them to get on their feet again. Frank hired one of the released convicts, a woman named Laura, as his new housekeeper and helped the others as he could. He took a special interest in the other "political," "Ella" Antolini, who, following her release from prison, was jailed in St. Louis pending a deportation hearing. After recruiting attorneys Luther Ely Smith and Edward D. Shea to defend Antolini, O'Hare raised her bail money by asking his readers to put up "a few loose Liberty Bonds."[46]

The seeming lack of interest in Kate's fight for freedom on the part of the Socialist party's Old Guard irritated the O'Hares no end. Faced with a long prison sentence and the prospect of being denied his seat in the House of Representatives (despite having won a plurality of votes), Victor Berger evidenced little sympathy for Kate's plight, complaining in August 1919 that "the Socialist press has made a lot of Gene Debs and Kate Richards O'Hare, who got only five and ten years respectively [*sic*]—but nobody seems to think much of the twenty years the rest of us received—in fact, some so-called radicals tacitly seem to approve the sentence." When Berger had the temerity to tell Frank "It would kill me to go to prison," O'Hare later recalled that "I looked at him coldly. 'My wife, Kate O'Hare, is in prison. You son-of-a-bitch, who do you think you are?' " By late 1919, the St. Louis local (still firm allies of the "yellows") had managed to raise only a paltry $42.22 for her case.[47]

On February 8, 1920, Kate wrote to Otto Branstetter that many members of the rank and file felt "that I have been most shamefully treated by the National Office." Having said that, she asked that Seymour Stedman or Comrade William Rempfer of South Dakota be allowed to assist her attorney Verner Lovell in securing evidence of perjury against the prosecution witnesses in her trial and that a press representative be dispatched to cover the story. Branstetter denied that the party had treated her badly, adding that "you and Frank are personally responsible for such unjustified resentment as does exist." The problem was that the party faced bankruptcy due to the drastic drop-off in membership. "My dear man," Kate replied, "what a case of nerves you must have developed." If her Democratic lawyer and the Nonpartisan League could stand by her, then surely the Socialist party should too. She wanted help from a Socialist lawyer and a reporter, not someone "doing a press agent stunt, God knows F. P. [O'Hare] is quite sufficient on that line." Once Lovell gathered further proof of her innocence, she would permit him to apply for a pardon. In closing, Kate could not resist taking another swipe at the hapless Branstetter (and Prohibition), writing revealingly that he should "relieve the racking nerve strain of your work by imbibing a little Freud since you can no longer imbibe Schlitz. Really my study of psychoanalysis has kept me sane during my imprisonment." At the next National Executive Committee meeting, another Socialist attorney, George Roewer, moved successfully that Rempfer be asked to help Kate to reopen her case. Branstetter soon broke the news to Frank that Rempfer had declined to help. The party was still willing to find someone else. As far as sending an investigator went, Branstetter wondered if Frank wanted the job for himself![48]

In response to all of this, Frank gambled on his longtime friendship with Branstetter (whom he had brought into the party years before in Oklahoma) by writing him in a personal and informal way. There had been trouble with the National Office ever since the indictment because Kate was "not calm and cool and efficient and normal." "Nerve specialists" the O'Hares had consulted told him that she suffered from shock "(and I suppose I was not free from aberrations myself) so as a result there was a hell of a mess." He had just returned from seeing his wife at Jefferson City, where she began the visit by accusing him of being glad she was in prison and saying that they did not love one another any more. Once he got her to laugh, she was herself again, but "her mind was playing tricks with her." After Zeuch had investigated the case independently, Frank had become convinced that her version of events was correct but not "her judgement and generalship." He still had hope that new evidence could be turned up. The friends receiving *Frank O'Hare's Bulletin* had been sending him an average of $150 per week and he believed he could raise another $10,000 on a special appeal. In closing, Frank proposed that the two men meet face-to-face so that they might "get something going."[49]

The candid exchange of views between the O'Hares and Otto Branstetter laid the groundwork for a new round of activity on Kate's behalf. After conferring with party leaders in Chicago in early March, Frank reported to his readers that "good work is going on . . . I am pledged to secrecy." Shortly thereafter, SP lawyer George Roewer spent ten days in North Dakota, where he wrote to Branstetter that state authorities would probably indict the prosecution witnesses for perjury if pushed by the Nonpartisan League. Roewer found that Verner Lovell had little interest in helping Kate. While he could understand how she might have fallen for such "a nice approachable chap," Lovell was the last person he would want working on her case. After meeting with William Lemke, the "Bishop" of the League in North Dakota (as he was known locally), Roewer reported that State's Attorney Allen would do whatever Lemke wanted; therefore, "I am to get the 'stuff' ready for him and he will tell Mr. Allen what to do." Roewer wired Frank O'Hare "that he had established the fact of the miscarriage of justice in Mrs. O'Hare's case." After visiting with Kate in prison and Frank at St. Louis, Branstetter returned to Chicago in early April to find that a committee of women from the Church Federation of Chicago had "a splendid program worked out in detail that promises to get the matter directly and personally before the President." He was confident enough that the committee would "get the ear of the President" to tell Roewer to stall the indictments in North Dakota. Frank felt "highly gratified" with the party's efforts, as he told Branstetter on May 3, saying by way of apology that "I meant to write but I am like a housewife—no time for the things I want to do, or too damn weary when I have time." A few days earlier, he chided Kate for not having written him for a few weeks. "We have been through a severe year," he concluded, "and we are all feeling the reaction of the strain. We shall get over this, I am sure, and be more equitable again."[50]

The letters soon resumed, with Kate tired but in good spirits. In mid-May, with no one else to turn to, the Socialist party nominated the imprisoned Eugene Debs as its presidential candidate. The Old Guard, firmly in charge of what remained of the party, beat back a movement by the Left to nominate Kate for vice president, choosing Seymour Stedman in her place by a vote of 106 to 26. Victor Berger then moved "that we send a telegram of sympathy and love to Comrade Kate Richards O'Hare." Kate had more important things to think about than party politics. Conversations with other inmates convinced her that she was extraordinarily fortunate to have such love and support from family and friends. "I can live thru the hell of prison life," she wrote on May 23, "I can rise above the petty persecutions of ignorance and venom because I have love—love that no bolts or bars or locks can shut out—love that is as bountiful as the gifts of God—love that can lift me out of the sordid, brutal ugliness of a convict's lot."[51]

Six days later, while Frank sat in his St. Louis office with children Dick and Kathleen, a reporter rushed in with a news bulletin from Washington announcing that Woodrow Wilson had commuted Kate's sentence to time served. The wife of pro-war Socialist journalist Charles Edward Russell had presented to Attorney General Palmer the results of George Roewer's investigation and supporting affidavits regarding the perjured testimony of the prosecution witnesses in Kate's trial. Otto Branstetter later wrote that "The information gathered by Comrade Roewer was largely, if not wholly, responsible for the release of Comrade O'Hare." Faced with this new evidence and the arguments of an SP delegation, Palmer had concluded "that aside from her distorted and erroneous views on sociological subjects, she is doubtless a sincere, earnest and worthy woman, [therefore] I think the ends of justice have been subserved." There remained only a final absurdity in the tragedy of Kate's imprisonment. She insisted that her release be set for the next afternoon to allow Frank time enough to meet her at the prison gates; Palmer demanded that she be set free at once. Warden Painter allowed her to remain in prison one more day. Taking the night train to Jefferson City, Frank picked her up in the morning. She returned home with him immediately, as a Justice Department agent reported, "amid the rejoicing of her St. Louis Socialist friends." Millions more who were not Socialists rejoiced as well at a time when the Red Scare was fading from the headlines, leaving Attorney General Palmer almost alone in shrieking about Bolshevism come to America. The *St. Louis Star* spoke for many in a May 31 editorial when it observed that if the facts unearthed in William Zeuch's investigation were true then Kate had been imprisoned thirteen and one-half months too long. "She never should have been convicted," the *Star* continued, "never should have been tried. Her release should increase the opposition to the un–American attempt to curb free speech with anti-sedition legislation." That was precisely what the O'Hares had in mind.[52]

Second Honeymoon

Frank and Kate O'Hare gave themselves ten days to, as Frank put it, "get our domestic affairs reorganized." They spent a good portion of their time receiving well-wishers. Kate announced to the press that she would devote herself to the cause of prison reform, adding cryptically that "Socialism doesn't need men." Eager to exploit the publicity of her release, Frank and Otto Branstetter arranged a twenty-day whirlwind tour of the East. Kicking off the trip in St. Louis on June 10, Kate told two thousand cheering followers that "I went in [to prison] a nice, ladylike pink, but I came out a genuine red." Frank later remembered the tour as a "tremendous, intoxicating chain of public receptions." They had begun their married life together with "a Socialist honeymoon," full of enthusiasm for the cause as they eagerly tried out what Walter Thomas Mills had taught them about speaking and organizing. Quite consciously, they regarded the postprison tour as a second honeymoon, a chance to renew their marital relationship and their professional partnership while reclaiming Kate's place as a leading light in the party.[53]

A frustrated Justice Department official told a field agent in Providence, Rhode Island, that because Kate could not be officially stopped from speaking, he should "cover speech very closely and forward report special delivery attention Mr. [J. Edgar] Hoover." A stenographic report made by two Providence police sergeants revealed that the evening began with piano and violin music. Frank then spoke, detailing his efforts to have Kate released. He talked about how the government had wrecked the old *Rip-Saw* and announced that he hoped to start an even better publication shortly. Socialism, he said, using a theme he had honed through the years (and cited by Friedrich Engels as the most basic of moral injunctions), could be boiled down to "thou shalt not steal." Unless his listeners were simply born rotten, they would "all catch socialism" if they listened long enough. After a plea for help in freeing the many political prisoners still jailed, especially Eugene Debs, Frank yielded the floor to Kate, who received a long ovation. She confined her remarks to commenting on the horrors of prison life. "There was no reference to revolution or violence," the police reported, "just a plea for the Socialist party." An agent in Washington, D.C., quoted Frank as boasting "that he had 'slipped the wool over Mr. Palmer's eyes and obtained her release after fourteen months and that they were now on their second honeymoon and having a wonderful time.' " The tour ended dramatically in Atlanta on July 2 when Kate visited Eugene Debs in prison. In public, the two agreed that the outlook for socialism seemed brighter than ever, although they expressed concern over what Kate called "differences of opinion among the so-called leaders of the movement." The reality was much more grim as the party had only seven fully functional state organizations, nineteen more existing only on paper, and none at all in twenty-two states.[54]

Upon returning to St. Louis, Frank wound down *O'Hare's Bulletin* since its raison d'être, freedom for his wife, had been achieved. He told his readers that the next objective would be a campaign to free all political prisoners. "Then," he wrote, looking down the road, "the fight for prison reform must be taken up." He closed with the announcement that Kate had made a report on prison conditions in the women's department of the Missouri State Penitentiary. Promoting Kate's sixty-four page pamphlet *In Prison,* O'Hare promised that "It gives facts more freely and adequately than was possible in the 'Letters.'" The report was little more than a hastily cobbled-together amalgam of her recent set speeches on prison life together with paraphrases of her letters and a detailed outline of a proposed case study in criminology, the last all that was left of almost two hundred detailed case studies of her fellow inmates that prison authorities confiscated and destroyed upon her release. Kate (and Frank) would spend the next two and one-half years working on an expanded version of this report.[55]

Frank and Kate O'Hare renewed their marriage with great hopes for the future. They suffered persecution at the hands of a government that justified prostituting liberty and justice at home in the name of safeguarding democracy abroad. Caught in the middle of a local political dispute, Kate had been brought to trial under a questionable indictment, found guilty on flimsy evidence by a jury stacked against her, and sentenced to prison by a deeply prejudiced judge. When the O'Hares complained too loudly about the process during her appeal, it cost Kate more time behind bars. She and her family were among the many martyrs to the cause of peace and freedom during a period of national delirium. By the time Frank escorted her out of the Missouri State Penitentiary, times had changed. The organization to which they had devoted their adult lives together, the Socialist party, was a mere shell of its former self, one of several small and ineffectual sects on the Left that despised one another even more than the system they hoped to overthrow. At times, imprisonment had put unbearable stresses and strains on their long season of personal and professional cooperation. Now, after a second honeymoon, they wanted desperately to pick up where they had left off before the war, to find the old magic that had defined their lives over the years.

5

"A Tragic Four Years," 1921–1924

In 1920, voters swept Republican Warren G. Harding into the White House on the vague and ungrammatical promise of "a return to normalcy." While Frank and Kate O'Hare (and some 915,000 others) cast their ballots for Eugene Debs, they shared with the mainstream the widespread craving for a reversion to the good old days; in their case, the days before their lives and the progress of the Socialist party were disrupted by the war, the party split, and the Red Scare. To this end, they reestablished the *National Rip-Saw* and launched campaigns to aid the Debs family financially, free the remaining political prisoners, and end the system of convict labor. Carrying out the dream of living socialism, they removed their magazine and their family to the promising New Llano colony in Louisiana. By 1924, though, the O'Hares were finished as a couple. Frank believed that he had lost everything: wife, children, friends, the magazine, his place in the party, and all of his money. Writing in 1960, shortly before his death, as he attempted to sort out more than eighty years of memories, he referred to this period as "a tragic four years." That the O'Hares failed in their personal quest for a return to normality should not surprise; that they faltered so miserably is more unexpected in light of their past endurance. The temper of the postwar world, changes in their personalities (at times subtle and at times prominent), and old character flaws combined to conspire against them as effective advocates of change, both as a couple and as individuals.[1]

Reviving the Rip-Saw

These four years were not all tragedy of course. Through the dark months of Kate's imprisonment, the thought of starting fresh in Ruskin had comforted them both, a dream nurtured by the arrival in early 1919 of a deed signed by George McKay Miller to seven lots in Commongood subdivision, Ruskin Colony. The land was theirs, provided that they upheld the covenant never to manufacture liquor or cigarettes or never to sell, lease, or convey the property "to any but white people." Unfortunately, as Frank later discovered, the deed did not amount to ownership. But in the summer of 1920, Frank and Kate had more pressing concerns than Florida real estate. Broke, as usual, they were determined to get back into publishing. Conversations with Emanuel Haldeman-Julius and Louis Kopelin, publishers of the new *Appeal to Reason* and owners of the mailing list of the defunct *Social Builder* (purchased from Phil Wagner for four hundred dollars in 1917), led to the revival of the *National Rip-Saw*. The arrangement, as Frank explained it to his readership, was deceptively simple: Emanuel and his wife, Marcet Haldeman, a Girard, Kansas, banking heiress, contributed one-half of the money and owned one-half of the paper, while the O'Hares put up the other half of the capital and also owned half of the *Rip-Saw*. To pay for their share, Kate and Frank borrowed five thousand dollars from Marcet Haldeman's bank at 6 percent interest. For the time being, the arrangement gave them what they wanted: complete editorial control of the paper. Frank received the title of manager, Kate that of editor. In reality, as in the old days, Kate wrote and made speeches while Frank edited the copy and ran the paper.[2]

Eager to get the first issue out before the November 1920 elections, Frank did not wait for the Post Office to process his application for second-class entry. Instead, he deposited $250 with postal authorities, one cent for each copy of the magazine printed in November, which he would get back, minus the cheaper second-class rate of one and one-half cents per pound, once the government approved the application. When the permit did not come through for several months due to a series of technicalities, the deposit money piled up, draining the paper of essential working capital. The Post Office claimed that the *Rip-Saw* did not qualify for the cheaper second-class rate because it contained too much advertising. Not fair, replied Frank, considering that the mainstream magazine *World's Work* contained 103 pages of ads and only 104 pages of reading material. But, said postal authorities, the overwhelming majority of the *Rip-Saw*'s advertisements came from just two sources, copy "boosting" the magazine (especially Kate's lectures) and *Appeal to Reason* books. Furthermore, the government questioned just how many copies of the *Rip-Saw* went to subscribers who paid the full price of one dollar per year as opposed to those paying the half-price club rate or people who had not paid at all. To end the petty harassment from the Post Office, still headed by the intolerant and unforgiving Albert S. Burleson, O'Hare launched a campaign for readers to send money for "legal" subscriptions. He cut back on *Rip-Saw* and *Appeal* advertisements in the magazine drastically and hired the firm of Fisher and Hightower of Chicago to sell advertisements for the magazine on the same basis as it had for the old *Rip-Saw*. O'Hare told his readership that he had given Harry Fisher instructions "to accept only ads from firms which are entirely reliable in every way." The second-class permit finally came through, but not before Burleson (nicknamed "the Cardinal" by Woodrow Wilson) had exacted the last bit of revenge against his old enemies and put the *Rip-Saw* deep in the red financially, a development that, in turn, created friction among the partners.[3]

In February 1921, the O'Hares put out a "Final Number" of *Frank O'Hare's Bulletin* both to thank the thousands of friends and acquaintances who had stood by Kate during her imprisonment and to promote the new magazine. Frank wrote that he was saying good-bye to "the combined personality of my 2300 readers . . . with a pang of something like regret." Kate had little to wax sentimental about, except to say that their second honeymoon had been "a joyous pageant of love and fellowship and thanksgiving everywhere." Turning to the present, she characterized the new *Rip-Saw* as "neither fashionable nor highbrow; but it is human." As to their lives in Girard, Kate asked the *Bulletin* readers to imagine "A modest cottage on a tree-lined street, a shabby office on a sleepy square where we find useful, joyous work to do; roaring presses and deft-handed girls sending out the Rip-saw to carry its message wherever that message is needed." This idyllic portrait of rural Socialists returned to their own version of pre-war "normalcy" passed over the most basic problem the O'Hares faced as publishers, for they needed more readers, lots of them, to make the new *Rip-Saw* a paying proposition.[4]

Frank urged the revamped "Rip-saw Army" to garner new subscriptions at every opportunity. Once circulation reached one hundred thousand, he promised, the magazine would derive enough revenue from advertisements to expand coverage of farm issues and to post their own correspondent in Washington to report "the news that YOU want but which the capitalist press does not care to give you." Rebuilding the magazine would not be easy, he realized. The Red Scare had passed, but socialism was no longer considered to be a respectable alternative to the two old parties in the new age of postwar conservatism. A mechanic had written to the *Rip-Saw* that he felt like a coward for not doing more for the movement. Any overt action on behalf of socialism, he feared, "would put me in bad shape and cost me my job." O'Hare used the letter to praise the workman as a thinker who understood that capitalism "defeats the very purpose of human existence." As an employee, he suffered from the loss of freedom to openly express an opinion at odds with the company's board of directors or the local chamber of commerce. O'Hare wrote that he understood the man's dilemma. He himself had a standing offer of a ten-thousand-dollar-a-year job in business—provided that he would renounce his "damned Socialism." Street corner agitators and writers did not make Socialists; rather, "The experiences of the individual under capitalism in actual production and distribution make all the Socialists that are made." Giving advice that applied to himself as much as to the anonymous mechanic, O'Hare wrote: "Simply stay on the job. Be true to yourself. Keep plugging away. It was a shout which shattered the walls of Jericho. Wait for the big shout."[5]

One of the effective ways of "plugging away," that is, selling enough magazines to cover operating expenses while providing "the shout," entailed routing the "star writers" to select towns in return for several hundred subscriptions per speech. This scheme had worked well for a time under Phil Wagner between 1911 and 1917, especially when the dates could be split among both O'Hares, Harry Tichenor, H. G. Creel, and Eugene Debs. With Frank managing the *Rip-Saw*, Tichenor too ill to contribute more than an occasional article, Creel having vanished, and Debs serving time in prison, Kate carried the full load of requests in the new *Rip-Saw* lecture bureau. She was willing to do it, but the one hundred dates Frank proposed added up to a grueling schedule for a woman, now middle-aged, who had suffered intensely from her time in prison. Kate actually began her *Rip-Saw* lecture tour before the new magazine rolled off the press in the fall of 1920, speaking in Minneapolis and other cities on the subject of prison reform. As in the old days, the Bureau of Investigation followed her movements ("KATE RICHARDS O'HARE . . . and others of like yolk [sic] are speaking at the Labor Lyceum") although agents no longer reported on what she said in any detail.[6]

Life on the road continued to be hazardous at times, as Kate discovered on July 1, 1921, when a group of American Legion vigilantes kidnapped her half-dressed from a private home in Twin Falls, Idaho, and drove her to the outskirts of Montello, Nevada, where she managed to escape. With daughter Kathleen prepared to go on in her place at the next stop, Pocatello, Kate arrived in time for the lecture only to find the doors to the hall locked. After speaking to a small group the next evening, she returned home to Girard to recover from the ordeal. Frank immediately sent out a circular to seven thousand friends and supporters appealing for donations to a fund to publicize the incident. This had to be done, he wrote, linking the kidnapping to his wife's wartime arrest and trial, "to drag the whole stinking mess of the crime against Kate O'Hare which started in Bowman, N.D., July, 1917, and ended in Twin Falls, Idaho, July, 1921, into the light." In the end, Idaho authorities declined to pursue the case.[7]

To pay the bills, Frank O'Hare took a part-time job in sales promotion for the Kansas City branch of the Apex Electric Company of Cleveland, collecting five dollars for every "beautiful $75 aluminum dust remover" sold by one of his salesmen. Working two jobs, he did not make the time to finish developing an ingenious automatic bookkeeping system he had devised in 1918, "a machine with a memory," as Kathleen O'Hare later described it. His friend, patent attorney Roy Eilers, told him in April 1921 that he owed it to himself and his family to patent what he had done as others (including Burroughs Adding Machine Company) were working along similar lines. Trying to prod O'Hare into action, Eilers wrote that he had no right "to expect an enfeebled mentality such as yours . . . to apply your negative intelligence to the securing of protection in your invention, you have such a colossal amount of Irish animosity towards law that it may be irritating you greatly to think of appealing to a law to give you protection on your so-called mental efforts." As with the Ruskin land deal a few years earlier, Frank simply let the proposition ride because he was busy with other things.[8]

Then there was the *Rip-Saw*, which, with a circulation of about forty thousand and few advertisements, continued to lose money. "I had hoped to get a couple thousand dollars for the Rip-saw from my friends," he wrote from St. Louis, where he had gone to see Roy Eilers in April 1921, "but did not have the heart to push matters." Animosity had already developed between the O'Hares and Haldeman-Julius, a man remarkable for both his idealism and his cynicism. Proud of his role in "Fordizing" literature, Haldeman-Julius hoped that his "Little Blue Books," paperback reprints of literary classics and Socialist brochures, would lead to self-education for the masses. On the other hand, Frank came to dislike him for being "a-social and a-moral. . . . He utterly despised those he thought were his inferiors." For his part, Julius could not stand Kate O'Hare, recalling that "I don't remember anyone who could quite equal her in self-satisfaction about so limited a set of talents. Everything she wrote was a pure masterpiece. She was a genius, and anyone who didn't recognize the fact was a fool or jealous."[9]

Further cooperation quickly became impossible. Haldeman-Julius made the first moves, attempting to merge the *Appeal* and the *Rip-Saw* behind the backs of his partners and, when that failed, firing the O'Hares from the *Rip-Saw*, claiming that they merely had an employment agreement with him. Upon the advice of attorney Jake Sheperd, Frank held his ground, reporting to the office as usual while his secretary, Mae Stalker, and two other trusted employees copied the precious mailing list and smuggled it out in their underclothes, hiding the names and addresses at the Tubbs's boarding house. The handshake partnership agreement was finally put into writing in July, with twenty-five thousand dollars in capital stock divided into 250 shares, issued to Kate (62 shares), Frank (63 shares), Marcet Haldeman-Julius (62 shares), Louis Kopelin (62 shares), and E. E. Haney (1 share). Assets of the company were valued at about six thousand dollars. When the Haldeman-Julius faction settled out of court by agreeing to sell their half to the O'Hares for seventy-five hundred dollars, to be paid in installments over a two-year period, Frank swallowed his pride and borrowed the money from his friends at the St. Louis City Club. As part of the settlement, he also agreed to use his talents as a "Taylorite" to help Haldeman-Julius put his line of Little Blue Books on an assembly line basis to keep the prices as low as possible.[10]

The O'Hares toyed with the idea of moving the *Rip-Saw* to Ruskin, Florida, but learned that they would have to pay $51.24 plus taxes and attorneys' fees to redeem title to their lots in the colony. Furthermore, a lawyer for the estate of George McKay Miller (who had died in August 1919) informed them that the six-thousand-acre tract that Frank had offered to buy in 1918 was now the subject of foreclosure proceedings. The holders of the mortgage would entertain a proposal to buy the bare land for forty thousand dollars, with all of the houses, farm buildings, and the college to be sold separately at near market value. Under the circumstances, living and teaching socialism on Tampa Bay was out of the question. In August, Frank and Kate brought the *Rip-Saw* back home to St. Louis. Keeping it going there proved to be even more difficult than escaping the clutches of the Haldeman-Juliuses.[11]

The move to St. Louis did not go unnoticed by an agent of the Bureau of Investigation, who reported in September 1921 that Frank had attended an SP picnic at Mueller's Grove, where he recounted "some of his experiences in the Socialist movement; also some of the recent adventures which have befallen MRS. O'HARE, who is now on a speaking tour throughout the country." "We're one year old today!" Frank told his *Rip-Saw* audience in October. "It has been a hard, toilsome and nerve-racking year. . . . We've been knifed from within and assaulted without, but we're still very much alive and still fighting for the truth as we see it." As for their magazine, the quality of the articles had remained reasonably high, although gone was the pre-war Socialist-style muckraking of the underside of capitalism. As in the old days, Harry Tichenor thundered against the hypocrisy of religion (he would die in 1922) and W. S. Morgan contributed a humor column. Kate provided the bulk of the copy, writing a series of articles on prostitution ("The War Against the Social Scourge"), popular psychology ("The Kind of People We Are"), the life of her friend Gabriella Antolini, and occasional pieces on prison reform. Seldom did she mention socialism in the coming years except in the context of the need for the Left to support a new political party of farmers and laborers, an indication that she had reverted to being "a nice ladylike pink" as opposed to "a genuine red." Frank wrote mostly to boost the magazine and Kate's lecture tours. The *Rip-Saw* also carried numerous articles from the labor press syndicate Federated Press and other magazines. Having congratulated himself for making it through the first twelve issues, Frank stated: "Next year must be a bigger, better year than last. ARE YOU WITH US?" He realized that the *Rip-Saw* faced an immediate crisis because most of those who had signed up for the paper a year earlier had not renewed their subscriptions. As he candidly explained some years later, the magazine had no wealthy "angel" to soak up red ink like *The Nation* and *New Republic*. Consequently, "The subscribers had to be stimulated into activity constantly by creating new dramatic situations."[12]

To this end, Frank dreamed up "the Katherine Debs Testimonial Edition of the Rip-saw." Many comrades had devoted themselves to working for the release of Eugene Debs from prison, he explained, but what of Mrs. Debs? Before the war, Kate O'Hare had found Katherine Debs beautiful and healthy; now she was "only a shadow of herself, desperately ill, ravished by sorrow and suspense, childless and lonely." Frank gave the *Rip-Saw* Army three weeks to send in donations for the Debs family and orders for the November special issue. And they did—much to the embarrassment of the Debs family. When Theodore Debs got wind of the plan, he demanded an explanation from his sister-in-law as to why she had permitted a collection to be taken up for her when the families of so many other political prisoners had nothing. Feebly, she denied all responsibility. Bowing to pressure from her brother-in-law, Katherine Debs wrote two letters to Kate O'Hare disavowing the appeal in late October. By then, it was far too late. The issue appeared as scheduled, free of all advertisements, with Kate pursuing the theme of Katherine Debs as the symbol of "all the suffering and the sacrifice that all the women through ages have borne who loved and served the men who served mankind." At one point she told the story of how, years before, a neighbor had bought Katherine a bicycle. "I determined," Kate wrote, "that somehow, by some hook or crook, I was going to get a little electric car that Katherine could drive, so she and her old, blind mother can go out into the sunshine and beauty of God's outdoors."[13]

To stave off disaster, Frank came to Terre Haute "wild with excitement," Theodore Debs remembered, shouting that he and Kate would be damned by their comrades and the *Rip-Saw* would face bankruptcy if the Debs family did not accept the money donated by his readers. They argued back and forth for a whole day, with Theodore Debs remaining adamant. The incident did not bring about a break in the long friendship between the O'Hares and the Debs family; if nothing else, the meeting with Frank convinced Theodore that Katherine Debs's "poor mouth" had been responsible for the testimonial idea. A few weeks later, Theodore wrote a long letter to Frank lamenting the ongoing bickering within the Socialist party and thanking him for sending a bundle of *Rip-Saw*s. In spite of the recent unpleasantness, he had enjoyed Frank's visit because "It is always exhilarating to clasp the hands of one of the 'old scouts' who is still in the trenches." His brother Eugene was equally forgiving, telling his wife that Kate O'Hare's tribute had been "masterly," while adding, "But you *must not* let her get you an electric car." Coming at a time when Debs was drained physically and depressed mentally, the O'Hares' efforts on his behalf had lifted his spirits. Theodore Debs came to see the campaign as "a monumental service inspired by the most magnanimous and unselfish spirit and made beautiful and radiant, even poetic in its appeal by the love which animated the precious service." While Frank subsequently explained to his readers that "every cent" had been returned to donators, some comrades were not as willing as the Debs brothers to overlook the Katherine Debs testimonial fiasco, especially those who had long disliked Frank and Kate. As Theodore Debs later told James Oneal, with considerable sympathy: "The outcome was that the O'Hares got hell from the comrades everywhere, charged with being the rankest kind of grafters. . . . The thing just about ruined their publication."[14]

The Children's Crusade

The O'Hares had another idea, one that had been brewing in their minds ever since Kate's release: to dramatize the plight of some 114 comrades still behind bars as a result of long sentences meted out during the war. The immediate impetus came when Dorothy Clark and Martha Reeder, wives of two political prisoners, stopped by the *Rip-Saw* office in St. Louis to ask for financial assistance in getting to Washington to plead their cases before President Harding in person. Frank suggested that they hold off while he gathered evidence and assembled as many wives and children of the prisoners as possible so they could march as a body to Washington. O'Hare asked Caroline A. Lowe, a wartime defense attorney for the IWW (whom he had inducted into the SP twenty years earlier), to come to St. Louis. Frank gave the briefs he had gathered to Charles R. Nagel, a law school professor and former secretary of commerce and labor during the Taft administration. Nagel would write in the *St. Louis Law Review* of prisoners "[in] whose cases the evidence was so technical and so inadequate that under normal conditions it is doubtful whether any judge would have permitted their cases to go to the jury." On January 21, 1922, Kate and Caroline Lowe called on Otto Branstetter in Chicago to ask for the party's support for a joint committee on amnesty to be composed of the SP, the IWW, the Civil Liberties Union, and the *Rip-Saw*. The magazine, Kate assured him, had no particular desire for credit or publicity. Branstetter pointed out that the National Executive Committee had considered similar schemes in the past and rejected them as counterproductive. Such a march to Washington might be undertaken after his executive assistant, Bertha Hale White, had completed her investigation of prisoners in Oklahoma convicted for their part in the "Green Corn Rebellion."[15]

A few days later, Branstetter was outraged by the receipt of a leaflet dated January 20 asking for renewal subscriptions to the *Rip-Saw* and contributions to bring the dependents of men still in prison to St. Louis. "You will admit that it is simply an inspiration, a stroke of genius, if you will," the circular read. This was intended to be strictly a preliminary to the crusade, for as Kate told Caroline Lowe several days later: "Naturally our plans are a little hazy, and it is best that they should be. Frank and I must be very careful not to give the impression that we are bossing the job." She should have told that to the inexperienced Dorothy Clark, who wrote to Branstetter demanding that the names of all wives and children of political prisoners be sent to the *Rip-Saw* immediately. To make matters worse, Clark attacked Caroline Lowe for criticizing the O'Hares' seemingly premature announcement of the crusade. Branstetter sent a cool reply to Mrs. Clark declining to participate in the crusade, observing "that your campaign bids fair to be more of a circularization campaign for the 'Rip Saw' than an Amnesty Campaign for the release of the prisoners."[16]

Branstetter's anger grew with a letter Frank wrote on January 28 saying that he had been trying to get current addresses for prisoners' dependents for a year from the SP's national office to distribute five hundred dollars in donations from *Rip-Saw* readers. You will note, O'Hare concluded, that you have nothing in your files from me asking you to help my wife during her time in prison, but you simply must help now. Branstetter later told party officials that this communication proved that the O'Hares had kept money intended for children's Christmas gifts for more than a year and they had not been interested enough to secure names and addresses "until they saw an opportunity of using them in a great circulation campaign by the Rip-Saw."[17]

As to Frank's comment that he had not written for help, this was "a tricky and contemptible sophistry" considering that he had asked the executive committee for assistance in person and George Roewer had subsequently secured the affidavits that led to Kate's release. There was truth in what Branstetter said because the party had, at Frank's request, helped win Kate O'Hare's freedom; the *Rip-Saw* had kept donations meant for dependents; and the Children's Crusade seemed to be self-serving, especially in light of

CIRCULAR 2C1

The Children's Crusade
to Free the Political Prisoners

Supported by the NATIONAL RIP-SAW MAGAZINE
and its Army of Volunteer Workers and Subscribers

1049a North Grand Ave., St. Louis, Mo.   March 10, 1922

Success Crowns Our First Effort!

Dear Rip-Saw Reader:

You have read of the Children's Crusade for the freedom of the men still confined in Federal Prisons charged with violation of the Espionage Act. You have learned of the plan to have the wives and children of the prisoners meet in St. Louis, and go to Washington, D. C., there to lay before the President of the United States the facts in the cases of these men, to present each case on its individual merits, but to present every case with a plea for Amnesty for all.

The funds for assembling the women and children have been raised, and are now in the bank. On the first call, sent to picked workers for the Rip-Saw, the members of the "Rip-Saw Family" contributed over a $1,000 for this purpose. This is probably all of the money that will be needed for paying the fares of the women and children to St. Louis, and their expenses while in St. Louis.

So much, so good.

This is a picture of Elbertine Reeder, the nine-year-old daughter of Walter Reeder, an Oklahoma Political. Elbertine is all ready to go with the Children's Crusade to Washington, to lay the facts regarding the political cases before President Harding.

Now to Provide the Big Book of Facts About the Politicals
for the Children to Take to the President

When the Children's Crusade starts to Washington, it cannot, of course, go empty-handed. It must be armed with the unanswerable arguments for general Amnesty, based on the protest against imprisoning men in America for actual or alleged expression of opinion, fortified by the history of each individual case, showing the many instances where injustice has been done. The work of collecting these facts and preparing the arguments is being rapidly carried forward. Thirty days ago we could publish hardly more than a bare list, and an imperfect list at that, of the political

A circular promoting the Children's Crusade of 1922, an effort that helped to free many political prisoners but landed the O'Hares in hot water with the Socialist party (courtesy Missouri Historical Society).

the recent Katherine Debs testimonial disaster. Yet during this same period, as Branstetter knew, the Socialist party had collected more than twenty thousand dollars in contributions from Kate's appearances while failing to pay her for contracted fees and expenses. He also knew the O'Hares well enough to realize that they were not exploiting the amnesty issue for personal profit. "Yes Ma'am!" Frank explained to his readership, answering Branstetter indirectly, "It IS a circulation scheme for the Rip-saw. And a dandy." The more *Rip-Saw*s that were sold, the more that could be done for amnesty. "You get us the subscribers," Frank promised, "and the Rip-saw will do the rest."[18]

Quickly, a simple misunderstanding over the preliminary announcement of the crusade had escalated into bitter charges and countercharges over past mistakes. Frank did not seem to grasp just how much the national office had grown to distrust his motives. When Branstetter asked him to explain his recent behavior, O'Hare answered: "Just excited. . . . The Children's Crusade is hitting BIG—never saw anything like it." He continued to insist that the *Rip-Saw* desired no general publicity and that the Socialist party and the IWW were behind the effort. On March 6, Branstetter informed him officially that neither organization would participate, citing "the subscription features of your first announcement" as well as "the unfortunate tone" of subsequent correspondence.[19]

Branstetter also thought it "a mistake to single out a crook and grafter like Clark and make special efforts in his behalf." Branstetter's reasoning made little sense to the O'Hares, who had carried a feature story on Stanley Clark's case as the first in a series of profiles on political prisoners. Frank had only asked his readers for money to bring the wives and children of all the prisoners to St. Louis. Mrs. Clark had come to St. Louis "almost hysterical"; as for her husband, O'Hare later admitted to journalist William Bradford Huie that Stanley Clark "had the most ignoble record of betrayal of every friend and every cause." Frank still remembered the time years before, when the two were pioneering the Texas Socialist encampment movement, that he had lent Clark his last twenty dollars only to find that his friend had gotten drunk and skipped town. More recently, Clark had betrayed the Socialist movement by supporting Woodrow Wilson and the war. But the government had thrown him into prison on framed-up charges for collecting food for striking Bisbee, Arizona, miners. The issue to Frank O'Hare was due process, not Stanley Clark's character. So, the Children's Crusade would go on, even if it meant further alienating his old party comrades. He and Otto Branstetter would never speak to one another again. Frank must have been cheered by another letter written the same day as Branstetter's, this one from Eugene Debs (freed from prison in December) praising Kate's "masterly article" in the February *Rip-Saw* on the Clark case.

"I yearn to be on the platform again," he wrote, "to do my share to get our comrades out of their hell-holes." As far as Debs was concerned, at least, Frank and Kate were doing more than their share.[20]

Through March, as the wives and children of "the politicals" made their way to St. Louis, Frank worked to organize an itinerary of sixteen cities to be visited en route to Washington and to raise more funds. He hoped to collect two thousand dollars to offset the costs of printing "The Big Book of Facts" on the cases of 113 imprisoned men, but when donations began to dwindle in April, that idea was scrapped as too expensive. To save money, Frank published a four-page edition of the magazine instead of the usual twenty pages. He asked the St. Louis local of the Socialist party for help in arranging a send-off meeting for the crusaders at the Odeon Theatre, which Kate said she had booked for April 16. The O'Hares, personae non grata with the local, which chose to side with Branstetter on the issue, sent Dorothy Clark to plead their case. While the party refused to sponsor the meeting, they agreed to provide some free publicity in *St. Louis Labor* and the *Arbeiter Zeitung* with copy to be provided by the O'Hares. Unfortunately for the Children's Crusade, Kate had not made the theater booking after all, leading to much anger and embarrassment among the St. Louis comrades. Instead, the O'Hares settled for a much smaller rally attended by about 150 people at another hall. The meeting to launch what Kate called "a petition that can't be tossed into a waste basket," made front-page news in the St. Louis *Post-Dispatch,* with Frank feeding details of the crusade to his friend, reporter Paul Y. Anderson. Many other Socialist and labor papers carried stories about "a huge and successful meeting at the Odeon," thanks to a press release that Frank had sent out several days earlier. Otto Branstetter used this incident as further proof of the O'Hares' supposed perfidy. The situation was probably best understood as an example of a growing problem in the O'Hare marriage: working at direct cross-purposes. Each thought they were in charge of the crusade; Frank because he had always run things from behind the scenes and Kate because she was a wife, a mother, and a former political prisoner herself. It was a serious problem that would only grow worse in the next two years.[21]

At the last minute, Frank decided to travel with the crusade, perhaps because he did not trust Kate and Dorothy Clark fully to handle day-to-day arrangements. He left the *Rip-Saw* in the hands of young Dick O'Hare and old friend and radical poet Covington Hall, hired, at least in part, because he was "loved and trusted by the IWW." At Union Station in St. Louis, Kate wrote, "the children found that first response to the words of the Nazarene . . . they found that a great, powerful corporation had heard and responded to their cry for justice and had placed at their service every resource of its great railway system." Actually, Frank had negotiated a

The National Executive Council, about 1921. Otto Branstetter (third from left), recruited into the SP as a college student by Frank O'Hare in Oklahoma, helped to win Kate's release from prison and denounced them both for acting too independently during the Children's Crusade (courtesy Perkins Library, Duke University).

group travel rate with the railroads for the thirty-three children and mothers in their own railcar. The first stop, Terre Haute, Indiana, proved to be a high point of the trip. For the first time since his return home from prison, Eugene Debs spoke in public, telling a large crowd that he would not rest until all of the prisoners had been freed. When the collection plate passed to him, the Socialist Hero dropped in a twenty-dollar gold piece. The reception was far different in Indianapolis, where no sympathizers welcomed them and authorities forbade all public activities. Already broke, the crusaders had to beg money for the hotel bill from a local trade union. Chicago was better, with Jane Addams arranging a meeting and providing enough money for expenses. After a warm welcome in Dayton, the crusade hit Cincinnati for another successful mass meeting. Mary D. Brite, local secretary of the American Civil Liberties Union, organized the day there so well that Frank talked her into becoming an advance agent to, as he put it, "checkmate

Hillquit and Berger," who were urging Socialists to boycott the O'Hares' campaign.[22]

The boycott was much in evidence several stops later in New York City, where the O'Hare's old friend, George Kirkpatrick of the Rand School, was singular among party regulars in defying Hillquit's edict. Elizabeth Gurley Flynn, the famed "Rebel Girl" of the IWW and a longtime friend of Kate's, handled the arrangements. After the train arrived in Grand Central Station from Buffalo, the tired crew of mothers and children unrolled their banners for a dramatic march through Manhattan with reporters, newsreel cameras, and a contingent from the New York City police bomb squad following. "This is a new sort of show," Mary Heaton Vorse wrote in the *Nation*, "This is a *grief parade*." They dined at the headquarters of the Amalgamated Food Workers on delicacies prepared by some of New York's leading chefs. The older children spent the afternoon at the circus while the mothers and their babies went on a sightseeing tour. Tea at the fashionable home of Mrs. Willard Straight rounded out the afternoon. That night, a mass meeting was held with a lineup of speakers calling for amnesty that read like a Who's Who of radical women, including Elizabeth Gurley Flynn, Mary Heaton Vorse, Crystal Eastman, Rose Scheiderman, Theresa Malkiel, and Caroline Lowe. Gurley Flynn remembered Kate above all: "tall, gaunt, standing there speaking, while she held Helen Keller Hicks asleep in her arms." After two more good days in Philadelphia and Baltimore, the crusaders arrived in Washington on April 29 with the hope of confronting the president of the United States.[23]

The O'Hares did not have to worry about finances once they reached Washington as Roger Baldwin's American Civil Liberties Union (one of only two official sponsors along with Gurley Flynn's National Defense Union) had agreed to pick up the tab. Upon arriving, the group began picketing along the sidewalk in front of the White House, a move that brought about a heated dispute between Kate and Baldwin on the one hand (who favored the public demonstration) and Frank on the other (who opposed it as counterproductive). After Baldwin intimated that it was his decision to make because the Civil Liberties Union controlled the purse strings and Frank threatened to spurn Baldwin's help, it was agreed that Dorothy Clark would make the decision once she had heard both sides. The group put aside their banners for the moment and a delegation led by Kate filed into the executive offices. "When the children reached the Mecca of their dreams, the goal of their tragic pilgrimage," Kate wrote, "policemen barred their way; the President was too busy receiving Lady Astor and a circus freak to see them." According to a White House press announcement, Harding would not meet the delegation because the Department of Justice handled such matters. That night, Dorothy Clark sided with Frank on the matter of picketing, although Baldwin always maintained, as he told an oral history interviewer, that once the crusade reached Washington "I took over."[24]

Eventually, the delegation got in to see Attorney General Harry S. Daugherty, who promised only to look at each case individually. The conversation between Kate and Daugherty grew lively at several points without anyone's mind being changed. In addition to their daily calls at the White House, the crusaders attempted to confront Harding in church; instead, authorities shunted them to a Sunday school in the annex. In mid-May, many of the crusaders departed after several of the children contracted mumps. Kate and a rump contingent vowed to stay on until the prisoners had been freed.[25]

Frank O'Hare returned to St. Louis upon receiving the news that daughter Kathleen had fallen ill and Covington Hall and Dick O'Hare were having trouble managing the *Rip-Saw*. Theodore Debs wrote on May 18 to say that he and his brother found the crusade to be an inspiration. Referring to Otto Branstetter's withering denunciations of the O'Hares at the recent Socialist party national convention, Debs said they were "not insensible . . . to the cold indifference of some and the cruel criticism of others that you have had to endure." Frank wrote back that he and Kate "will not permit ourselves to grieve over the opposition from those to whom we have a right to look for cooperation" because the good had far outweighed the bad in the crusade. He had received a disturbing letter from Kate indicating that "she has apparently permitted herself to work too hard on this, and seems to be on the verge of collapse, and I am now trying to frame a telegram to her that will take all the pressure off and permit her to breathe freely and return home." He hoped to convince the crusaders to move to the shadow of the federal prison at Leavenworth, Kansas, until their loved ones came out, but Kate would have none of it. She stayed on in Washington long enough to be denounced on the floor of the House of Representatives by an opponent of amnesty for using a "disgraceful, unpatriotic, and unfair method" of trying to force the president to take action. Kate was quoted as saying that although the White House had turned the crusaders away twenty times, they would not leave "until we have succeeded in getting the administration to meet this issue squarely." By mid-June, all but four of the families represented in the crusade had been reunited with their men as the administration quietly released the prisoners individually. Having made their point, Kate and Mary Brite departed, leaving Dorothy Clark in charge.[26]

In St. Louis, Frank O'Hare had a more pressing concern to deal with: survival of the magazine in the face of continuing losses. Theodore Debs tried to console him with the observation that the crusade had succeeded.

"The financial difficulties you are now experiencing," he continued, "is a part of the price you are having to pay for this noble service." The August *Rip-Saw* declared the Children's Crusade to be over, with the number of federal politicals reduced from 114 to 76 as the administration continued to release them at a trickle to minimize the fallout from hard-liners. The July and August issues of the magazine contained only eight pages each. In September, Frank asked his volunteer subscription hustlers to get busy. "Frankly," he explained, "we had a narrow squeeze this summer. . . . But we gritted our teeth and held on." From Lindlahr Sanitarium, Eugene Debs wrote: "You nobly laid your all on the altar for this cause, so it is a shame that you had to bear the greatest part of the sacrifice alone. Is the Rip-Saw running or did you have to suspend for a time?" The magazine was still going, Frank replied; "True we have to buck the line pretty hard, but we will feel fine when we have busted through and victory perches etc." Perhaps as a way of making amends for snubbing the crusade, Otto Branstetter agreed to pay Kate five hundred dollars that the party had owed her for more than two years. She had resumed her lecturing and while the fees amounted to little, Frank approved because "it rests her, I believe to get away from housekeeping and the office for a while. She has been mighty brave and sweet and patient while we have been having this rocky time."[27]

If Frank had launched the Children's Crusade, as Otto Branstetter charged, just as a subscription stunt, then it was a failure. If he did so, as he said, to right a series of terrible wrongs, then the crusade succeeded. Elizabeth Gurley Flynn believed that the Children's Crusade had highlighted political injustice and hastened the day of freedom for the political prisoners. So did the Debs brothers. Ralph Chaplin, whose son Vonnie had been one of the child stars of the crusade, emphasized in his *Autobiography* that many groups had fought for his freedom. Roger Baldwin later would claim that the American Civil Liberties Union had been responsible for freeing the politicals. Before the O'Hares jumped in, the amnesty movement had been ineffectual because, like the Left in general, it was badly divided. Having reached a stalemate, Frank wrote, "Nothing but a highly humanized appeal would reach the people." He put the prisoners' dependents in the public eye and let others denounce him, "none of which hurt my feelings, as I started the Crusade to arouse the country, and if it incidently aroused the S. P. so much the better. It needed arousing." In the end, the Crusade played a pivotal role in dramatizing the issue of political prisoners, won the release of the men whose wives and children had appeared at the gates of the White House, and helped pave the way for President Calvin Coolidge's commutation of the last of those jailed on December 15, 1923. Years later, Frank O'Hare called the Children's Crusade "the last satisfactory thing I have done."[28]

The Children's Crusade was also the last campaign Frank and Kate conducted as members of the Socialist party. In mid-1922, at the behest of *St. Louis Labor* editor Gus Hoehn, a firm ally of the Center-Right, the O'Hares were read out of the party by the St. Louis chapter on the technical grounds that they had not taken part recently in the work of the local and were in arrears in the payment of dues. Five years later, when Kate went public with her version of the incident, Bertha Hale [White] King issued a rejoinder that "the real reason why the national organization was dissatisfied with Mrs. O'Hare was her refusal to co-operate with the national office in its efforts to provide for the defense of all those who were victimized by the Espionage Act." Following her release from prison, she and Frank had gone on tour for the party, contributing all monies raised minus expenses and fees, yet "she refused—as usual—to make necessary reports or to work with the office," all the while denouncing the party " 'officialdom' " for its lack of support. The final blow, King continued, reviving Branstetter's charges, came with the Children's Crusade, undertaken as a way to sell magazines and without party approval. The O'Hares' former comrade at the old pre-war *Rip-Saw,* James Oneal, chimed in that Kate had made the decision for the crusade and then insisted that the party approve the plan. "It was another case of 'free lancing' and another demonstration of inability to co-operate with a movement."[29]

Finally warming to his real agenda, Oneal charged that Kate (and, by implication, Frank, Debs, and other hinterland comrades) had always been too independent of the national office, writing that "In the West, where Mrs. O'Hare did most of her work, she either made independent arrangements or induced organizations to accept her terms, and they often did so, as they did not have the knowledge of discipline and sense of organized team-work that organizations in the East did."[30]

Furious with these criticisms, Kate lashed out some months later against the person she was certain stood behind her ouster, Morris Hillquit. The party's refusal to aid in her defense had nothing to do with lack of funds "but because I was disliked by the individual who always had, and still does dominate the S. P. as his personal property." Hillquit had come to hate her not on ideological grounds as "I was always 'regular' and 'right-wing.' " Rather, he had retaliated after losing out to her as international secretary in 1913 and for the chairmanship of the committee that wrote the War Manifesto in 1917. By the time of her trial, she continued, "I had long been a thorn in the flesh of the dictator of the S. P. and my election to these coveted positions wounded his morbid ego until he felt that my arrest and imprisonment was a 'Divine dispensation.' " The charge that she had failed to keep in contact with the NEC during her many Western barnstorming swings was "silly" since, like Debs, she toured under the auspices of state organizations and the *Rip-Saw.* "We were both handled by Frank O'Hare," Kate concluded, "and he is a report crank."[31]

The bitter exchange between former comrades revealed much about the inner workings of the Socialist party. The O'Hares had been purged on a pretext. Their real crime had been acting too independently for years from the authority of the Center-Right, even if they had been, for the most part, "always regular and 'right-wing'" as Kate had said. Now they had nowhere to go, except to carry on (as Hillquit had said of them years before) as "an unmitigated nuisance."[32]

New Llano

Financially, the *Rip-Saw* limped through the year 1922. "The Children's Crusade operation had been a great success," O'Hare wrote, "but it had killed the 'doctor.'" Searching for a fresh start, the O'Hares decided to rename the magazine *American Vanguard* as more reflective of their mission "to educate mankind, that it may rebuild war-wrecked civilization upon the solid rock of social justice." Eugene Debs wrote approvingly that the name change "will give you a wider appeal," which is what they had in mind, considering the new objective, which Frank defined as "to help build up a real, constructive, honest-to-God American Labor Movement." New subscribers and a return to the policy of accepting all advertisements, however outrageous ("Live Forever with a Perfectly Balanced Glandular System" one proclaimed) allowed the magazine to keep publishing. Job Harriman, once a leading light in the Socialist party, approached Frank about advertising his Llano Colony in the magazine, an offer O'Hare refused, having been badly burned in the Ruskin venture. "The fake advertising we carried was obviously what it was," he later explained, "and it fooled no Socialists. But Harriman was promoting Socialism!" Dissatisfied with her life as the star attraction of the faltering *Vanguard,* Kate O'Hare had not abandoned her dream of returning to rural life and teaching in a college for workers as she and Frank had done briefly at Ruskin before her indictment disrupted their lives.[33]

As the Socialist party crumbled and the movement for a farm-labor coalition fizzled, she became more convinced than ever that worker education in the area of cooperation offered the best hope for a new world. Intrigued by the possibility of starting such an educational program at Harriman's New Llano, recently relocated to Louisiana, Kate arranged for a week-long inspection of the colony in early 1923.[34]

New Llano buzzed with excitement over the prospect of the famous Kate O'Hare visiting the colony. At one of the weekly "psychological meetings,"

The O'Hare family arrives at New Llano in 1923, with the four "short hares" looking less than enthusiastic at the prospect of living socialism in rural Louisiana (courtesy Perkins Library, Duke University).

members were told that great advantages might be reaped if she came away impressed. One colonist, Fred M. Goodhue, remembered her as "tall, not bad looking, possessing a strong, kindly face; very much a lady and evidently very capable." Kate looked at everything, held lengthy conversations with General Manager George Pickett, and interviewed many of the colonists to see why they had come, what they liked and disliked, and what they thought about the future of New Llano. Returning to St. Louis, Frank recalled, "she was up in the air. This was THE place. . . . [She] was as wildly enthusiastic over it as many of my friends, in the 20's were over Soviet Russia." When Kate pressed Frank to relocate following a formal invitation from Pickett, he did not resist. They were heavily in debt and the colony's terms seemed very generous. The move offered them both something beyond the very real opportunity to live socialism: for Frank it meant saving the magazine while for Kate it was the opportunity to become involved in starting a workers' college. Had they known more about the troubled history of the colony—and the current intramural war of words—they might have thought better of once again risking their all.[35]

Llano Colony was the largest and most long-lasting of the experiments in communal living prompted by the nineteenth-century vision of a Cooperative Commonwealth. After years of activity in the Socialist movement, founder Job Harriman wrote, "I came to the conclusion that we should have to add economic activities to our political activities, or we should never succeed." To this end, he tried to create a cooperative society based on parity in ownership, wages, and opportunity on several thousand acres of dryland in Antelope Valley, California, beginning in 1914. Criticized by the state of California for wasting water, Harriman reincorporated the colony as Llano del Rio of Nevada, a legal sleight of hand that kept the experiment alive. While Llano had attracted more than eleven hundred settlers by mid-1917, it was not a success in either the financial or the philosophical sense. Coming to the realization that the colony could never have access to sufficient amounts of water, Harriman began looking for another location. The search ended when the Gulf Lumber Company of St. Louis agreed to sell the colony some nineteen thousand acres of land in Louisiana (where much of the pine had been cut) complete with the abandoned mill town of Stables for the price of $150,000, payable on easy terms. Beginning in the fall of 1917, Harriman stripped the California colony of most of its industrial property, including the print shop. New Llano, as Stables was renamed, contained enough facilities for the colonists to move in immediately, although the next three years were marked chiefly by hardship and bickering between factions from California and Texas. With Harriman absent for most of the time, leadership gravitated toward the dynamic and dictatorial George Pickett and his handpicked board of directors. After three subsequent years of relative peace, a new power struggle loomed in 1923 between Harriman (returned from a lengthy health cure in Brazil) and Pickett, just as the O'Hares appeared on the scene.[36]

Kate O'Hare's close investigation of the place had failed to detect the fundamental flaws in the community as a Socialist scheme. From the beginning, the colonists had shared, but unequally. Rather than hewing to the ideal of a truly collectivist society and opting for slow and steady growth, Harriman (and then Pickett) managed the colony in opportunistic fashion, without a consistent plan, admitting anyone who could come up with the two-thousand-dollar admission fee, regardless of their ideology, and practicing only partial cooperation. While the colonists owned the land, farm machinery, and livestock in common, members kept their private property rights in regard to their homes, their household goods, and even their automobiles, as well as worldly goods and investments held outside of Llano. Freed of the financial insecurities that went with life in a market economy, the comrades' fidelity to traditional American private property rights remained untouched. Individualism combined with a strictly voluntary system of cooperation in production did not add up to a new way of life based on collectivism that Harriman had hoped to initiate. The colony also did not come to grips with the matter of democratic governance. As a result, as Paul Conkin has observed, "Its history was constantly marred by jealousy, factionalism, and even revolution." From the start to the bankrupt finish in 1939, the Llano experiment hovered always on the brink of financial collapse, a reflection of the failure to create a better way than competition, a cooperative society grounded in a sound economy. This was the worst shortcoming of all; for while the political infighting created bitterness and splits, economic insufficiencies would eventually bring the colony to ruin.[37]

Under the terms of agreement as outlined in a letter written by George Pickett to Frank O'Hare on February 5, 1923, Frank was to occupy the position of "general production manager," responsible for the colony's budgeting. Regarding the *Vanguard*, the colony would provide the labor for typesetting, press work, and mailing; office space and housing; and pay the staff in kind at the same rates as other members of the commune. The O'Hares had complete control over the content of the magazine and accepted the responsibility of paying off previous debts within one year. After that, ownership of the *Vanguard* would pass to the colony. Meanwhile, a board of directors consisting of the O'Hares, Pickett, Ernest Wooster (Harriman's former resident manager), Covington Hall, and George Cantrell (the colony's printer), would oversee the management of the paper. As Frank later told his fellow colonist A. James McDonald: "Of course I never functioned as production manager and general budget director etc. I really didn't want to, as I'm a lazy bum, and believed that concentration on the publications would be plenty to occupy my mind." The move to New Llano appeared to make good sense for all concerned. The colony had bagged the most famous Socialist husband-wife team in the country. Their paper, with a circulation hovering between twenty and twenty-five thousand, could be a very effective recruiting medium for New Llano. For the O'Hares, the colony's promised subsidies were the "angel" they needed to pull the *Vanguard* out of debt. Frank went so far as to promise the readership that "the economies which result from the change" could lead to a semimonthly magazine in the near future. Kate could pursue her dream of effective worker education. The restless O'Hare children, their parents hoped, might find communal life to be a character-building experience. Finally, as Frank later wrote, "This looked like a chance for a rest for one and all after a pretty hectic five years."[38]

Fred Goodhue later remembered the "tall and attenuated" Frank O'Hare he befriended in 1923:

> His face, strongly outlined, was one of intellect and interest. He was a "practical dreamer," that is, full of schemes and ideas. Behind all this, once convinced of their worth, he had the power to push on so long as there remained reason for pushing. If a scheme failed he probably

would carry it so far as was reasonable and then gracefully drop it—
with regrets! He was musical, artistic, pleasant, ingenuous, transparent,
and fairly deep.

New Llano was not what Frank expected. Without having to worry about
paid labor, he assigned the many tasks he had done for years to others. Kate
and Covington Hall continued to write most of the stories. Dick O'Hare,
now age twenty, ran the office. Ivy Van Etten, equally young, doubled as
circulation manager ("Comrade Frank O'Hare has asked me to conduct a
special column for the Vanguard Army") and bookkeeper. The irreplaceable
Mae Stalker rejoined the staff in the spring. George Cantrell imitated the
dress of the magazine on the colony's relatively primitive equipment so well
that Frank did not even miss the services of his longtime friend and printer
Albert Von Hoffman of St. Louis. Frank discovered that what remained to be
done (reading the mail, dictating letters, looking over accounts) took about
thirty minutes per day. Thus the publisher of the *Vanguard* and production
manager of Llano Colony found that he had very little to do. "It did not take
F.[rank] P. long," Goodhue wrote, "to see that, so far as he was concerned,
he had been merely given something to play with and his reaction was
rather sad."[39]

Frank adjusted to the unaccustomed situation by lowering his hopes
for New Llano. "I never expected TOO MUCH from the colony," he later
explained, "I expected to be satisfied with very little, and as a matter
of fact I was more than satisfied." He plunged into projects to improve
the colony, quietly taking over general supervision of children's activities,
described by Goodhue as including "their work, 'pep,' propaganda, and
entertainment." He taught high school geometry and English. Landscaping
around the central square and the school, he shoveled, planted, and raked
while thinking about the next edition of the *Vanguard*. He helped to put on
plays in the colony's little theater, tooted the alto saxophone in the orchestra,
built sidewalks, made bricks, worked in the planing mill, and conducted
funerals. As long as he stayed out of colony politics, he was happy. Like
most of the other residents, O'Hare liked New Llano most for what Mc-
Donald, a fellow colonist, called "the beautiful social life" that resembled
an idealized version of the simple diversions of a typical small town. For
the first time in his long career of agitating for socialism, he was finally
living it: telephone, electricity, delivered laundry, groceries, shoes, work
clothes, entertainment, boardinghouse-style meals, medical care—and no
bills. "From each according to his ability, to each according to what is to be
portioned out," is how he later described New Llano, "Believe it or not."[40]

Kate O'Hare told her *Vanguard* readers that "Children and young people
who have not been warped by contact with the capitalist struggle or

existence take to Colony life like ducks to water." In the case of the O'Hare children, that was only partially true. Their eldest son Dick proved to be so competent in his work with the *Vanguard* that Frank gave him significant responsibilities. Adjustment to colony life for the twins, Victor and Eugene, bright, street-smart city boys just discovering their sexuality, proved to be more difficult. Eventually, as the colony's other teenagers accepted their leadership, the twins became reasonably content. "Gene is well loved," Frank told his sister, "and Vic is getting better liked as time goes on. He certainly cut up some didoes, but has been a pretty good kid (for him)." The fractious Victor eventually found his niche in the colony's bakery. As for Kathleen, "Colony life palled on her," as Frank put it. Described by Goodhue as "sixteen, good looking, smartly set up, and very much the young lady of 'the period,' " she hated using the outhouse, eating her meals at the hotel dining room, and the food itself, which consisted principally of sweet potatoes, rice cane syrup, peanuts, and bread. New Llano, she later said, "completely soured me on the idea of socialism and communism." Fleeing at the first opportunity, she boarded in St. Louis with the Browns, old friends of the family whose son Harold came to New Llano to work with Kate and Frank on the *Vanguard.* By December 1923, Frank could report to Gertie Petzold that "Kathleen acted up a while, tried the outside world, and then shinned home when she found that the world is a hard place. She is adjusting herself better now and will come out of it all right." Unfortunately for the O'Hare family, the adjustment of troubled Kathleen would prove to be quite temporary.[41]

Kate divided her time among writing for the *Vanguard;* putting the finishing touches on her book *In Prison;* planning for the worker's college; and coaching, costuming, and producing plays for the theater. "I probably was too busy to be tactful," Kate later confessed. Disgusted by the unsanitary conditions in the common dining room, she monitored the young waiters and waitresses closely, much to the anger of their mothers. She clashed with Pickett over what she called "his passionate espousal of quacks, the quackier the more ardently he took them to his bosom." Theorizing that "all human ills [are] caused by overeating," Pickett refused to consider contaminated drinking water as the source for persistent impetigo, diphtheria, and typhoid among the colonists and criticized Kate for treating sick children with medicine donated by a Memphis doctor. Late in the spring of 1923, her health campaign ended when she contracted typhoid fever herself, losing thirty pounds before checking into the colony hospital.[42]

Frank tried to warn her "not to expect too much, and to be satisfied with little," lest she become disillusioned. She wrote a series of articles for the *Vanguard* comparing New Llano to the Kuzbas, a colony of Americans (including Bill Haywood for a time) in the Kuznetz Basin of Soviet Russia, charged with developing mining and chemical operations. "KRO," Frank wrote of his wife, "in her Kuzbas stories, wanted to go all out, whole hog, in her report. I blue pencilled her stuff mercilessly, and Pickett knew it." These stories, strung together in a pamphlet entitled *Kuzbasing in Dixie*, portrayed the New Llano colony as a "little world" where capitalism and exploitation had been eliminated. Yet problems remained, especially the unfair division of labor based on gender, with men doing "the big, interesting, creative things that give a worker a sense of power" while the women did "the drab, uninteresting maintenance work." She used her illness, which lasted through the summer, to make the point that the colony had taken very good care of both her and her family. "We seem to have solved the vexing problem of wages," she concluded, "but we are of 'the earth, earthy' and have no desire right now to achieve Heaven, either here or somewhere else. The earth looks pretty good to us and we are going to make it look better." Ironically, these reports, responsible for luring many *Vanguard* readers to the colony, would later be used against the O'Hares by George Pickett because of a few veiled criticisms of his leadership.[43]

Returning to her desk in September 1923, Kate wrote the forward to *In Prison*, which Alfred A. Knopf published later in the year. Her time as a political prisoner had led to the understanding, she observed in the book, that "Only in prisons are the crudities, stupidities, barbarities, and brutalities of slavery, feudalism, and capitalism concentrated into the narrow confines of four walls where one may see and feel and suffer them all to the nth degree." The heart of the 210-page study, her personal experience as a prisoner, was based on the 64-page version published by Frank O'Hare in 1920, with several pages reprinted verbatim from the earlier work. Frank wrote on the flyleaf of his own copy of the book that he had "prepared the systematic sociological material"; as usual, he had edited her prose as well. His St. Louis friends, attorneys Luther Ely Smith and Elmer E. Pearcy, read the manuscript and the first proofs carefully, making their own suggestions. "It is shocking," one critic wrote, "that the extremity of martyrdom should have been necessary to produce this brilliant study in criminology." As to the future, Kate suggested at the conclusion of *In Prison*, the solution "possibly" would be found in socialism, but as this would come about only gradually, "we must patch up what we have." Her recommendations included counseling and better medical care, simplification of criminal laws, professionalization of jailers, and an end to exploitative convict labor, the last an especially pressing personal concern considering her own galling, sweated labor sewing overalls for pennies a day. Kate broke no new ground in her insistence that most criminals were victims of their environment, but the vivid firsthand description of prison life, combined with her analysis as an amateur criminologist and psychologist, made for a potent indictment of the American penal system.[44]

In the spring of 1923, once the O'Hares had settled in at New Llano, Frank wrote to William E. Zeuch "that 'this is the place,'" meaning, the ideal location to set up the kind of school the two of them—and, of course, Kate—had dreamed of since their days together at Ruskin. Here was the perfect opportunity to create a resident college for workers and farmers to study the liberal arts while gaining technical skills in a Socialist environment. Zeuch, who had been corresponding with Pickett since 1920, came to New Llano to help the O'Hares negotiate an agreement with the colony creating the Commonwealth College Association. Three trustees—Kate, Zeuch, and Pickett's representative, A. James McDonald—were to oversee the operation of the college. In theory, the interests of the colony and the college, Goodhue wrote, "in general, would run on parallel tracks but would never interfere with each other." The college could help the colony by attracting idealistic young people while New Llano would benefit from the labor of students, set at twenty-four hours per week, given in return for room and board. Commonwealth received a deed for forty acres of land for a campus, a part of the agreement that Kate and Zeuch should have examined more closely since, as it turned out, the property did not actually belong to New Llano. Zeuch hurried back to Urbana to finish his contract as a fledgling instructor of economics at the University of Illinois, designing the curriculum at a long distance while typhoid-ridden Kate did her best to oversee the many tasks that needed to be completed before the opening of the first semester in October.[45]

Frank and Kate used the *Vanguard* to spread the good news about Commonwealth. Beginning with a special "Educational Edition" published in May, the O'Hares went all out to promote the college as "an institution of higher learning for the masses." One unsigned article in the September issue (written by Zeuch) damned American higher education for producing a series of four-year country clubs for the elite, "training schools turning out cogs for the current commercial life." Commonwealth put a good education within the reach of any working-class boy or girl willing to learn and labor. The school would begin with a three-year high school curriculum and a freshman year of college with two more years of college to be added later. Promised classes included mathematics, three foreign languages, English, science, economics (to be taught by Frank O'Hare), history, and psychology. The college opened formally on September 30, 1923, in a festive dedication held on the roof garden (converted from a huge lumber-drying shed) of Llano Colony. After an overture from the Llano orchestra, Educational Director Zeuch delivered an address, explaining that "This school is a protest against evil conditions that prevail in our present educational systems." Speaking next, Kate called Commonwealth "a new adventure in working-class education," and pledged that the institution would "build a culture in overalls and work-marked hands; a culture whose ideal is a working class fit to inherit and hold the earth." Finally, George Pickett spoke on the relation of the college to Llano Colony. Somewhat ominously, he chose to emphasize the college's dependence on the colony, reminding the audience that New Llano provided the land, raw materials, machinery, skilled directors, and the means for teachers and students to earn their livelihood.[46]

"The lovefeast of Founders' Day," Covington Hall later recalled, "was hardly over before the struggle to control the community began." Long before the college opened, Kate and Zeuch came to resent McDonald, the third trustee, a man described by Goodhue as a "willing tool of Pickett, dour and egotistic in his rectitude." Years later, Kate told McDonald that Pickett had said to her that he would represent the colony on college matters, not his bookkeeper, McDonald. After Zeuch returned to the University of Illinois to finish his term there in the spring of 1923, McDonald wrote to Pickett, complaining that Kate was ignoring him. When McDonald showed her the letter, she told him that he was being difficult. "You have a badly ingrown case of inferiority complex," Kate continued, perhaps hoping to gauge his reaction to a calculated insult, as she had to Roger Baldwin and others since the time in 1917 when her friend Zeuch had first interested her in psychology. It took McDonald almost a quarter-century to reply that she seemed to think that she had a right to judge him on the basis of very little information. To make matters worse, Zeuch indirectly expressed his reservations about New Llano by sending Pickett a bitter critique of the colony written by a former member, charging the general manager with being undemocratic in his management. Upon his return to Llano, Zeuch treated McDonald no better than Kate had, preferring to make important decisions in consultation with her outside of the formal trustee meetings. Intimidated but determined to carry out what he thought was his role as a full-fledged trustee, McDonald could only sputter in protest at the ambitious program of expansion that Kate and Zeuch envisioned.[47]

Fred Goodhue (who also taught at Commonwealth) and Zeuch designed a central building for the campus to replace the college's makeshift facilities. The layout, complete with a large auditorium, classrooms, offices, and a formal garden, would have cost nearly fifty thousand dollars to construct under normal circumstances; Goodhue and Zeuch estimated that with colony labor and locally manufactured bricks, it could be built for less than half of that, still a huge sum for a struggling commune. Horrified, McDonald told the ever-suspicious Pickett (sequestered in New Jersey for treatment of his bad back) that a conspiracy was developing against him. "He was glad," Goodhue wrote of McDonald, "to report the matter to the Colony as an entering wedge leading to College domination and assumption of management in the Colony." McDonald had fired the first shot in what became known in the annals of the colony as "the big fight," a battle that caught the O'Hares in a withering cross fire of charges and recriminations.[48]

Kate O'Hare did not wait for Commonwealth's first term to end before hitting the road to lecture and raise funds for the college in mid-November 1923, suffering from what Frank described as a "bad nervous condition." She returned before Christmas happy and having gained back several pounds. Two weeks later, she went out again, this time for three months, in her role as field director of the college, in search of a large grant from the American Fund for Public Service of New York. The Garland Fund, as it was called, had been set up by Charles Garland of Boston to disperse his unwanted two-million-dollar inheritance among left-wing causes as quickly as possible. With a board of directors that included such friends of the O'Hares as Roger Baldwin, Scott Nearing, and Elizabeth Gurley Flynn, the prospects for a generous gift for Commonwealth seemed auspicious. The O'Hares had made some progress in paying off their debts. Frank predicted to his sister that if they had "a fairly good year" in 1924, they would be able to square all of their past accounts. He had even canceled his longstanding arrangement with Harry R. Fisher's agency, which had provided the sleazy advertisements for mail-order cure-alls and get-rich-quick schemes. "Kate could get a high salaried job with the UMW [United Mine Workers] but she will not take it, as we are committed to this proposition. . . . Yep—its [sic] a great life if you don't weaken."[49]

The Last Crusade

In the January 1924 *Vanguard,* Frank O'Hare announced that his wife was in the process of visiting seventeen states "gathering evidence exposing a great gruesome crime of politicians and private interests against the people." In truth, progress toward climbing out of debt had been painfully slow in spite of the advantage of printing at New Llano and a badly needed infusion of cash from the Brown family of St. Louis, enough capital that the O'Hares made Commonwealth student Harold Z. Brown a silent partner in the *Vanguard.* Frank and Kate had been casting about for another crusade. "Therefore (to their everlasting credit and ingenuity,)" Goodhue wrote, "they found one: a 'Crusade against prison contract labor.'" It was a natural, given Kate's own nightmarish experience, her firsthand reports in the *Vanguard* and *In Prison,* and the growing interest in the problem in the mainstream press. The Crusade against Prison Contract Labor, Frank promised in January, "will be the great public-service effort of the Vanguard for 1924." Kate clearly enjoyed her investigative forays and lecturing on both prison reform and Commonwealth. "I am having a wonderfully interesting trip," she wrote to Alice Stone Blackwell, "For the most part I am speaking to an entirely new group and find the ferment of unrest and the longing for something substantial to which the human soul may be anchored is very strong." The crusade opened with the April issue of the *Vanguard*, with Kate presenting an overview of convict labor as a multimillion-dollar enterprise that exploited the imprisoned, corrupted state officials, party bosses, and labor unions, and undercut legitimate garment manufacturers. Subsequent issues, Frank declared, would zero in on particular prison-made commodities to show consumers, merchants, and workers how they were being bilked and what they could do about it. Furthermore, his wife "will personally go into the field leading a crusade that will get the country by the ears." Readers could help the cause by selling subscriptions to the *Vanguard* and ordering bundles of the current issue for their friends. "You have been waiting a long time for a scrap to start in which you could enter whole-heartedly and with enthusiasm," he concluded. "Here it is."[50]

Meanwhile, the O'Hares found themselves caught in a scrap at home that threatened not only their crusade but the very existence of their magazine. The feud between followers of George Pickett and Job Harriman had broken into the open in early 1924, with the college and the *Vanguard* squarely in the middle. McDonald warned Pickett (still in New Jersey) that a cabal was forming against him. Kate's search for funding outside of the colony fueled the bookkeeper's suspicion that the college would go its own way. At the same time, McDonald fretted that Commonwealth might become a financial drag, hindering future plans to increase New Llano's agricultural and industrial productive capacity. When Kate and Zeuch ignored these jeremiads, McDonald, as he later admitted, "stopped reasoning and expostulating and began to fight."[51]

Returning to the colony in February, Pickett asked New Llano's board of directors to give him a vote of confidence in his leadership and industrial program, a move, Zeuch charged, that would effectively lead to a dictatorship. Pickett had applied to the Garland Fund for a fifty-thousand-dollar grant to improve New Llano's water system only to learn that Kate had already asked the same organization to fund Commonwealth's new central building. In reply, the Fund's president, the O'Hares' old chum Roger Baldwin, wrote that Commonwealth and New Llano would have to decide which enterprise was more important, a condition that neither side was prepared to meet. Rather than discussing the matter openly with his comrades, Pickett decided to throttle Commonwealth College. In early April McDonald recommended to the board that it rescind the agreement between the colony and the college, replacing it with one that would put Commonwealth firmly under the control of New Llano. "We feel," Zeuch and Kate wrote in reply, "that any college run as a department of the colony would sooner or later suffer from integral coercion, just as the ordinary colleges of today suffer from capitalistic domination." At a general meeting of April 17, Pickett railed against the college at length, citing the competing grant applications as evidence of a conflict of interest between Commonwealth and New Llano that could be remedied only by Zeuch's surrender to the colony. For good measure, he added that "Quite a bit of feeling has been raised in the Colony and outside of the Colony because the Vanguard has boosted specially the College and not the Colony."[52]

Having linked the college and the *Vanguard*, Pickett moved next against the O'Hares' magazine. On April 23, his followers asked the board to look into the agreement that had brought the *Vanguard* to New Llano. Because the general membership had not been consulted beforehand, the compact should be declared null and void, the petitioners said. They charged that the "exacting demands" the *Vanguard* made on the print shop "inconvenienced and retarded" the colony's other publications. The O'Hares menaced the future of the colony "by the belligerently destructive attacks made upon social problems," referring, presumably, to a few passing lines on sexism in the colony in Kate's laudatory series on New Llano, *Kuzbasing in Dixie*. The O'Hare family, the indictment continued, "seems to be a law unto itself in the matter of labor" because the *Vanguard* had used free colony labor in the print shop. "They seem to enjoy" better food, clothing, and housing than others. Finally, Pickett's minions voiced resentment that the O'Hares had not yet become paying members of the colony. This absurd indictment revealed not only Pickett's demagoguery but a deep undercurrent of anger in the colony that the general manager was willing to exploit for his own ends. The fight against the O'Hares, Goodhue commented, was "marked by fully as intense a bitterness on the part of the Colony as had been its previous desire to get them."[53]

As part of his defense against the charges made against the *Vanguard*, Frank O'Hare produced a report showing that the magazine had brought $6,721.94 in liabilities to the colony and paid off $2,538.85, leaving an indebtedness of $4,183.09. He included other figures to show that his family had not been enriched and that colony labor on behalf of the *Vanguard* was not unreasonable. McDonald later claimed that Pickett had offered Frank the opportunity to continue publishing the *Vanguard* "under the existing contract with some minor changes." But the unreasoning attacks on both the college and the O'Hares' magazine embittered them against the colony.

Kate and Zeuch attached themselves to the Job Harriman faction, which, as early as April 1924, began talking about seceding from New Llano. To this end, they sent out an advance scouting party to search for a new site. By the time the O'Hares launched their Crusade against Prison Contract Labor in May, they had had quite enough of New Llano.[54]

Neatly summarizing what would be Kate and Frank's last crusade together, Fred Goodhue explained:

> So here was an issue and the O'Hares, with all the ingenuity of the Irish; with all the experience and ability of the dynamic personality of Mrs. O'Hare, went into it and they made a great stab for prominence . . . and for a time illuminated the horizon with an iridescence that betokened a conflagration of the first magnitude. It was really spectacular.

The May 1924 issue of the *Vanguard* announced that Kate O'Hare "and a picked crew of expert helpers" would soon set out on a nationwide publicity tour to fight against the manufacture and sale of prison-made goods. Following up on an article in the April issue, Kate set her sights on the Reliance Manufacturing Company, which, in 1924, along with its subsidiaries, produced more than sixteen million work shirts in seventeen prison sweatshops under various brand names including "Big Yank." She detailed her visits to the prison shirt factories in Oklahoma, Indiana, and Kentucky, comparing them with her own sweated labor at Jefferson City. The article included the names and locations of the directors, plants, and corporations involved in the "prison factory trust" as well as a sample prison factory contract. Advertisements of the Reliance Company were included to show how it used patriotism to sell "Big Yank" to Americans while making a larger percentage of profits than any other corporation. "It is a huge, filthy, corruption-breeding, death-dealing monster," Kate wrote, "and yet as defenceless as a devil-fish on land . . . [as] the Prison Factory Trust can be killed in ninety days by publicity."[55]

Having launched the crusade, Frank wrote a long letter to Eugene Debs on May 25, explaining that Kate, Dick, Kathleen, and Harold Brown were in Springfield, Illinois, to publicize the sale of prison goods, forcing retailers to clear their counters of prison-made clothing. His plan was to "get out say three or four slashing issues" of the *Vanguard* covering the prison contract labor system from every angle. He hoped the Socialist Hero would have a chance to meet Zeuch, promising, "You will love this durn rebel teacher. . . . I have made mistakes frequently in sizing men up—but I think I got Zeuch's number the first time I saw him." Frank did not mention the bitter controversy raging in the colony or the fact that his magazine's future hung in the balance; instead he observed that while "building colonies is not all beer and skittles. . . . It is amazing that so large a family should get along so well." His tone was entirely different two days later, in a memorandum to the "field force" in Springfield. Why had they not reported to him more frequently? Send me news, he demanded, adding, "This should be very plain, when I have explained it over and over."[56]

The bitter feud between Pickett and Harriman reached a head when the two sides agreed to a special election, with the losing side to pack up and go elsewhere. Pickett's forces easily carried the day, a problematic victory considering that Harriman's followers had not yet chosen a new site. Zeuch answered complaints lodged against the college by Pickett's henchman, George Sutherland, with a blistering attack on the general manager, calling him an incompetent, a liar, and a fraud. Three days later, the Pickett faction canceled Zeuch's membership in the colony and gave him ten days to leave, a meaningless edict as he lived at the college, not at New Llano. While mounting his defense, Zeuch came across a carbon copy of a letter written by the Pickett administration to Ruskin colony seeking to "get the lowdown" on the O'Hares. While this tack came to naught, the board dutifully voted to suspend publication of the *Vanguard* at New Llano within sixty days.[57]

All of this might have been bearable for Frank (after all, the magazine still belonged to him) if the Crusade against Prison Contract Labor had been going well. Although he boasted to his readers in the June *Vanguard* that "The job of closing the markets of the United States to Prison Factory Trust goods is really going to be like taking candy from a baby," he and Kate had been at loggerheads over tactics and financing from the beginning of their offensive. She was tired of Frank's old formula of hustling subscriptions and underwriting the magazine through her lecturing for one hundred or more dates per year. Also, as Frank later admitted, Kate felt "very anxious to 'get from under' my galling management and try her own wings." After failing to obtain a large grant from a labor union to underwrite the crusade, they had agreed as a compromise to launch a series of public demonstrations beginning in Springfield to force stores to stop doing business with the prison factory trust. Revealing his own feelings about what he felt their relationship should have been, O'Hare wrote: "She was a great person when she played catch to my pitch. Or pitched to my coaching. We accomplished our purpose." But Kate chafed under the new assignment—which essentially asked her to both pitch and catch—and she was angry with the coach as well. The O'Hares had been effective over the years precisely because Frank had organized and Kate had agitated.[58]

Little wonder, then, that she and her inexperienced crew floundered. Frank's anger boiled over in a memorandum to the "field force" of June 18:

I know perfectly well what KRO can do. I know perfectly well what she don't like to do, and what she WILL NOT UNDER ANY CIRCUM-STANCES do. And she has a right to do as she pleases just as you have a right to do as you please and just as I have a right to do as I please. Just now I am pleasing to try to build a real movement that will function now, and be ready for the next move after this one is put over.

The next day, he threatened to call the crusade off after learning that instead of organizing a peaceful picket line around a store selling prison-made goods, the field force had marched in to confront the frightened proprietor at the head of an angry mob.[59]

The July *Vanguard* reported in the Commonwealth "News and Views" department that "F. P. O'Hare, Professor of Genetic Economics, is now in the North on a mission connected with his magazine work." Fred Goodhue, by then Dean of Commonwealth, remembered that the O'Hares, "finally seeing how impossible it was that they could remain with any self respect, at last left, he to Chicago, 'on the night train' to take up the Prison Reform Crusade, and Mrs. O'Hare on the road. Thus ended their sojourn at Llano." Frank had brought Zeuch on board the *Vanguard* as a director in the hope that he might "arbitrate" between him and his wife as Phil Wagner had during the pre-war period. What Frank really wanted was for Zeuch, Kate's most recent intellectual mentor, to side with him in his plan to restart the crusade with Kate lecturing once again as she had in the old days. To Frank's astonishment, his old friend had supported Kate in her plan to underwrite the crusade with union donations. "Not that I blame them," Frank later wrote, "for they were perfectly honest. But neither had the slightest idea of how to manage an institution." After a violent argument in which Frank predicted that the *Vanguard* and the college would fail unless they adopted his plan and Zeuch accused him of being a supreme egotist, the two men ended their close friendship—at least for the next fifteen years.[60]

"It was painful to leave," he later told an old comrade; the night before departing New Llano, he wept along with two close friends. Not having expected much from the colony allowed Frank to exit without lingering feelings of anger. He recognized that under the circumstances George Pickett faced almost insurmountable difficulties. The colony was undercapitalized and could not even feed itself. Economic difficulties led to a political split that Frank had wanted no part of because he saw no necessity for it. He admired Job Harriman, but the dynamic man he had first met in 1902 ("clad in immaculate white, handsome, virile, forensic") was old now, spitting up pus and phlegm, yet still beguiling enough to convince Kate and Zeuch (two avid students of psychology) to follow him into another promised land. Frank resisted the secessionist impulse of the Harriman–Zeuch–Kate

O'Hare "brush gang," he wrote, so they "expelled me from their councils." Describing himself at this point as "almost nuts," Frank approached Harriman for advice about what to do next. When Harriman snapped that Frank would have to solve his own personal problems, O'Hare decided to retake direct control of the crusade.[61]

Frank joined the "Crusade Bombing Squad" consisting of Kate, their daughter Kathleen, and Commonwealth students Harold Brown, Ivy Van Etten, and William Beavers in Chicago, where they lived at Hull House. Covington Hall put out the *Vanguard* from New Llano in July, August, and September. While the paper made no mention of the O'Hares' problems with the Pickett faction, Hall took a swipe at William Zeuch, observing that "Zeuch wants a 'Dictatorship of the Technicians,' but, as for Covami, I prefer the Boss-ship of the Rockefords, and the Morganheims to that of their house slaves." Frank moved the magazine to Chicago in September, managing to put out one last issue of the *Vanguard* the next month, but after that he could only wait for another financial angel to appear. While *Vanguard* readers sent in more than two thousand dollars in contributions toward the crusade in September, this was eaten up quickly by expenses. There were old debts from St. Louis still to be settled and the matter of $345 that the Pickett group insisted would have to be paid before they would release the O'Hares' personal effects left behind at New Llano. "The Vanguard," Goodhue later wrote, "inspiration of a clientele of perhaps five to eight thousand readers, departed this life without a murmur. The O'Hares saved their face however, for the paper did not expire at the Colony, which was what the Colony wanted."[62]

Relations between Frank and the rest of the family continued to deteriorate. "KRO has one of her periods of misery on again, and for a while I was driven almost insane," he explained to his half sister that fall, revealing how strained his marriage had become. "I had to pull myself together, and ask her not to write except on business." Kate had gone to New York in September to apply again for a large grant from the Garland Fund, this time for the new colony and the college as well as lobbying labor unions on behalf of the crusade. "Have also," she told Frank in a businesslike letter of October 10, "been doing quite a bit of speaking for the LaFollette Campaign Committee which is wearing but has made it possible for me to meet my expenses and wait for the labor unions to take action." By November 1, 1924, with donations falling off sharply, Frank let all of his staff go except for Bill Beavers, whom he had retained as a bodyguard after intruders broke into his office and threats were put out against the crusade. Informed that help would not be forthcoming from either the Chicago offices of the International Ladies Garment Workers Union or the American Federation of Labor, Frank reported to Kate glumly that he could only pin his hopes on donations from union-made clothing manufacturers and the U.S. Chamber of Commerce, both scheduled to meet in New York in December.[63]

Two weeks later his mood swung around completely to optimism once again. He had enough money to stay in Chicago for another month; any additional donations would be sent to Dick O'Hare and Covington Hall in Mena, Arkansas, and Wilbur Benton in nearby Ink in order to restart the magazine. "The situation is clearing nicely," he wrote. "The Crusade is in excellent shape—the Vanguard can be brought up to par with vigorous and peppy work by Hall and Dick during November . . . and if KRO is in shape now to lay off for a while and rest all will be jake." He met with Job Harriman, who seemed supportive. "Personally, I feel like a million dollars," he concluded, "as I have gotten a number of perplexing problems off of my mind, and I am able to go right ahead on the division of work I have in hand. I have a hunch that we are over the worst."[64]

Kate was "reasonably sure" that Roger Baldwin and the Garland Fund would give the college twenty thousand dollars as a gift and provide another fifty thousand in loans. This was not an unrealistic hope considering her connections with the fund's board and the "fancy sums" (as Baldwin later put it) lavished on experiments in labor education. When asked about the bewildering factionalism in New Llano, Kate blamed it all on the general manager, observing that "Pickett is a psychopath—a plain nut." Job Harriman had joined Kate O'Hare and fellow colonist Alice Chown in New York, where the women found him to be "a great asset," as she told Frank on October 10. But Harriman, who had begun to build another colony incorporated as Commonwealth Community Corporation on a site adjacent to Ink, Arkansas, came to New York with his own agenda.[65]

In a tragic-comic repeat of Pickett's sabotaging of Kate's first application to the Garland Fund, Harriman charmed Kate and Roger Baldwin into rewriting the grant so that a goodly portion of the money would go to the colony, this in spite of a solemn promise to Zeuch that he would not encroach on this promising source of revenue for the college. By the time Zeuch caught wind of Harriman's scheme, the Garland Fund had dispatched a check to Alice Chown for thirty-five thousand dollars, with only fifteen thousand dollars designated for the college. Chown could not release the money until a merger between the college and the Ink colony had taken place. After Harriman's small advance party at Ink beat back Zeuch's charges of treason, the college director rallied the bulk of the Ink sympathizers, long stranded in New Llano, to his side. In a showdown at New Llano between Zeuch and Harriman, interrupted for a time when Pickett was spotted in a nearby tree spying on the proceedings, the Zeuch faction succeeded in blocking the merger. Zeuch pulled off this maneuver because Dick O'Hare, who had admittance to the Ink colony, provided him

The last photograph of the O'Hare family together, taken at Ink, Arkansas, in late 1924 (courtesy Perkins Library, Duke University).

with details of Harriman's every move. Young O'Hare nurtured the hope that the reestablishment of the college on a firm financial footing would bring his parents back together and help to revive the moribund *Vanguard*. Frank had gone so far as to draw up an agreement between Commonwealth Community and his Rip-Saw Publishing Company. With the two factions hopelessly split, Alice Chown saw no alternative but to return the check uncashed to the Garland Fund. Thus, Kate O'Hare's year-long effort to secure underwriting from friends for her dream came to naught.[66]

Frank O'Hare's whole world had begun to fall apart. "I wish I could write you some very good news," he told his half sister on November 19, "but nothing of that sort seems to be in the air at this time." Two of his children, Kathleen and Victor, were giving him great trouble. He had heard that his daughter "had been running around with a terrible bunch of newspaper sports" and even some of his "hard-boiled" friends seemed worried about her. After taking dancing lessons, she was thinking about looking for work

The *Vanguard* crew takes a break (left to right, Lottie Brown, Harold Z. Brown, and Ivy Van Etten). Courtesy Special Collections, University of Arkansas Libraries, Fayetteville.

in a cabaret. While some hope remained that the Crusade might receive outside funding, "It looks as though everything that we have touched since January 1, 1917 has been a large and juicy lemon." He longed for the simple life: a cottage in the country, a garden, and a few friends to play cards. He had enjoyed living at the colony, although Kate's unhappiness and the antics of Kathleen and Victor had made him feel miserable at times there. "I have gotten myself into a campaign that I have to stick to until it is either a success or a failure. I hope to know which by the first of the year." Worst of all, Frank wrote, Kate remained convinced that he had "gone nutty," attributing this opinion (in a tacit admission of its veracity) to the tendency of "a great many women [to] break the same way when their husbands get up against the real thing in this joyous struggle for existence."[67]

Kathleen O'Hare continued to be a great worry to both of her parents. After life at New Llano, she found tough, corrupt, vice-ridden Chicago to be "very exciting." She had indeed fallen in with "newspaper sports" after Kate wangled a press pass for her to the sensational Leopold-Loeb trial. Socialism bored her although she enjoyed (at least for a time) working on the Crusade against Prison Contract Labor, electing to stay in Chicago when Kate went to New York to lobby the Garland Fund. As Kathleen later explained, she wanted more than anything "to get out and be my own person. If I had to scrub floors I was not going to be a little Kate Richards O'Hare and I was not going to be a little Frank O'Hare. I just wanted to get away from the whole situation." She did considerably more than scrub floors. Threatening to use her newspaper friends to wreck the crusade, the headstrong eighteen-year-old demanded complete freedom from parental control, which Frank granted with great reluctance following Kathleen's expulsion from their residence at Hull House for repeatedly violating curfew.[68]

During the fall of 1924, after drifting from job to job, Kathleen accepted a position as an assistant to Ben Reitman, a former longtime paramour

The students and faculty of Commonwealth College, New Llano, about 1924 (seated, left to right, Frank O'Hare, Wilbur C. Benton, A. James McDonald, Howard Buck, William E. Zeuch, Kate Richards O'Hare, Ernest Wooster, George [?], F. M. Goodhue, and C [?]). Courtesy Special Collections, University of Arkansas Libraries, Fayetteville.

of Emma Goldman and Chicago's legendary Hobo King and whorehouse physician. Reitman, she told an interviewer, "wanted someone who was young, who was innocent, who had empathy and who was bright . . . because he wanted the real story of the prostitutes" for a book he was writing. She assisted him in his medical examinations of streetwalkers and interviewed them "to get the real story." All of this seemed perfectly natural to the daughter of a woman whose empathy for prostitutes had propelled her into social activism thirty years earlier. At a time when the South Side's largest and most notorious brothel, the Granville Hotel, was being raided almost nightly, it is possible that the pretty young assistant to the house physician ("Doc" Reitman) may have been caught in a police dragnet— or she may have been spotted there by one of Frank's concerned friends. Kathleen could not resist the impulse to taunt her mother, writing what Frank later described to Kate as "the famous letter to you about the river and the brothel." After a frantic search, they found her "living in a brothel on Ohio Street." Regardless of what Kathleen was actually doing there, circumstantial evidence pointing to her involvement in prostitution in late 1924 proved to be devastating emotionally for both of her parents. "Is it any wonder," Frank later asked, "that KRO and I went nuts that winter?"[69]

"Dear Kate," Frank began on December 23 in response to a letter from his wife, "We should make a formal announcement of our separation, just as soon as possible—say by January 1." In a year of misfortunes, their formal separation should not have shocked anyone who knew them well. They had been living apart since May 7 (except for a brief reunion at Hull House that summer) and their relationship had been strictly business for several months. She had been saying for some time that he had "gone nutty"; he was equally convinced that she had become "hysterical." Kathleen's troubles and the disastrous end to the Garland campaign may have triggered Kate's decision to end her marriage, but the relationship had begun to deteriorate years earlier. In prison, Frank later observed, Kate "had risen to the highest spiritual heights, truly heroic and saintly. Afterward there was nothing that would give her peace of mind." She no longer wanted or needed to be managed by her husband—and he resented it. The triumphant second honeymoon, the restarting of the old Rip-Saw, the attempt to live socialism at New Llano and the crusades merely postponed the end of their marriage. Without money, a home, a brood of dependent children, or the glue of socialism, there was very little left to hold them together, only the "business" of ending prison contract labor, which had helped to make Kate's time in prison so torturous. Probably, she had not loved him for some time. Unfortunately for Frank, he would never stop loving her, at least the "great soul" she had been before prison. "To me," he wrote of their marriage, "its dissolution was unthinkable."[70]

In spite of their many troubles, the O'Hares both believed that some source of financing might yet be found that would allow the Crusade against Prison Contract Labor to continue. Frank's contact in the Union-Made Garment Manufacturers' Association in Chicago had expressed interest in using Vanguard reprints and new pamphlets as the basis for its forthcoming campaign against contract prison labor, promising "to pay us 'as soon as there was money in sight.'" He believed that he already had an oral agreement to funnel enough money into the crusade to pay off five thousand dollars in debts and provide them with a decent compensation for all of their work. If the UMGM came through as promised, Frank told Kate, "This will involve further temporary business relations between me and you, which is extremely distasteful to me." The same day as he wrote these words (December 23), Kate wrote that Thomas A. Rickert, president of the United Garment Workers of America, "put me through a three hour grill" covering the O'Hares' activities of the past quarter-century "and finally indicated that I had stood the examination 100%." This was a sure sign that the union was on the verge of offering them both employment. "Your work," she continued, "will be so completely separate from mine that there will not be the slightest conflict." Frank found this news to be "very welcome." They stood to make plenty of money from the *Vanguard* reprints in the coming year. He advised her to hold out for straight salaries of one hundred dollars per week for each of them. "I have developed some new kinks in the Crusade," he concluded, "that will tickle everybody." She replied to him coldly, saying he would have to make his own deal. For good measure, she added: "I would suggest also that it will be better for you if you manage to get your proposition in shape without finding it necessary to make critical remarks concerning me." Before writing again, she continued, have someone else read over your letter "and eliminate the evidences of your complexes."[71]

The tone of this letter should have suggested to him what would happen next. Following a joint meeting of the United Garment Workers and the Union-Made Garment Manufacturers, Kate was offered the position of directing publicist at a generous salary. "Everything went very smoothly," she told him, at least for *her*. As for him, "None of them doubt your ability, but they do have reservations concerning your stability, and nothing I could say made the slightest impression." So there would be no job for Frank. Where and how these sudden doubts about his stability arose she did not say, although it is quite possible that they originated with her. "I am sorry," she continued, "but there is nothing I can do. You will have to make whatever arrangements is [sic] possible." Their last crusade together had crashed, but not the cause. Kate spent much of the next three years crisscrossing the country, campaigning against prison labor as pressure from special interests mounted on Congress. One of many companies that Frank had embarrassed through publicity, a St. Louis broom wholesaler, appealed for help to Congressman (and soon Senator) Harry B. Hawes. What began as an effort to aid a manufacturing constituent ended as the Hawes-Cooper Act of 1929, which all but eradicated the interstate sale of prison goods. While many groups and individuals deserve credit for ending contract convict labor, the O'Hares' last crusade certainly made an important contribution to the effort.[72]

Devastated by what he regarded as Kate's rank betrayal, Frank O'Hare sank into a deep mental depression in early 1925. He later wrote: "I dragged myself back to St. Louis, in debt to every friend, without wife, children, self-respect or money." His personal and professional partnership with his wife had meant everything to him. He had long regarded her "as a gifted individual with a unique call to serve humanity." With his help, she had done that. As he came to see it, "All domestic, and personal interests were sacrificed in order to keep her where she could function most adequately. In my 'over-evaluation of the object of my affection' I was blinded to many things. I had to pay bitterly for this blindness." The O'Hares had never fully resolved the tension between their dual roles as "manager" and "star" on the one hand and husband and wife on the other. For all of his talk of being a feminist, Frank wanted Kate to be a wife and mother first. Despite her insistence that she was a domestic-minded woman above all, she usually gave her work in the public sphere first priority. For years they subordinated these underlying tensions, balancing family concerns with devotion to larger causes, as during their two Socialist honeymoons and in the rhythms of daily life developed in the intervening years. After serving her sentence in the penitentiary, Kate forged new commitments to the causes of prison reform and labor education. Frank shared her enthusiasms but primarily as vehicles for continuing his renewed dedication as a Socialist publisher, this at a time when the movement was evaporating.[73]

The O'Hares had worked at basic cross-purposes for much of what Frank later regarded as "four tragic years," tragic in the sense that they were increasingly incapable of performing their accustomed roles as public and private partners. The time was a tragic one also because the interests of their children suffered. Too much had changed for any kind of meaningful "Return to Normalcy" for the O'Hares, as it had for the country. After Kate left him behind, Frank was, as he put it, "in a hell of a fix which took me years to get over." He would spend the next several years trying to make a new life, torturing himself with the futile hope that he might win back his lost love.[74]

6

Hard Times,
1925–1940

"Coming back to St. Louis to live was a terrific ordeal," Frank O'Hare later confessed to his daughter. He grew increasingly dispirited during the first months of 1925 as his wife and children vented their anger against him. Suffering through the worst emotional crisis of his life, O'Hare slowly pulled himself together, living on the hope that he might yet patch up his marriage and win back the love of his family. After a fruitless attempt at reconciliation, Frank and Kate divorced and married other people in 1928. The Great Depression interrupted Frank's new life, propelling him back into the radical movement. Like many Americans, he spent most of the 1930s on the edge of abject poverty. Near the end of the decade, he renewed his friendship with Oscar Ameringer and William E. Zeuch for the purpose of launching "Abundance for All," a joint crusade against the Great Depression. But as in 1917, when war derailed the Socialist movement and O'Hare's personal life, the coming of World War II quickly wrecked his modest political comeback. By 1940, Frank O'Hare felt that he had seen it all—twice over.[1]

"Completely Busted"

Sometime in their forties, many males undergo a midlife crisis. The most basic symptom is depression, characterized by physical ills and feelings of hopelessness, helplessness, and loss of self-worth. A sense of profound crisis can be triggered during a time of multiple concurrent demands for personality reformation. The causes include endocrine changes, a sense of unachieved aspirations, the reemergence of youthful dreams long suppressed, generally felt stagnation, confrontation with death, changing relationships within the family, and alterations in social status and social role. Sometimes this series of challenges takes place over an extended period of time, as long as twenty years.[2]

In the case of Frank O'Hare, a series of personal and professional setbacks in 1924 brought on a midlife crisis very quickly. The first symptoms can be seen as early as 1917 when he walked away from the *Rip-Saw* and attempted to assert his power as a familial patriarch. At that time, though, there was no dramatic break with his lifelong dream of socialism in that he was merely substituting one form of activity (defacto editor) with another (recruiting for Ruskin). The O'Hares' second honeymoon temporarily resolved the emotional upheaval caused by Kate's conviction and imprisonment. Subsequently, a series of "crusades" designed both to further worthy causes and to preserve his niche in the movement postponed Frank's realization that he had been pushed out of the Socialist party and that his wife's own personal development demanded an end to her dependency on him. In 1924, in rapid succession, Frank was expelled from New Llano, forced to suspend his magazine, saw his last crusade wrecked, witnessed the rebellion of his now grown children, and was faced with his wife's final declaration of independence. His self-esteem almost completely shattered as he "crept home" to St. Louis, he could no longer postpone a confrontation with failure and mortality.

Kate's letter announcing that she would be carrying on the Crusade against Prison Labor without Frank contained another revelation. On January 17, weeks after being "rescued" from a Chicago brothel, Kathleen O'Hare had married Charles Bae "Chick" Zalliel, a twenty-nine-year-old Russian Jewish artist. Writing to Kate ("Dear Love"), Frank could only express regret over his recent differences with his daughter and ask that his good wishes be relayed to her. "She is not altogether to blame for having been trying," he told Kate on January 20, "nor for having shared in part at least in a crisis having arisen that was painful, nay tragic to me, and no doubt to her." Frank told his estranged wife that they had been through many crises before and she "will perhaps come back to a cleared view of things." He wrote again the next day to wish her luck in the new job. They had been "merely the victim of brainstorms." The crusade had been sound to the point that it should have succeeded, "But a house divided against itself must fall, so we fell." His attitude toward her had not changed at all. "I have always put *your* success first," he reminded her, adding, "You are wilful as Kathleen, and your judgement is sometimes very punk." That was as close as he came to rebuking her, for he still had every hope that they might yet get back together.[3]

Kathleen O'Hare strikes a defiant pose, sometime in the mid-1920s. She was alienated from her father for ten years before deciding that he was the parent who really loved her (courtesy Missouri Historical Society).

By his own account, it was the lowest point in his life. Frank later described himself as "completely 'busted' and 'flattened out' as ever Job was. I was so wobbly that I could not endure a two-block walk." He continued to write Kate through the spring, but received no reply. Her cold indifference to his plight deepened his sense of crisis. All of his aspirations had come to naught. His greatest achievement, the shaping of Kate Richards O'Hare into a respected advocate of change, offered little consolation considering her complete rejection of him. Disowned first by the Socialist party and then by New Llano, he had no way of furthering his youthful dream of being a part of the Cooperative Commonwealth. Without his magazine, he was saddled with a mountain of debts and no source of income. Kathleen's marriage and the hostility of his grown children brought him face-to-face with a central feature of the midlife crisis: confrontation with his own mortality. Three of Frank's close associates from his early business career committed suicide rather than face the realities of financial ruin; one of them, his first mentor, Tom Meston, had ended his life a few years earlier, in 1922. As he pondered his mortality, Frank O'Hare too thought about suicide. "In my 'class,'" he later explained, "the proper thing is for a guy to do as many of my friends have done. Pistol, high window, cyanide of potass[ium]. And leave a hefty insurance policy to widow and orphans."[4]

Frank O'Hare never tired of telling the story of how his old friend Covington Hall stopped by on his way through St. Louis one day, listened to him pour out his troubles, and then laughed in his face. After recounting his own struggles with mental depression, Hall told O'Hare to "Change your pattern of life. Start fresh with a clean slate." This advice, while simple and obvious, is not unlike what a professional expert on the male midlife crisis might suggest; the major psychological burdens that must be overcome for a middle-aged person to begin recovery are resignation to mortality and a reordering of one's life priorities. The effect of this simple wisdom, coming from an old and respected comrade, Frank found to be "electric." It would take him years to recoup completely, but he began to make his new start immediately. First, he answered a newspaper advertisement for a position in the mail-order division at Shapleigh Hardware Company. His experience at Simmons Hardware in 1911 (undertaken following his last prolonged bout with depression) landed him the job. Second, in a conscious act of catharsis, he burned most of his files in the basement furnace, especially the letters that he and Kate had written to one another over a period that spanned almost a quarter-century. Only the correspondence with Eugene Debs and a few legal papers escaped the paper inferno. While he later regretted consigning this priceless record to the flames, it did help him, he felt, to start fresh.[5]

For the next year, the lifelong night owl arose daily at 6 A.M. to walk to work, arriving in time to punch a time clock at 7. He spent most of his day filling order after order from "the dumb hardware dealer in the hick town." He often felt "loopy." "Some days," he later wrote, "I would have to grasp the arms of my swivel chair—and hold on with every ounce of power." In June 1925 he described his existence to feminist leader Alice Stone Blackwell:

> It is an excellent substitute for living. It absorbs, what with coming and going, some sixty hours of the week. These sixty hours are as near as zero as one could look for . . . [for] the two thousand of us engaged in this distributing unit there is no politics, except as permitting us to buy German hair clippers cheaply. . . . This life is like life in a test-tube. This is taking a necessary rest from the activities of the past twenty-five years. Vegetating to let the vegetative processes improve as much as they can under such treatment. Up to a certain point the treatment is probably beneficial.

Formerly gregarious, O'Hare spent most of his free time alone in a rented room, avoiding the rest of his family and his friends, except for an occasional evening at the home of Edward and Lucy Henschel, longtime Socialist comrades. "Gradually," he later observed to his son Gene, "the joy of living began to appear—like buds under the soggy dead leaves."[6]

Family problems interrupted his recovery that summer. Kate spent several days in St. Louis without bothering to call, an act that left him "grievously disappointed." Then, his son-in-law Chick and Victor O'Hare stopped by to inform him that, at the behest of Kate, they had filed for patents on a new kind of bookmaking process and an automatic interleavering machine. This interleaving device (which Frank had invented), when attached to a mimeograph or small press, allowed a single operator to print, collate, and bind several pages at a time into book form easily and efficiently. Surely a disinterested person would conclude, Frank wrote to Kate on August 2, "that you had attempted to 'clean me.'" He poured his heart out to her in a long letter that was alternately angry and loving. Six months ago, "mental conflicts" had sapped his strength; now he was building a life again. The thought of "the supremely happiest time in my life," their second honeymoon of 1920, gave hope "there may be other bright days to come." Working through his problems, he hoped soon to be in a position to give her "rest and love and peace." He had prayed for that outcome every night since returning to St. Louis. "I think there is something in this prayer business," he observed, "for I have attained a measure of peace and efficiency. And if my days are not happy, they are at least calm." He would only stay with the hardware company until he had recovered completely. But he was through with politics as a profession forever. If they ever got back together, he would not permit her to disrupt their lives with prolonged periods on the road. She would have to live according to his means. If she could not accept those terms at the present time, he would wait until she was ready. "I have made up my mind," he concluded, "to go on letting myself love you no matter whether you want me to or not. So that's that."[7]

Kate O'Hare had no intention of reconciling with Frank—at least not strictly on his terms. In retrospect, Frank came to realize that she too was dealing with a protracted midlife crisis. He admired her sensible attitude in continuing to lecture, feeling that she would come back to him, even if it meant waiting several years. Frank was equally sure that she would fail without him, especially his blue pencil, which he had never hesitated to wield on her speeches and essays, and his skillful management of her career. On her own, Kate had composed a manuscript on life at New Llano. "All the pent up hates of her life," Frank wrote, "were liberated in this writing. I would say it is not so much a book about Llano as about FPO and children." He later told his son Victor that it was "an *impossible* book" because it was solely her work. Frank's analysis seemed to be confirmed by a profile of Kate published in *The World Tomorrow* in early 1926. In an otherwise laudatory tribute, "Harold Bronco" (a pseudonym for Harold Brown and other Commonwealth admirers) observed that "she lacks ability to plan

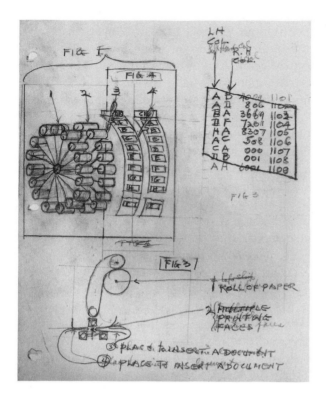

Frank O'Hare's diagram of his "automatic interleavering machine" that Kate O'Hare, Kathleen O'Hare's new husband, and Victor O'Hare tried to patent behind his back in 1925 (courtesy Missouri Historical Society).

and organize. For this phase of her work she has always been indebted to some one—usually her husband, Frank O'Hare." But if Frank remained confident through the mid-1920s that his wife would return to the fold, Kate gave little evidence of wanting anything but a divorce.[8]

Meanwhile, O'Hare continued to slowly recover from his midlife crisis. After convincing Chick Zalliel and Victor to drop their patent applications, he renewed his own labors on the automatic interleavering machine. Four years after his attorney had urged him to protect his work on his accounting mechanism with a memory, he went so far as to draw up patent specifications. In typical fashion, though, he went no further, failing to file a patent for this or any of his many other inventions, either for lack of money or lack of further interest. When the Daily Worker Publishing Company threatened to undertake legal proceedings against him to collect a debt from the Crusade against Prison Labor, Frank suggested that they send the bill to his wife as he had nothing to spare. "At the end of the year," he later wrote, "I was again functioning."[9]

In early 1926, he accepted an executive position with the Caradine Hat Company as an efficiency expert at what he considered to be a decent salary. O'Hare had done "Tayloring" work before, first under Tom Meston at Simmons Hardware and Emerson Electric, then in New York in 1903 and during Kate's imprisonment. Ironically, Frank's onetime Socialist party ally (at least on the "farm question"), Algie Martin Simons, had become a champion of scientific management following his expulsion from the party for supporting Wilson's war. Although some Socialists had castigated Frederick Winslow Taylor and the efficiency movement as just another form of capitalist exploitation, others viewed scientific management as a step in the direction of socialism and an effort to make work less tedious and more humane. Simons had made this argument as early as 1912, while the O'Hares had praised Henry Ford's five-dollar day and worker education program in a series of articles in the *Rip-Saw* in 1916. Like Simons, who taught personnel management and wrote extensively on the subject in the 1920s, Frank O'Hare believed that he had finally found a second career, one not totally inconsistent with his continuing Socialist sympathies. Inconsistent enough, though, that he would write: "The only work worth while is the tearing down of capitalism and the building of Socialism. There is an overproduction of men for production. I must compete other men out of jobs to have one for myself. I must invent and install labor displacing methods to earn a living for myself."[10]

Newly self-confident, he began renewing old acquaintances and made new friends as well, including Emmanuale Grossman, president of the Public Question Club. By the end of the year, Frank would be invited to join this exclusive group of "two-story thinkers" who met every Thursday evening to discuss philosophy and politics. To O'Hare this was further evidence that he was "fit for human society again." He loved being "a red hot Socialist" in the public arena again, if only for a few hours a week, and the give-and-take of lively intellectual exchange among friends, including baseball executive Branch Rickey, publisher Flint Garrison, and law professor Wiley Rutledge. Yet his life was still very incomplete without Kate Richards O'Hare.[11]

In a letter of March 24, 1926, Kate reminded him that they had been living apart for almost two years. "I simply cannot conceive," she informed him, "going back to the stress and strain, conflicts and brain storms, wretchedness and misery of other days." She wanted him to file for a divorce on the basis of her desertion. If he would not, then she would secure one in Mexico, where she "will be compelled to file [on] grounds which are most objectionable to me." She did not elaborate further on this veiled threat of exposé. When Frank refused anyway, she wrote again to say "that all the love I once had for you is quite dead . . . as dead as my youth." Frank's suggestion of a trial reconciliation filled her with anxiety. She insisted that she was not bitter, just in "sick dread of being driven beyond my strength, harassed, criticized and being subjected to humiliations and brainstorms."[12]

Having slammed the door on all of his hopes, she then opened it a crack in bitter, calculated terms. Of course, it was possible that he had finally gotten hold of himself "and found the man that I hoped existed, but never could find, for so many years." It could be "that I would not drive you to do insane things, as I always did," but she did not think that he would ever let her live in peace. He was not a bad man, he just had "a warped, sick soul and mind." Still, she might consider a reconciliation if his doctor assured her that he had recovered completely. She would see him on her next trip through St. Louis, so, she advised, "have something concrete for me when I arrive." She ended her amateur psychoanalyzing with a telling comment on their professional relationship. She had done her best, but it was not good enough for him. "You wanted more than I was, wanted me to give more than I could—and—well it was just hell." Three weeks later, after hearing from him again and receiving candy and flowers, she had second thoughts about a possible reunion. Exhausted from a tour of western cities, she wrote "that the Kate of other days is dead. . . . I think what you are clinging to is the memory of what I was in other days, and what I can never be again."[13]

Divorce and Remarriage

While Frank O'Hare may have recovered substantially from his midlife crisis in 1926, he continued to suffer a terrible longing for his estranged wife and daughter. When Kate and Kathleen came to St. Louis that summer, though, the long-anticipated reunion with Frank did not go well. Kate told her daughter that she had packed their things and moved "to a place where I will feel safe." She would consent to meet Frank only in the safety of a psychiatrist's office. Kathleen could stay with him if she so chose, Kate wrote, "But it is out of the question for me to see your father unless there is some man present to protect my person." That fall, news of the death of his longtime idol, Eugene Debs, came as another terrible blow. Two weeks after the funeral, O'Hare apologized to Theodore Debs for not having attended, explaining that "Personal conditions were against my going to Terre Haute, though you know I was there in spirit." During the Christmas season of 1926, Frank expressed gratitude for the "sweet and loving thoughts from my three boys." In counting his blessings, he included "a more or less secure job . . . good health, many warm friends . . . a vivid pleasure in most of the events of the day . . . and the fact that I am clear of many small and harassing debts." As the twenty-fifth anniversary of

Morris Hillquit speaking at the funeral of Eugene V. Debs on October 23, 1926 (foreground, left to right, Norman Thomas and Algernon Lee). Courtesy State Historical Society of Wisconsin.

his marriage approached, though, he lamented that "my two ewe lambs are . . . still out of the fold." After years of thought about his mistakes, he concluded that Kate and Kathleen were "both built into the structure of my mind and heart." He had become close to Irene Reynolds, a plain, soft-spoken, unmarried woman fifteen years his junior, whom he had known since her childhood. While Irene regarded him as a potential husband, Frank looked on her primarily as a friend as he persevered in his longing for Kate.[14]

Frank O'Hare finally got his chance at reconciliation with Kate in the fall of 1927. The *Post-Dispatch* reported that "Mrs. O'Hare is taking a brief vacation here with her husband, Frank P. O'Hare, and their children, at 2303 Minnesota Avenue." The reunion went well enough that Frank and Kate decided to drive together from St. Louis to Mena, Arkansas, where she had resumed her work as field secretary and professor at Commonwealth College. It took them several days to make the trip owing to a series of minor mishaps in an automobile with a top speed of twenty miles per hour. Along the way, Kate taught fifty-one-year-old Frank O'Hare how to drive. From Mena, Frank wrote to Irene Reynolds that if only she and Kate had been friends, he would have invited her along too. "The last time KRO was to visit me," he continued, "we were both in such nervous condition that it was *orful* but now we both seem to be in a pleasant, equable frame of mind, and everything is lovely and restful." Reynolds wrote back to say that if he still cared for his wife she never wanted to see him again. As he later told his daughter-in-law Bobbie O'Hare, he was not then "passionately in love" with Reynolds. At the same time, the trip to Commonwealth had made him realize "that I had become very objective to KRO. She was simply another person, and no longer bone of my bone, etc." After spending a few days fixing up Kate's quarters for her, Frank took the train back to St. Louis, his longtime obsession with Kate Richards O'Hare apparently over.[15]

Kate's next letter to him, written a few weeks later, was full of cordiality and gossip about the college. Gone was the bitterness and anger that she had poured out in her communications to him over the last years. "I am so glad you finished the chimney for me," she wrote, "it will be a pleasant reminder." She ended with the news that Victor was working at the National Suit Company for "mean-spirited, grasping, gouging, yelling Jews." She had once worked in the very same factory briefly as undercover writer Kitty Kelly. "Funny isn't it," she asked, "twenty five years ago when I was doing my 'Modern Pied Piper' I worked there, and [it] was just the same. Evidently the management has learned nothing in a quarter of a century." With their lives thus having come around full circle, Kate Richards O'Hare was, in her own way, saying good-bye to her husband.[16]

When Frank remained adamant in his refusal to initiate a divorce, Kate hired her old suitor and O'Hare family friend Wilbur Benton to file from Mena, where he taught at Commonwealth College. Under Arkansas's strict divorce laws, she would have to charge him with either adultery or some form of extreme cruelty. According to Frank, Benton "cooked up" a case alleging that he had attempted to murder Kate on a Jefferson Avenue streetcar in St. Louis. O'Hare always claimed that the incident had been made up out of whole cloth, citing as evidence the fact that Kate had driven with him, unchaperoned, to Mena ("and she seemed to be having a swell time") some time after the abusive episode supposedly took place. He later claimed to have a letter from Kate in which "she admits that she had to perjure herself considerably in order to sue me for divorce in Arkansas. . . . She warned me what she intended to do, so I made no defense to save my own reputation." In the spring of 1928, at Kate's behest, Wilbur Benton filed the divorce brief in an Arkansas court. Frank wrote a letter threatening his former comrade with "elimination" from Commonwealth if he proceeded further. Nonplussed, Benton wrote back, advising "that the situation demands a divorce." The threat of elimination carried no weight, he continued, as Zeuch was in the process of easing him out of the college already and he was preparing to practice law full-time.[17]

Having huffed and puffed one last time, Frank acquiesced in the inevitable. His growing love for Irene Reynolds and the realization of what he called "my 'over-evaluation of the object of my affection'" took much of the sting out of what he had long hoped to avoid. What seemed to concern him most was the loss of his hard-won bourgeois respectability among his friends when news of the divorce hit the newspapers. The *Post-Dispatch* reported on March 22 that Kate "visited her family in St. Louis last September, and at the time apparently was on good terms with her husband." In the divorce suit, she had charged her spouse "with general indignities." As for the always quotable Frank, the story continued, "O'Hare said today he was unable to explain his wife's suit and would not comment." The next day, the *St. Louis Daily Globe-Democrat* repeated the same story almost word for word. Much to his relief, Frank's chums at the Public Question Club did not shun their token radical; on the contrary, they feted him in a night he remembered as "about as beautiful [a] thing as ever happened to me in my life." The Arkansas divorce became final in June 1928.[18]

Five months later, on November 28, Frank married Irene Reynolds in a civil ceremony. Poking fun at himself, Frank told his cousin Susie that "The Groom wore coat, vest and trousers, shirt, collar, tie, sox, shoes and BVDs." Guests at the reception that followed included Frank's son Dick, his half sister Gertie Petzold, his half brother George, and a few close friends. At one point, a reporter telephoned Frank with the news that Kate Richards O'Hare had, that very day, married Charles Cunningham, an Alabama landowner, in San Jose, California. Frank was quoted as saying that "The former Mrs. O'Hare was a wonderful woman and I was afraid she would be lonely." Breaking his public silence on the divorce, O'Hare told a reporter from the *Post-Dispatch* that "he assented to his former wife's wish for a divorce because she was 'emotionally unhappy' after her release from the penitentiary in 1920," a sophistry that belied his own emotional problems. St. Louis newspapers gave greater play to the remarriages than to the divorce, in part, because Frank and Kate had both taken their new nuptial vows on the same day during midweek in November. But it was the whiff of scandal that turned matrimony into tabloid-style news stories when Frank told reporters that when he married Kate, Walter Thomas Mills had said: "I pronounce you man and wife as long as life or love shall last." This variation on the usual marriage formula, the *St. Louis Star-Times* reported, "furnishes the ground for O'Hare's hope that the marriage, from which four children were born, will be declared never to have existed." A devout

Catholic, Irene O'Hare desperately wanted Frank's first marriage annulled so that her church would bless their union. If she had not persisted in this wish, Kate and Frank might have remained friends at a safe distance for the rest of their lives.[19]

The ensuing controversy embittered them all over again. Kate refused to give Frank the public declaration he wanted because it would imply that she had believed in "trial marriage" and "free love." On March 19, 1929, Kate wrote that Kathleen was "in Chicago sick and in trouble." If Frank could arrange for her transportation to California, she would take care of the rest. In regard to the annulment, Kate concluded, have a priest draw up something and she would sign it "if I can do so." Ten days later, she wrote again to request Kathleen's travel money and to ex-

Newlyweds Frank and Irene O'Hare share breakfast in 1928 (courtesy Missouri Historical Society).

plain that she could not possibly agree to sign a statement about her first marriage without the consent of her new spouse, whom she described as "an old fashioned Southern gentleman." Eugene O'Hare urged his father not to send Kathleen any money as he had heard from one of her former boyfriends (she had long since ditched Chick Zalliel) that she was "just the same old Katz. You never know where or what she is." When Frank took this advice, Kate demanded that her former husband "come across just once in a whole lifetime and do a man's part." If he would not help Kathleen, she would not agree to the annulment.[20]

Frank could not have helped his daughter even if he had been so inclined. His household records for the summer months of 1929 reveal that his "executive position," really part-time consulting work, paid less than one hundred dollars per month, a condition he was loathe to reveal to his former wife. Frank had no way of knowing at the time that Eugene O'Hare had been wrong about "the same old Katz," for Kathleen would give birth out of wedlock to Victoria Hope Von Hagen on July 13. In the fall of 1929, O'Hare tried another approach to the annulment dilemma, asking Hilda Mills and Wilbur Benton (who had both attended the 1902 ceremony) to make sworn statements about the marriage vows. They both complied, but without Kate's cooperation there would be no annulment. Two years later, Charles Cunningham finally put an end to the controversy with the announcement that his wife had nothing more to say about her first marriage. Frank and Kate's paths crossed just once more, in Washington, D.C., in 1937, when Frank called on her to ask if she had changed her mind about the annulment. "I was cured forever that day," he wrote a few years later. After that they never communicated directly again.[21]

Federated Press

The Great Depression spread over the United States in late 1929, sowing countless misery for the next decade. When the sale of hats dropped off, Frank, like millions of others (including fellow Taylorite Algie Martin Simons), found himself without a job by the middle of the next year. Shortly thereafter, Irene Reynolds lost her position in a post office cafeteria. Employment prospects for a fifty-four-year-old man with a long record of radical activism seemed grim. While he allowed his mostly liberal and conservative friends at the Public Question Club to tease him about having once been "a REAL RED RANTER" (as the *Saint Louis Optimist* put it), O'Hare never turned his back on socialism in the late 1920s when he worked in business. "I speak once in a while to service clubs of business men, in church parlors, to brotherhoods, etc," he wrote in mid-1929. "The audiences seem to like the Socialist gospel as I render it. And I have built up a circle of liberal friends who seem to like my iconoclasm." Too proud to apply for reinstatement to the party that had expelled him, nevertheless, he had sent a detailed Marxian analysis of economic conditions in St. Louis in 1929 to Norman Thomas, then emerging as the titular leader of the revived Socialist party. At the behest of his son Eugene, O'Hare started writing freelance articles to make ends meet. He wrote a humorous piece on the "University of Hard Knocks" for a St. Louis Rotarian magazine. In July 1930 he received plaudits for a story in the *Post-Dispatch* on his old friend James Eads How, heir to a large fortune, who had lived and died as a hobo. He remembered How bumming around with Jack London and the many times when his friend asked him to speak before groups of hoboes. His life, Frank wrote, paralleled that of St. Francis of Assisi. While many thought him insane in forsaking the Social Register for the cross of Nazarene, O'Hare found him "marvelously sane."[22]

The next month, he wrote a feature for the *Post-Dispatch*'s *Sunday Magazine* on "The Rise and Fall of the Soap-Boxer." Chronicling his own experiences as an ardent missionary for socialism in rural, pre-war America, O'Hare remembered that "the soapboxer felt that he was a herald of a new day, that he was called to proclaim a living gospel, that would sweep the earth and make the whole planet a commonwealth—a worker republic, where war and poverty would be no more." The Great War and the new age of automobiles, radios, and movies all contributed to the demise of the soapboxer. Still, independent political action from the bottom up will surface again, he predicted, if Marx's prophesies about capitalism proved correct, and privately he was certain that they still would. The new Socialist movement, he concluded, "will have a different technique. And I can't guess what it will be like."[23]

O'Hare did not have to wait long to find out about his new role in the movement. When word of his impoverishment reached New York that summer, his adoring daughter-in-law, Jule Seibol (who had called him "Father FPO" even before marrying Dick O'Hare) mentioned his name to her bosses, Carl Haessler, managing editor of Federated Press and his Eastern Bureau manager, Harvey O'Connor. Formed in 1919 as a press service for leftist newspapers (the revived *Rip-Saw* had been a client), by 1930 Federated Press supplied news stories to eighty publications with a combined readership of about two million people and published *Labor's News*, a weekly summary of press dispatches primarily for labor editors. The service was also running a deficit of about ten thousand dollars annually, which promised only to get worse as the depression deepened. Page one of the September 13, 1930, *Labor's News* announced "the enlistment of Frank P. O'Hare, labor editor and lecturer, on its staff 'for the duration of the war or until 100,000 minds in America have tuned in on the LABOR'S NEWS broadcast.'" Explaining his assignment, Frank wrote that "I'd rejoice if I could put in my time editorializing . . . but I just have to take over the other job—to tell you about the work of the devoted, competent and tireless F[ederated] P[ress] staff." No longer the soapboxer, now he was to be a "salesman-soldier" of the Left once again. His job was to sell one thousand associate memberships in FP at ten dollars each to erase the deficit. He pledged to do it by the following March.[24]

O'Hare threw himself into his new job with all the energy and enthusiasm he had given to Phil Wagner when he had been the circulation manager and de facto editor of the pre-war *Rip-Saw*. Carl Haessler gave him a three-paragraph space on page one of *Labor's News*, a weekly "Builders' Column" inside the paper, and a modest expense account. When Irene insisted on accompanying him, they decided to give up their St. Louis rental and live out of suitcases. Frank spent most of his time traveling from city to city in the Northeast, with only an occasional respite in New York. First, with the help of a few of Federated Press's established contacts, he would develop a list of likely donors from among college and university faculty, social workers, public officials, newspapermen, clergy, lawyers, doctors, business persons, and labor leaders. Then he would call on each one to ask for a donation of ten dollars. Results of the week's work appeared in his column along with a few folksy observations on life and politics in a style that echoed J. A. Wayland. "The farmer's granaries are bursting," he wrote in typical fashion, "He's bursted too. Funny world. That's another reason for Federated Press."[25]

It was grueling work, but Frank met his quotas and enjoyed talking with his contacts as well as visiting many of the old haunts from his days as a Socialist lecturer twenty years earlier. He wrote of standing on a hilltop outside of Pittsburgh one night, noting the absence of the glow from the great blast furnaces that lit up the sky during prosperous times. Descending into the city, he saw thousands of homeless queued in front of shelters in anticipation of a bowl of stew and a "flop" for the night. The next week, it was New York, where he observed the unemployed selling apples on street corners and an odd joint committee of Franciscans and American Legionnaires serving hot coffee to the shivering poor. By the end of the year, having sold 269 associate memberships, O'Hare pushed back his target date for enlisting one thousand. He began to emphasize the selling of individual subscriptions to *Labor's News* for two dollars per year when it became apparent that "Readers like their news raw" and he could still wipe out Federated Press's deficit if enough individuals subscribed to the weekly. Just as he had once had a *"Rip-Saw* Army" of volunteers hustling subscribers, he recruited a "Sub-Card Brigade" (including his son Dick) to sell *Labor's News*. By March, Frank O'Hare and his minions had doubled the paper's circulation.[26]

While O'Hare boosted Federated Press as a service to labor, farmers, and liberal newspapers, his own commitment to socialism remained as strong as ever. "There is no capitalist on the job [at FP]," he reminded his readers, "Purely cooperative. Is there anything you can take more pleasure in helping to build?" The list of associate members contained the names of old Socialists, Progressives, and Liberals including Reinhold Niebuhr, Lynn Frazier, Roger Baldwin, Heywood Broun, Harry Elmer Barnes, Amos Pinchot, Herbert Bigelow, Bruce Bliven, Harry Laidler, Art Young, and Norman Thomas, as well as many academics, rabbis, and ministers. In Chicago, O'Hare called on Fred D. Warren, who had edited the *Appeal to Reason* for J. A. Wayland years earlier. For old time's sake, they "marked up" an issue of *Labor's News,* with Warren pronouncing it "good, breezy, [and] exclusive" as he handed Frank the money for a subscription.[27]

He spoke before men's clubs and lectured in a college journalism class and a course in economics at Northwestern University. In Minneapolis, he enjoyed attending the National Conference of Social Work, where forty of the advertised speakers held associate memberships in Federated Press. "Poor Herb Hoover," he observed, "would have felt badly to have been here incog[nito], and learned how the world's greatest humanitarian, the world's greatest engineer, and the greatest president since Cal Coolidge fared at the hands of the folks who are taking care of his ragged individuals." The recent election of the Farmer-Labor candidate to the governorship of Minnesota and Socialist William A. Anderson's victory in the Minneapolis mayoral contest gave him hope that the state might prove to be "the American laboratory where . . . the structure of the new American industrial democracy is being erected."[28]

Boarding a train for the trip home to St. Louis after ten months on the road, he believed it had been "perhaps the happiest tour I ever made." Hard as he had worked, though, Federated Press was still deeply in debt and *Labor's News* had been cut down to only four pages. Back in St. Louis, after regaling the Public Question Club with an account of his work, he received a lucrative offer to sell bonds that he spurned because he found his work for Federated Press to be more satisfactory than "pecuniary pursuits."[29]

Before returning to New York, O'Hare wrote an article for the *Post-Dispatch* in which he attempted to come to grips with the economic nightmare scientific management had helped to create. Recently, he had visited a gigantic factory in Milwaukee that produced enough oil and gas pipelines to satisfy the needs of the entire country, as well as ten thousand car frames per day, in a "manless" system almost completely automated from start to finish. Observing the operation from a catwalk, he felt thrilled and speechless, yet horrified that "Less and less of more and more finds itself accessible to the ultimate consumer." He advanced the Marxian argument that if the ongoing revolution in production led, in turn, to a revolution in social relations, "It is conceivable that unhampered social engineering can work out new systems of social control, of planned production and planned compensation, which will permit the universal expansion of the manless factory, to the greater happiness and security of man." What O'Hare left unsaid was that such a scenario could take place (at least according to Marx) only after a Socialist revolution. Still, he had managed to present a distinctly Marxian solution to the depression in what was then arguably the best mainstream newspaper in the country. Most of O'Hare's articles from this period appeared on the "dignity page" controlled by the *Post-Dispatch*'s legendary managing editor, Oliver K. Bovard, who had become convinced that democratic socialism offered a reasonable middle ground between capitalism and communism.[30]

Through the summer of 1931, Frank O'Hare continued to see "deep stirrings" in the American people against a system that had produced the Great Depression. As a Marxist, he had always believed that an economic smashup would sweep capitalism away and provide the opportunity for socialism. Yet inexplicably, capitalism had survived. "The outside of the cocoon has not changed," he wrote, "but the animal within is changing. Otherwise one would have to believe that vast economic changes had no psychological effect, which would contradict all history." With donations and subscriptions falling off, O'Hare told his *Labor's News* readership that "the so-called capitalist press" had hypnotized the nation into inertia. As "the one uncontrolled defender of whatever rights man may have," the labor press had to remain vital for the coming battle. So, he was asking for one thousand volunteers to secure ten new readers each for *Labor's News* in the next few months to keep Federated Press operating. He would set out immediately to visit the same sixteen cities as he had on his previous tour.[31]

After enlisting several volunteers in St. Louis, he hit Cincinnati, where Mary D. Brite, savior of the Children's Crusade, agreed to recruit subscribers. On October 27, 1931, Frank L. Palmer, who had replaced Harvey O'Connor as his immediate supervisor, wrote to say that he did not know how much longer *Labor's News* could continue to be published, "But there doesn't seem to be anything to do about it." Sometime in the future, the paper would become bigger and better "with pictures and everything." That was only a distant hope at a time when the country faced yet another financial panic.[32]

"I feel that Federated Press is just beginning to hit its stride," O'Hare wrote bravely in the paper a few days later. He apologized to his readers for a "rather jerky" weekly essay because his index finger had been crushed when Carl Haessler had accidentally slammed a car door on it. By the time he had a new fingernail, he predicted, the depression would have deepened to the point where "more and more people will have decided that the profit motive is about played out, and that the use or service era is desirable, attainable, and inevitable." It was his last column. Haessler had decided to slam the door on *Labor's News* with that issue. O'Hare hung on with Federated Press for a while longer, accepting his reassignment to New York and the loss of his expense account. But the disappointment of losing his public forum in "Ellen" (*LN*), differences of opinion with the laconic Frank Palmer, and the difficulty of selling memberships in the now frill-less press service took most of the fun out of the job. By the spring of 1932, Frank O'Hare was once again unemployed.[33]

This time, it would be several years before he found another full-time job. The twenty months at Federated Press had not been a waste. O'Hare raised thousands of dollars for a worthy cause under the worst possible economic circumstances. The assignment had done him a world of good psychologically, boosting his self-esteem and reconnecting him with the radical roots of his younger days. He gained many new friends, none more important than one made during a sales pitch at Ohio State University. In his final column for *Labor's News*, he had listed the week's contributors to the List of 1,000 Federated Press Associates; among them (number 650) was "Prof. H. B., Columbus Ohio." Professor Henry Blumberg had given O'Hare a ten-dollar check and, in less than an hour, kindled Frank's interest in higher mathematics. O'Hare would return to Blumberg's home for several weeks nearly every year for the next two decades so that this mathematician, highly respected in academic circles, could continue the process of, as Frank put it, "reorienting my mind," which meant learning math for the purpose of integrating scientific thinking with social theory. He found higher mathematics to be "joyous, thrilling, poetic, marvelous, and exciting in every way." For his part, Blumberg, a great admirer of Eugene Debs, was fascinated with Frank O'Hare as a man of action who had played an important role in the "Golden Age" of socialism. Blumberg gave O'Hare a mental companionship he had been searching for ever since his break with Tom Meston before the turn of the century. In the coming years of enforced idleness, higher mathematics provided him with a cerebral outlet for his creative genius and the wherewithal to become a nonacademic intellectual.[34]

A *"Simply Gruelling Experience"*

Frank O'Hare was unemployed most of the time from 1932 until early 1939, a "simply gruelling experience" as he told his son Dick in 1938, adding that he had remained "fairly serene" most of the time. He and Irene stayed on in New York City for a year to look for work and to be near two of his sons. Living in a series of cold-water flats, he wrote freelance articles and did part-time work for Federated Press. "If a guy didn't have to sleep and eat, New York City would be just fine," is how he began an article for the *Post-Dispatch* on life in America's largest city at the nadir of the depression. Some days, he would join throngs of old leftists at the International Labor Defense offices to read magazines and play cards. Thirty years earlier, Bernarr Macfadden kept Frank and Kate O'Hare from going hungry by paying them for articles in his *Fair Play* magazine. Now, he provided a similar service in his cafeteria on Third Avenue, where Frank and Irene could dine on small portions of boiled cracked wheat, bread, and milk for one cent per item. O'Hare observed hundreds of people on West Street digging six-by-six holes in the ground, covering these "kennels" for primitive shelters. He had never seen people so dispirited; except for the rattle of the elevated trains, New York sounded like turn-of-the-century Tulsa. "Nobody feels sorry for the unemployed," he wrote. "Everybody is too busy feeling sorry for himself." New Yorkers were uncharacteristically polite, considerate, and quiet, "just like at a funeral." Observing the mass psychosis of the unemployed, O'Hare wondered what the long-term effect would be on the country when so many felt so utterly unwanted and useless.[35]

In an article published for the June 1932 *Railway Clerk*, O'Hare described the scene inside S. Klein's store, a "clerkless shop" (the retail equivalent of the "manless factory") where consumers purchased cut-rate garments, without the aid of salespeople, under the watchful gaze of a small army of private police. Walking out into the sunshine on the square, he watched as a Communist speaker told a crowd of unemployed men and women: "Fellow workers, a great change must be made! The workers must organize and seize. . . ." While he was neither prepared to mount a soapbox again himself nor join a political party of the Left, clearly O'Hare identified at a distance with the agitator, not as a Communist but as a fellow disciple of Marx. Years later he would write to a Communist soapboxer whose path he had crossed during the depression: "Your gesture was sublime. Your judgement was rotten. For you were not reaching the vigorous working people, but the defeated victims of the depression." Yet, he still thought he scented revolution in the air. "It would be fine to be 24 again," he wrote wistfully to a friend, "and get into the thick of it." Harvey O'Connor tried to cheer him up, observing that while he wished Frank could join him for a May Day workers' forum outside Pittsburgh, he understood that "Enough nomading is enough." In early 1933, O'Hare wrote to a friend at New Llano that "Here, in the outside world, everything is crashing. . . . Every face you see on the street is gray and drawn."[36]

That spring, the O'Hares moved back to St. Louis on the strength of an offer of part-time work from his old boss Ed Witcoff, who had merged his Superior Hat Company with Caradine Hat as a minority owner. "I have far too much time on my hands," he wrote his son Dick. "Fortunately I am able to get some kick out of reading, mathematics, and meeting my friends." With "the old sinner" Gus Hoehn no longer the boss of the Socialist party's St. Louis local, Frank became a regular at meetings again. He had no interest in rejoining the SP, which, under the leadership of Norman Thomas, had evolved into a leftist-Progressive organization more comfortable with carrying on the imagined legacies of Bryan, Theodore Roosevelt, and Wilson than the ideology of Marx. Much to O'Hare's surprise, capitalism had still not collapsed. Writing during the first one hundred days of the New Deal, O'Hare denounced Franklin Roosevelt for merely "tinkering" with the economy. "Nothing short of universal collectivism will save the situation," he observed, while conceding that the American people had "great enthusiasm" for the president. He remained confident that once New Deal liberalism failed, socialism would sweep the country. Meanwhile, Ed Witcoff's partners had expressed their displeasure over the part-time employment of "Red" Frank. "Caradine and Christmas," Frank explained about his bosses, "are fine people of the old school (the school which thinks folks like me ought to be deported.)" Witcoff had no choice but to let Frank go for the second time in three years.[37]

The "gruelling experience" of poverty and unemployment continued for the O'Hares through 1933 and 1934. In 1935, after more than a decade of estrangement, Kathleen O'Hare wrote "that now I have been able to really love you and admire you, father—I do understand how tortured your life has been." She had come to this conclusion following an extended visit with Kate Richards O'Hare (still her pen name) that had left her disillusioned "for, I am afraid, the last time." Just as Frank was making peace with the last of his children, his sons Dick and Eugene invited him to New York as a partner in their furniture factory. Unfortunately, a fire and subsequent lawsuits soon wiped out the family venture. "I worked hard as hell on it, with the old pep and enthusiasm," he told a friend, "but alas and alack! One more corpse had to be buried." He continued to insist that Marx had been right in seeing that history would sweep capitalism away. Because the world had gone through such enormous changes since his death "without corresponding changes in the ideology of the masses, it is likely that the immediate future will be marked by a destructive breakup of the old ideology. In fact it is already here."[38]

In the spring of 1936, after several more hard months "at leisure," he dropped in with a contingent of teachers in a Communist-sponsored Labor Day parade in New York. The sight and sound of thousands of marchers singing the Internationale and old labor songs made him believe "that at last an American socialism is on the way." The limited accomplishments of the New Deal had at least replaced the mood of melancholy O'Hare had reported in 1932 with a potentially volatile mixture of hope and frustration four years later. After all, social revolutions usually take place after the nadir has passed, driven by a sense of soaring expectations. Yet O'Hare came to see that New Deal liberalism had undermined class discontent successfully with the make-work doles, especially the Works Progress Administration (WPA). Instead of jailing leftists, Roosevelt, with extraordinary common sense, had them "busy digging post holes and filling them up again," a temporary expedient that put food on the table while preserving capitalism and upholding traditional American values of individualism and consumption. As for his own circumstances, "I would be much happier if I were slashing away effectively at the menace."[39]

His sons had been urging him to resume his freelance writing, but his output lately had been "dull as ditch water." His best ideas came to him when he was making a speech or writing to friends. "A guy like me," he lamented, "has to own his own paper, as I once did." For the first time in years, he signed his letters off, "Yours for the Revolution." A request that he send greetings to a Socialist "Oldtimers Party" commemorating the twentieth anniversary of the St. Louis antiwar convention buoyed O'Hare's spirits in April 1937. He responded with a fiery full-dress speech, read in his absence, which began with the assertion that he regretted nothing. The Socialist party had not been taken in by government slogans; Wilson declared war in 1917 not to make the world safe for democracy but to save capitalism. Unfortunately, he continued, "The American working class was immature," accepting a wartime dictatorship, the mothballing of the Constitution, and "murder in the name of the Prince of Peace." Twenty years later, he saw hope in workers' cooperatives in Scandinavia and "In Russia [where] we see a complete economy existing and marvelously expanding without private capital." Socialists should be ready to engage in "the war to end capitalism and fascism" through the education of the working class. "The corpse will be buried," he promised, "Socialism will come."[40]

In the spring of 1937, after another year of doing "absolutely nothing significant . . . which is hard if you ask me," Frank and Irene O'Hare returned to St. Louis, this time for good. Working again part-time with the Caradine Hat Company, he was "paid for projects 'as adopted,'" an arrangement that netted him only fifteen dollars for the month of April. To make ends meet, Frank borrowed against their only asset (the household furnishings) and then, to avoid eviction, he had to ask his children to write a letter guaranteeing that his rent would be paid. With the Congress of Industrial Organizations (CIO) unionizing mass production workers successfully under the Wagner Act, he applied for a position in St. Louis with CIO officials who "'knew me when.'" He was downtown every morning looking for work. "Since I have my store teeth," he told Dick O'Hare, "my health, my breath, my appearance and my morale have bettered enormously. The old bean is not completely ossified." If nothing else turned up, he promised to swallow his pride and apply to the WPA. Having received some encouragement from the CIO, O'Hare went to Washington, D.C., for an interview. Irene wrote him there to say that she felt "very uneasy and worried about you." She hoped that his son Gene had sent him a little money so that he would not have to do without food and tobacco. Hearing that Frank had encountered Kate O'Hare briefly, Irene (still hoping for an annulment of his first marriage) asked if he had spoken to a priest about the matter. Had he seen Kate again? "Was she nice to you?" His first conversation with his former wife in ten years had been unpleasant enough that they would never speak to one another again. As for the job, he was sure that he could do it. "I will have no trouble . . ." he wrote. "In case of a strike they send in hardened veterans who are young and can take it. My work would be pleasant." Yet, the sixty-one-year-old O'Hare admitted that "They do not give a damn what I have done in the past—what can I do now is the question." He left Washington two weeks later without a job offer.[41]

In July 1937, having gained control of Caradine Hat over his partners, Ed Witcoff hired Frank full-time as "consulting manager." "For the time being, for me," O'Hare wrote a few months later, "the depression is over. Back at my old job. Very comfortable and happy in it." Frank's employment came along in time to save the eyesight of Irene O'Hare, who underwent extensive surgery that fall. He continued to fret about the state of the nation, predicting that open class warfare was not far off. To his friend Flint Garrison, he fantasized about preparing "for the long eventless days when I will be # 1,768,433 in concentration camp 769." Ironically, his lack of faith in the limited economic recovery seemed justified when a recession hit the country in early 1938, once again wiping out his job at the hat company. Breaking the news to his son Victor, he merely noted that he was "in a waiting position . . . but by no means washed up." He then went on to describe, in great detail, his latest invention: a "microscopic and projective system," a kind of horizontal microscope fashioned out of tin cans, foil, cardboard, and old camera lenses.[42]

O'Hare began to look for work again, failing to get very far once he told interviewers that he was sixty-two. The WPA pronounced O'Hare eligible for a make-work job and put him on a waiting list. He and Irene lived on a budget of ten dollars per week borrowed (and, though Frank would not admit it, begged) from friends and family. He staved off eviction only by getting his children to guarantee his rent against the proceeds of a life insurance policy willed to them by his half sister Gertie, who died in August 1938. O'Hare began to grasp at straws, offering to act as a consultant for a local tobacco company for fifty dollars a month and even auditioning for a children's radio program on WTMV in East St. Louis. About all that he could say about himself was that he had "managed to keep looking fit." Listening to the radio, he concluded that "We are living in a 24-hour per day megalomaniac medicine show." After a decade of economic depression, he found the American people to be bewildered, lacking immediate enthusiasm and faith in the future. And why not? Labor unions lived in the past, Roosevelt was "shallow," and Congress seemed

A working model of another O'Hare invention, a "microscopic and projective system," a kind of horizontal microscope fashioned out of tin cans, foil, cardboard, and old camera lenses, 1939 (courtesy Vince Peciulis).

to be embracing a new Inquisition in the form of the Red-hunting Dies Committee. As for political alternatives, he found Norman Thomas of the SP "awful weak" and Dr. Francis Townsend's Old Age Pension Plan and California's "Ham and Eggs" campaign "insane panaceas." O'Hare's only satisfaction came from Marx's observation that every action taken by capitalism ultimately would hasten the debacle to come.[43]

Frank penned a spirited rejoinder to an essay by William Henry Chamberlin in the *Post-Dispatch* (excerpted from *American Mercury*) entitled "Karl Marx, a Discredited Prophet." Chamberlin had merely succeeded in being "tricky" and "not quite honest" by twisting Marx's words to make an argument against all forms of collectivism. O'Hare would not defend the lack of democracy in the Soviet Union; Chamberlin had been to Russia and he had not. "It may be terrible in Russia . . ." he wrote, "There may be no more real democracy in Russia than there is in the Metropolitan Life Insurance Co[mpany]." Besides, Stalinism was certainly not Marxism and Marx bore no responsibility for it. What mattered was Marx's analysis of capitalism as well as his "explanation of the world we live in as a gigantic intellectual achievement." The Marx he so admired was "a meliorist . . . believing and teaching that the world had an end—a good end. That some day a real democracy would exist, enfranchising every human being, and releasing untold human powers for the continued conquest of nature."[44]

Unlike many other American leftists in the 1930s, O'Hare refused to equate socialism with Soviet communism, an intellectual trap, as Richard Pells has observed, that led many radicals to become obsessed with Stalin rather than exploring Marxism and defining concrete goals. Thus, while O'Hare admired certain aspects of the Soviet system, the revelations in years to come concerning the brutal nature of Stalinism did not lessen his faith in Marx the meliorist or the possibilities of an American Marxism. At the time, his defense of Marx proved to be cold comfort, considering that the Post-Dispatch refused to print the essay as his longtime champion, Oliver Bovard, had resigned some months earlier in a showdown with publisher Joseph Pulitzer II. Impecunious and politically voiceless, by 1939 Frank O'Hare had hit bottom again.[45]

"Abundance for All"

Two of Frank's former friends, Oscar Ameringer and William E. Zeuch, rescued him from a further downward spiral into poverty. The close friendship between O'Hare and Ameringer had cooled years before, when Ameringer left the Oklahoma movement to work for Victor Berger. Ironically, Berger's recruitment of the "Funny Dutchman" nearly undid him financially after Ameringer talked him into underwriting the Oklahoma Leader in 1919 in a bold bid to restart the shattered Oklahoma Socialist movement, a scheme that drowned Berger's Milwaukee Social Democratic Publishing Company in red ink through the 1920s. Following Berger's untimely death in 1929, the Milwaukee organization sold its interest in the Oklahoma paper to the Ameringer family and former Berger crony John Hagel, who then renamed their paper American Guardian. Ameringer, his son Siegfried, his wife Freda, and his father-in-law Dan Hogan (who had helped to organize Arkansas with Frank for the SP years before) kept alive the militant spirit of Southwestern radicalism in the 1930s through their lively weekly newspaper.[46]

With Victor Berger gone, Frank reconciled with his old friend in 1934, contributing two essays to the Guardian that year, one a film review on the life of Eugene Debs and the other a nostalgic piece on pre-war soapboxers. On December 30, 1938, Ameringer announced the opening of a campaign he called "Abundance for All" (AFA) to prevent economic depressions, pay off public debts, abolish taxes, and end poverty through the payment of an annual guaranteed income to every American. This would be accomplished by a National Abundance Bill providing for the nationalization of all banks and monopolies; the funding of all local, state, and national debts into one public debt; the setting up of government agencies to coordinate national industries, employment, price fixing, and guaranteed incomes; the replacement of current taxes with a "Social Overhead" (a value-added tax); and a massive conservation program funded through rent on land. Boiled down to its essence, Ameringer described AFA as "a program to provide plenty for all our people through an expansion of industries brought about by the direct and widespread distribution of purchasing power."[47]

Ameringer's humorous alter ego, "Adam Coaldigger," explained that coauthors of the plan included Moses, the prophets, Christ, Plato, the church fathers, Marx, Henry George, Bellamy, Veblen, and Charles Steinmetz. "I mention these illustrious co-workers by name," he wrote, "because being dead, Brother [Congressman Martin] Dies can't put the red label on them without making himself still more ridiculous—which hardly seems possible, but safety first." While his point was well taken, Ameringer's proposal amounted to a circuitous route to an American socialism not unlike Upton Sinclair's End Poverty in California (EPIC) program of a few years earlier. It also bore close resemblance to another scheme Ameringer had been involved with in 1933, the "Continental Congress on Economic Reconstruction," which had flopped badly. Whether or not AFA could work was a moot point unless this country editor publicized the plan well beyond his weekly readership of fifty thousand. First came the word, he wrote, but "it's also gospel truth that words are mere wind unless they are hitched to deeds." He began by incorporating AFA as "a non-profit, non-political, non-sectarian, non-excluding, purely educational and 101% patriotic society." Three trustees were to govern the organization: Ameringer; Michael S. Shadid, a veteran Socialist who had founded the nation's first cooperative hospital at Elk City, Oklahoma; and William E. Zeuch.[48]

In the fifteen years since Frank and Zeuch quarreled over the future course of the Prison Labor Crusade, Zeuch had reestablished Commonwealth College at Mena, Arkansas, serving as director (and welcoming Kate Richards O'Hare back into the fold in 1926) until being eased out in 1931. He spent a year in Europe on a Guggenheim Fellowship, then joined the New Deal as chief of initiation and planning of subsistence in the Resettlement Administration. Between 1936 and 1938, Zeuch served as an informal adviser to the Mexican government and head of Anglo-American Studies at an institute in Mexico City. At the time he hooked up with Ameringer, he was teaching economics at Black Mountain College in North Carolina. Among the three trustees, Ameringer provided the ideas and the publicity through the *Guardian,* Dr. Shadid added little more than the prestige of his name, while Zeuch was to develop AFA as a serious economic proposal and lecture on the plan. None of them had any real experience in promoting a national educational and political scheme. So they turned to Frank O'Hare.[49]

The agreement reached in April 1939 between AFA and Frank O'Hare read like his job description under Phil Wagner and the old *Rip-Saw*, except that this time, instead of a salary, he would be paid strictly on a commission basis. He was to arrange speaking engagements for Zeuch and other AFA lecturers. For every new subscription to the *Guardian* sold at one dollar per year, he would give fifty cents to the paper, thirty cents to AFA, and keep twenty cents for himself. AFA would pay fees and expenses for the speakers while Frank footed promotional costs. He also received a percentage on the sale of AFA memberships (forty cents each) and 40 percent of the profits on books and pamphlets sold at the lectures. Organizations wishing to book AFA speakers paid for the privilege through subscriptions to the *Guardian*. The agreement gave O'Hare full control over all AFA promotions. He was also to have his own weekly column in the *Guardian*, with the rather awkward punning title "O Hear Ye O'Hare!" His resentments against his old chums evaporated in an atmosphere of goodwill as Oscar Ameringer came to St. Louis to work out the final arrangements. Now Frank ranked Ameringer with J. A. Wayland and Gaylord Wilshire as model Socialist publishers. He found the matured Zeuch to be "thorough, conscientious, patient, implacably determined, experimental, skeptical, (used to be horribly tactless)."[50]

"I'm having a lotta fun lately," O'Hare wrote in May, after speaking to the St. Louis Abundance Club. "Didn't think enthusiasm could boil up again but it does." His ardor for AFA was such that he called on most of the two hundred *Guardian* subscribers in St. Louis and the surrounding area "to see what they look like, what they think, how they will behave." He enjoyed the freedom of operating independently of the faction-ridden Socialist and Communist parties, which, between them, had garnered less than 1 percent of presidential votes cast in Missouri in 1936. Furthermore, "I can talk to ANY BODY about it without running into resistances that confront the labelled S. P. or C. P. It is simply common sense strategy to talk united states and not to build up artificial barriers between yourself and the public." Still traumatized from the experience of World War I, he fretted that the government might swoop down on AFA if it became a popular movement. The Post Office and the FBI had developed "splendid technique" in their snooping on criminals, he wrote, adding sarcastically, "but of course that will NEVER NEVER be used for political purposes." His fear of government snooping was well founded. While the FBI had never ceased spying on radical movements, Director J. Edgar Hoover had reestablished the General Intelligence Section to compile information systematically on suspected radicals. A few years later, O'Hare would once again feel the government's sting personally.[51]

In addition to meeting *Guardian* subscribers and hustling new readers, O'Hare studied Ameringer's AFA handbook and corresponded with Zeuch, "getting the idea clearer in my head." Concluding that the explanation of AFA "was surrounded with considerable excess baggage in the form of words," he squeezed his conception of what Ameringer and Zeuch's ideas meant onto a single sheet of paper. "A Proposed Solution for the Depression by Frank P. O'Hare" argued that there was a fundamental difference between "little business," which harmed no one in a competitive system, and "almost entirely parasitical and predatory" big business. The combination of big business and the banks held back buying power and caused economic depression. Therefore, the government should take over rapacious private interests for the sake of labor and small business. This could be accomplished if voters put pressure on every congressional candidate in the 1940 primaries and general elections to endorse the National Abundance Bill, which Congress would then pass.[52]

O'Hare circulated his solution among trusted friends to gauge their reactions, explaining that "The AFA program is not presented as COMPLETE, but as something to be further developed." His draft, he told his old professor, Walter Thomas Mills, "appeals especially to the business and professional classes, which, as Marx predicted, have been proletarianized. They are wide open to instruction now." The verdict from his friends was not encouraging. Publisher Flint Garrison informed Frank that he could accept his diagnosis of what had caused the depression, but not the proposed solution. Better to stick with the Socialist party, his old comrade Ralph Fuchs wrote, dismissing the AFA as nothing more than "a combination of economic ideas, slogans, and over-simple proposals." Writing back, Frank admitted that Zeuch, by then the movement's chief theoretician, had obscured the program with "impractical and undigested detail." Businessmen wanted to talk about the depression, not collectivism.[53]

In a recent visit to St. Louis, Norman Thomas, successor to Debs as standard bearer of the SP, had not even mentioned socialism. "The heart of Marxian Socialism, and of the AFA are identical. . . ." O'Hare argued, "Marx stated that ORGANS of Socialism would be developed WITHIN capitalism," so he would work with a movement that was "yet in a very nascent, plastic condition." In his columns and articles for the *Guardian*, Frank, like Norman Thomas, shied away from talk about socialism as he continued to reach out to the small-business class. At the behest of former New Llano boss George Pickett, O'Hare and Ameringer also tried to recruit AFA members from the ranks of the Townsend Clubs, whose members (numbering in the millions) had extracted promises of support from some one hundred congressmen for a scheme to provide generous old-age pensions as a means of curing the depression. O'Hare could not mask his devotion to old Socialist ideals completely, though, in articles such as "Americanism," in which he wrote that the Fourth of July would remain a mockery until all races had access to the vote and the people enjoyed equal economic opportunity. That piece was good enough that a newspaper in Lineville, Iowa, asked him for permission to reprint it. By all means, Frank wrote back, remembering that he had napped on a printer's blanket sixty years earlier in nearby New Hampton while his brother George cranked out the paper there by hand. Now he was a columnist. "Just a typewriter, a box of stogies, plenty of No. 1 news print . . . ," he wrote, "and we can tell the cockeyed world what we think of it."[54]

Explaining "The Philosophy of the AFA" in late August 1939, Zeuch denounced "a Left group wanting abundance . . . by way of a r-r-revolution. . . . Americans are just too skeptical to accept abundance, or salvation of any sort, at the hands of the dialectic, the materialistic dialectic, whatever that may be." The AFA, he insisted, was neither Left nor Right. Undaunted by this pronouncement, O'Hare went so far as to advance in print his thesis that the petit bourgeois business class had effectively been reduced to proletarian status by the depression, meaning that the vast majority of Americans would be better off "if we had a breakdown of the 'profits' of the various sizes of business concerns in this country." The outbreak of war in Europe following Hitler's invasion of Poland gave new urgency to the task. "To hell with the European wars," O'Hare wrote, "OPEN THE AMERICAN FACTORIES! DISTRIBUTE PURCHASING POWER! When Europe sees what we have done, war will be DEAD!" The next week he warned that the big capitalists were "licking their chops" over the profits to be made in the manufacture of armaments. "Can the American people," he asked, "organize QUICKLY ENOUGH to elect a 77th Congress which will create PEACEFUL NATIONAL ABUNDANCE TO PREVENT ANOTHER BETRAYAL OF HUMANITY?" To further this end, he created the National Abundance Campaign Bureau, pledging to establish an organization in each congressional district to elect as many "Abundance pledged congressmen" as possible in 1940. Every volunteer who sold ten subscriptions to the *American Guardian* would become a deputy district director charged with finding another ten volunteers to sell their own ten subscriptions. A district that sold at least 550 subs would be eligible for a Congressional district conference conducted by William Zeuch to whip up enthusiasm for the National Abundance Bill drawn up by Oscar Ameringer and his son Siegfried.[55]

Thus O'Hare proposed to route Zeuch in much the same way he had managed the speaking tours of Kate Richards before the last war. "Time is short," O'Hare pleaded, "We must work fast." It was a bold, Quixotic scheme driven by the desperate desire to outrace the firestorm of war that had engulfed the activists of 1917 and now threatened to do so again in 1939.[56]

It was sure to fail, but driven by the prospect of reliving an old nightmare and of the tantalizing examples of the Townsend Clubs and the "Ham and Eggs" campaign ("$30—every Thursday") being waged in California, O'Hare plunged what little money he had and all that he could borrow from his friends into the Abundance campaign. "I am almost crushed by the bad turn things have taken," he confessed to a creditor in November. The campaign had begun well enough, but "the damn War" quickly stalled his scheme. While he faced "a terrible five or six weeks ahead," at least he had "the groundwork laid, ready for the harvest season," which would come when the political campaigning began early in 1940.[57]

To make matters worse, Zeuch had quarreled with the Ameringers over the future of AFA, demanding that Frank's Abundance Campaign Bureau be disbanded at once. In retaliation, Siegfried Ameringer cut back on the amount of space in the *Guardian* devoted to Abundance and refused to publish any more of Zeuch's theorizing. "If we are to help in building up some one in the AFA," Siegfried explained to O'Hare, "we should try and select a person who is more democratic in his relations to both membership and fellow workers—plus having the ability and the desire to organize." O'Hare refused to give up on AFA; after all, even though the California "Ham and Eggs" pension proposal had gone down to defeat in a recent California referendum, more than one million people had voted for it, conjuring up the specter among mainstream politicians of a "gray rising." Zeuch's endless pedantries were counterproductive, Frank told Upton Sinclair in early 1940. "The more detail the less appeal," he reasoned, adding that he preferred to hammer home in his weekly columns the necessity of a simple four-point program: nationalization of the trusts, mutualization of credit facilities, public works programs, and an adequate old age pension, the last point added to appeal to the millions who supported Ham and Eggs, the Townsend Plan, and Sinclair's own EPIC proposal. He favored presenting Abundance only in "the most *general* terms, leaving details of actual legislation to the to-be-hoped-for block of representatives elected."[58]

O'Hare attempted to reach an understanding with Zeuch, writing that "it would be a grand thing if you could hitchhike to St. Louis. We could then find out what we each have in view and to what extent adjustments must be made on both sides." The movement needed his genius as "a teacher of teachers." His writings on Abundance, though "masterly" in presentation, were not effective propaganda since "the average business man is simply lost in it (to my astonishment)." He ended by saying that Zeuch had "made me use my noggin considerably during the past ten months, for which I am truly grateful." Zeuch's reply was anything but conciliatory. He was "rather surprised" to have heard from Frank at all. "Had made up my mind," Zeuch wrote, sounding like a latter-day Kate O'Hare, "that despite your earlier protestations you were still suffering from some of the old complexes." He had given the Abundance leadership "[the] opportunity to strut your stuff." Oscar and Siegfried Ameringer and Michael Shadid had all failed to deliver. As for Frank, "You go into your shell and mope." "You master builders" had floundered in the attempt to organize the movement. Armed with the mailing list and a revised version of the Abundance handbook, Zeuch would carry on in his own way. "I may try lecturing later," he continued, "just to show you wise guys how wet you are . . . I will get to it if I live long enough. Wait and see." In closing, he warned O'Hare not to trust the Ameringers, whom he branded as "progressives for profit and for no other reason, and personal profit at that."[59]

Frank wrote back that he suffered from only one complex: "gradual cessation of income," thanks to the failure of Abundance to coalesce as a movement. The only proper answer to Zeuch's behavior, which he likened to "a stage brigand calling for wine at a moment of severe strain" was "go to hell." O'Hare reiterated his belief that a movement could be built only by publicizing a set of basic principles, not a detailed Abundance bill. "Just now," he concluded, "things are pretty baffling, but light may dawn."[60]

With both men refusing to budge, Abundance carried on along parallel, contradictory lines, with Director Zeuch operating on one track and O'Hare and the Ameringers on the other, while executive secretary John Wall (a young Zeuch protégé) tried to play the role of peacemaker. "Well, kid," O'Hare wrote his son Gene, "I wish I could write you a sparkling, chatty, inspiring letter. A year ago things looked somewhat hopeful to me. About the first of the year tough sledding began again." He still wrote his weekly column, although the Ameringers had not paid him in some time, "claiming no jack." Ed Witcoff offered him work, then backed off. O'Hare wanted to write articles for hobby magazines on how to make telescopes, microscopes, projectors, and enlargers out of tin cans and lenses, but the proffered fees were not worth the trouble. He was surprised to hear that his son had joined the Communist party. "I doubt that I could feel at home in the cp," Frank observed, adding that he was still quite certain "that capitalism simply cannot function beyond a certain point." The future of AFA also seemed quite uncertain. "I should have known," he added bitterly, "that Zeuch would run out as soon as he got into difficulties." The only rays of hope for AFA lay in John Wall ("very brilliant but inexperienced") and another newcomer, Walter Meyer, an AFA organizer who wanted to run for Congress in the Democratic party primary as an Abundance candidate. In April, Wall launched what he called "my last trump," the *AFA Organizer*, a four-page monthly tabloid dedicated to spreading the message of Abundance. "We'll work out the best compensation arrangement for you we can," Wall pledged to O'Hare, "Right now only God knows what we'll be able to do."[61]

The May edition of the *Organizer*, which listed O'Hare and Zeuch as coeditors, carried Frank's four-point program of the AFA on the editorial page as well as two articles by Zeuch, one predicting that "The Big Business–New Deal planned economy for scarcity can end only in fascism" and the other explaining that AFA "is neither Old Deal or New Deal—but New Deck." On page one, the *Organizer* featured Frank's keynote address to the Metropolitan St. Louis Abundance Club. Before World War I wrecked "the liberal movement," the paper reported, "O'Hare was recognized as one of the strongest orators ever to kindle hope for a better day in the heart of a western wheat farmer." He told the delegates that the depression had lasted for ten long years, affecting everyone except a few giant corporations. This was the first of what he hoped would be many AFA conferences to draft congressional candidates. Congress already had the power to control industry and the banks. In order to save themselves, industrialists in Italy, Germany, and Spain had supported the rise to power of dictatorial thugs—and it could happen in the United States as well. The common people "have nobody to vote for except a slate of $10,000 a year Charley McCarthies who are handpicked in advance." The St. Louis conference had the opportunity to choose a nonpartisan candidate for Congress who would support Abundance and serve as an example of grassroots democracy. As expected, the conference endorsed Walter C. Meyer, a thirty-seven-year-old businessman, to run as the AFA candidate in Missouri's twelfth district, composed of St. Louis County and the southern third of the city. Before the end of the year, the paper predicted, there would be an Abundance Campaign Bureau in every congressional district.[62]

A week after the second edition of the *Organizer* appeared, John Wall promised O'Hare that "If you can keep from starving for another month, the N[ational] O[ffice] will be able to take care of you. This is no bull." Praising his "genius as a propagandist and organizer," he advised him not to become embroiled "in local tugs of war." If Frank found himself hungry, Wall would slip him a ten-dollar bill or two. "Don't hit up the St. Louis crowd anymore if you can help it," he wrote, finally coming to the point, "They are beginning to resent your touches to the extent that they overlook your tremendous value to the movement." In addition to "hitting up" AFA supporters for money one too many times, O'Hare faced a rebellion by the St. Louis executive committee, which wanted to dump Walter Meyer for behaving like a martinet in favor of a candidate from their own ranks. Wall warned O'Hare that such a move "*would* make [a] laughing stock of the Metro St. Louis AFA members in general, and FPO in particular." Better to work for a stronger AFA so that "Little Caesars" like Meyer could be forced into line.[63]

Realizing too late that Meyer had used him to secure a base of support, Frank felt the old impulse to hit the road, proposing a speaking tour of towns between St. Louis and Oklahoma City, modeled after his work with the old *Rip-Saw*. Because he did not own a car, he would need money for bus and rail tickets. Subsequently, O'Hare agreed with Wall that opposing Meyer now "would pull the entire house of cards down," although he lamented: "Jesus, if we only had a competent candidate in another district (St. Louis) little Walter [Meyer] would not be able to do any harm." For the time being, he would settle for Wall sending him three ten-dollar bills so he could get through the month.[64]

On May 21, 1940, John Wall broke the bad news to Frank: "The war ballyhoo has backed AFA clear off the map." While Zeuch had found O'Hare's St. Louis keynote speech to be "the best thing by you he had ever read," only fifteen new members had joined the organization in the past month. People in Oklahoma "are simply crazy with war hysteria." Veterans groups had blocked attempts to book Municipal Auditorium in Oklahoma City for an AFA Fourth of July rally. Local newspapers had branded AFA as communistic in recent news stories and editorials. "Siegfried," Wall continued, "is scared shitless for fear the Guardian will be connected with the AFA in the minds of local brass hats." The Ameringers were also angry because the AFA had not been able to pay for recent ads in the *Guardian*. Dead broke, Wall was about to hitchhike to his parents' home in Akron, Ohio, where he would try to carry on the movement. A week later, he had changed his mind. He would stay in Oklahoma, find a job, and promote AFA "as the ONLY WAY TO BUILD UP AN ADEQUATE DEFENSE AGAINST AGGRESSION."[65]

As Wall soon discovered, without money or an outlet for publicity, Abundance was dead. In the end, Frank blamed his old pal Oscar Ameringer for the AFA fiasco. "You gotta hand it to Oscar," he wrote the next year, "I have know him for 34 years, working intimately with him, and I now recollect that I never saw him hand *anything out* though he is very elegant at taking things in." What O'Hare did not know was that Ameringer was on the verge of financial ruin and very ill. The *Guardian* ceased operation in 1941; Ameringer died two years later. O'Hare, Ameringer, and Zeuch had all been swimming against the tide in their quest to resurrect socialism by other means. Their nascent movement had only replicated in miniature the sectarianism that had kept the Left weak and divided for so long. As their organization crumbled in 1940, America was gearing up for war through a military Keynesianism that at last put an end to the Great Depression. The call for "Abundance for All" came about after all, but through a reinvigorated capitalism and another world war.[66]

In his final column for the *Guardian*, Frank O'Hare looked to the future with characteristic optimism. He had been talking with college students and was disappointed to hear the same old platitudes about "survival of the fittest" he had been hearing all of his life. "That's the trouble with most of us," he wrote, "We have a lot of intellectual lumber saved from the ox-cart days and it blocks our thinking." Times had changed but "our youth are brought up on the old wheezes, and thus are victims of the smarties who have grabbed off the nation's oil, lumber, copper, aluminum, electricity, banking and what not." As presently constituted, "schools actually conceal the facts of national life from the pupils!" It did not have to be that way. Students could be prepared to rule the country through their votes and to help solve the problems of today. In the last words he would ever write from a national forum, O'Hare asked: "What are YOU doing about it?"[67]

Personally, as he admitted privately, he was "completely washed up." The abrupt end of AFA left him "without a dime, the room-rent a week over due, a hard-boiled landlord who had given us notice. No food in the house." In some ways, he was back to where he had been in 1924: deeply in debt, unemployed, and alienated from his old comrades in the movement. He had been through a midlife crisis, a bitter divorce, the disappointment of giving his all for Federated Press only to be let go, several years of punishing unemployment, and the failure of Abundance.[68]

Sixteen years wiser, he could still poke fun at himself, writing that "poor little FPO saw his elegant plans fade into dust." O'Hare had nothing left but faith:

> For forty years I have been right about one thing—that the world was due for an earth-wide smash. It is here. I was not able to find a way of security for myself while the smash is on. I had looked for development of a great constructive movement of the people to take over. It has not appeared.

He had been down and out for so long that the end of what he had described to Upton Sinclair as "my coming back, in a modest way, into the arena" did not faze him for long. A few years later, he would tell his son Gene that "The sweetest, in many ways, of the years of my life have been SINCE that nadir of 1924–25." At age sixty-three, he would pick himself up and earn his daily bread the best that he could while carving out a final niche as a Debsian docent, asking again and again: "What are YOU doing about it?"[69]

7

Gadfly and Sage,
1941–1960

Frank O'Hare was "down and out" again in 1940, but unlike his midlife crisis in the 1920s, this time he turned willingly to an extensive network of friends in St. Louis for emotional and financial succor. Above all, he had the love and devotion of his wife, Irene. "As the years have gone on she has become ever more precious," he told Bobbie O'Hare, adding, "And I am much wiser and more tactful than in an earlier life." In his later years, O'Hare worked for money when he could, although that was not often. He tinkered with ideas for inventions that poured out of his fertile imagination. He organized a luncheon club and published a newsletter as forums for his many opinions. Mostly, he read and wrote and argued, always teaching and never losing his faith in the possibilities of the Cooperative Commonwealth. "They tell me that I have been a 'gad-fly' here in St. Louis," he wrote to Margaret Sanger. But to his legion of friends and admirers, he became considerably more than an irritating holdout against the often mindless social and political conformity of the postwar years. "Thanks for the philosophy, affection and faith in the goodness of living," Roger Baldwin wrote by way of a New Year's greeting. "Few reach your state of consciousness in their routines of habit—and I rejoice in yours, alive with the sense of discovery and the freshness of the day." To another of his friends, a professor of psychology, the Frank O'Hare he knew was nothing less than a sage. By the time he died in 1960, he had become an anachronism, the last of the Debsian Socialists, mourned by the many whose lives he had touched.[1]

Frustrated Inventor

Following the collapse of AFA, O'Hare dragged through the rest of 1940 at "25% efficiency . . . as it is hard to concentrate when your immediate necessity is to get say a half-dollar cash." The next year, he began life anew as he had in 1924—by feeding many of his papers into the basement furnace. Having burned his files on "Abundance," he wrote a postmortem on the movement to William E. Zeuch in March 1941. They had blundered in announcing all of the specifics of their program in advance. They had dared to defy the "warmongers" and had been crushed as a result. Once the United States became involved in the war, there would be little opposition as "Those living remember what war objectors got 25 years ago, and feel the hopelessness of any resistance." Ultimately, AFA had failed because the subject of economic determinism had become taboo. "It cannot be discussed in polite society, for if one is factual, realistic, and truthful," he wrote, "he is stamped a Commie or at least subversive." Personally, O'Hare opposed American military involvement in the European war, as he had in 1917. "But as our monopoly capitalists have exactly the same aims and the same modes of obtaining profit as the Kaiser's and Hitler's, they will not endure the exposure of the anatomy and physiology of the system."[2]

As if to prove his point, O'Hare was the subject of an FBI internal security investigation in the summer of 1941 that involved interviewing at least one informant and looking into his credit reports and criminal records. The report concluded that the information gathered "is not of a derogatory nature," hardly surprising since he had refused to join any organized party of the Left for almost twenty years. After attending a speech by Norman Thomas, O'Hare wondered why the SP leader had even bothered. "If he has deep thoughts," he wrote, "and makes just one speech expressing them, he will be shut off the air, shut out of the Post-Dispatch, and possibly be shut up in jail." While he retained his faith in Marx, world socialism had been "a hopeless failure." As for Stalinism, while admitting that "I have no more means of knowing what is going on in Russia than I have of knowing what is going on in the atom," Frank feared "that it is NOT a workers government, but a bureaucratic dictatorship."[3]

Germany's invasion of the Soviet Union and the Japanese attack on Pearl Harbor swung O'Hare around completely. "It is swell to be 'at one' with most everybody, as I am now," he explained in early 1942. "In the first world war I simply couldn't see it. It was a scrap between two rival racketeers, Germany and England. . . . Now it is a fight of the decent half of the world against the deluded half of the world." The prospects for socialism seemed bright again because, as he told one of his sons, "Russia at last stands vindicated—the exemplar. So, hooray and hoorah!" Finding himself in step with the majority for one of the few times in his life, O'Hare longed to make a contribution to the war effort.[4]

At the age of sixty-four, Frank had trouble finding employment of any kind, much less war work. After the end of AFA, Ed Witcoff of Caradine Hat Company took him back again as a part-time consultant at twenty-five dollars per week, although, as O'Hare complained, Witcoff "has given me about fifteen minutes of his time in the past three months, except for one occasion in which he got me jingled on high-balls." His underemployment afforded him the opportunity to resume work on his many inventions, including an automatic mapmaking device, a cutting tool that sharpened like a lead pencil, an improved wood screw, and a home desk, the last described as "a complete office . . . I have such a desk in use in my corner of the present O'Hare dump. It does everything I need except light my pipe." He also developed some more practical money-making schemes such as a slide rule instruction book, a loose-leaf rule for salesmen, and a "Tayloring" consultation service. O'Hare described his hobbies at this time as "everything—photography, cabinet work, horseshoe pitching, penuchle [pinocle], mathematics, teaching seven year old kids to read as well as they speak," the last the result of observing "how Henry Ford mass educated 14,000 bohunks in 39 one-hour lessons."[5]

His son Victor interrupted the daily routine in the basement workshop with a visit, inflicting on Frank an extended and brutal character analysis not unlike his father's own "brainstorming" sessions that Kate Richards O'Hare had grown to dread years earlier. "The boy kept on," Frank reported, "his cold, level voice penetrating to the remote corner of the seat where I collapsed. Being as he had inherited many of my faults as well as some of my few virtues, he knew exactly what he was talking about." After a subsequent bout of mental depression, O'Hare emerged renewed. "Well, life really begins over again at whatever age, whenever new enthusiasms boil up," he told a friend, "I have lived very many lives, every one darn interesting, some of them excruciatingly painful, some gloriously exuberant. Now I am in an exuberant phase." Without money and the proper equipment, though, O'Hare would remain frustrated in his attempts to fully develop his ideas.[6]

Strapped for cash, as always, Frank asked Ed Witcoff to give him full-time work, promising that he could make the Caradine Hat Company sales force more productive with his ideas. Witcoff declined the offer, citing as a bar his partner J. T. Caradine's continuing dislike for O'Hare's unrepentant radicalism. He did agree to give Frank office space and to let him use the hat factory as a kind of laboratory for constructing improved conveyers, skids, and production control apparatuses. "So, in some strange way, something IS keeping my bottom warm," he wrote Roy Eilers, a patent attorney who had been waiting for more than twenty years for O'Hare to bring him a finished, patentable project. In September 1941 another attorney friend, Rodney Bedell, conducted a patent search on Frank's mapmaking device, concluding that it was "novel and patentable." When months went by without O'Hare making a formal application, an exasperated Eilers wrote (as he had many years before) that "I think you have the qualities of an optimist with all the shiftlessness of a Communist. In other words, I think you have a good brain but it needs somebody to give you a good swift kick every few hours in order to get it to work." O'Hare finally filed for a patent on his "Map and Method of Making the Same" in the fall of 1942.[7]

He told another longtime friend, Wiley B. Rutledge (recently appointed an Associate Justice on the Supreme Court) that "At last, like Riley, I am leading my own ideal of a life." For the time being, he was happy to work for a few hours at the hat company, to tinker with his projects, and to do a little writing. He claimed to be making significant progress on ten of his inventions, hoping to raise three thousand dollars to finish developing them and file patents. Then, "if just one clicks, it wins a jackpot." To this end, he created "O'Hare and Associates," a scheme whereby investors would pay him ten dollars a month each for the chance to share in the profits from his inventions.[8]

In reality, he had only written a few chapters of his slide rule text; the other ideas, including a projectile system ("an astonishing proposition") existed only as crude models or drawings in a large notebook of ideas he kept on his desk. Not surprisingly, O'Hare's friends greeted his partnership proposal with polite skepticism, while a few donated their professional services or slipped him some cash. Two years later, he was still seeking investors, describing "several projects in process" and the completed mapping system. When the Patent Office informed him that another inventor had registered a map scheme similar to his in 1940, he was determined to file an appeal. "Unfortunately for the O'Hare estate," he wrote his attorneys, "too many of my inventions (and they ARE inventions) have been in the unprotected field." While his friends finally ponied up the money for the appeal, characteristically, O'Hare did not follow up. In 1947, the government turned down his appeal with the note: "Appellant has filed no brief and did not appear at the hearing." By then, Frank had long since given up any hope of making money from his inventions, although as late as the 1950s, one neighbor remembered, "he was often in the basement 'inventing' things albeit severely limited by a lack of materials."[9]

In the spring of 1944, O'Hare found himself seated at a luncheon next to Stuart Symington, then president of Emerson Electric, who was fascinated to hear that Frank had worked for Tom Meston at Emerson in the late 1890s. Symington urged him to apply for a position as an engineer. O'Hare later told C. Wright Mills that when he reported for work the first day, "My questionnaire was taken, also my photograph and finger-prints. The doctor also examined my penis." O'Hare discovered that there was actually very little for him to do, so he spent most of his time "visiting," doing about two days of solid work in two months before receiving a pink slip. "Perhaps the FBI had reported that my name was in their files," he told his son Victor, although "I have always been careful not to knowing work with C. P. people as they struck me as being 50% undercover people and 50% fanatics." It was the last full-time job he ever held.[10]

Frustrated Public Man

During the war years, O'Hare spent much of his time at the typewriter, composing missives to friends, family, and "people everywhere who stick their necks out." He struck up a correspondence with H. Allen Smith, the writer of a humorous syndicated newspaper column. Smith's reminiscence about an absurd, chaotic shipside press conference he attended some years earlier with a bewildered Albert Einstein ended with the observation that he wished he understood the theory of relativity. Frank promptly wrote to "Brother Smith," explaining relativity in laymen's terms using an elaborate analogy involving electric lights surrounded by onion skins in a glass room. In a column of December 17, 1941, Smith reported that he had received many letters about Einstein, only two of which he found to be really interesting. "One is from a Mr. F. P. O'Hare," Smith wrote, "and contains 19 pages, single-spaced. . . . He says it has something to do with onion skins." After repeating the beginning of Frank's explanation, Smith observed: "I could go on quoting O'Hare like this for hours, but you probably already understand the Einstein Onion Skin Theory, so I won't bother you with any more light bulbs in rooms with transparent walls." O'Hare loved the column, laughing at his own pretensions and reveling in the subsequent publicity linking his name with that of one of his mathematical heroes.[11]

He wrote Eleanor Roosevelt in October 1943 that "No one, living in the White House has ever before told so much truth as frankly as you have." Sticking her neck out, the president's wife had penned an article in *Negro Digest* arguing that if her skin was black, she "would have moments of great bitterness. It would be hard for me to sustain my faith in democracy and to build up a sense of goodwill toward men of other races." Conceding that African Americans had made much progress toward equality in a relatively short time, she wrote that black people should appreciate that "Even women of the white race still suffer inequalities and injustices, and many groups of white people in my country are the slaves of economic conditions." While Roosevelt concluded that African Americans ought to continue to prove their equality rather than "do too much demanding," O'Hare found her words to be an inspiration. He had spent the past forty-two years of his life, he told her, "centered on the battle for emancipation of Jews, women, colored races, workers (and even capitalists) even as you have." Your Frank need not be jealous of other Franks who love you for your courage, he wrote. "In an earlier age," he continued, "you would be in line for the title 'St. Eleanor.' " O'Hare admired her more than any other public figure. Unattractive physically, bold, caring, and courageous, she reminded him, he later confessed, of Kate Richards O'Hare at her best—and what might have been in his own life.[12]

Being " 'at one' with most everybody," O'Hare found that he once again had entrée to the editorial page of the *Post-Dispatch*. Never did he waver in the belief that socialism would yet triumph; indeed, he came to the conclusion that the world war would hasten the day of the Cooperative Commonwealth. Still, without the left-leaning Oliver K. Bovard in the editor's chair, O'Hare downplayed his Marxism in order to be "a public man" during the war. In the spring of 1942, responding to an editorial crediting Henry Ford as "the father of mass production," Frank wrote a column arguing that Tom Meston's uncle had developed this process in the 1880s while supervising the production of freight cars. Ford had merely modified and expanded the Meston system. The Detroit automaker "has a moral compulsion to help win this war," O'Hare argued, considering that Ford had helped teach the Germans how to produce its war machine. He still held the Ford system in high regard as a step above " 'free' (anarchistic) enterprise," fostering efficient industrial giants ripe for government intervention on behalf of workers. O'Hare saw the war as a prelude to the rise of a new worldwide system. "If Hitler wins," he concluded, "the system will be despotic, tyrannical. If the democracies win, the system will be, we have every hope, far more 'democratic' than the supplanted 'capitalist' system."[13]

Still sensitive to the xenophobia of World War I that had wrecked the Socialist party, he wrote a sarcastic rejoinder to a letter denouncing murals in the St. Louis Post Office as somehow unpatriotic because they had been painted by a foreign-born artist. It made little sense to stop with art, Frank wisecracked. Why not ban such un–American inventions as radio, diesel engines, lithography, photography, higher mathematics, electric dynamos, telescopes, and synthetic dyes too? The love of Greek, Roman, and French architecture similarly reflected "our supreme ignorance of the fact that everything foreign is poisonous!" In another letter, he argued that the war presented an opportunity to make industry more efficient through systematic recycling. The government ought to establish research laboratories to discover new means of reclamation. "All hail the junk man!" he wrote, "Enfranchise him—educate him, and let him help us win whatever 'wars' turn up—wars against Hitler, or wars against want." An editorial demanding that more American history be taught in public schools led O'Hare to respond that "Very wisely, the schools have left this hot potato strictly alone" because it was impossible to agree on the proper interpretation of the Palmer Red raids, the Civil War, and American labor history, to name just a few areas of historical controversy. "Columbus discovered America in 1492," he observed. "Why go into the horrible details of the events which followed? Leave that for adult minds." Public school history, he feared, amounted to little more than "memorizing of approved prejudices."[14]

O'Hare became a regular book reviewer for the *Post-Dispatch*, writing some thirty essays between mid-1942 and the end of the war. One-half of his reviews covered books on philosophy, economics, science, exploration, and labor, as well as *The Handbook for Home Mechanics* by Eugene O'Hare, which Papa Frank praised (with considerable restraint) as "a good job." There was little evidence of his socialism in these reviews, although he could not resist concluding his commentary on the autobiography of capitalist Tom Girdler with the observation that perhaps the book should not be marketed overseas lest other democratic peoples be left with the impression that company towns, electric fences, tear gas, and private police "are America's contribution to the Century of the Common Man." The other half of O'Hare's reviews dealt with books on the war. He was unrestrained in his praise of works recounting British and Russian bravery. In one review, he saw the Red Army as the new embodiment of the Soviet system, "the great reconditioning or educational instrument by means of which all Russia is brought to effective national solidarity." A book on Russian tanks, *White Mammoths*, "made real and understandable to us the magnificent performance of peasants turned into industrialists and warriors, and the true ingenuity with which they navigate, repair and operate their mighty land battleships." That was as close as he came to joining in what William L. O'Neill has called the "pro-Soviet gush" that dominated the mass media and progressive journals early in the war. Like most Americans, O'Hare believed the Soviets (and the British for that matter) to be valiant allies, regardless of any pre-war failings.[15]

While Frank O'Hare had no trouble publishing his book reviews, he soon discovered the limits the *Post-Dispatch* placed on his political opinions. In a letter of May 6, 1943, he questioned the assertion of the Episcopal archbishop of St. Louis that people do not learn from history. During World War I, O'Hare observed, the government had rewarded "good" labor leaders (those who supported the administration) and had thrown "bad" ones into prison "under highly phoney 'espionage act' charges." Now, labor, capital, and the government were getting along and that, he concluded, "suits me fine." But the *Post-Dispatch* declined to print the final paragraph of his letter, which made the point that peace prevailed on the home front in spite of the newspaper's antilabor editorials and because "allegedly God-appointed trustees of American productive property have no successors." Therefore, "There is no red-eyed Palmer to raid anybody. The foul Burns sleuths have not been called from their kennels." That is what had suited him fine in the original letter, not the seeming subservience of labor.[16]

The *Post-Dispatch* printed his next communiqué verbatim, a closely reasoned jeremiad against what he saw as growing American arrogance in the world. How can the United States teach "backward nations" about democracy, he asked, when a "dictatorship of the vigilantes" still governed the American South and "municipal boss rule" predominated in much of the North? During his lifetime, the country had become less democratic. "New democratic forms suitable to the existing centralized collectivization have not yet emerged," he wrote, adding with Debsian optimism, "I believe they are on the way." Until then, he urged Americans to develop a degree of humility "if we aim to big-brother the rest of the universe." In a subsequent letter, when he complained that the Missouri legislature had decided on its own to revise the state constitution, the *Post-Dispatch* let O'Hare have his say—until he wrote "They tell me" that in the Soviet Union, Communist party members fought and died with the common people on the battlefield while in Missouri politicians merely "get to the public teat and suck." Again, the paper refused to print his punch line.[17]

After that, the editor published two sentences from a missive demanding that the St. Louis Police Board resign for allegedly whitewashing the fatal beating of a Mexican-American prisoner and one sentence from another expressing joy that the Red Army had recaptured Kiev. A letter praising Wendell Wilkie's book *One World* for its exposé of "contending exploitative world-trade empires" fared better, perhaps because the *Post-Dispatch* had endorsed Wilkie over Roosevelt in 1940. In late 1943, O'Hare wrote to criticize Professor L. F. Jaffe, head of the ACLU in Buffalo, New York, who had quit the group rather than join in protesting the denial of Fascist sympathizer Gerald L. K. Smith's right to speak. "Jaffe, how could you?" he wrote. "Are your principles so feeble that Smith can upset them? Let Smith talk and let the common sense of Buffalo (if any) answer. Talk is not that which creates strife. Underlying conditions create strife." His words were aimed as much at his employer, the *Post-Dispatch,* as Professor Jaffe. He had pushed his right of free speech in wartime and found not a "red-eyed

Palmer" waiting to jail him but an editor ready with a blue pencil instead. To O'Hare, one preemption was as bad as the other. He simply had to find another public forum.[18]

The Dunkers

In spite of his continuing poverty and the inability to follow through on his ideas, O'Hare enjoyed life because of his extensive social network. "All of my personal friends ante my KRO connection," he wrote in 1942, "have taken me back to their hearts, and Irene and I after fourteen years of companionship, some of which were years of tough sledding, are as happy and enthusiastic as kids." That was not enough for the still gregarious O'Hare, who dearly missed the camaraderie of the old City Club of the pre–World War I years and the Public Question Club of the 1920s. In 1934, he had tried to organize a weekly luncheon club of people interested in mathematics and science, but found little interest. "After living in this man's town for nigh onto sixty years," he explained, "I was lonesome as hell for contacts with my old friends and boxing partners." In 1943, he began having lunch every Monday with five or six close friends and a few special guests to talk about politics and ideas well into the afternoon. "My latest caper is a sheer delight," he proclaimed—and his friends agreed.[19]

He invited more and more people to the lunches, organizing them eventually as "The St. Louis Refectory Global Federation of Orthodox and Uninhibited Dunkers." The next year, O'Hare began publishing *Dunkerdo-ings*, a weekly newsletter that not only publicized the "Dunker" luncheons but also served as a vehicle for his opinions. Between selling subscriptions at one dollar per year to what he described as "a real newspaper" and brokering the luncheon arrangements, he managed to break even on the venture. More importantly, he had become Frank P. O'Hare, editor, again. It was not the *Rip-Saw* or the *Vanguard*, but as one of his friends observed, "so long as Frank presented himself to the public as an active editor he could impress. He had prestige. Never mind the importance of the publication. It was a wonderful entree. It was his lifeline."[20]

Eugene O'Hare believed that his father could do better. The author of successful books on home repair and furniture making, Eugene accused Frank of being neurotic for merely talking about writing a book on slide rules rather than finishing it. Playing the amateur psychologist, as his mother and twin brother had before him, he scolded:

> You are bouncy—full of piss and vinegar, trenchant, brilliant, and po-tentially useful to society. You just negate your potentiality by thrusting

into your own path the fatal obstruction of building a dream-self. . . .
So please get up off your heine, stir your stirrups, write the goddamned
rottenest or goddamned best book on anything—not a scramble of
flashes.

Everything about him was sloppy, wrote Eugene: his letters, the copy for
his *Post-Dispatch* book reviews, and parts of the Dunker bulletins. Even his
personal appearance in recent years reeked of "infernal sloppiness." Frank
simply had to stop "puffing on the opium pipe you have kept lit 'till now."
As for the Dunkers, it was merely his father's way of "hiding from the real
day's work—which is a job—or a book—or books." O'Hare could only try
to explain to his son that *Dunkerdoings* "has been a life saver for me, given
me many valuable contacts and new friends."[21]

This acute reproach, coming from Eugene O'Hare, whose accomplishments had made Frank proud, must have wounded him deeply, in part
because it had the ring of truth. There was something neurotic about his
inability to complete his projects and a touch of pathos in the former
"Dude Socialist" traipsing around St. Louis unshaven, in ragged clothes,
and without his false teeth.

Yet his friends looked beyond his personal appearance because they
saw in him a zest and a courage that they admired. O'Hare's friend,
Professor of Mathematics Henry Blumberg, congratulated him for "tack-
ling quintessences" in *Dunkerdoings*. The newsletter "cannot but stir every
Christian minister not befogged by 'scholarship' and undigested reading
and fear." O'Hare was "firing away . . . genially, cheerfully, in faith. So did
Emerson and Whitman, who knew the dark better than the shrewdest
cynics." Seemingly just a newsletter of a luncheon club for middle-class
teachers, newspaper writers, engineers, employers, managers, labor leaders, and realtors, *Dunkerdoings* provided a way for O'Hare to carry on the
crusading spirit of left-wing periodicals that helped to make socialism a
mass movement before World War I. In his own way, he believed that he
was helping to prepare the country for "the big show" of socialism. As he
commented to Blumberg:

More and more my admiration grows for Dr. Karl Marx, who so positively announced that when the debacle came whole sections of the
bourgeoisie would join up with the revolution. Not one bit of true
educational work during the past sixty years has been wasted. . . .
Socialism not only has never been tried, but it has never come to
life until now, and I do not mean that poor bumfoozled Norman
Thomas. Poor Norman has missed the bus. In fact he never even saw
the bus.[22]

He hated racial segregation ("my primitive ideas about 'racial inferiority' were exploded years ago"), arguing, in Debsian fashion, that it was an offshoot of the class issue. O'Hare would not be bought. Indignantly, he refused to let a local politician pay his printing bill, observing that "it never occurred to this bimbo that DUNKERDOINGS is not on the market." He would not be silenced. For example, in the July 24, 1944, issue, in his Waylandesque column "They Say" (meaning, of course "I Say"), Frank took a swipe at the war effort, observing "That the damned Roosians don't bother to sell war bonds. They use the paper to make explosives." On free enterprise: "They say . . . That the wonderful folks in Adam Smith's time invented a scheme of economics that works under our mass-production scheme. Or does it?" The same issue of the paper ended with a denunciation of the world capitalist system whereby factory workers in Allied and Axis countries alike "are bled white to extort export surpluses."[23]

O'Hare also devoted space to science and philosophy. He sent a sample newsletter and a copy of the *Post-Dispatch* book review he had written of Vilhjalmur Stefansson's *Arctic Manual* to the famed arctic explorer. Stefansson sent Frank a copy of his long-out-of-print *Standardization of Error* and the right to serialize it in return for a one-year subscription to *Dunkerdoings*. The work, described by O'Hare as "the completely dehydrated residue of some 20,000 tomes of philosophic discussion," ran in twenty weekly installments and helped to sell lots of subscriptions. Little wonder that Frank O'Hare paid scant attention to his other projects once *Dunkerdoings* hit its stride. Like his hero J. A. Wayland, he had again become a "one-hoss editor."[24]

Unlike Wayland, who had a knack for making money, Frank O'Hare continued to live on the edge of poverty. He managed to scrape together enough money to take a six-week trip in the summer of 1944, first visiting Henry Blumberg in Columbus, Ohio, for his yearly immersion into higher mathematics and then bunking with sons Victor in Washington, D.C., Dick in New York, and Eugene in New Jersey. On his return to St. Louis, he told his luncheon club that "the moment seems ripe for the foundation of dunkerdens in every section of the country." A bout with illness in early 1945 reminded him of just how precarious life could be running a one-man show. Broke, Frank and Irene moved to cheaper lodgings and he suspended *Dunkerdoings*. The newsletter, Henry Blumberg consoled him, "is too hot for most people's touch, and you're having trouble giving away subs." His friends chipped in enough money to revive the paper and even provided some cash for a "traveling fellowship" the next summer.[25]

In the spring of 1945, Samuel Castleton, a Socialist attorney who had worked to get Eugene Debs out of prison after World War I, invited Frank to Boston to collaborate on a biography of Debs. Explaining that *Dunkerdoings*, with a circulation of well over one thousand, "involves as much work as getting out a little country weekly," O'Hare replied that he would come to Boston only if Castleton would sell one hundred subscriptions in return. Henry Blumberg urged him to write his own biography of Debs, suggesting that he could support the project with a lecture tour on the Socialist Hero. As an inducement, Blumberg sent Frank fifty dollars "for the splendid, alluring cause." Frank liked the idea of lecturing again, but only "to further work I am doing, not celebrate past achievements." He would present "An Evening with Debs" in several cities, setting up Dunkers' Clubs wherever he went, just as he had organized locals of the Socialist party so many years ago. Blumberg warned against the scheme, arguing that the St. Louis club "owes its being to a certain friend of ours, poet and artist, a genius in blazing new patterns of living together, a gifted and practiced political activist." Going national with the Dunkers "might tax even FPO." When Frank failed to take this broad hint, the mathematician grew more blunt, telling him in subsequent letters that people were not interested in subscribing to *Dunkerdoings* beyond St. Louis and his time would be better spent writing a book or editing a collection of his essays.[26]

The lure of hitting the road again proved irresistible: eight weeks, sixteen cities, organizing for the Dunkers, selling subscriptions, and collecting "Debsiana" for historians, as well as venturing "Into newsrooms, on campuses, into boozing dens, and greasy spoons, to see how the years have dealt with men and things." He promoted the trip in rhetorical terms meant to conjure up the old magic. "After a year of intense propaganda, originating in St. Louis," he announced, "the Northeastern Region of the U.S.A. is softened up sufficiently to warrant an expedition—a penetration by Dunking." Besides, compared to what he had going in St. Louis, this was important. He worked thirty minutes a week for the hat company, he told Roger Baldwin, "[and] for this half-hour weekly service I get the highest rate per half-hour in St. Louis but what in hell is a half hour?"[27]

He had become embroiled in a controversy played out on the editorial page of the *Post-Dispatch* over the city's wartime effort to stem the deterioration of inner St. Louis with federally aided public housing. O'Hare ridiculed the charge that the program amounted to Bolshevik-style communism. St. Louis, he claimed, "attained an all-time high for slumminess among American cities. Free enterprise in housing had had 140 years of freedom to do its stuff." When the Chamber of Commerce announced that it would oppose any more subsidized housing, he responded with another letter arguing that slums were a loss for everyone. While public housing offered only a partial and imperfect solution to the foul decay of poor neighborhoods, he contended that wealthy landowners and their minions had lost their right to give advice. "Like the 'nobility' of Poland, whom they much resemble in their achievements," O'Hare concluded, "they will eventually be swept aside by a thoroughly disgusted community." By the time this letter appeared in the newspaper in July of 1945, Poland had become the focal point of Anglo-American mistrust of the Soviet Union, owing to Stalin's determination to impose his own system on that country in apparent violation of the Yalta Agreement. O'Hare's Polish analogy did not sit well with Joseph Pulitzer II and the *Post-Dispatch* editorial staff. He was not asked to write another book review for a year and a half, and the paper would not publish any of his letters or articles for more than five years. With seemingly little to lose, then, O'Hare was determined to press on with his "penetration by Dunking" rather than sink back into the despair of poverty and voiceless failure.[28]

From the first stop in Chicago, he reported that "there was a roomful of people at the potty last night, none of whom had met each other before (except a few husbands and wives), yet for a couple hours there was 100% participation." In his absence, his fellow Dunkers edited the newsletter, filling it with their own observations and the "Ohareagraphs" that Frank mailed in. One article paid tribute to him as a Marxist who had "reconstructed his philosophy to live somewhat rebelliously in a capitalist system. . . . His brain is teeming with ideas, and he must have an audience to shock by his exposition of them." No one agrees with everything he has to say, the article concluded, "But if you knew him, your outlook would be broader and your life would be richer for the experience." Before leaving, Frank admitted that there seemed to be little interest in establishing Dunkers' clubs in several cities on his itinerary, including Detroit and Cleveland ("not one durned letter"), Boston ("not as yet all steamed up about dunking"), Baltimore ("another town where positively NO ONE has written"), and Pittsburgh and Cincinnati ("Arrangements going on slowly"). He continued anyway and held successful gatherings in New York, Washington, D.C., and three other locales.[29]

O'Hare returned to St. Louis exhausted in mid-October, having sold several hundred subscriptions to *Dunkerdoings,* which brought circulation up to nearly two thousand. He flailed away against what he regarded as the absurdity of the postwar scene, which gave him "the willies." "Imagine the world from now on," he wrote with considerable prescience, "held in check by some 'good' nations in a constant state of war preparedness, a large section of the population laboring like a blinded Samson, under secret rulers, every other guy a sleuth. What a happy outcome! Practically a global booby-hatch!" In December 1945, he was forced to suspend the newsletter after suffering a mild heart attack. Characteristically, he regretted only that he would have continued to expand the subscription rate at 100 percent per year until it turned a healthy profit if he had not become ill. His latest stint as a one-hoss editor, he later remembered, "was lots of fun."[30]

From his sickbed, O'Hare brooded over the state of the world. After studying the report prepared under the direction of Dean Acheson and David Lilienthal on the international control of atomic energy, he feared that the American elite would be left with "terrific powers of coercion, against which there is no defense." Then he asked what was for him a terrible question: "Is it too late for the democratic revolution—the transfer of all power to the people, by destroying the concept of property—oh inheritance?" This was as close as he would come to the realization that American socialism and all that he had stood for had become irrelevant by midcentury. But when his strength returned, he made the conscious decision to carry on as before, alone if necessary, because he could not live without his lifelong faith in the Debsian dream.[31]

After a short recuperation, O'Hare resumed his place as "Public Dunker No. 1," as *Post-Dispatch* cartoonist Daniel Fitzpatrick dubbed him in a birthday caricature. Feisty as ever, he enjoyed arguing with friends and acquaintances in person and by mail. Frank wrote a long letter to Joseph Pulitzer II to "unleash my grouches" about being dropped as a book reviewer and to tell the publisher exactly what was wrong with his newspaper, reminding him along the way of the family legend that his Uncle Gerard had given Pulitzer's father his first job in St. Louis, as a stable boy. He chided old chum William E. Zeuch in a letter of June 6, 1947, over his ignorance of mathematics, claiming he could prove with a series of formulas that Marx had been right about class action. Also, Frank expressed his renewed faith in Debsian socialism and his right to preach it:

> Just because Marx is suppressed and forbidden, I will fight for him. I will not let some ignorant janissary of the cormorant class shush me down. Nor will I let the stool-pigeon ruled communist parties mislead me as to Marx' doctrines. . . . Now the crack-pots are demanding to know why Marx did not anticipate in detail what has happened since his time. When did he ever claim that he could foresee in detail. He promised an end result.

A few weeks after writing this, O'Hare suffered a severe heart attack. He came back home after what he described as "a four weeks vacation at the Joosh Hospital. Under house arrest as it were." At the urging of Blumberg, he amused himself by beginning a manuscript on higher mathematics as a creative thought process for the layman. "Can I dress this up so it looks like fun?" he asked his friend. "You will be the judge."[32]

On January 10, 1948, as Frank O'Hare was sitting down to dinner with his son Gene and daughter Kathleen, Dick O'Hare telephoned with the news that Kate Richards Cunningham had died of a heart attack. "Now,"

Frank told Zeuch, "all the faults and failings are forgotten, and the things she accomplished stand out." He assured his son Dick that "It was no little thing that your mother spoke to millions of people, stirring them to realize the dignity of being men; and at her highest there was no one who gave everything so unselfishly 'that others might have life and life more abundant.' "[33]

O'Hare pretended that the past did not matter to him, observing: "How little I care for history and biography, knowing how it is written. Those who know cannot write it; Those who write it cannot know." But it bothered him that his place in the Socialist movement seemed to have been forgotten. Oscar Ameringer had not even mentioned him in his lively *Autobiography* published a few years earlier. Zeuch consoled O'Hare that there were "many missing

PUBLIC DUNKER NO. I.

A caricature of Frank O'Hare, drawn by *St. Louis Post-Dispatch* cartoonist Daniel Fitzpatrick for FPO's seventieth birthday (courtesy Alice Swantner).

chapters" from the original manuscript that Ameringer had shown to him, speculating that Oscar's family had edited both of them out for spite in the aftermath of the "Abundance" disaster. Increasingly, his thoughts turned to his greatest hero, Eugene Debs, "the nearest approach to an *American Jeshua* [the historical Jesus] there has been in my time." When Ray Ginger, a young graduate student, wrote requesting information about Debs for a biography, O'Hare was glad to reply, providing a wealth of detail emphasizing the differences between the pre-war Socialist movement and the recent pronouncements by "the last word in despicability," Norman Thomas. The contrast between Debs and Thomas could not have been greater. O'Hare's hero had been a labor leader with little education exhorting socialism to the working class whereas Thomas was a highly educated minister who preached largely to other intellectuals and evidenced little understanding of working people. But Thomas's chief sin, in O'Hare's eyes, was that he was no Eugene Debs.[34]

O'Hare continued to bask in the spotlight of the weekly Dunker luncheons. A room full of friends "had a hell of a good time" celebrating the club's fifth anniversary in March of 1948. "Naturally," O'Hare wrote, "they were 74 to one against me, the founder, and razzed hell out of me (they all know my hectic record) but they said it was a hell of a good thing to have a place where men could say what they damn please and get away with it." He did little else but "dunk" and write for the next year after Ed Witcoff cut off his small retainer from Caradine Hat. A visit from Henry Blumberg in May 1949 provided "a solid week of mathematical dynamite" and renewed his enthusiasm for working on his math book. He vowed to write sixteen pages a day until it was done. And he did write—hundreds of pages in which he struggled to translate what he had learned into layperson's terms, just as he had once boiled Marx down to vulgarities on the Socialist hustings. "Not that I am sure," he told his friend, "that you will think so well of everything I have written, but that you have OPENED UP MATHEMATICS to me, and WITH TIME I may yet write a chapter that will do for many what you have done for me."[35]

As always, his mind was easily diverted to politics. In his letters to Blumberg, he preferred to discuss the world situation or dispense advice about how the professor should handle his dean. In one missive, he paused for breath on page nine long enough to observe: "So you see, Henry, why I dare not start a letter to you. It goes on and on. And mathematics waits." A few days later he apologized (again) to Blumberg, saying he was "fully intending to whack a chapter into shape" that day but he simply had to write a long letter to historian Ray Ginger instead. By the end of July the impulse to write math had dissolved into frustration. He had grappled the entire day to write one page of text, he told Blumberg, so the time had come for some relaxation. Then followed five thousand words of monologue on the Supreme Court, the coal situation, education, diet, Erskine Caldwell, religion, and Marx.[36]

Nothing put O'Hare off the track of math in 1949 more than the growing climate of fear engendered by the Cold War, especially after one friend told him that "Perhaps the Dunkers have at last been submerged by hush hush." A year earlier, he had treated a telephone call from the FBI about the activities of a fellow Dunker as a joke, advising the agent that he was welcome to attend a meeting, provided that he would flash his badge and shout " 'This is the F.B.I. The joint is raided. Everybody keep your seats!' " Now, O'Hare sensed a palpable erosion of free speech. He told his friend Luther Ely Smith that he hated the way newspaper reporters and editors were being turned into

cooperative stooges of State and Industry . . . to carefully ladle out the Dickensien gruel and treacle to the 130,000,000 nonprivileged suckers who support the papers by buying from the advertisers. . . . It is now ALMOST axiomatic that any one who believes in collective democracy is subversive, but that monopoly for profit alone is American, Democratic, Christian, etc. ideology.[37]

In early 1949, the *Post-Dispatch* published a feature under his byline for the first time in years, not exactly "Dickensien gruel and treacle," but a nonetheless nostalgic piece entitled "Kerry Patch—A Vivid Closeup" that drew a flood of favorable responses from old residents of the slum. He devoted most of his time to keeping the Dunkers going as a haven of free speech. When attendance continued to fall off, he recruited new members. Once they felt welcome, several prominent professional women became regular Dunkers. O'Hare had to work harder to convince representatives from organized labor to attend. It was an old story, he told his friend Frank J. Swantner, manager of the St. Louis local of the Textile Workers Union; before World War I, Frank O'Hare had been "the only professional labor–Socialist person" in the City Club. After several months of letters and phone calls, Swantner and other labor figures became fixtures at O'Hare's lunches and parties.[38]

At a time when strict segregation of the races was still the rule in St. Louis, O'Hare also recruited African Americans into the Dunkers. That news caused "many inquiries" in the African American community, observed Howard B. Woods, editor of the black weekly *Saint Louis Argus*. O'Hare, Woods wrote, wanted to "See that ALL the intelligence and public spirit of St. Louis is appealed to, and enlisted." He invited African Americans to join Dunker activities "Not as 'toleration,' but as mutual acceptance. Not as a gift or favor, but as an equal exchange." Only one white person had refused to attend when told that people of color would be present and she changed her mind in time to attend the next meeting.[39]

Frank orchestrated the seating arrangements so that there was "one labor man, one management man at each table. That leaves seats for 6 others, one of whom should be a Negro." Having reconstituted the Dunkers to reach across lines of gender, class, and race, he made the lunch club an important progressive political force. St. Louis Mayor Joseph M. Darst used an appearance at the eighth anniversary meeting of the Dunkers to announce plans to spend thirty-eight million dollars on civic improvements and to drum up support for further slum clearance projects. A photograph taken that day by the *Post-Dispatch* shows a smiling O'Hare dressed in a suit and sweater vest holding his emcee's notes, posed next to artist Rose Propper and her portrait of FPO (an eighth anniversary gift) that captured a more severe countenance, and, almost squeezed out of the picture, Mayor Darst.[40]

O'Hare resumed publishing *Dunkerdoings* in 1950. Blithely, he listed the June 20 issue as Number 379, with "256 numbers skipped," while adding that weekly lunch sessions had continued without interruption for seven years. Henry Blumberg's sudden death at the age of sixty-four a week later left Frank depressed and guilt-ridden that he had not finished the math text his friend had encouraged him to write for years. "He was a great soul—and a great teacher, a great citizen," he told Ed Witcoff. Broke and bereft of the closest friend he had ever had, O'Hare tried to bury himself in work, asking his old boss to take him back as an adviser. Finding Frank's pleas to be irresistible, Witcoff put him back on the payroll for a few hours a week one last time. The final blowup between the two men was not long in coming, with the contents of O'Hare's office being removed in such haste that his carefully arranged files ended up in a jumble that has still not been completely sorted out. Looking back on his on-again, off-again "Tayloring" career a few years later, he wrote that "all my life, I have had to compromise. I have had to do my work as an industrial engineer, reducing working men and women to button pushing robots. Or . . . shoving some other man who could do the same work out into the army of the unemployed. There is nothing any one can do that does not cause injury to his fellow workers under capitalism." Frank O'Hare's final retirement from business was softened by the discovery that he qualified for monthly Social Security payments of $42.50. With the Dunkers on an even keel, he allowed his friend Art Kuhl, a reporter for the *Star-Times*, to talk him into writing his autobiography. All Frank had to do was sit down and write; Kuhl would edit the work for publication.[41]

He worked at the autobiography diligently in late 1950, banging out five thousand words a day on his typewriter for more than a month. "We will try to tell the story as History should be told—" he promised, "in such a way as to reveal and illustrate the law of its growth." He began well, writing in the first four chapters of his boyhood in Iowa and St. Louis, his career in business and subsequent conversion to Marxism, and his meeting Kate Richards at the Mills School. Conveying the excitement of life on the road as a Socialist organizer, O'Hare wrote extensively of the mobs he had faced, the many kindnesses he had received from strangers who had also found the faith, and of the special comradeship of Debs, Ameringer, and countless members of the SP's rank and file.[42]

In his haste to put his life on paper, he began to lose his sense of narrative, spewing out anecdotes as they occurred to him in the hope that Kuhl would be able to make sense of it all later. With memories of his salad days before World War I seemingly exhausted, he faltered in the face of reliving the painful story of the party's and his family's persecution. "Up to this time," he announced in the middle of chapter fifteen, "the writing of these recollections has been easy—very easy. But now I begin to feel the labor, the travail, of trying to give a picture of the years that

An "art party" sponsored by Frank O'Hare's Dunkers, which, at his insistence, included his many African American friends (courtesy Missouri Historical Society).

followed, 1914, 1916, 1918, 1920, when the old world blew up." Rather than dealing with Kate's arrest, trial, and imprisonment, he next wrote a chapter on the happiest memory of his childhood: a patchwork quilt his mother had made for him. Then another followed on Ruskin College, where he had taken the family in early 1917 in a futile bid to escape the whirlwind of Wilson's dragonnade. From there, he skipped to life at New Llano and then back to the pre-war era for more anecdotes about party organizing. Except for a few pages on his life in New York in the 1930s and two chapters on the O'Hare's housekeeper Anna, the last third of his manuscript consisted largely of musings on communications, Marx, and science. As for Art Kuhl, O'Hare wrote in a rare flash of bitterness, "the bum egged me on, each time he received a new one of the thirty 'chapters.'" When the *Star-Times* went out of business, Kuhl moved to Washington to take a job as a publicist and never got around to editing or even acknowledging Frank's efforts. O'Hare filed the manuscript away with his math text and a dozen other half-finished writings, never to work on it again.[43]

At about this time, he turned his attention back to an idea that had run through his mind on and off for twenty years, ever since Henry Blumberg introduced him to the then mysterious world of higher mathematics. In 1933 he had written an essay entitled "Can Mathematics Be Applied to Economics?" and came to the rather fuzzy conclusion (after nine pages) that "By the answer to this question all other temporal questions shall be answered." Almost twenty years later, having become a largely self-taught intellectual, he hypothesized that "One can laugh at the massive power of entrenched privilege if he believes he can discern as Jesus thought he discerned, as Marx thought he discerned, the existence of a 'differential' a rate of instantaneous change (however small that change) working through TIME." Just as scientists had recently discovered a minute differential of change in the earth's orbit over time, human progress must be measurable mathematically, a complex task, he admitted, as progress was not linear. Nor could progress even be plotted on a curve as one cannot know the direction of the curve after taking the latest measurements. He hoped that the many defeats suffered by the forces of economic democracy over the years had produced a pruning effect, with the root system developing more strongly as a result. In the end, O'Hare concluded, it came down to faith, "Faith that 'God' would not play such cruel tricks with us as to make all historical knowledge, all learning futile." He was not any closer in 1951 to answering the question he had first posed in 1933 about applying higher mathematics to social engineering, but he still had his faith that it would someday be answered in the affirmative and he would never cease in his search for that will-o'-the-wisp until the day he died.[44]

In the immediacy of the present, the Dunkers continued to be his first love. To save money, he mimeographed *Dunkerdoings* onto four-by-six-inch slips of paper and stapled together anywhere from eight to sixteen pages, depending on how much copy he had gathered for the week. "Gee, I'm having fun," he announced in the April 24, 1951, issue. "One loves to do again what one was happy doing in one's youth. I'm reporter, editor, subscription hustler, advertising manager, proof reader, 'n everything on a thumbnail publication." A week later, when it was Howard Wood's turn to act as emcee for the first time, O'Hare felt compelled to explain that "The Dunkers is the only downtown luncheon club in the only club building (Columbian Club) where men of all complexions may enter and be treated with the consideration due to all human beings. This party is not racial or bi-racial, or any other racial. It is Woods' party." When the post office threatened to pull his bulk mail permit because he could not prove how many of his subscribers had actually paid, he kept the paper going by giving it away and relying on donations. The FBI office in St. Louis began monitoring his activities again, hamhandedly, but it did not bother him.

At a Dunker meeting of June 12, 1951, the guest speaker, in his remarks, denounced O'Hare's lifelong adherence to socialism as "fanatical." Noting his nonplussed reaction, one guest was heard to remark to another that "the nicest thing about Frank is that he doesn't scare worth a damn." As Roger Baldwin later wrote of Frank O'Hare, Dunker:

> He was grammatical and colloquial; his dress was commonplace, his manner warm—punctuated at times by an intensity that could nail a listener by his piercing eyes. . . . Though Frank loved good talk, he left aside his emotions; I never saw him angry nor indignant, but he could inject cutting wit and sharp condemnation into any subject.

In addition to promoting upcoming events and reporting on Dunker meetings, there was plenty of space left in *Dunkerdoings* for O'Hare's essays on subjects ranging from the historic Jesus to freedom of speech. He filled the paper with irreverent comments on contemporary society and politics, such as his observation that Washington, D.C., was a place "where rival politicians eager to serve massive wealth call each other Commies and traitors."[45]

Ironically, at the height of the McCarthy Red Scare, O'Hare found that he continued to have entrée to the *Post-Dispatch*, thanks largely to his friend and fellow Dunker, Irving Dilliard, who had become editor of the editorial page in mid-1949. Frank wrote a memorable feature on the good old days "When Pigs Died Happy." Ham used to be much better, he claimed, when pigs lived on kitchen scraps and were well-loved members of the homestead full of the joy of living until the painless coup de grâce. The contrast between the delicate taste of ham from such "pampered hedonists" and today's mass-produced pork amounted to the difference between attending a play and watching television. The loss of old-fashioned Missouri ham was symbolic of the price one paid for living in a mass society. "This new generation," he lamented, "will have no memories—only books, television, gas fumes and cash in the bank. They will ask each other 'What is life for?' And they will die feeling somehow that they have never 'lived' but have only endured a series of emergencies." Irving Dilliard wrote an editorial about "Editor O'Hare," characterizing him as "indefatigable" and plugging "his unique little publication, *Dunkerdoings*." A few days earlier, Frank had strolled down to the riverfront to see if the Mississippi had risen as high after a series of recent storms as it had in the great flood of 1892, but with all of the old buildings gone he reported that he could not tell. Dilliard wondered if he had checked the still visible high-water mark on the old Eads Bridge, a subtle reminder to his friend that the past had not been forgotten—and neither had he.[46]

As long as the donations kept coming in, Frank O'Hare continued to publish *Dunkerdoings,* although attendance at the luncheons slowly diminished to a mere handful. "Still," he later wrote, "it was a haven. There at least one did not hear the yammering about communism and loyalty and so forth that hounds his reading and listening hours. McCarthy loomed larger than Jesus Christ." Caroline Nations was one of the few Dunkers who seldom missed a meeting. A prim and proper liberal professional woman, Nations found herself both repelled and fascinated by O'Hare, whom she labeled as "much better known than understood. . . . Incorrigibly forgiving himself he expects to be forgiven seventy times seven regardless of the enormity of his petty offenses." At the same time, she wrote, "Frank's insight into the marrow of men, and his genius at infecting others with his Whitmanish spirit tends to give solidarity to human relationship in this city." For his part, O'Hare enjoyed playing the part of Groucho Marx to Nation's Margaret Dumont, skewering her pretenses at every opportunity while delighting in her company.[47]

He also cherished the friendship of Gloria Pritchard, an African American welfare worker, poet, and broadcaster for KATZ radio, who, like O'Hare, had remained optimistic and radiant after a lifetime of trying experiences. When his friends Will and Rose Propper gave him a subscription to the Mercantile Lending Library, he filled *Dunkerdoings* with book reviews. He took the occasion of a dinner honoring the memory of Eugene Debs to comment acidly that the guest of honor, Norman Thomas, "presented some obscure carping criticism far far from the analytical clarity of Debs." He went on to explain why he so admired Debs in terms that revealed much about his own beliefs. "Jesus, (Jeshua) the Jew Carpenter, was to Debs the exalted Exemplar. Marx gave Debs the 'mathematics' of mundane life to which Debs added the poetry, love, sublime purposeness of existence." O'Hare published the newsletter until April 1952, when he ran out of funds. His friends put together an appeal, writing in a circular that "Frank Peter O'Hare is in the hole, and how!" They asked for donations to "help straighten out FPO's accounts" in time for his seventy-fifth birthday a few weeks hence. While they collected enough to get him and Irene back on their feet and Frank announced that he was merely taking a vacation from *Dunkerdoings,* he was through as a publisher. He discovered once again that life was not the same without his own sheet. "In some strange way I manage to survive," he wrote Zeuch at the end of the year.[48]

One Million More Words

Financially, he barely managed to survive. His sons Gene and Dick alternated sending monthly forty-dollar checks, which, when added to social security, gave him an income of eighty-five dollars a month plus a few dollars from the *Post-Dispatch*. He told Victor O'Hare that "If worst comes to the worst, I can let my friends know, but I hate to do this before I am at least 80 years old." His budget did not allow for the purchase of new clothes; he simply wore old ones while Irene donned hand-me-downs from a wealthy aunt in California. His friends kept him in liquor, which he drank only sparingly, and the son of his longtime physician treated him for free. Irene's sister Kathryn, employed as a secretary, proved to be "an ideal paying guest," buying the groceries as her share of the rent. "Of course I feel like a bum," he wrote his son Gene, "but that is one of the penalties of a badly planned financial career."[49]

By 1953, the *Post-Dispatch* had stopped publishing his articles "despite the great love the many department editors profess for me." Irving Dilliard had given O'Hare many assignments over the years, publishing his essays whenever possible directly under the political cartoons of Daniel Fitzpatrick and printing his letters verbatim. While recognizing that O'Hare's Marxism made him "controversial with some people," Dilliard, an absolutist in regard to freedom of speech, had continued to use Frank's features because they "reached into situations that concerned people." So long as O'Hare could use his own publication as a forum for Debsian socialism, he enjoyed the prestige and extra income that went with his mostly nostalgic and apolitical *Post-Dispatch* articles. Following the demise of *Dunkerdoings*, though, he told his son Victor he resented that Dilliard would only publish pieces that made him "appear as a mere comic." At a time when publisher Joseph Pulitzer II was growing increasingly uneasy about Dilliard's zealous denunciations of the Red Scare phenomenon in general and Senator Joseph McCarthy in particular, O'Hare had chosen a poor moment to demand to be taken more seriously. Frank's letter published in the *Post-Dispatch* on January 16, 1953, damning the death sentences of Julius and Ethel Rosenberg was his last contribution for three years.[50]

The decision to drop him from the paper did not affect the warm friendship between O'Hare and Dilliard. Once the Red Scare abated, they reached a unique and unspoken compromise whereby Dilliard continued to publish Frank's jottings as letters to the editor and paid him for them. In subsequent years, O'Hare carried on his role as the "gad-fly" of St. Louis through published letters on a number of public issues including government agricultural policy, juvenile delinquency, protection of his beloved parks, TVA, saving public landmarks, the erection of a monument to the slave Dred Scott, nuclear war, and (on his deathbed) public transit.[51]

Broke, a failed memorialist, and an editor without a sheet of his own, Frank kept his mind active by continuing to preside over Dunker functions (which he orchestrated as monthly theme parties) and by writing letters. Upon rising late in the morning or early in the afternoon, he would pour out his thoughts on paper to a friend, a member of his family, or a stranger who had written or broadcast something that had stimulated him. He sent carbon copies to the Missouri Historical Society for the growing collection of Frank O'Hare Papers. In a long missive to his daughter-in-law Bobbie O'Hare, he explained:

> As you see, this letter is really a journal—a flow. If you read it, or do not read it, O.K., It goes in the file. Then, some day the 1,000,000 words will be read by some one, who will excise 950,000 of them. The 50,000 remainder will be what Henry Blumberg expected to be the "cream" of what I have to say.[52]

For example, he wrote to Harvard historian Arthur Schlesinger Jr. to say that he had recently dropped a line to Max Eastman, once a leading light of the pre-war "Lyrical Left" and now an equally outspoken member of the Far Right, asking "a few harmless (I thought) questions" about an Eastman essay in *Reader's Digest.* Eastman had replied: "You're an awful fool to write letters like that to your old friends. If you haven't learned a thing in these forty years of the world's agony you ought to keep mum about it." O'Hare had no intention of engaging in a controversy with the "very slippery" Eastman, he told Schlesinger, observing: "Poor Max. He fools nobody but himself." His old friend now reminded him of Whittaker Chambers, who had created a sensation by accusing Alger Hiss of being a Communist agent, as both Eastman and Chambers had become obsessed with "The threat," internal subversion. Schlesinger replied that while he was a Roosevelt liberal and not a Socialist, he too deplored Eastman, adding, "there would be a certain pathos in the Eastman performance, except for the fact that he can do—and is perhaps doing—a lot of damage." O'Hare was less cordial in a letter to another leading historian, Walter Prescott Webb, lambasting his book *The Great Frontier* for major blunders in astronomy, Darwin, economics, and labor history.[53]

O'Hare especially enjoyed writing to the editors of the few remaining publications of the Socialist Left, men he regarded as his successors and who understood and admired him. To Cedric Belfrage, editor of the *National Guardian,* O'Hare expressed the hope that old mistakes would not be repeated. "WE failed," he wrote, speaking for his generation, "because we underestimated the intelligence of the enemy." Today, the obstacles were even greater because the minions of capitalism had mastered the use of psychological warfare in order to attain complete social control. He praised Harvey O'Connor (an old comrade from Federated Press) who wrote for the independent Socialist *Monthly Review* and Leo Huberman, one of the coeditors, for keeping up the good fight, observing that "The

Socialist movement in USA is of course deader than a fried egg. But the THOUGHT never was of higher urgency." He told Huberman he wished he could help to boost *Monthly Review*'s circulation. In the old days, he could have at least sold subscriptions to his friends, but "I can't do that now. People are actually scared stiff at the idea of having their name on a 'left' publication list."[54]

If the impotence of the contemporary Left saddened and frustrated him, the antics of Red Scare politicians in Washington turned his stomach. "Enough comes over the radio," he remarked, "to show beyond all question of doubt what a swine [Senator Joseph] McCarthy is—how unfit he is to contaminate the atmosphere that decent people must breathe." Two world wars and two Red Scares had not changed Frank P. O'Hare: "I am today, as in 1902, a clear cut, uncompromising, class-conscious, revolutionary Socialist."[55]

Through the 1950s, O'Hare continued to despair over what he regarded as a tenuous totalitarianism that had crept over the country as a result of the Cold War. "Terror is in the hearts of many of my old time newspaper friends," he wrote to Margaret Sanger. "Yep. We done won birth-control. We now have thought-control." To publisher Theodore Lentz, he observed:

A writer who merely writes is a fart in a windstorm. No man who failed to organize men ever *moved* men. That is why ORGANIZA- TION for peace is not legally FORBIDDEN in America, but simply made IMPOSSIBLE. To organize the grassroots is proof of communist– atheist–treasonable subversion. Any ORGANIZATION not approved by the Chamber of Commerce, by the officially recognized churches, by government authority of one sort or another, is prima facie suspect. The Attorney General's list is GROWING. Men fear to send written orders to you for your books. Those who advocate peace fly counter to the program of the "Power Elite."[56]

In spite of this cant, O'Hare continued to enjoy life and retained his Debsian optimism that a better future lay ahead. "I will confide to you," he wrote to Anna Louise Strong, "that I think that I have had more *fun* in the last ten years than in any other decade of my life." O'Hare said much the same thing during a panel discussion at a conference on aging at Washington University, where Dean Willis Reals introduced him as "'well known for at least 100 years' . . . a St. Louis institution." Frank described himself as "frisky, and if you ask me, having a hell of a good time." His advice to those contemplating retirement was simple: "lose all your money, discover who your friends are, and whether your wife really loves you. Then you will have no 'old-age' problem to be solved for you by professional do-gooders." As he saw it, after a lifetime of generating wealth for the capitalists, "the aged USA proletariat" could no longer take care of itself—and that would have to change. "I demand partnership in the enterprise," O'Hare continued, "—and on Walt Whitman's terms, that every man be a democrat in economic democracy. I have been a rebel against fascism, incipient or attained, all of my life." Like many older people, he felt "pulled both ways" between the future and the past. He was not afraid to die, he concluded, but he wanted to stick around because "life is *so* sweet, people are so sweet, the world is so beautiful." Life remained beautiful for O'Hare because of continuing opportunities to teach, persuade, and on this occasion, to again hold an audience in the hollow of his hand for fifteen minutes.[57]

Frank O'Hare felt neither old nor poor, because "To surround yourself with eager YOUNG people, is the answer to Ponce de Leon's quest." While the Dunkers ceased meeting publicly in 1953, Frank explained, "What I did do was to build a university around *me*. This university is yet very much alive." Several of the Dunkers continued to gather at O'Hare's home, where he presided over a salon of St. Louis liberal and radical intellectuals. The conversation was wide-ranging, with no holds barred. One visitor recorded in FPO's guest book: "Mr. O'Hare has insulted me 18 times in the last 2 hours but he has not the heart to hurt me personally. He is 78 years old and is prepared to convert St. Peter as well as to give him hell!" He remained as intense personally as ever, although old age mellowed his Irish temper. His neighbor Gene Peciulis remembered that "Love for his fellow man dominated his character. In the final analysis his motives were self-transcending. He had such drive that the surroundings shook." O'Hare's old friend Roger Baldwin wrote in 1956 that he admired him more than ever, although he disagreed with his unbending faith in democratic socialism. "You got a vision once and you stick to it, as you should," Baldwin observed, "embellished with perhaps more love and tolerance than before, which is as you should too . . . keep right on, as you will, loving and cussing and believing."[58]

One of the things that kept O'Hare buoyantly optimistic was the faith that, properly publicized, the injustices of the world and the power of Marx would lead the younger generation to embrace a new radicalism, just as he and Kate Richards had at the turn of the century. He thought he detected the first stirring of long-awaited renaissance in the publication of *The Power Elite* by C. Wright Mills, a professor of sociology at Columbia University. Mills examined an "interlocking directorate" that had come to dominate modern capitalist society, explaining that "the leading men in each of the three domains of power—the warlords, the corporation chieftains, the political directorate—tend to come together, to form the power elite of America." Consciously eschewing the Marxian conception of the ruling class as overly

Frank O'Hare's "salon" sometime in the mid-1950s (top row, left to right, Gene Peciulis, Ray Witcoff, Irene O'Hare, Rose and Will Propper, unidentified, and Caroline Nations). Seated, third from right, is Irene's sister Kathryn, "an ideal paying guest," as Frank called her. O'Hare is seated at lower left, holding his customary King Edward (courtesy Vince Peciulis).

simple, he argued that economic determinism had to be elaborated by the equally important political and military determinisms that combined to form the power elite, an ever-shifting triumvirate of hierarchies without any real ideology, perpetuating itself through shameless manipulation for immoral ends. The call to action against the "crackpot realists" was unmistakable. "We study history, it has been said, to rid ourselves of it," Mills wrote, "and the history of the power elite is a clear case for which this maxim is correct."[59]

Plainly delighted, O'Hare wrote to Mills: "I am having as many barrels of fun out of ELITE as I got out of Veblen 54 years ago." Reading his "heavily freighted" text, "I check what you say against my own observations and experiences. Nowhere, nowhere, do I quarrel with you. Except of course the sense of futility, helplessness that your pages convey. The defeatism." Enough reviewers of *The Power Elite* had complained of Mills's pessimism that he felt compelled to answer that what such people wanted was "less of a program than a lyric upsurge—at least at the end. . . . But the world I'm trying to understand does not make me politically hopeful and morally complacent, which is to say, I find it difficult to play the cheerful idiot. . . . Personally, as you know, I'm a very cheerful type." Nearing the end of his long life, eighty-year-old Frank O'Hare understandably was looking for a "lyric upsurge." Yet he too had balked at playing "the cheerful idiot," even when it meant losing his forum in the *Post-Dispatch*.[60]

Mills articulated in academic terms what O'Hare had been saying for years about an allegedly classless society tightly controlled from the top with the help of a captive press. What Ralph Miliband said of Mills could be applied to O'Hare in the second half of his life as well: "He was a man on his own, with both the strength and also the weakness which go with that solitude. He was on the Left, but not of the Left, a deliberately lone guerilla, not a regular soldier." A decade earlier, O'Hare had told Ray Ginger that "I cannot conform. I do not want to conform. I have tested myself before a million persons in person, and a few millions *via* print, and I am not apologizing to anybody. What the hell." Frank's instincts about Mills had been correct. The most potent critic of the American social order since Veblen, Mills would influence (posthumously) a generation of university-centered activists whom he was among the first to call "The New Left."[61]

O'Hare had long since realized that the Cooperative Commonwealth would never come about in his lifetime. Once a mass movement, the Socialist party had shriveled to a handful of locals presided over by "Gloomy Gus," one of his more polite nicknames for Norman Thomas, a man he continued to see as "ignorant, shallow, oratorical, and supercilious—and when we meet, we clash." The world (and the Socialist party) had changed, but not Frank P. O'Hare. He would continue the struggle as long as he had the strength to teach and publicize, explaining: "I am a Socialist. . . . My job is not immediate victory, but the long-time view. My job is to announce the goal—A nation in which every PRIVATE necessity is at the command of every work-willing citizen. And NO public necessity is monopolized." He could not let go because socialism had been his lifelong faith. The justness and the inevitability of socialism had not yet been proven, he observed, any more than Newton's belief in the calculus had until centuries after his death.[62]

Like Veblen, he continued to believe that science would prove him right in the end. "There is no explaining how one may accept a *faith* that afterwards is enfolded in science," he wrote. "I feel that my faith of 1900 is more and more enfolded in science." He did what he could to hearten the faithful, writing in *American Socialist* that "all I can hope is that the younger generation of socialists is having as much fun as we-all did so long, long ago. We sure had fun, to balance all the hard work." He encouraged teachers to organize into unions, rather than complaining about their low salaries, as they had on a television news program he had watched. When the *Post-Dispatch* refused to print his letter on the subject, he sent it to a Teamsters' Union newspaper, which not only published it but called O'Hare "one of the truly great men of St. Louis—possibly the ONLY one." He signed the article "Frank P. O'Hare, sometime high school and academy teacher who wouldn't take nobody's dust."[63]

"Such Zest for Living"

He continued to push himself relentlessly, as he had for most of his life. In June 1958, O'Hare wrote that he woke up every afternoon promising today he would not write a letter. Instead he would read or work on his files, or make a garden or just sit under a tree and enjoy the sounds of children at play—and every day the typewriter and the telephone would continue to beckon. The pattern ended a few months later when he was diagnosed with stomach cancer. O'Hare survived an operation in which surgeons removed four pounds of cancerous tissue and sewed up what remained of his stomach into a walnut-sized configuration. Recovery was slow, with Irene faithfully spoon-feeding him nourishment every few hours. When his strength began to return, he took up pen and paper as a way of banishing the demons from his sickroom and affirming that his life had not been a waste.[64]

His mind as restless and active as ever, Frank meditated on the meaning of his life and his hopes and dreams. In November 1959 he wrote Irving Dilliard:

> Even though a man lives obscurely in his lifetime and his writings are ignored for fifty years he may, like VICO, inform, influence, guide the thinkers of the whole world. This is attained immortality. This is the criterion of morality. This is the wedding of materialism and religion, of science and philosophy, of individualism and communism. This demonstrates Jeshuah ben Josef, Marx, Tolstoi, and I humbly hope, myself.

After a lifetime of struggle for socialism, he had little to show for the effort. Like the Italian philosopher Giovanni Battista Vico (1668–1744), whose application of science to history went unappreciated in his lifetime, Frank had led an inconspicuous existence. The magazines he had published, the articles, Kate's work that he had done so much to shape, and "the 1,000,000 words" he wrote in his private letters, were the raw materials for his attained immortality. Having labored in his own vulgar way to unify scientific, economic, and political thought as he understood it, he wished to be linked in serial immortality to the great men who had inspired him to strive for justice and equality. He would never be Vico, but a third of a century after receiving O'Hare's letter, Irving Dilliard remembered his friend fondly as "a different person in his concerns, interests, and way of life. He was [pausing] Frank P. O'Hare."[65]

While conceding that "Irene and I for 18 months have been through hell," O'Hare swore that his doctor had pronounced him cured. Excited by the prospect of a new generation vying for the White House in 1960, he dictated a letter to Dilliard regarding Robert Kennedy's appearance on Jack Parr's *Tonight Show*. While Kennedy's denunciation of Teamster's president Jimmy Hoffa reminded him of the persecution of the Socialists during World War I, he saw some hope in the "honest, searching, accurate, extremely brave" report Kennedy gave on the terrible poverty he had seen in West Virginia. O'Hare plunged back into community activism too, inviting friends to his home to help organize a cultural exchange program between St. Louis and Stuttgart, Germany. Left with a mountain of medical bills, he needed money desperately. His friend Will Propper had offered to take care of everything, including a monthly stipend, but Frank would not hear of it. "WE CANNOT accept money that is offered for our living expenses from *anyone*," he wrote, "It must be to support our WORK—and NO LARGE amount from any one person."[66]

He had a more dignified way to go out in mind. On May 12, 1960, he sent a circular to friends explaining: "I am now very tired of being retired, and am announcing to this cock-eyed world the fact that I am starting my thirteenth newspaper." *Frank O'Hare's Weekly Commentary* would cost one dollar for twenty-six issues. Still the promoter, he asked thirty-six of the old Dunkers and his newer friends to sell thirty subscriptions each for "what will probably be the world's best thumbnail newspaper or the greatest small newspaper in the English-speaking world." Once he had banked at least one thousand dollars, the first issue would roll off the press.[67]

As the money began to come in, he learned that cancer had spread to the organs surrounding his stomach. Frank O'Hare died on July 16, 1960. Irene O'Hare used the subscription money to have his remains cremated and buried in Calvary Cemetery. She died in 1969. Three months after Frank O'Hare's death, Irving Dilliard paid an extraordinary tribute to his friend in a remembrance that took up most of a page in the *Post-Dispatch*. He summarized his life's work as "rebel against prejudice and injustice, organizer of the Socialist tent encampments, editor of the Rip-Saw, Dunker, efficiency statistician, unhurried essayist for hurried newspaper readers— the Celtic leprechaun." As for his work as a fighting editor, "the National

Rip-Saw, in the hands of Frank O'Hare, lived up to its name and then some." The timing of Dilliard's piece would have pleased Frank, for it was meant not only as an encomium but as publicity for a memorial service to be held the following week. "Mourning and dirges," Dilliard announced, "have been ruled out as un-O'Hareian." So were all formalities. Dilliard, Roger Baldwin, Howard Woods, and Caroline Nations spoke along with other close friends. He had lived a long and mostly happy life without accomplishing much that could be quantified. Phil Hickey, longtime Superintendent of Public Schools in St. Louis, captured what O'Hare had meant to those who knew him and those who read what he had published, observing at Frank's eightieth birthday celebration that "No one that I have known has had such zest for living and such a willingness to share it." After sixty years of swimming against the tide as a rebel against injustice, it was a good way to be remembered. Roger Baldwin had once advised him to "Just keep your sanities and your freedom to think and kick, and if you don't amount to a damn, at least you'll have the satisfaction of going to the devil your own way with your torch still alight and your faith undimmed." That is exactly what Frank O'Hare did—and he would not have had it any other way.[68]

Notes

Abbreviations

AG   *American Guardian*

AV   *American Vanguard*

AtR   *Appeal to Reason*

CDP   *Chandler Daily Publicist* (Okla.)

CN (RH)   *Coming Nation* (Rich Hill, Mo.)

DD   *Dunkerdoings*

DS   KRO, *"Dear Sweethearts": Letters from Kate Richards O'Hare to Her Family* St. Louis: Frank O'Hare, 1920

EVD   Eugene V. Debs

EVDL   *Letters of Eugene V. Debs*, J. Robert Constantine, ed., 3 vols. Urbana: University of Illinois Press, 1990

FMGN   Fred Miner Goodhue, "Notes," 1931, Richard W. St. John Collection, Newllano Colony Papers, University of Arkansas Libraries, Fayetteville, Arkansas, Box 1

FOB   *Frank O'Hare's Bulletin*

FPO   Frank P. O'Hare

FOP   Frank P. O'Hare Papers, Missouri Historical Society, St. Louis

FOP Mss   Frank P. O'Hare, unpublished autobiographical manuscript, O'Hare Papers, Missouri Historical Society, St. Louis

FOP (Pec) Frank P. O'Hare Papers, Gene Peciulis Collection, Baltimore, Maryland

KRO   Kate Richards O'Hare

LN   *Labor's News*

NR-S   *National Rip-Saw*

RB   Roger Baldwin

SLPD   *St. Louis Post-Dispatch*

SR   *Social Revolution*

WEZ   William E. Zeuch

Introduction

1. Caroline G. Nations to James F. Hornback, November 2, 1960, Records of the Ethical Society of St. Louis, Western Manuscript Collection, University of Missouri–St. Louis, Box 26; "Register of Friends Attending Memorial to Frank P. O'Hare," FOP; Roger Baldwin, unpublished manuscript, FOP (Pec). Box numbers have not been used when referring to the O'Hare Papers because the collection has been reboxed several times in recent years. A detailed guide to the use of the collection can be found in the bibliography.

2. FOP Mss, 1 and FPO to WEZ, January 15, 1948, FOP.

3. FPO to Dave, August 20, 1942, FOP; FPO to RB, December 25, 1958, FOP; and FPO to Sarah Rhue, March 6, 1958, FOP (Pec).

4. Stephen B. Oates, "Biography as High Adventure," in Stephen B. Oates, ed., *Biography as High Adventure* (Amherst: University of Massachusetts Press, 1986), 129; and Leon Edel, "The Figure Under the Carpet," in Oates, *Biography,* 24.

5. FOP Mss, 29; FPO to Ira Kipnis, February 3, 1953, FOP; Neil K. Basen, "Kate Richards O'Hare: The 'First Lady' of American Socialism, 1901–1917," *Labor History* 21 (spring 1980): 172; and FPO to Brown, November 23, 1942, FOP.

6. Irving Stone to FPO, December 29, 1944, FOP.

1. The Making of a Socialist, 1877–1902

1. FOP Mss, 1 and FPO to Walter Thomas Mills, July 13, 1939, FOP.

2. "F. P. O'Hare Outline of Life," and family Bible, FOP; FOP Mss, 1; "Frank P. O'Hare to Mrs. Margretta Scott Lawler and Miss Mary Porter Scott," *Bulletin of the Missouri Historical Society* 20 (1963): 56–57. The 1880 census lists Peter O'Hair [*sic*] as 35 years old and his wife as 34. See U.S. Bureau of the Census, 1880, New Hampton Village, Iowa.

3. Peter O'Hare to Elizabeth O'Hare, May 27, 1882, FOP; *Mesa County Mail,* January 20, 1905; August Petzold to Gertrude Petzold, December 16, 1880, FOP; FOP Mss, 1; and Ted C. Hinckley, "When the Boer War Came to St. Louis," *Missouri Historical Review* 61 (April 1967): 285–302.

4. FPO to Victor O'Hare, January 18, 1955; FPO to WEZ, March 17, 1947; and FPO to Bobbie O'Hare, n.d. [1955], FOP.

5. FPO to Bobbie O'Hare, n.d. [1955]; FPO to "Dear Friend," May 12, 1960; and Report cards, New Hampton Public Schools, FOP; and Irving Dilliard, "The Boy from Kerry Patch," *SLPD,* October 23, 1960.

6. FOP Mss, 1; FPO, unpublished mss., n.d. [1930s], FOP; and Julian S. Rammelkamp, "St. Louis in the Early 'Eighties," *Bulletin of the Missouri Historical Society* 19 (July 1963): 328–39.

7. FPO, "Kerry Patch—A Vivid Closeup," *SLPD,* February 13, 1949; FPO to Gertrude Klosterman, August 30, 1958, FOP; Etan Diamond, "Kerry Patch: Irish Immigrant Life in St. Louis," *Gateway Heritage* (fall 1989): 23–30; James N. Primm,

Lion of the Valley: St. Louis, Missouri, 2d ed. (Boulder: Pruett, 1990), 357–58; and *SLPD,* March 6, 1949.

8. FPO to Bobbie O'Hare, n.d. [1955]; FPO to Victor O'Hare, January 8, 1954; FPO to Bobbie O'Hare, January 6, 1952; FPO to Margery, January 20, 1952, FOP and FPO to Victor O'Hare, n.d. [1955], FOP (Pec).

9. FPO to WEZ, March 17, 1947; FPO to Leo Huberman, September 14, 1957; and FPO to Upton Sinclair, January 3, 1958, FOP. On the significance of dime novels to working-class culture, see Michael Denning, *Mechanic Accents: Dime Novels and Working-Class Culture in America* (New York: Verso, 1987).

10. C. M. Frazier to FPO, December 29, 1942; FPO to Frank Lynch, July 9, 1939; FPO to Andy O'Hare, January 24, 1947; FPO to Bobbie O'Hare, April 6, 1943; FPO to Nellie Joyce, n.d.; and FPO to Joseph Pulitzer II, April 12, 1947, FOP; *St. Louis Star-Times,* January 30, 1948; *St. Louis Star,* June 5, 1900; and Selwyn K. Troen and Glen E. Holt, eds., *St. Louis* (New York: Franklin Watts, 1977), 91–95.

11. *St. Louis Star-Times,* June 23, 1944; FOP Mss, 1; and Diary of Gertrude Petzold; FPO to Rose and Will Propper, March 10, 1955; and FPO to David Shannon, February 9, 1949, FOP.

12. FPO to Gertie Petzold, August 6, 1894, FOP; *St. Louis Star-Times,* June 23, 1944; FPO to Phil Hickey, January 12, 1946; FPO to Irving Dilliard, June 24 and 28, 1955; and FPO to Russell Sharp, January 19, 1944, FOP; and Primm, *Lion of the Valley,* 311.

13. FPO to Harvey O'Connor, March 17, 1954; FPO to Susan Meston, February 1, 1941; and FPO, "O'Hare Book," June 1951, FOP.

14. FPO to Corliss Lamont, n.d. [c. 1950], FOP (Pec); FPO to Susan Meston, February 1, 1941; Life Insurance Application, 1915; and FPO, "O'Hare Book," June 1951, FOP; Daniel Nelson, *Managers and Workers: Origins of the New Factory System in the United States, 1880–1920* (Madison: University of Wisconsin Press, 1975), 55–61; and Daniel Nelson, *Frederick W. Taylor and the Rise of Scientific Management* (Madison: University of Wisconsin Press, 1980), 38–75.

15. Martin J. Sklar, *The Corporate Reconstruction of American Capitalism, 1890–1916* (New York: Cambridge University Press, 1988), 1–40; Primm, *Lion of the Valley,* 346–47; and Paul Buhle, *Marxism in the United States* (New York: Verso, 1991), 61–79.

16. FOP Mss, 2; FPO to Bobbie O'Hare, n.d., FOP; and FPO to Jim, April 18, 1958, Records of the Ethical Society of St. Louis, Western Manuscript Collection, University of Missouri–St. Louis, Box 26.

17. Herron quoted in Robert T. Handy, "George D. Herron and the Social Gospel in American Protestantism, 1890–1901" (Ph.D. diss., University of Chicago, 1949), 144; FPO, "Book," June 1951; Charles Hanaway to FPO and FPO to Charles Hanaway, September 21, 1899; FPO to Margery, January 20, 1952; and FPO to Susan Meston, February 1, 1941, FOP; *Social Democratic Herald* (Chicago), February 3, 1900; Howard H. Quint, *The Forging of American Socialism* (Indianapolis: Bobbs-Merrill, 1953), 126–35; and James Dombrowski, *The Early Days of Christian Socialism in America* (New York: Columbia University Press, 1936), 171–93.

18. *DD,* May 14, 1945; FOP Mss, 2; and FPO to Fred Adam, April 20, 1947, FOP.

19. *Missouri Socialist,* June 1, 1901; Primm, *Lion of the Valley,* 380–81; FPO to Corliss Lamont, n.d. [c. 1950], FOP (Pec); FPO to Harry Slattery, n.d. [1945], FOP; and David Loth, *Swope of G. E.* (New York: Simon and Schuster, 1958), 43–45.

20. FPO to Lancelot Hogben, August 1, 1937; FPO to Bobbie O'Hare, April 6, 1943; and FPO to Dick and Bobbie O'Hare, September 10, 1943, FOP.

21. John Graham, ed., *"Yours for the Revolution": The Appeal to Reason, 1895–1922* (Lincoln: University of Nebraska Press, 1990), 33; Elliott Shore, *Talkin' Socialism: J. A. Wayland and the Role of the Press in American Radicalism, 1890–1912* (Lawrence: University of Kansas Press, 1988), 32–54 and 103–112; FPO to John Granbery, April 9, 1946, FOP; and FOP Mss, 8.

22. FPO, untitled essay, December 17, 1958, FOP and James R. Green, "The 'SALESMEN-SOLDIERS' of the 'APPEAL ARMY': A Profile of Rank-and-File Socialist Agitators," Bruce M. Stave, ed., *Socialism and the Cities* (Port Washington, N.Y.: Kennikat, 1975): 13–40.

23. Walter Thomas Mills, *How to Work for Socialism* (Chicago: Charles H. Kerr, 1900) and Shore, *Talkin' Socialism,* 123.

24. *Missouri Socialist,* January 5, February 23, March 30, April 13, June 1, June 8, and December 7, 1901; Walter Thomas Mills, *The Struggle for Existence* (Chicago: International School of Social Economy, 1904); Buhle, *Marxism in the United States,* 91; and Paul M. Buhle, "Marxism in the United States, 1900–1940" (Ph.D. diss., University of Wisconsin, 1975), 6–8.

25. *St. Louis Labor,* December 10, 1898, and January 21, 1899; *Missouri Socialist,* January 12 and March 23, 1901; *Social Democratic Herald* (Chicago), July 9, 1898, and March 17 and 31, 1900; and Ira Kipnis, *The American Socialist Movement, 1897–1912* (New York: Columbia University Press, 1952), 43–80.

26. Kipnis, *Socialist Movement,* 81–99; Quint, *American Socialism,* 319–72; and James Weinstein, *Ambiguous Legacy: The Left in American Politics* (New York: Franklin Watts, 1975), 4–5.

27. FPO, untitled essay, n.d.; FPO to Leo Huberman, September 14, 1957; and FPO to Theodore Lentz, January 1, 1957, FOP and FPO Mss, 2.

28. FPO to Thais Magrane Prescott, March 11, 1955; FPO to Victor O'Hare, January 24, 1953; and FPO to Nellie Joyce, n.d., FOP.

29. *SLPD,* October 10, 1900; FPO to Samuel Castleton, March 31, 1945, FOP; *Social Democratic Herald,* October 20, 1900; FPO to Samuel Castleton, April 13, 1945, FOP; FPO to Theodore Debs, March 17, 1937, *Papers of Eugene V. Debs 1834–1945,* microfilm edition (Glen Rock, N.J.: Microfilming Corporation of America, 1983), reel 5; and Nick Salvatore, *Eugene V. Debs: Citizen and Socialist* (Urbana: University of Illinois Press, 1982), 310–11.

30. Quint, *American Socialism,* 373; *Missouri Socialist,* January 5, 1901; and Kipnis, *Socialist Movement,* 99–102.

31. *Missouri Socialist,* January 12 and February 2, 1901, and FPO to Commonwealth College Comrades, December 1, 1936, FOP. See also *Missouri Socialist,* January 19, February 9, March 2, and July 13, 1901.

32. Morris Hillquit, *History of Socialism in the United States* (New York: Dover, 1971), 308–9; Norma Fain Pratt, *Morris Hillquit: A Political History of an American*

Jewish Socialist (Westport, Conn.: Greenwood, 1979), 8–55; Quint, *American Socialism,* 374–88; David A. Shannon, *The Socialist Party of America* (New York: Macmillan, 1955), 3–17; and James Weinstein, *The Decline of Socialism in America, 1912–1925* (New York: Vintage, 1969), 5–26.

33. "Proceedings of Socialist Unity Convention, Indianapolis, Indiana, 1901," *Socialist Party of America Papers,* microfilm edition (Glen Rock, N.J.: Microfilming Corporation of America 1975), reel 1; *Missouri Socialist,* August 3, 1901; Quint, *American Socialism,* 382–88; and Kipnis, *Socialist Movement,* 104–6.

34. FOP Mss, 2; FPO to John Stewart, April 1, 1948; FPO to Commonwealth College Comrades, December 1, 1936; and FPO to Dick and Bobbie O'Hare, September 10, 1943, FOP; *Missouri Socialist,* June 8, 1901; and *Social Democratic Herald,* February 16, 1901.

35. FPO to Irving Stone, December 8, 1944, FOP and *The Republic,* December 17, 1901.

36. *Missouri Socialist,* September 21, 1901; *The Republic,* August 20, 1901; and FPO to Fred Adam, April 20, 1947, FOP.

37. FOP Mss, 2 and 3; FPO to J. W. Parker et al., February 18, 1956, and FPO to Upton Sinclair, January 3, 1958, FOP; *AtR,* October 3, 1901; and *St. Louis Labor,* March 15, 1902.

38. FPO to Will and Gertie Petzold, September 17, 1901, FOP; *AtR,* August 17, 1901; and Shore, *Talkin' Socialism,* 83 and 90–93.

39. *Girard Press,* October 10, 1901; FPO to Gertie Petzold, October 3, 1901, FOP; and FOP Mss, 3.

40. *SLPD,* March 15, 1914; *Newport Daily Independent* (Ark.), November 19, 1907; KRO, "Dives and Lazarus," *NR-S,* September 1911; KRO, "How I Became a Socialist Agitator," in Philip S. Foner and Sally M. Miller, eds., *Kate Richards O'Hare: Selected Writings and Speeches* (Baton Rouge: Louisiana State University Press, 1982), 35–38; KRO, "The Girl Who Would," *Selected Writings,* 41–44; Basen, "Kate Richards O'Hare" 169–71; and Sally M. Miller, *From Prairie to Prison: The Life of Social Activist Kate Richards O'Hare* (Columbia: University of Missouri Press, 1993), 4–17. Obituaries of Kate Richards O'Hare listed her year of birth as 1877. See, for example, *SLPD,* January 12, 1948. Her friend William E. Zeuch claimed that "Her brother John told me she was born in 1875," a date that she acknowledged to be the correct one, according to Zeuch. See WEZ to FPO, May 18, 1948, FOP. The consensus among Kate O'Hare scholars is that she was born in 1876.

41. KRO, "How I Became a Socialist Agitator," 38–39; KRO, "Mother Jones of the Revolution," *NR-S,* August 1913; Basen, "Kate Richards O'Hare," 172; and Miller, *From Prairie to Prison,* 17–21.

42. FPO to Thais Magrane Prescott, March 11, 1955, and FPO to Irving Stone, December 8, 1944, FOP and FOP Mss, 3.

43. *Girard Press,* November 28, 1901; Kate Richards to Gertic Petzold, November 3, 1901, FOP; *AtR,* January 11, 1902; FPO to Gertie Petzold, December 12, 1901, and FPO to Ray Ginger, n.d. [1949], FOP; *Girard Press,* December 5, 1901; and *AtR,* October 19, November 2 and 6, and December 21, 1901.

44. *The Republic,* December 17, 1901; Leonard D. Abbott, "A Socialist Wedding," *International Socialist Review* 2 (July 1901): 14–20; FPO to Hilda Mills and Wilbur C.

Benton, September 23, 1929; Sworn Statements of Hilda Mills and Wilbur C. Benton, November 8, 1929; FPO to Ray Ginger, n.d. [1949]; and FPO to Henry Blumberg, May 5, 1949, FOP; *AtR*, January 4, 1902; FPO to Angela Leyton, April 23, 1958, FOP; *Missouri Socialist*, December 14, 1901; and *Girard Press*, January 9, 1902.

2. *Missionary Career, 1902–1911*

1. Kate Richards to Gertie Petzold, November 3, 1901, FOP.

2. *St. Louis Labor*, January 11, 1902; *AtR*, January 18, 1902; *Daily Mail* (Nevada, Mo.), January 6, 1902; *St. Louis Labor*, January 18 and February 8, 1902; and FOP Mss, 3.

3. *AtR*, March 1, 1902; FOP Mss, 3; FPO to Eugene O'Hare, February 5, 1955, FOP; and *St. Louis Labor*, February 8, 1902.

4. *Kansas City Journal*, January 14, 1902, quoted in *Girard Press*, January 16, 1902; *Kansas City Journal*, February 17, 1902; KRO to Gertie Petzold, February 7, 1902, and FPO to Eugene O'Hare, February 5, 1955, FOP; and FOP Mss, 3.

5. KRO, "For the Fair Ones," *CN* (RH), April 12, 1902; *CN* (RH), September 13, 1902; *Kansas City Star*, quoted in "Cooperation and Socialism," *CN* (RH), May 31, 1902; *AtR*, February 22 and March 8, 1902; *St. Louis Labor*, March 8, 1902; *CN* (RH), May 3, August 30, October 4, 1902; and FPO to J. W. Parker et al., February 18, 1956, FOP. Socialist organizer and writer Oscar Ameringer formed a similar partnership with a traveling hypnotist and mind reader in Oklahoma. See Oscar Ameringer, *If You Don't Weaken* (Norman: University of Oklahoma Press, reprint, 1983), 244–52.

6. *Kansas City World*, quoted in *AtR*, March 22, 1902; *St. Louis Labor*, March 8, 1902; KRO, "For the Fair Ones," *CN* (RH), March 22, 1902; FPO, "The Reward of Industry," *CN* (RH), April 5, 1902; "An Impossible Story," *CN* (RH), May 10, 1902; FPO, "Observations," *CN* (RH), April 12, 1902; FPO, "Thought Starters," *CN* (RH), May 31, 1902; "O'Hare's Thots," *CN* (RH), July 26, 1902; and Shore, *Talkin' Socialism*, 123 and 146–52.

7. *St. Louis Labor*, May 31, 1902; FPO to Thais Magrane, April 6, 1947, FOP; *The Socialist* (Seattle), June 8, 1902; *St. Louis Labor*, May 17 and June 14, 1902; *Girard Press*, August 21, 1902; *CN* (RH), May 31, June 7 and 21, July 5, and September 20, 1902; and FPO Mss, 3 and 5.

8. Daniel Bell, "Marxian Socialism in the United States," in Donald D. Egbert and Stow Persons, eds., *Socialism and American Life*, 2 vols. (Princeton: Princeton University Press, 1952), vol. 1, 269; KRO to Samuel Castleton, September 16, 1945, Samuel Castleton Papers, Eugene V. Debs Collection, Tamiment Library, New York, Box 3; FOP Mss, 3; *Beloit Daily Call* (Kans.), September 13, 1902; and KRO, "Women's Department," *CN* (RH), October 4, 1902.

9. *CN* (RH), October 18, 1902; *Hazleton Plain Speaker* (Pa.), quoted in *Frank P. O'Hare* (n.p. [Girard, Kans.], n.d. [1907]); Kipnis, *Socialist Movement*, 139; and FOP Mss, 4.

10. *The Socialist*, November 2, 1902; KRO, "Women's Department," *CN* (RH), November 1, 1902; KRO to Gertie Petzold, October 30, 1902, FOP; *The Worker* (New York), October 19, 1902; and *CN* (RH), October 25, 1902.

11. *Brooklyn Standard-Eagle,* quoted in *Frank P. O'Hare;* FPO to Henry Blumberg, May 7, 1945, and FPO to Ira Kipnis, February 3, 1953, FOP; FOP Mss, 4; KRO, "Women's Department," *CN* (RH), November 15 and December 13, 1902; and Salvatore, *Debs,* 197.

12. FOP Mss, 4; FPO to Ralph Korngold, June 6, 1939; FPO to Ira Kipnis, February 3, 1953; FPO to WEZ, January 8, 1957; and FPO to Max Eastman, June 6, 1958, FOP; and *CN* (RH), February 21, 1903. In later life, O'Hare was proud of the accomplishments of the boys who had studied under him, including Adolph Held (bank president and left-wing activist); Harry Rogoff (managing editor of the *Jewish Daily Forward*); Henry Greenfield (manager of the Debs Memorial Radio station, WEVD); and William Carlin (labor lawyer and Socialist New York Assemblyman). See Adolph Held to FPO, January 19, 1944, FOP.

13. KRO, "Women's Department," *CN* (RH), December 13, 1902, and February 21, 1903; Kate Richards O'Hare, *The Sorrows of Cupid* (St. Louis: National Rip-Saw, 1912), 38; and *CDP,* February 20, 1905. See also *CDP,* November 19 and 21, 1904, January 10, 11, 12, 13, 18, 19, 23, 24, 25, and 28, 1905, and February 2, 3, 4, 6, 8, 11, 13, 15, and 18, 1905; KRO, "Women's Department," *CN* (RH), February 21, 1903; "A Week with the Rank and File," *Fair Play,* March 28, 1903, and Basen, "Kate Richards O'Hare," 173.

14. *CN* (RH), January 10, 1903; *Iowa Socialist* (Dubuque), December 20, 1902; FPO, "Kate Richards O'Hare: A Portrait," *The Call Magazine* (February 1918), annotated copy and FPO to George Petzold (not sent), n.d. [March 1903], FOP; *Cleveland Citizen,* November 22 and 29, 1902; *CN* (RH), December 13 and 27, 1902, January 3 and 17, and February 21, 1903; FPO to Gertie Petzold, March 7, 1903; FPO to Upton Sinclair, January 3, 1958; and FPO to Ralph Korngold, June 6, 1939, FOP; and FOP Mss, 4.

15. FPO to George Petzold (not sent), n.d. [March 1903]; FPO to Irving Dilliard, March 25, 1954; and FPO to Gertie Petzold, March 7, 1903, FOP; *Kansas Agitator* (Garnett), February 27, 1903; and *Girard Press,* January 15 and February 26, 1903.

16. FPO, "The Rise and Fall of the Soap-Boxer," *SLPD,* August 24, 1930; *CN* (RH), July 18, 1903; *Evening Times* (Rochester, N.Y.), May 2, 1903; *Toledo Evening News,* May 18 and June 6, 1903; *Toledo Bee,* June 6, 1903; *CN* (RH), May 23, June 13, July 4, and August 1, 1903; FOP Mss, 10; FPO to Irving Dilliard, n.d. [1957], FOP (Pec); and FPO to Gertie Petzold, June 26, 1903, FOP.

17. *Brown City Banner* (Mich.), July 10 and 17, 1903; *CN* (RH), August 1, 1903; *American Labor Union Journal* (Butte, Mont.), June 25, 1903; *CN* (RH), July 4, 1903; FPO to J. W. Parker et al., February 18, 1956, FOP; FOP Mss, 10; and Alexander Trachtenberg, ed., *The American Labor Year Book, 1917–1918* (New York: Rand School, 1918), 339.

18. *Parkersburg News,* quoted in *Frank P. O'Hare; Wheeling Register,* August 18, 1903; *CN* (RH), August 1, 1903; *Wheeling Register,* August 16 and 19, 1903; FPO to Bobbie O'Hare, n.d. [1955] and FPO to Upton Sinclair, January 3, 1958, FOP; and FOP Mss, 10.

19. *Wheeling Register,* September 1, 2, and 8, 1903; *Cleveland Citizen,* September 26, 1903; *CN* (RH), September 5 and 19, and October 10 and 17, 1903; *Wheeling Register,*

September 4 and 5, 1903; FPO to Bobbie O'Hare, January 6, 1952, FOP; and FOP Mss, 10.

20. Morris Hillquit to Vera Hillquit, January 30, 1903, and Job Harriman to Morris Hillquit, May 2, 1903, Morris Hillquit Papers, State Historical Society of Wisconsin, Madison, Wisc., 1969, microfilm, reel 1; and Kipnis, *Socialist Movement*, 143–49.

21. William Mailly to Morris Hillquit, May 8, 1903, Hillquit Papers, reel 3; William Mailly to Joe Jahn, July 27, 1903, *Socialist Party of America Papers*, reel 3; William Mailly to Morris Hillquit, July 17, October 9, and November 17, 1903, Hillquit Papers, reel 3; and Kipnis, *Socialist Movement*, 176 and 180.

22. *Ohio Socialist* (Dayton), October 10, 1903; FPO to Victor O'Hare, January 24, 1953; FPO to Upton Sinclair, January 3, 1958; FPO to Bobbie O'Hare, January 6, 1952; FPO to Bobbie O'Hare, n.d. [1955], FOP; *Ohio Socialist*, October 17, 1903; and *Cleveland Citizen*, September 26, October 10, 17, 24, and 31 and November 7, 1903.

23. *CDP*, March 20, 1905; Kate Richards O'Hare, *What Happened to Dan* (n.p., n.d.); FPO to Ira Kipnis, February 3, 1953, and FPO to Irving Dilliard, March 25, 1954, FOP; *CN* (RH), May 9, 1903; and Basen, "Kate Richards O'Hare," 173–74.

24. FOP Mss, 5; FPO to Theda Savage, June 21, 1957, and FPO to Gene O'Hare, February 5, 1955, FOP and FPO to Roz Peciulis, October 6, 1959, FOP (Pec).

25. *Neodesha Daily Sun* (Kans.), February 19, 1904, and FPO to Gene O'Hare, February 5, 1955, FOP.

26. FOP Mss, 3; and FPO to Gene O'Hare, February 5, 1955; FPO to Thais Magrane Prescott, March 11, 1955; and FPO to Victor O'Hare, January 24, 1953, FOP.

27. *AtR*, June 18, 1904; FPO, "The Conquest of Coalgate," *Erie People* (Pa.), April 16, 1904; *AtR*, March 26, April 16 and 30, 1904; *Dallas Morning News*, March 17, 1904; Shore, *Talkin' Socialism*, 146; Howard Lynn Meredith, "A History of the Socialist Party in Oklahoma" (Ph.D. diss., University of Oklahoma, 1970), 41–49.

28. *CDP*, June 21, 1904; FPO to Charles A. Smart, February 20, 1939, FOP; *CDP*, April 25, May 16, and June 22, 1904.

29. *Dallas Morning News*, August 8, 1904; FOP Mss, 5; FPO, "Notes on the History of the Socialist Party of Oklahoma," April 15, 1956; FPO to Lucy Henschel, September 8, 1942; FPO to Irving Dilliard, April 12, 1956; FPO to Maury Maverick, November 1, 1940; and FPO, unpublished essay, n.d., FOP; Margaret E. Hall, *A History of Van Zandt County* (Austin, Tex.: Jenkins, 1976), 68–69; and James R. Green, *Grass-Roots Socialism: Radical Movements in the Southwest, 1895–1943* (Baton Rouge: Louisiana State University Press, 1978), 38–40.

30. *Iowa Socialist*, November 12, 1904.

31. Weinstein, *Ambiguous Legacy*, 4–5, and Sklar, *Corporate Reconstruction*, 441.

32. KRO to Gertie Petzold, December 16, 1904, FOP and FOP Mss, 21.

33. *CDP*, January 5 and 10, 1905; FOP Mss, 6 and 21; FPO to Theda Savage, June 21, 1957, and FPO to RB, December 25, 1958, FOP.

34. EVD to Marguerite Bettrich Debs, March 17, 1905, *EVDL*, vol. 1, 203–4; *CDP*, March 21, 1905; and FPO to Roz Peciulis, May 10, 1958, FOP. On Debs, see Ray Ginger, *The Bending Cross* (New Brunswick: Rutgers University Press, 1949), 234–37; Scott Molloy, "Eugene V. Debs," in Mari Jo Buhle, Paul Buhle, and Dan Georgakas, eds., *Encyclopedia of the American Left* (Urbana: University of Illinois

Press, 1992), 184–87; Salvatore, *Debs*, 191–94; Shannon, *Socialist Party*, 12–13; and Weinstein, *Decline of Socialism*, 25–26.

35. *CDP*, April 7, May 30, and June 27, 1905.

36. *CDP*, June 27, 1905; *Oklahoma City Times-Journal*, quoted in *CDP*, June 19, 1905; and *AtR*, June 24 and July 1, 1905.

37. *CDP*, July 5, 1905.

38. James R. Scales and Danny Goble, *Oklahoma Politics: A History* (Norman: University of Oklahoma Press, 1982), 65–67; *Muskogee Times*, July 21, 1905; *AtR*, August 26, 1905; *CDP*, July 5, 1905; FOP Mss, 8 and 9; FPO to Margaret Sanger, January 6, 1956, FOP; and Kate Richards O'Hare, "The Land of Graft," *International Socialist Review* 6 (1906): 603.

39. FPO to George Petzold (not sent), n.d. [March 1903], FOP; Kathleen O'Hare interview with Meredith Tax, July 4, 1971, New York; FOP Mss, 6; FPO to Irving Stone, December 8, 1944, FOP; KRO to Alice Stone Blackwell, January 22, 1924, National American Woman Suffrage Association (NAWSA) Papers, Library of Congress, Washington, D.C.; and *CDP*, September 11, 1905.

40. FPO to Bobbie O'Hare, n.d. [1955], FOP; KRO to Fred Warren, August 5, 1906, J. A. Wayland Collection, Axe Library, Pittsburg State University, Pittsburg, Kans.; FPO to Gene O'Hare, March 28, 1947; FPO to John Stewart, December 16, 1952; FPO to Mrs. Biese, May 22, 1956; and KRO to Gertie Petzold, December 17, 1906, FOP; and FOP Mss, 21.

41. FPO to WEZ, April 1, 1942, FOP; FPO, "The Oklahoma Vote," *International Socialist Review* 9 (1909): 519; Meredith, "Socialist Party in Oklahoma," 51–53; Green, *Grass-Roots Socialism*, 41; and Salvatore, *Debs*, 236.

42. *AtR*, September 8, July 21, August 11, and September 1, 15, and 22, 1906, and Salvatore, *Debs*, 37–38.

43. FPO to Paul Dennie, September 1957, FOP; FPO to Theodore Debs, November 10, 1925, *Debs Papers*, reel 5; *AtR*, October 20, 1906; Ginger, *Bending Cross*, 244–55; FPO to Ralph Chaplin, n.d. [1948] and FPO, "Debs," n.d. [1930s], FOP; FOP Mss, 14; William D. Haywood, *The Autobiography of Big Bill Haywood* (New York: International, 1983), 190–206; and Shore, *Talkin' Socialism*, 177.

44. *AtR*, December 15, 1906; FPO to Gertie Petzold, February 2, 1907, FOP; and *Frank P. O'Hare.*

45. KRO to Gertie Petzold, April 9 and 21, 1907, FOP.

46. *AtR*, June 1, 1907; *Frank P. O'Hare*; *Arkansas Sentinel* (Fayetteville), April 3, 1907; *AtR*, March 23 and 30, April 13 and 27, and May 4, 1907; *Newport Daily Independent*, May 31, 1907; FPO Mss, 18; FPO to "brother in X-to Rains," February 17, 1954, and FPO to Irving Dilliard, January 21, 1950, FOP.

47. *Commercial Appeal* (Memphis), May 13, 1907.

48. Ameringer, *If You Don't Weaken*, Introduction by James Green, 233. See also xvii–xxxviii and 227–42; FPO, "We Didn't Make Much Money but We Had a Lot of Fun," *American Socialist* 5 (March 1958): 17; FOP Mss, 6; FPO to Irving Dilliard, June 24, 1958; FPO, "Obituary notes," November 10, 1943; FPO to John McManus, August 1, 1957, FOP; *St. Louis Star*, November 12, 1943; and FPO to RB, n.d. [1955], FOP (Pec). Ameringer does not mention Frank O'Hare in his *Autobiography*,

although, as will be seen, this was probably due to a break between the two men when they worked together at the *American Guardian*. Ameringer's references to "my companion" (*If You Don't Weaken*, 237–38) are clearly to Frank O'Hare.

49. *Newport Daily Independent*, November 19, 1907; FPO, "Kate Richards O'Hare: A Portrait"; FOP Mss, 18; and John M. Work, *What's So and What Isn't* (New York: Vanguard, 1905; reprint, 1927).

50. Kipnis, *Socialist Movement*, 199–206; Victor Berger to Morris Hillquit, March 29, 1909, Hillquit Papers, reel 1; Salvatore, *Debs*, 211–12; Ginger, *Bending Cross*, 262–63; Pratt, *Hillquit*, 12–13 and 56–83; Weinstein, *Decline of Socialism*, 25–26; and Shannon, *Socialist Party*, 12–17.

51. Salvatore, *Debs*, 220–21.

52. *Chicago Daily Socialist*, June 10, 1908; Meredith, "Socialist Party in Oklahoma," 58–71; Green, *Grass-Roots Socialism*, 39 and 233–34; Danny Goble, *Progressive Oklahoma: The Making of a New Kind of State* (Norman: University of Oklahoma Press, 1980), 112–13; *AtR*, October 5, 1907; and *South West American* (Ark.), April 3, 1907.

53. Socialist Party, *Proceedings of the National Convention* (Chicago: Socialist Party, 1908), 21, 182, and 179; Ernest Poole, "Harnessing Socialism," *American Magazine* 66 (September 1908): 427–32; Green, *Grass-Roots Socialism*, 79–80; and Kipnis, *Socialist Movement*, 218. On Simons and the farm question, see Algie M. Simons, *The American Farmer* (Chicago: Charles Kerr, 1908), 38–44 and 83–95, and Kent Kreuter and Gretchen Kreuter, *An American Dissenter: The Life of Algie Martin Simons, 1870–1950* (Lexington: University of Kentucky Press, 1969), 59–60.

54. *Proceedings of the National Convention*, 150 (see also 148–65); Kreuter and Kreuter, *Simons*, 99–106; Ginger, *Bending Cross*, 262–64; Salvatore, *Debs*, 221–23; and Kipnis, *Socialist Movement*, 207–9 and 293.

55. *AtR*, October 31, 1908; KRO to Gertie Petzold, October 28, 1908, FOP; *AtR*, August 22, 1908; FOP Mss, 9; KRO to Gertie Petzold, June 30, 1908, and FPO to Irving Stone, December 8, 1944, FOP; and KRO to Alice Stone Blackwell, January 22, 1924, NAWSA Papers.

56. *AtR*, July 25 and August 22, 1908; FPO, "The Oklahoma Vote," 519; Meredith, "Socialist Party in Oklahoma," 78–82; Ginger, *Bending Cross*, 269–84; Green, *Grass-Roots Socialism*, 72–75; Kipnis, *Socialist Movement*, 212–13; and Salvatore, *Debs*, 224.

57. FPO, "The Oklahoma Vote," 519–20; FPO, *Putting Socialism Across* (St. Louis: National Ripsaw, 1916); FPO to Irving Dilliard, April 12, 1956; FPO, "Notes on the History of the Socialist Party of Oklahoma," April 15, 1956; FPO to Ray Ginger, n.d. [1949]; and FPO, unpublished essay, n.d., FOP; FOP Mss, 6, 7, and 9; *AtR*, October 2, 1909; Richey Alexander, "The Socialist Encampment," *Southern Worker* (Huntington, Ark.) (April–May 1913): 7–8; "The Oklahoma Encampment," International Socialist Review 10 (September 1909): 278–79; and Ameringer, *If You Don't Weaken*, 265–67.

58. FOP Mss, 9; and FPO to Ralph, January 3, 1957, and FPO to Tom Hennings Jr., July 2, 1957 (not sent), FOP. For a summary of recent scientific literature on the connection between malaria and mental disorder, see "The Interrelationship of Tropical Disease and Mental Disorder: Conceptual Framework and Literature Review: I. Malaria," *Culture, Medicine and Psychiatry* 9 (June 1985): 121–200.

59. FOP Mss, 14 and 9; FPO to Tom Hennings Jr., July 2, 1957 (not sent), FOP; and FPO to Irving Dilliard, 1957, FOP (Pec); FPO, *Putting Socialism Across* (St. Louis: National Ripsaw, 1916); and *Chicago Daily Socialist,* January 18 and May 17, 1910.

60. Ameringer, *If You Don't Weaken,* 269; FPO to Gertie Petzold, May 1, 1910, KRO to Gertie Petzold, May 30, 1910, and FPO to Gertie Petzold, May 25, 1910, FOP.

61. *Kansas City Daily Journal,* June 26, 1910; KRO, "How Oklahoma Talks Socialism to the Farmer," *Chicago Daily Socialist,* September 16, 1910; *Kansas City Times,* November 7, 1910; *AtR,* June 11 and July 16, 1910; *Kansas City Star,* September 11, 1910; *Kansas City Times,* September 20, 1910; Sally M. Miller, "Kate Richards O'Hare: Progression toward Feminism," *Kansas History* 7 (winter 1984–1985): 271, and Basen, "Kate Richards O'Hare," 186–88.

62. KRO to Gertie Petzold, February 25, 1911, FOP; FPO, "Kate Richards O'Hare: A Portrait"; FOP Mss, 14 and 15; and KRO to Samuel Castleton, September 16, 1945, Castleton Papers, Box 3.

63. *AtR,* January 4, 1902.

3. Editorial Career, 1911–1917

1. FPO to Gertie Petzold, February 2, 1907, FOP; FOP Mss, 15; and Miller, *From Prairie to Prison,* 80–81.

2. Gary M. Fink, "The Evolution of Social and Political Attitudes in the Missouri Labor Movement, 1900–1940" (Ph.D. diss., University of Missouri–Columbia, 1968), 4–59.

3. Marie Algor, "Gottlieb Hoehn—A Labor and Socialist Pioneer"; Martin A. Dillmon, "William A. Brandt—Labor Pioneer"; and Memorandum, William A. Brandt, June 24, 1914, Socialist Party of St. Louis and Missouri Records, 1909–1964, Western Historical Manuscript Collection, University of Missouri–St. Louis, Box 7; Weinstein, *Ambiguous Legacy,* 9–13; Salvatore, *Debs,* 246–47; and Miller, *From Prairie to Prison,* 52–53 and 83–87.

4. FOP Mss, 15 and FPO to Ralph Korngold, May 13, 1939, FOP.

5. FOP Mss, 15; FPO to J. W. Parker, February 18, 1956, FOP; EVD to Fred D. Warren, January 19, 1914, *EVDL,* vol. 2, 93; and KRO to Samuel Castleton, September 16, 1945, Castleton Papers, Box 3.

6. FPO to Victor O'Hare, January 18, 1955, FOP; FPO to Roz Peciulis, November 6, 1959, FOP (Pec); and FPO to Victor O'Hare, December 15, 1952, FOP.

7. FPO to Thais Magrane Prescott, March 11, 1955, and FPO to Upton Sinclair, January 3, 1958, FOP.

8. Kathleen O'Hare interview with Meredith Tax, July 4, 1971.

9. KRO, "What Shall I Do?" *Reedy's Mirror* (St. Louis), May 11, 1911, 13–14.

10. *NR-S* (June 1911), 5; "Colonel Maple Quits," *NR-S* (August 1911), 1; "Sept. Rip-Saw Lectures," *NR-S* (November 1911), 22; *NR-S* (February 1913), 14; *NR-S* (March 1914), 18; and FPO, *Putting Socialism Across* (St. Louis: National Ripsaw, 1916).

11. FPO, "How the Socialist Party Is Managed," *NR-S* (September 1911), 6; "Circulation Chat," *NR-S* (September 1911), 29; "Circulation Chat," *NR-S* (October 1911), 14–15; "The Winona Encampment," *NR-S* (October 1911), 21; "Sept. Rip-Saw Lectures," *NR-S* (November 1911), 22; and "Circulation Chat," *NR-S* (December 1911), 30.

12. KRO to Gertie Petzold, February 3, 1912, FOP; *Chicago Daily Socialist*, February 24, 1912; FPO to Ray Ginger, January 3, 1950, FOP; "Circulation Chat," *NR-S* (July 1912), 9; "Mrs. O'Hare at Home," *NR-S* (April 1912), 30; *NR-S* (September 1912), 4; FPO, "Kate Richards O'Hare: A Portrait," *The Call Magazine* (February 1918), annotated copy, FOP; and KRO to family, October 4, 1912, FOP. The literature on the history and neurophysiology of cocaine is enormous, but see Lester Grunspoon and James B. Bakalar, *Cocaine: A Drug and Its Social Evolution* (New York: Basic, 1976), 40–41; David F. Musto, "America's First Cocaine Epidemic," *Wilson Quarterly* 13 (summer 1989): 59–64; Robert M. Malow and Jeffrey A. West, "Personality Disorders Classification and Symptoms in Cocaine and Opioid Addicts," *Journal of Consulting and Clinical Psychology* 57 (1989): 765–67; Sally L. Satel et al., "Clinical Phenomenology and Neurobiology of Cocaine Abstinence: A Prospective Inpatient Study," *American Journal of Psychiatry* 148 (1991): 1712–16; and Frank H. Gawin, "Cocaine Addiction: Psychology and Neurophysiology," *Science,* March 29, 1991, 1580–85.

13. FPO to Victor O'Hare, n.d., FOP (Pec) and Kathleen O'Hare interview with Meredith Tax, July 4, 1971.

14. FPO to James Aronson, November 14, 1955, FOP and "Circulation Chat," *NR-S* (May 1912), 28.

15. FPO, "The National Socialist Convention," *NR-S* (June 1912), 6–7; Socialist Party, *National Convention of the Socialist Party Held at Indianapolis, May 12 to 18, 1912* (Chicago: Socialist Party, 1912), 122–41; Ginger, *Bending Cross,* 308–10; Kipnis, *Socialist Movement,* 396–407; and Salvatore, *Debs,* 248.

16. FPO, "The National Socialist Convention," *NR-S* (June 1912), 6–7; Salvatore, *Debs,* 249; Morris Hillquit to Victor Berger, July 22, 1912, Victor L. Berger Papers, Wisconsin State Historical Society, Madison, Wisc., Box 12; Socialist Party, *National Convention, 1912,* 4–5 and 164–65; *Christian Socialist* (Chicago), June 27, 1912; Ginger, *Bending Cross,* 310; Kipnis, *Socialist Movement,* 408–10; and Weinstein, *Decline of Socialism,* 93 and 103.

17. "The Rip-Saw Illustrated Lectures," *NR-S* (September 1912), 24.

18. "Rip-Saw Picture Show Informs and Enthuses Thousands," *NR-S* (November 1912), 24; *Birmingham Age-Herald,* October 21, 1912; *Labor Advocate* (Birmingham), October 25, 1912; and *Winston-Salem Journal,* November 1, 1912; Robert B. Ringler to Fred Warren, May 28, 1912, and Warren to Ringler, May 31, 1912, J. A. Wayland Collection, Axe Library, Pittsburg State University, Pittsburg, Kans.; and "Everybody's Doin' It!" *NR-S* (December 1912), 20–21.

19. *Tampa Morning Tribune,* October 28, 1912; FPO to KRO, October 29, 1912, FOP; and KRO, "Coming Out of the Night," *NR-S* (December 1912), 30.

20. KRO quoted in Ginger, *Bending Cross,* 314; Shore, *Talkin' Socialism,* 217–18; Salvatore, *Debs,* 392n25; H. G. Creel, "A Memory of Wayland," *NR-S* (December

1912), 22; FPO to Henry Blumberg, May 5, 1949, FOP; *AtR,* November 23, 1912; and *Girard Press,* November 14, 1912.

21. "Circulation Chat," *NR-S* (March 1913), 28–29; "Circulation Chat," *NR-S* (April 1913), 31; "Circulation Chat," *NR-S* (May 1913), 23; "Circulation Chat," *NR-S* (July 1913), 15; "Everybody's Doin' It!" *NR-S* (December 1912), 20–21; and Shannon, *Socialist Party,* 77–78.

22. *Industrial Worker* (Spokane, Wash.), May 22 and July 3, 1913; *AtR,* May 24 and August 9, 1902, and November 12, 1910; Salvatore, *Debs,* 252–56; and Miller, *From Prairie to Prison,* 99–100.

23. "Frank O'Hare Visits Ruskin," *NR-S* (May 1913), 22; "Ruskin and Morris Park Colonies," *NR-S* (June 1913), 3; "Get a Home in Florida," *NR-S* (May 1913), 2; "Get Insured Land for a Home in South Florida," *NR-S* (October 1913), 19; FPO to Aurora Miller, March 26, 1949, FOP; and Miller, *From Prairie to Prison,* 104–5.

24. "Socialists and the Little Hookworm," *NR-S* (April 1913), 20 and FPO to Irving Dilliard, June 24, 1958, FOP.

25. Victor Berger to Morris Hillquit, October 23, 1913, and Algie Martin Simons to Morris Hillquit, January 22, 1914, Hillquit Papers, reel 2 and Sally M. Miller, *Victor Berger and the Promise of Constructive Socialism, 1910–1920* (Westport, Conn.: Greenwood, 1973), 61–62.

26. *Party Builder* (Chicago), November 1, 1913; FPO to Corliss Lamont, April 30, 1954, FOP (Pec); KRO to Samuel Castleton, September 16, 1945, Castleton Papers, Box 3; KRO, "The Ghost of the Past and the Spirit of the Future," *NR-S* (February 1914), 6–7, 20, and 22; Sally M. Miller, "Americans and the Second International," *Proceedings of the American Philosophical Society* 120 (1976): 375 and 377; Shannon, *Socialist Party,* 26; and *Party Builder,* December 20, 1913, and January 3, 1914.

27. *NR-S* (January 1914), 22–23; *Hamilton Evening Journal* (Ohio), January 13, 1914; *Cambridge Daily Jeffersonian* (Ohio), January 5, 1914; "Picture Show Notes," *NR-S* (February 1914), 27; "Stereo Opticon Sources of Information," n.d. [c. 1914–1915], Socialist Party Papers, State Historical Society of Wisconsin, Box 10; and *Sunlight* (Carmen, Okla.), August 7, 1914.

28. "Now, Darn You, Will You Get Busy," *NR-S* (February 1914), 24; FPO to James Aronson, November 14, 1955, FOP (Pec); EVD to Fred Warren, January 19, 1914, and EVD to Walter Lanfersiek, July 8, 1914, *EVDL,* vol. 2, 93 and 105; FPO to Ira Kipnis, February 3, 1953; FPO, unpublished draft, "Debs," n.d.; and FPO to WEZ, n.d. [1942], FOP.

29. EVD to FPO, February 14, 1915, *EVDL,* vol. 2, 128–29; EVD to FPO, July 1, 1915, *EVDL,* vol. 2, 170–71; EVD to FPO, December 31, 1915, *EVDL,* vol. 2, 215–18; FPO to Theodore Debs, n.d. [1916], *EVDL,* vol. 2, 219–21; Theodore Debs to Phil Wagner, September 30, 1915, *EVDL,* vol. 2, 193–94; and "Debs—Rip-Saw Rallies— Kate O'Hare," *NR-S* (January 1916), 18.

30. "Statement by the Rip-Saw," *American Socialist* (Chicago), September 12, 1914; FPO, *Putting Socialism Across;* and FPO to Ralph Korngold, May 13, 1939, FOP.

31. "Why Is a Local?" *NR-S* (February 1914), 36–37; "Why Is a Party?" *NR-S* (April 1914), 18; and "State Organization," *NR-S* (March 1914), 44.

32. Basen, "Kate Richards O'Hare," 176–79.

33. Allan L. Benson to EVD, March 24, 1915, *EVDL,* vol. 2, 146 and Weinstein, *Decline of Socialism,* 103–15.

34. Robert H. Ferrell, *Woodrow Wilson and World War I, 1917–1921* (New York: Harper and Row, 1985), 8–9; Shannon, *Socialist Party,* 90–91; Weinstein, *Decline of Socialism,* 120–25; and Alexander Trachtenberg, ed., *The American Labor Year Book, 1916* (New York: Rand School, 1916), 29.

35. "Our Martyred Comrade," *NR-S* (September 1914), 10–11, and FPO to Frank Lynch, July 9, 1939, FOP.

36. "The Bankers' Pool," *NR-S* (November 1914), 18–19; "Open Letter to President Wilson," *NR-S* (February 1915), 5; FPO, "Kate Richards O'Hare: A Portrait"; "I Denounce," *NR-S* (March 1915), 1; "Shall Red Hell Rage?" *NR-S* (June 1915), 6–7; "To the Mothers and Maids of America," *NR-S* (August 1915), 5–6; "Breed, Mother, Breed," *NR-S* (September 1915), 5–6; FPO and KRO, *World Peace* (St. Louis: National Ripsaw, 1915); and Weinstein, *Decline of Socialism,* 124–25.

37. Arthur S. Link, *Wilson,* vol. 3, *The Struggle for Neutrality* (Princeton: Princeton University Press, 1960), 27; Link, *Wilson,* vol. 4, *Confusions and Crises, 1915–1916* (Princeton: Princeton University Press, 1964), 26–27; FOP Mss, 15; FPO to Florence Moog, May 27, 1955, FOP; Peggy Lamson, *Roger Baldwin: Founder of the American Civil Liberties Union* (Boston: Houghton Mifflin, 1976), 49; *SLPD,* May 2 and 3 and December 1, 1914, January 25, May 2, and September 30, 1915; *St. Louis Globe-Democrat,* May 3, 1914; "Report of the Labor Committee to the Mayor's Conference on Unemployment, St. Louis," December 18, 1914, Socialist Party Papers (Madison, Wisc.), Box 1; and FPO to William Korfmacher, April 7, 1945, FOP.

38. "Has Henry Ford Made Good?" *NR-S* (January 1916), 6, 8–10; "Some More 'Ford,'" *NR-S* (February 1916), 6, 8–11, and 13; and Philip S. Foner, *History of the Labor Movement in the United States,* vol. 6, *On the Eve of America's Entrance into World War I* (New York: International, 1982), 5–12.

39. FOP Mss, 26; "A Conversation with Henry Ford," *NR-S* (March 1916), 6, 8–9, and 23; and FPO to Leo Huberman, September 14, 1957, and FPO to Harvey O'Connor, March 17, 1954, FOP.

40. Debs quoted in Ginger, *Bending Cross,* 332–33; "The Oklahoma Earthquake," *NR-S* (September 1916), 6 and 8; Trachtenberg, ed., *American Labor Year Book, 1917–1918,* 336–38; Link, *Wilson,* vol. 5, *Campaigns for Progressivism and Peace, 1916–1917* (Princeton: Princeton University Press, 1965), 125; J. A. H. Hopkins to Woodrow Wilson, November 14, 1916, in Arthur S. Link et al., eds., *The Papers of Woodrow Wilson* (Princeton: Princeton University Press, 1967–1994), vol. 38, 642; and Basen, "Kate Richards O'Hare," 188–89.

41. "A Trip to Old Kentucky," *NR-S* (January 1917), 21 and 27, and FPO, "Kate Richards O'Hare: A Portrait."

42. KRO to Phil Wagner, March 2, 1918, FOP; Wilbur S. Shepperson, *Retreat to Nevada: A Socialist Colony of World War I* (Reno: University of Nevada Press, 1966), 66–71; and Phil Wagner, "Llano Del Rio Colony," *SR* (October 1917), 23.

43. "Social Revolution," *SR* (March 1917), 1.

44. *SR* (March 1917), 13 and FPO to "brother in X-to Rains," February 17, 1954, FOP.

45. KRO, "My Country," *SR* (April 1917), 5 and FOP Mss, 15.

46. Morris Hillquit, *Loose Leaves from a Busy Life* (New York: Macmillan, 1934), 165; Trachtenberg, ed., *American Labor Year Book, 1917–1918*, 50–53 and 373–79; Pratt, *Hillquit*, 116–22; and *Proceedings, Emergency Convention of the Socialist Party of America* (Chicago: Socialist Party, 1917), second day, morning session, 12–13.

47. Hillquit, *Loose Leaves*, 167; KRO to Samuel Castleton, September 16, 1945, Castleton Papers, Box 3; and Foner, *History of the Labor Movement in the United States*, vol. 7, *Labor and World War I* (New York: International, 1987), 34.

48. KRO, "You Are Playing with Fire, Gentlemen!" *SR* (May 1917), 8; Irving Howe, *Socialism and America* (New York: Harcourt Brace Jovanovich, 1985), 44–45: and William Preston Jr., *Aliens and Dissenters: Federal Suppression of Radicals, 1903–1933* (New York: Harper and Row, 1963), 46–49.

49. Woodrow Wilson to Robert Lansing, May 11, 1917, *Wilson Papers*, vol. 42, 274; Joseph P. Tumulty to Woodrow Wilson, May 8, 1917, *Wilson Papers*, vol. 42, 245–47; U.S. Congress, *40 Stat*, 219 (1917); Richard Polenberg, *Fighting Faiths: The Abrams Case, the Supreme Court, and Free Speech* (New York: Viking, 1987), 27–28; H. C. Peterson and Gilbert C. Fite, *Opponents of War, 1917–1918* (Seattle: University of Washington Press, reprint, 1968), 15–17; *SR* (May 1917), 1; and Ferrell, *Woodrow Wilson and World War I*, 202–3.

50. "Mrs. Kate Richards O'Hare's Address at Atlanta," April 17, 1917," U.S. Department of Justice, Records of the Federal Bureau of Investigation, Record Group 65, Investigative Case Files of the Bureau of Investigation, Old German Files [OG] 11324, National Archives, Washington, D.C., and *SLPD*, April 30, 1917.

51. KRO to O'Hare children, May 18, 1917; FPO to Marius Hansome, October 23, 1940; FPO to Gertie Petzold, October 25, 1917; and John C. Granbery, "William Edward Zeuch, Apostle of Abundance," n.d. [1939], FOP.

52. "To Our Readers," *SR* (August 1917), 1; "Rally to the Rescue, Comrades, *SR* (November 1917), 3; and FPO to Paul, n.d. [1952], FOP.

53. Woodrow Wilson to Albert S. Burleson, July 13, 1917, *Wilson Papers*, vol. 43, 164; Wilson to William Kent, July 17, 1917, *Wilson Papers*, vol. 43, 193; Edward M. House to Wilson, October 17, 1917, *Wilson Papers*, vol. 44, 393; and P. E. Marrinan, "Re—Kate Richards O'Hare, Socialist Activities," July 21, 1917, OG11324. See also Woodrow Wilson to Amos Pinchot, July 13, 1917; Max Eastman, Amos Pinchot, and John Reed to Wilson, July 12, 1917; and William Kent to Wilson, July 16, 1917, *Wilson Papers*, vol. 43, 164–66, 190, and 193, and Joseph P. Tumulty to Wilson, October 30, 1917; Upton Sinclair to Wilson, October 22, 1917; and Wilson to Burleson, October 30, 1917, *Wilson Papers*, vol. 44, 467–73.

54. *Congressional Record*, 65th Cong., 1st sess., 5390; Indictment, *United States v. Kate Richards O'Hare*, Records of U.S. Attorney and Marshals, District of North Dakota, Record Group 118, National Archives, Kansas City, Box 1; "A Criminal at the Bar of Justice: A Personal Narrative, *SR* (September 1917), 2 and 5; Miller, *From Prairie to Prison*, 145; and WEZ, *The Truth about the Kate Richards O'Hare Case* (St. Louis: Frank O'Hare, 1919), 8–13.

4. Family Martyrdom, 1917–1920

1. FPO to Kathleen O'Hare, n.d. [c. 1940] and Kathleen O'Hare to FPO, February 14, 1945, FOP.

2. FPO to Harvey O'Connor, August 2, 1956, FOP; "Join Us in Florida," *SR* (September 1917), 11; and KRO, "A Criminal at the Bar of Justice," *SR* (September 1917), 2 and 5. On the Green Corn Rebellion, see Green, *Grass-Roots Socialism*, 358–72; Ameringer, *If You Don't Weaken*, 347–56; Shannon, *Socialist Party*, 106–9; and H. C. Peterson and Gilbert C. Fite, *Opponents of War, 1917–1918* (Seattle: University of Washington Press, reprint, 1968), 40–41.

3. FPO to Gertie Petzold, October 25, 1917, and Kitty to Gertie Petzold, n.d. [fall 1917], FOP; "I Want Successful Farmers" and KRO, "Waiting!," *SR* (December 1917), 10 and 4; "Bills Paid in Oct. 1917," FOP; Kathleen O'Hare interview with Meredith Tax, July 4, 1971; and C. S. Weakley to Department of Justice, November 3, 1917, U.S. Department of Justice, Records of the Federal Bureau of Investigation, Record Group 65, Investigative Case Files of the Bureau of Investigation, Old German Files [OG] 11324, National Archives, Washington, D.C.

4. Victor Berger to Robert La Follette, October 23, 1917, Berger Papers, Box 10; J. Louis Engdahl, "Socialist Electoral Results in 1917," in Trachtenberg, ed., *American Labor Year Book, 1917–1918*, 341–42; Morris Hillquit to Victor Berger, November 13, 1917, Berger Papers, Box 10; Eugene V. Debs, "The November Elections," *SR* (December 1917), 5; and Weinstein, *Decline of Socialism*, 145–76. On the liberal protest vote, see Walter Lippmann to Edward M. House, October 17, 1917, and Herbert Croly to Wilson, October 19, 1917, Link et al., eds., *Papers of Woodrow Wilson*, vol. 44, 393–94 and 408–10.

5. Gregory quoted in Peterson and Fite, *Opponents of War*, 148–49; EVD to Louis Kopelin, December 14, 1917, *EVDL*, vol. 2, 348; Foner, *History of the Labor Movement in the United States*, vol. 7, *Labor and World War I*, 315–16; Weinstein, *Decline of Socialism*, 162; Salvatore, *Debs*, 289; and Louis Kopelin to Wilson, December 4, 1917, *Wilson Papers*, 45: 203.

6. WEZ, *The Truth about the Kate Richards O'Hare Case* (St. Louis: Frank O'Hare, 1919), 4–13.

7. WEZ, *The Truth*, 14, and KRO, *Socialism and the World War* (St. Louis: Frank P. O'Hare, 1919), 1, 20, and 30.

8. "Indictment," *United States v. Kate Richards O'Hare*, Records of U.S. Attorney and Marshals, District of North Dakota, Record Group 118, National Archives, Kansas City, Box 1; "Transcript of Testimony," Records of U.S. Attorney and Marshals, District of North Dakota, Record Group 118, National Archives, Kansas City, Box 1, 1–44; and Frank P. O'Hare, "The Case of Kate Richards O'Hare" in Alexander Trachtenberg, ed., *The American Labor Year Book, 1919–1920* (New York: Rand School, 1920), 103–4.

9. "Transcript of Testimony," 45–52.

10. Ibid., 54–65.

11. Ibid., 65–123.

12. Ibid., 125–42.

13. KRO, "Guilty!" *SR* (February 1918), 2, and Edward J. Brennan to H. G. Clabaugh, December 8, 1917; W. H. Lamar to Martin J. Wade, December 10, 1917, and Martin J. Wade to Albert S. Burleson, December 17 [*sic* December 7], 1917, OG11324.

14. "Proceedings on the Sentencing of Mrs. Kate Richards O'Hare," December 14, 1917, *United States v. Kate Richards O'Hare*, 6–21.

15. Ibid., 24–45, and *New York Times*, December 15, 1917.

16. KRO, "Guilty!" *SR* (February 1918), 2; KRO to Phil Wagner, March 2, 1918, FOP; and WEZ, *The Truth*, 15–19.

17. FPO to EVD, December 27, 1917, *EVDL*, vol. 2, 349–51.

18. EVD to FPO, January 2 and 12, 1918, *EVDL*, vol. 2, 353–60 and 363–64.

19. KRO to FPO, January 5, 1920, *DS*.

20. FPO to Ray Ginger, August 30, 1948, FOP; FPO to EVD, March 4, 1918, *EVDL*, vol. 2, 380–81; Morris Hillquit to Adolph Germer, February 12, 1918, Hillquit Papers, reel 2; FPO to Kathleen O'Hare, n.d. [c. 1940] and FPO to A. James McDonald, February 24, 1947, FOP; and Adolph Germer to Morris Hillquit, February 8, 1918, Hillquit Papers, reel 2.

21. EVD to FPO, March 2, 1918; and FPO to EVD, February 28, 1918, *EVDL*, vol. 2, 375–78; *New York Call*, February 17, 1918; and FPO, "Kate Richards O'Hare."

22. Phil Wagner to KRO, February 26, 1918; KRO to Wagner, March 2, 1918; FPO to Phil Wagner and EVD, March 12, 1918; and FPO to EVD, March 31, 1918, FOP.

23. Charles Barrett to Commanding Officer, February 1918, U.S., *Surveillance of Radicals in the United States, 1917–1941* (Frederick, Md.: University Publications of America, 1984), microfilm, reel 6; and Arthur L. Barkey to Department of Justice, March 1, 1918; Robert B. Judge to Department of Justice, April 4, 1918; and John E. Farley to Department of Justice, April 29, 1918, OG11324.

24. FPO to Phil Wagner and EVD, March 12, 1918, and FPO to EVD, March 31, 1918, FOP; FPO to EVD, February 28, 1918, *EVDL*, vol. 2, 375–77; FPO to R. W. Earlywine, March 1, 1918, FOP; EVD to FPO, April 1, 1918, *EVDL*, vol. 2, 392–93; and FPO to Eugene and Theodore Debs, April 3, 1918, FOP.

25. "Declaratory," *The Social Builder* (May 1918), 8; Phil Wagner to EVD, May 17, 1918, *EVDL*, vol. 2, 417; FPO to Ralph Korngold, May 13, 1939, FOP; Martin J. Wade to Julius L. O'Brien, April 28, 1918, U.S. Department of Justice, Record Group 60, Classified Subject Files, 186233–225, National Archives, Washington, D.C.; Melvin Hildreth to B. R. Goggins, April 8, 1918, *United States v. Kate Richards O'Hare*, Box 1; FPO to Frank Lynch, July 9, 1939, and FPO to Max Eastman, June 6, 1958, FOP; "Liberty Defense Union Sweeping the Country," *The Social Builder* (May 1918), 8; FPO to EVD, February 28, 1918, *EVDL*, vol. 2, 375–77 and KRO, "Why We Are Weary," *Unity*, May 16, 1927, 174–75.

26. R. W. Finch to Department of Justice, October 23, 1918, and Special Employee Akers to Department of Justice, October 3, 1918, OG11324; Kathleen O'Hare interview with Meredith Tax, July 4, 1971; Dwight MacDonald, "In Defense of Everybody, II," *New Yorker*, July 18, 1953, 35; and *O'Hare v. United States*, October 23, 1918, 253 *Federal Reporter*.

27. Philip S. Foner, *History of the Labor Movement in the United States*, vol. 8, *Postwar Struggles, 1918–1920* (New York: International, 1988), 237–38; Burl Noggle, *Into the*

Twenties: The United States from Armistice to Normalcy (Urbana: University of Illinois Press, 1974), 84–102; and Weinstein, *Decline of Socialism,* 172–86.

28. *Iowa Unionist* (Des Moines), January 23, 1919; J. H. Daly to Department of Justice, January 25, 1919, and S. M. Cox to Department of Justice, January 22, 1919, OG11324; and Augustus Graham to Intelligence Office, Camp Dodge, January 20, 1919, *Surveillance of Radicals.*

29. A. P. Sherwood to Department of Justice, March 11, 1919, OG 11324; KRO, *Americanism and Bolshevism* (St. Louis: Frank O'Hare, 1919), 5; and *New York Times,* March 4, 1919.

30. FPO foreword in KRO, *Americanism and Bolshevism,* 3 and Louis Lobl to Department of Justice, April 2, 1919, OG11324.

31. Lynn J. Frazier to FPO, April 8, 1919, and Edward W. Herbert to Department of Justice, March 22, 1919, Classified Subject Files, 186233–225.

32. Adolph Germer to Morris Hillquit, April 9 and March 22, 1919, Hillquit Papers, reel 2.

33. FPO to A. Mitchell Palmer, April 16, 1919, Classified Subject Files, 186233-225; FPO, "Note" in KRO to FPO, March 17, 1920, DS; and J. Louis Engdahl, *Debs and O'Hare in Prison* (Chicago: Socialist Party, 1919), 40–42.

34. Alfred Bettman to John Lord O'Brian, March 6, 1919; Bettman to O'Brian, April 8, 1919; Alexander King to O'Brian, May 19, 1919; O'Brian to A. Mitchell Palmer, May 27 and 28, 1919; Palmer to O'Brian, April 8, 1919; Bettman to Harold Hanes, April 16, 1919; Hanes to Bettman, April 17, 1919; Bettman to O'Brian, April 25, 1919; O'Brian to King, May 17, 1919; and Woodrow Wilson, Executive Clemency for Kate Richards O'Hare, n.d. [1919], U.S. Department of Justice, Records of the Pardon Attorney, Record Group 204, Case File 35-30, National Archives, Washington, D.C.

35. Martin J. Wade to A. Mitchell Palmer, June 11, 1919, Classified Subject Files, 186233-225; "Petition of American War Mothers Chapter No. 1," February 2, 1920, and Palmer to Woodrow Wilson, May 28, 1920, Records of the Pardon Attorney; and George S. Johns to John T. Creighton, March 26, 1920, Classified Subjects Files, 9-19-603-99.

36. FPO to Ray Ginger, August 30, 1948, FOP and *FOB,* November 8, 1919. See also *FOB,* September 12 and 19, 1919, and February 16, 1921, and Kathleen O'Hare interview with Meredith Tax, July 4, 1971.

37. KRO to FPO, April 20, 1919, *Kate O'Hare's Prison Letters* (Girard, Kans.: Appeal to Reason, 1919), 3; FPO to *Unity,* May 6, 1928, FOP; and *Prison Letters,* 68n1. Sally Miller has observed that "it is feasible to assume that the fact of the onset of menopause added an additional complication for Kate O'Hare." See Miller, *From Prairie to Prison,* 169.

38. KRO to FPO, June 8, and April 20, 1919, *Prison Letters,* 33 and 4; KRO to FPO, May, 3, 1919, *DS;* Emma Goldman, *Living My Life,* Richard and Anna Maria Drinnon, eds. (New York: Meridian, 1977, reprint), 677–78; and Foner and Miller, eds., *Kate Richards O'Hare,* 27.

39. FPO to Friends, July, 3, 1919, *DS;* J. F. Fishman to Attorney General, August 27, 1919, FOP; and KRO to FPO, August 21, 1919, *DS.*

40. KRO to FPO, August 10, 1919, *Prison Letters*, 72; KRO to FPO, August 28, 1919, *DS;* and Weinstein, *Decline of Socialism,* 192–210.

41. KRO to FPO, September 7, 1919, *DS;* Foner, *Postwar Struggles,* 239–48; and Weinstein, *Decline of Socialism,* 210–22.

42. Basen, "Kate Richards O'Hare," 176–77.

43. KRO to FPO, November 16, 1919, *DS; FOB,* December 13, 1919; KRO to FPO, December 7, 1919, *DS;* Foner, *Postwar Struggles,* 263; Weinstein, *Decline of Socialism,* 229–30; Lincoln Colcord, "The Committee of Forty-Eight," *Nation* 109 (December 27, 1919): 821–22; and Stanley Shapiro, "The Twilight of Reform: Advanced Progressives After the Armistice," *The Historian* (May 1971): 349–64.

44. William Brandt to Otto Branstetter, March 2, 1920, *Socialist Party of America Papers,* reel 9. On the O'Hare's disenchantment with the Committee of Forty-Eight, see KRO to FPO, April 6, 1920, *DS.* On the St. Louis City Club "Nuts' Table" (or "Crank's Table" as Roger Baldwin called it), see Lamson, *Roger Baldwin,* 63.

45. FPO to Bill, June 1954, FOP (Pec); *FOB,* February 21, 1920, and January 31, 1920; KRO to FPO, September 7, 1919, *DS;* Shore, *Talkin' Socialism,* 220; and Emanuel Haldeman-Julius, *My Second 25 Years: Instead of a Footnote, an Autobiography* (Girard, Kans.: Haldeman-Julius, 1949), 70.

46. KRO to FPO, August 17, 1919, *Prison Letters,* 77; KRO to FPO, October 11, 1919, and February 28, 1920, *DS;* Emma Goldman, "Kate Richards O'Hare Testimonial Dinner Address, November 17, 1919," Alexander Berkman Papers, Tamiment Library, New York, Box 1; *FOB,* January 17, 1920; KRO to FPO, September 28 and November 23, 1919; January 5 and March 27, 1920, *DS; FOB,* January 10 and 31 and July 17, 1920; and KRO to FPO, June 8 and 15, 1919, *Prison Letters,* 33 and 37. A copy of the January 17, 1920, *FOB* was seized by postal authorities at Jacksonville, Florida, and forwarded to the Department of Justice as "mail matter of questionable character" under the Espionage Act. See Postmaster, Jacksonville, Florida to Solicitor General, Post Office Department, January 26, 1920, U.S. Post Office Department, Records of the Post Office Department, Record Group 28, B 308.

47. Victor Berger to Morris Hillquit, August 20, 1919, Hillquit Papers, reel 2; FPO to John McManus, August 1, 1957, FOP; and KRO to FPO, May 31, 1919, *Prison Letters,* 28.

48. KRO to Otto Branstetter, February 8, 1920; Branstetter to KRO, February 14, 1920; KRO to Branstetter, February 24, 1920; Branstetter to KRO, February 26, 1920; and Branstetter to FPO, February 26, 1920, *Socialist Party Papers,* reel 9 and Socialist Party of St. Louis, Official Minutes, General Committee, November 3, 1919, Socialist Party of St. Louis and Missouri Records, 1909–1964, Western Historical Manuscript Collection, University of Missouri–St. Louis, Box 1.

49. FPO to Branstetter, n.d. [c. March 1, 1920], *Socialist Party Papers,* reel 9.

50. *FOB,* March 13, 1920; George Roewer to Otto Branstetter, March 12 and 13, 1920, *Socialist Party Papers,* reel 9; *FOB,* May 29, 1920; Branstetter to FPO, April 10, 1920, and FPO to Branstetter, May 3, 1920, *Socialist Party Papers,* reel 9; FPO to Dick O'Hare and KRO, April 30, 1920, FOP; KRO, "Why We Are Weary," *Unity,* May 16, 1927, 174–75; KRO to FPO, April 17 and 22, 1920, *DS;* and Robert L.

Morlan, *Political Prairie Fire: The Nonpartisan League, 1915–1922* (St. Paul: Minnesota Historical Society Press, reprint, 1985), 250.

51. Socialist Party, National Convention Proceedings, 1920, *Socialist Party Papers,* reel 76; KRO to FPO, May 23, 1920, FOP; Shannon, *Socialist Party,* 155–56; and *New York Times,* May 14, 1920.

52. Otto Branstetter, "Amnesty Work of the Socialist Party," n.d. [1922], *Socialist Party Papers,* reel 77; A. Mitchell Palmer to Woodrow Wilson, May 28, 1920, Records of Pardon Attorney; E. A. Solanka to Department of Justice, June 19, 1920, OG11324; *St. Louis Star* quoted in Solanka to Department of Justice, June 19, 1920, OG11324; *FOB,* May 15 and June 12, 1920; *New York Times,* May 30, 1920; and Elizabeth Glendower Evans to A. Mitchell Palmer, May 14, 1920; Palmer to Evans, May 21, 1920; Palmer to Pardon Attorney, May 21, 1920; W. H. Painter to Palmer, May 29, 1920; and Palmer to Painter, May 29, 1920, Records of Pardon Attorney.

53. *FOB,* June 12, 1920; *New York Times,* June 1, 1920; E. A. Solanka to Department of Justice, June 19, 1920, OG11324; and FPO to Corliss Lamont, August 15, 1955; FPO to Anna Louise Strong, August 8, 1957; FPO to Samuel Castleton, April 19, 1945; and FPO to Ammon Hennacy, October 5, 1957, FOP.

54. Burke to Callaghan, June 21, 1920, OG11324; John Maguire to Peter Gilmartin, June 22, 1920, OG386508; Robert Healey to Department of Justice, June 30, 1920, OG11324; "Kate O'Hare Visits Debs," *Socialist World* (July 1920), 8–9; Morris Hillquit to Eugene Debs, June 20, 1920, Hillquit Papers, reel 2; and Weinstein, *Decline of Socialism,* 235–36. For Engels's essay "On Morality," see Robert C. Tucker, ed., *The Marx-Engels Reader* (New York: Norton, 1972), 667.

55. *FOB,* July 17, 1920; Kate Richards O'Hare, *In Prison* (St. Louis: Frank O'Hare, 1920); and Polenberg, *Fighting Faiths,* 317.

5. "A Tragic Four Years," 1921–1924

1. FPO to Eugene, Berta, and Michael O'Hare, April 28, 1960, FOP. On "normalcy," see John F. Wilson, "Harding's Rhetoric of Normalcy, 1920–1923," *Quarterly Journal of Speech* 48 (December 1962): 406–11.

2. Warranty Deed, February 5, 1919; FPO to Robert Brodie, August 5, 1921; FPO to Mary Brite, July 16, 1929; FPO to Victor O'Hare, January 8, 1954; FPO, letter fragment, n.d. [1957]; and "Outline Agreement," January 1921, FOP and *NR-S* (February 1921), 4.

3. *NR-S* (April 1921), 4 and "Agreement Between the National Rip-saw Publishing Company and Fisher and Hightower," March 15, 1921, FOP.

4. *FOB,* February 16, 1921.

5. *NR-S* (April 1921), 4 and FPO, "Keep Plugging Away," *NR-S* (May 1921), 5.

6. E. W. Hosa, "Radical Situation," Omaha, Nebraska, December 14, 1920, U.S. Department of Justice, Records of the Federal Bureau of Investigation, Record Group 65, Bureau Section Files, 202600; Circular, "The Rip-saw Rallies for 1921," December 11, 1920, FOP; and Lt. Col. Gordon Johnston to Director of Military Intelligence, October 21, 1920, U.S., *Surveillance of Radicals,* reel 6.

7. "Plans Perfected for the Prosecution of Twin Falls Kidnappers," *NR-S* (September 1921), 5; *NR-S* (August 1921), 1–6; D. F. Costello to General Intelligence Division, July 3, 1921, U.S. Department of Justice, Record Group 60, Classified Subject Files, 9-19-603, National Archives, Washington, D.C.; *New York Times*, July 2, 3, and 5, 1921; and Hugh Lovin, "The Banishment of Kate Richards O'Hare," *Idaho Yesterdays* 22 (spring 1978): 20–25.

8. *DD*, April 10, 1944; Kathleen O'Hare interview with Meredith Tax, July 4, 1971; and Roy Eilers to FPO, April 2, 1921; FPO to Ed Wittcoff, n.d. [1942]; and FPO, Drawing and Specifications, December 7, 1918, FOP. On the history of adding and calculating machines, see James W. Cortada, *Before the Computer: IBM, NCR, Burroughs, and Remington Rand and the Industry They Created, 1865–1956* (Princeton: Princeton University Press, 1993), 25–43.

9. FPO to Swift, April 7, 1921, and FPO to A. James McDonald, October 7, 1952, FOP; Haldeman-Julius, *My Second 25 Years*, 70–71; Paul M. Buhle, "The Appeal to Reason," in Joseph R. Conlon, ed., *The American Radical Press*, 2 vols. (Westport, Conn.: Greenwood, 1974), vol. 1, 58–59; and Gene DeGruson, "Little Blue Books," *Encyclopedia of the American Left*, 429–30.

10. FOP mss., 7 and Memorandum, March 16, 1921; FPO, letter fragment, n.d. [1957]; Agreement, July 14, 1921; Stock Certificates, July 15, 1921; FPO to Victor O'Hare, December 15, 1952; FPO to Caroline, n.d. [1952]; and FPO to John, September 26, 1956, FOP.

11. *New York Times*, August 10, 1919, and Robert Brodie to KRO, June 8, 1921, and FPO to Robert Brodie, August 5, 1921, FOP.

12. Emil A. Solanka, "General Intelligence Report," St. Louis, September 10, 1921, Bureau Section Files, 202600; "We're One Year Old Today," *NR-S* (October 1921), 4 and FPO to Mary Brite, July 16, 1929, FOP.

13. "The November Issue," *NR-S* (October 1921), 3; *NR-S* (November 1921), 2 and 10; and Katherine Debs to KRO, October 17 and 29, 1921, *EVDL*, vol. 3, 252 and 260–61.

14. Theodore Debs to Jim [James Oneal], April 1, 1927, Castleton Papers, Box 3; Theodore Debs to FPO, November 9, 1921; Katherine Debs to KRO, December 7, 1921, and Theodore Debs to FPO, December 22, 1923, FOP; *NR-S* (January 1922), 5; and Salvatore, *Debs*, 326–27.

15. Nagel quoted in *New York Call*, September 10, 1922; KRO, "Political Prisoners' Dependents," *NR-S* (February 1921), 11; American Civil Liberties Union, "Federal Political Prisoners Still in Prison," (n.p., 1922); Theodore Debs to FPO, January 21 and 28, 1922; FPO to Mary Brite, July 16, 1929; and FPO to Ralph Chaplin, n.d. [1948], FOP; and Otto Branstetter, "The Children's Crusade: Supplemental Report on Amnesty Work by the National Executive Committee to the National Convention," 1922, *Socialist Party of America Papers*, reel 9. This last document contains several letters written back and forth between the National Office and the O'Hares.

16. Branstetter, "The Children's Crusade"; KRO to Caroline Lowe, January 26, 1922, FOP; and "The Children's Crusade for Amnesty," *NR-S* (February 1922), 5.

17. Branstetter, "The Children's Crusade."

18. Ibid. and FPO, "Only a Subscription Campaign!" *NR-S* (March 1922), 4.

19. Branstetter, "The Children's Crusade."

20. Ibid.; FPO to Mary Brite, July 16, 1929, and FPO to William Bradford Huie, June 7, 1956, FOP; EVD to FPO, March 6, 1922, *EVDL*, vol. 3, 296–97, and KRO, "The Case of Stanley J. Clark," *NR-S* (February 1922), 7.

21. *SLPD*, April 17, 1922; Branstetter, "The Children's Crusade"; "The Children's Crusade," March 10, 1922, Circular 2C1; FPO to *Unity*, May 6, 1928; and FPO, fragmentary letter, n.d. [1942], FOP; "All for Amnesty," *NR-S* (April 1922), 2; and *New York Times*, March 29, 1922.

22. FPO to Lucy Henschel, September 13, 1942, FOP; KRO, "The Children's Crusade" in Foner and Miller, eds., *Kate Richards O'Hare*, 334–37; FPO to John, September 26, 1956; FPO, "The Children's Crusade for Amnesty," April 13, 1922, Circular 2C9; FPO to Mary Brite, July 16, 1929; and FPO to WEZ and Covington Hall, February 24, 1945, FOP; *SLPD*, April 18, 19, and 27, 1922; and *Terre Haute Post*, April 18, 1922.

23. Mary Heaton Vorse, "The Children's Crusade for Amnesty," in Dee Garrison, ed., *Rebel Pen: The Writings of Mary Heaton Vorse* (New York: Monthly Review, 1985), 95; Elizabeth Gurley Flynn, *The Rebel Girl* (New York: International, reprint, 1982), 292–96; FPO to Iris Kipnis, February 3, 1953; FPO to John, September 26, 1956; and FPO to Corliss Lamont, August 15, 1955, FOP; Elizabeth Gurley Flynn, "The Hotel Workers Union and the Children," in Rosalyn F. Baxandall, ed., *Words on Fire: The Life and Writing of Elizabeth Gurley Flynn* (New Brunswick: Rutgers University Press, 1987), 176–78; *SLPD*, April 27, 1922; and KRO, "The Children's Crusade," 338–39.

24. KRO, "The Children's Crusade," 339; Roger N. Baldwin, *The Reminiscences of Roger Nash Baldwin* (Glen Rock, N.J.: Microfilming Corporation of America, 1972), 295; and FPO to Irene Peciulis, March 7, 1958, and FPO to Mary Brite, July 16, 1929, FOP.

25. FOP mss., 29; *Washington Evening Star*, April 29 and May 6, 8, and 11, 1922; and Murray E. King, "Washington Receives Children's Crusade," *NR-S* (April–May 1922), 9.

26. Theodore Debs to FPO, May 18, 1922, and FPO to Theodore Debs, May 19, 1922, FOP; *Congressional Record*, 67th Cong., 2d sess., June 7, 1922, 8353; Theodore Debs to FPO, May 20, 1922, FOP; "The Crusade Holds the Fort, *NR-S* (June 1922), 2 and "The Children's Crusade Still Game," *NR-S* (July 1922), 5.

27. Theodore Debs to FPO, July 6, 1922, FOP; "Let's Get Busy," *NR-S* (September 1922), 4; EVD to KRO and FPO, September 27 [1922], and FPO to EVD, October 5, 1922, FOP; and "The Crusade Rests," *NR-S* (August 1922), 7.

28. FPO to Mary Brite, July 16, 1929; FPO to Charles A. Smart, February 20, 1939; EVD to FPO, October 7 [1922]; FPO to Eugene, Katherine, and Theodore Debs, December 19, 1923; and FPO to Lucy Henschel, September 1942, FOP; Flynn, *Rebel Girl*, 296; Salvatore, *Debs*, 326; Ralph Chaplin, *Wobbly: The Rough-and-Tumble Story of an American Radical* (Chicago: University of Chicago Press, 1948), 311–24; Dwight MacDonald, "In Defense of Everybody, II," *New Yorker*, July 18, 1953, 35, 36; and Peterson and Fite, *Opponents of War*, 284.

29. Bertha Hale King letter, *Unity,* July 11, 1927, 276–77; James Oneal letter, *Unity,* July 11, 1927, 277; FPO to Max Eastman, June 6, 1958, and FPO to Ralph Chaplin, n.d. [1948], FOP; and KRO, "Why We Are Weary," *Unity,* May 16, 1927, 174–75.

30. James Oneal letter, *Unity,* 277.

31. KRO letter, *Unity,* May 7, 1928, 194–95.

32. Morris Hillquit to Adolph Germer, February 12, 1918, Hillquit Papers, reel 2.

33. FOP Mss, 17; *NR-S* (October 1922), 6; *AV* (November 1922): 4–8 and 11; and FPO to Walter Groth, June 1, 1948, FOP.

34. KRO, "Are We Headed Straight for Perdition?" *AV* (November 1923): 1.

35. FMGN, 1–2, and FOP Mss, 17. For Pickett's own version of events at New Llano, see "Life History Document of Mr. George T. Pickett," in Fred Hanover, "Llano Cooperative Colony: An American Rural Community Experiment," MSW thesis, Tulane University, 1936, 225–30.

36. Ernest S. Wooster, *Communities of the Past and Present* (New York: AMS, 1974, reprint), iii and 117–31; Paul K. Conkin, *Two Paths to Utopia: The Hutterites and the Llano Colony* (Lincoln: University of Nebraska Press, 1964), 103–17; Robert V. Hine, *California's Utopian Colonies* (New Haven: Yale University Press, 1966), 114–31; A. James McDonald, *The Llano Co-operative Colony and What It Taught* (Leesville, La.: privately printed, 1950), 11–30; and Edward K. Spann, *Brotherly Tomorrows: Movements for a Cooperative Society in America, 1820–1920* (New York: Columbia University Press, 1989), 269–71.

37. Conkin, *Two Paths,* 126 (see also 103–67) and Henrik Infield, *Cooperative Communities at Work* (New York: Dryden, 1945), 37–52.

38. George Pickett to FPO, February 5, 1923, and FPO to A. James McDonald, April 11, 1948, FOP; *AV* (February 1923): 4; FOP Mss, 17; KRO to A. James Mc-Donald, n.d. [1947], FOP; and McDonald, *Llano,* 31.

39. FMGN, 2–3; "Shake Hands with the Vanguard Army," *AV* (September 1923): 14; "Comrade Kate's Shop Talks," *AV* (April 1923): 3; FPO to Corliss Lamont, November 1956, FOP (Pec); FOP Mss, 17; and FPO to Irving Dilliard, June 5, 1952, and FPO to A. James McDonald, August 21, 1947, FOP.

40. FPO to A. James McDonald, August 21, 1947, FOP; FMGN, 3; A. James McDonald to Walter Groth, May 24, 1948, FOP; FOP Mss, 17; and FPO to Winfield Gaylord, January 24, 1933; FPO to Joshua and David, October 28, 1954; FPO Journal, April 26, 1959; and FPO to Charles Smart, February 20, 1939, FOP.

41. KRO, *Kuzbasing in Dixie* (New Llano, La.: New Llano Publications, 1926), 5; FPO to Gertie Petzold, December 26 and July 2, 1923, FOP; FMGN, 4; Kathleen O'Hare interview with Meredith Tax, July 4, 1971; Raymond and Charlotte Koch, *Educational Commune: The Story of Commonwealth College* (New York: Schocken, 1972), 19; and FPO to Doris Wheeler, April 22, 1954, FOP.

42. KRO to A. James McDonald, n.d. [1947], FOP.

43. FPO to Gertie Petzold, July 2, 1923; FPO to Walter Groth, June 1, 1948, and FPO to A. James McDonald, August 21, 1947, FOP; KRO, *Kuzbasing in Dixie,* 2–4 and 24; A. James McDonald to FPO, November 5, 1953, FOP; Haywood, *Autobiography of Big Bill Haywood,* 364; and McDonald, *Llano,* 32.

44. KRO, *In Prison* (New York: Knopf, 1923), 19 and 165; FPO, flyleaf inscription, July 10, 1952, FOP (Pec); *Book Review Digest* (New York: H. W. Wilson, 1924), 443;

FPO to Victor O'Hare, December 15, 1952, and FPO to Irving Dilliard, December 24, 1954, FOP; Foner and Miller, *Selected Writings*, 24–28; and Jack M. Holl, Introduction to *In Prison*, by KRO (Seattle: University of Washington Press, reprint, 1976), xvii–xix.

45. FPO to Selig Perlman, October 3, 1956, FOP; FMGN, 5; FPO, "A Dream Come True—Commonwealth College Here!" *AV* (April 1923): 8–9; Koch and Koch, *Educational Commune*, 13; William H. Cobb, "Commonwealth College Comes to Arkansas, 1923–1925," *Arkansas Historical Quarterly* 23 (summer 1964): 104–5; and McDonald, *Llano*, 32–33.

46. "Commonwealth College Opens Monday, October 1st, 1923," *AV* (May 1923): 13 and "Commonwealth College Opens," *AV* (October 1923): 3, 6, 7, and 10.

47. Hall quoted in Koch and Koch, *Educational Commune*, 17; FMGN, 72; A. James McDonald to KRO, July 7, 1947, FOP; and George Pickett to WEZ, August 12, 1923, Henry Edward Wilson Collection, Newllano Colony Papers, University of Arkansas Libraries, Fayetteville, Ark.

48. FMGN, 32–33; A. James McDonald to KRO, July 7, 1947, FOP; George Pickett to WEZ, August 12, 1923, and A. James McDonald to Pickett, January 24, 1923 [*sic,* 1924], Wilson Collection.

49. FPO to Gertie Petzold, December 26, 1923, FOP; RB, *Reminiscences*, 325; and Lamson, *Roger Baldwin*, 148–49.

50. *AV* (January 1924): 3; FMGN, 11; KRO to Alice Stone Blackwell, February 6, 1924, NAWSA Papers; FPO, "Now to Destroy the Prison Factory Trust!" *AV* (April 1924): 1; "Statement of Ownership," *AV* (November 1923): 15; *AV* (February 1924): 1; and KRO, "Prisons, Profits, Politics, and Patriotism," *AV* (April 1924): 8, 9, 12, 13. On the general interest in the problem of prison labor in the mainstream press during this time, see Bruce P. Disque, "Prison Progress," *Atlantic* 9 (March 1922): 330–37; "Convict Labor: 1923," *Monthly Labor Review* 18 (April 1924): 699–731; "Forward, March!" *Nation* 117 (October 3, 1923): 342; "A Victim of Convict 'Slavery,' " *Literary Digest* 77 (April 21, 1923): 41–44 and 46; Adolph Lewison, "Prisons and Prison Labor," *Century* 106 (July 1923): 399–404; and *New York Times*, January 13, May 20 and 21, August 5 and 19, September 2, November 18 and 28, 1923, and March 2, 1924.

51. McDonald, *Llano*, 33–34 and A. James McDonald to Pickett, January 24, 1923 [*sic,* 1924] and February 3, 1924, Wilson Collection.

52. WEZ and KRO to Llano Board, April 14, 1924; "A Paper Read . . . by Geo. T. Pickett," April 17, 1924; WEZ to George Pickett, February 17, 1924; Pickett to WEZ, February 18, 1924; and RB to Pickett, March 28, 1924, Wilson Collection.

53. Petition, April 23, 1924, William A. Gilbert Papers, University of Arkansas Libraries, Fayetteville, Ark., and FMGN, 72.

54. McDonald, *Llano*, 36; "Vanguard Monthly Labor Report," May 16, 1924, Gilbert Papers; and Cobb, "Commonwealth College," 1.

55. FMGN, 12; "The Prison Factory Trust!" *AV* (May 1924): 1; and KRO, "The Story of the 'Big Yank'," *AV* (May 1924): 6–12.

56. FPO to EVD, May 25, 1924; FPO to A. James McDonald, February 24, 1947; and FPO, "Memorandum to Field Force," May 27, 1924, FOP.

57. FMGN, 76; WEZ, "The Purpose of the Free Forum Meeting Was to Present Charges against the Management of the Llano Co-Operative Colony," June 23, 1924,

Wilson Collection; Cobb, "Commonwealth College," 113; McDonald, *Llano*, 35; and FPO to "Field Force," June 18, 1924, FOP.

58. *AV* (June 1924): 1 and FPO to A. James McDonald, April 11, 1948, and FPO to Duncan McDonald, October 30, 1950, FOP.

59. FPO to "Field Force," June 18, 1924, and FPO to "Bombing Squad," June 19, 1924, FOP.

60. "Commonwealth News and Views," *AV* (July 1924): 8; FMGN, 14; and FPO to Victor O'Hare, December 15, 1952; FPO to A. James McDonald, April 11, 1948; FPO to Harold Z. Brown, June 25, 1924; and FPO to Duncan McDonald, October 30, 1950, FOP.

61. FPO to Winfield Gaylord, January 24, 1933; FPO to Walter Groth, June 1, 1948; FPO to A. James McDonald, August 21, 1947; and FPO to A. James McDonald, October 7, 1952, FOP; and FOP Mss, 17.

62. *AV* (September 1924): 11; FMGN, 9 and 22; KRO, "Wayside Tales," *AV* (August 1924): 3; and FPO to Gertie Petzold, November 19, 1924, and FPO to KRO, August 28, 1924, FOP.

63. FPO to Gertie Petzold, November 19, 1924; KRO to FPO, October 10, 1924; FPO to KRO, August 28, 1924; and FPO to KRO, November 1, 1924, FOP.

64. FPO to KRO, Dick O'Hare, and Wilbur C. Benton, November 13, 1924, FOP.

65. KRO to FPO, October 10, 1924, FOP; Baldwin, *Reminiscences*, 328; and Walter Groth to A. James McDonald, May 20, 1948, FOP.

66. FMGN, 7, 16–23, and 52; Koch and Koch, *Educational Commune*, 20–21; A. James McDonald to Walter Groth, May 24, 1948; Walter Groth to A. James McDonald, May 20, 1948; and "Memorandum," n.d. [1924], FOP; Conkin, *Two Paths*, 153; and Infield, *Cooperative Communities*, 47.

67. FPO to Gertie Petzold, November 19, 1924, FOP.

68. Kathleen O'Hare interview with Meredith Tax, July 4, 1971; and FPO to KRO, August 2, 1925, FOP.

69. Kathleen O'Hare interview with Meredith Tax, July 4, 1971; FPO to KRO, August 2, 1925, and FPO to Bobbie O'Hare, n.d. [c. 1942], FOP; and Roger A. Bruns, *The Damndest Radical: The Life and World of Ben Reitman* (Urbana: University of Illinois Press, 1987), 221–23.

70. FPO to KRO, December 23, 1924; FPO to Victor O'Hare, January 2, 1953; FPO to Ammon Henacy, October 5, 1957; and FPO to A. James McDonald, November 9, 1953, FOP.

71. FPO to KRO, December 23, 1924; KRO to FPO, December 23, 1924; FPO to KRO, December 26, 1924; KRO to FPO, December 29, 1924; and FPO to Victor O'Hare, December 15, 1952, FOP.

72. KRO to FPO, January 19, 1925; FPO to Duncan McDonald, October 30, 1950; FPO to A. James McDonald, February 24, 1947; and FPO to Spurgeon O'Dell, June 12, 1939, FOP; *Oregon Daily Journal*, April 3, 1926; FPO to Victor O'Hare, December 15, 1952, FOP; FPO, "How the Prison Racket Was Beaten," *SLPD*, April 1, 1943; *New York Times*, April 10, December 18 and 20, 1928, and August 21, 1929; Louis N. Robinson, *Should Prisoners Work?* (Chicago: Winston, 1931), 90–118; and Holl, "Introduction," xxv–xxvi.

73. FPO to Spurgeon O'Dell, June 12, 1939, and FPO to Mary D. Brite, July 16, 1929, FOP.

74. FPO to Ralph Korngold, June 6, 1939, FOP.

6. Hard Times, 1925–1940

1. FPO to Kathleen O'Hare, n.d. [1940], FOP.

2. Orville G. Brim Jr., "Theories of the Male Mid-Life Crisis," *Counseling Psychologist* 6 (1976): 2–9 and Daniel J. Levinson et al., *The Seasons of a Man's Life* (New York: Knopf, 1978), 192–259.

3. FPO to KRO, January 20 and 21, 1925, and KRO to Folks and KRO to FPO, January 19, 1925, FOP.

4. FPO to Gene O'Hare, March 28, 1947, FOP (Pec); FPO to Tom Hennings Jr., July 2, 1957; FPO to KRO, April 26, 1925; and FPO to Susan Meston, February 1, 1941, FOP; and FPO to Ray, January 21, 1944, FOP (Pec).

5. FPO to Tom Hennings Jr., July 2, 1957; FPO to Duncan McDonald, October 30, 1950; FPO to Victor O'Hare, January 2, 1953; FPO to WEZ, September 7, 1942; FPO to Dick O'Hare, October 26, 1938; FPO to A. James McDonald, November 9, 1953; and FPO to Doris, n.d. [1950], FOP, and FPO to Corliss Lamont, April 30, 1954, and FPO to Gene O'Hare, March 28, 1947, FOP (Pec). When Gertie Petzold died in 1938, Frank discovered that his half sister had saved all of the letters that he and Kate had written to her. This correspondence is now part of the O'Hare collection at the Missouri Historical Society. Ironically, a few years after Frank's bonfire, Kate O'Hare's collection of papers "was destroyed by a fanatical young female Communist at Commonwealth College because 'they were not class-conscious.' " KRO to Samuel Castleton, September 16, 1945, Castleton Papers, Box 3.

6. FPO to Gene O'Hare, March 28, 1947, FOP (Pec) and FPO to Alice Stone Blackwell, June 14, 1925, NAWSA Papers.

7. FPO to KRO, August 2, 1925; Charles R. Zalliel, "Specification," July 1925; and FPO to Bobbie O'Hare, n.d. (April 1943), FOP.

8. FPO to A. James McDonald, April 23, 1947, and FPO to Victor O'Hare, December 15, 1952, FOP; and Harold Bronco [Harold Brown et al.], "The Family Album," *The World Tomorrow* 9 (February 1926): 55–56; and FPO to Ray, January 21, 1944, FOP (Pec).

9. FPO to Gene O'Hare, March 28, 1947, FOP (Pec) and FPO, "Specifications," n.d. [1925]; Roy Eilers to FPO, August 7, 1925; and FPO to Loeb, August 23, 1925, FOP.

10. FPO to Mary D. Brite, July 16, 1929, FOP; Samuel Haber, *Efficiency and Uplift: Scientific Management in the Progressive Era, 1890–1920* (Chicago: University of Chicago Press, 1964), 65 and 153–55; and Kreuter and Kreuter, *Simons,* 201–10.

11. Julian Glasgow to FPO, November 1, 1926; FPO to Tom Hennings Jr., July 2, 1957; FPO to Duncan McDonald, October 30, 1950; and FPO to Kathleen O'Hare, January 19, 1943, FOP; and *Saint Louis Optimist,* November 16, 1927.

12. KRO to FPO, March 24 and April 4, 1926, FOP.

13. KRO to FPO, April 4 and 26, 1926, FOP.

14. KRO to Kathleen O'Hare, n.d. [1926], FOP; FPO to Theodore Debs, November 10, 1926, *Papers of Eugene V. Debs,* reel 5; and FPO to Dick O'Hare, December 18, 1926; FPO to Bobbie O'Hare, n.d. (1942); and FPO to Eugene, Berta, and Michael O'Hare, April 28, 1960, FOP.

15. *SLPD,* September 13, 1927, and FPO to Irene Reynolds, September 25, 1927, and FPO to Bobbie O'Hare, n.d. (1942), FOP.

16. KRO to FPO, October 13, 1927, FOP.

17. FPO to WEZ and Covington Hall, February 24, 1945; FPO to Russell Wilbur, October 16, 1931; and Wilbur Benton to FPO, April 11, 1928, FOP.

18. FPO to Mary D. Brite, July 16, 1929, FOP; *SLPD,* March 22, 1928; FPO to Duncan McDonald, October 30, 1950, FOP; *St. Louis Daily Globe-Democrat,* March 23, 1928; and FPO to Spurgeon O'Dell, June 12, 1939, FOP.

19. FPO to Cousin Susie, November 29, 1928, FOP; *New York Times,* November 30, 1928; *SLPD,* November 30, 1928; *St. Louis Star-Times,* November 30, 1928; *St. Louis Daily Globe-Democrat,* November 29 and 30, 1928; and *Commonwealth College Fortnightly,* December 15, 1928.

20. KRO to FPO, March 4, 1929; KRO to FPO, March 19, 1929; KRO to FPO, March 29, 1929; Eugene O'Hare to FPO, March 31, 1929; KRO to FPO, April 20, 1929, and Telegram, Kathleen O'Hare to KRO, March 17, 1929, FOP.

21. FPO to Spurgeon O'Dell, June 12, 1939; FPO, "Accounts Payable," 1929; FPO to Bobbie O'Hare, n.d. [April 1943]; FPO to Hilda Mills and Wilbur C. Benton, September 23, 1929; Sworn Statements of Hilda Mills and Wilbur C. Benton, November 8, 1929; and Charles Cunningham to Russell Wilbur, October 2, 1931, FOP.

22. *Saint Louis Optimist,* November 16, 1927; FPO to Mary D. Brite, July 16, 1929, FOP; FPO, "James Eads How Seen through Eyes of an Old Friend," *SLPD,* July 27, 1930; FPO to Doris, n.d. [1950], FOP; Kreuter and Kreuter, *Simons,* 210; Norman Thomas to FPO, March 25, 1929, and Eugene O'Hare to FPO, March 13, 1930, FOP; and [St. Louis] *Pepperbox,* April 15, 1930, 3–4.

23. FPO, "The Rise and Fall of the Soap-Boxer," *SLPD,* August 24, 1930.

24. *LN,* September 13, 1930, 1; *LN,* September 20, 1930, 8; Doug Reynolds, "Federated Press," *Encyclopedia of the American Left,* 225–27; and Jesse L. O'Connor, Harvey O'Connor, and Susan M. Bowler, *Harvey and Jesse: A Couple of Radicals* (Philadelphia: Temple University Press, 1988), 49.

25. *LN,* October 11, 1930, 8, and "Cleveland O'Hare List of 1000," FOP Mss 22.

26. *LN,* May 9, 1931, 4; December 6, 1930, 8; December 6, 1930, 8; January 3, 1931, 8; January 10, 1931, 1 and 8 and March 28, 1931, 8.

27. *LN,* April 4, 1931, 4; May 9, 1931, 4; November 22, 1930, 8; May 2, 1931, 8; and Harvey O'Connor, Press Release, March 16, 1931, and "Federated Press Associates," n.d. [1931], FOP.

28. *LN,* June 27, 1931, 4 and July 11, 1931, 4.

29. *LN,* July 11, 1931, 4 and July 18, 1931, 4.

30. FPO, "Manufacturing without Men," *SLPD,* August 17, 1931; Simon Mohun, "Automation," in Tom Bottomore, ed., *A Dictionary of Marxist Thought* (Cambridge: Harvard University Press, 1983), 39–40; James W. Markham, *Bovard of the*

Post-Dispatch (Baton Rouge: Louisiana State University Press, 1954), 179–94; and Daniel W. Pfaff, *Joseph Pulitzer II and the Post-Dispatch* (University Park: Pennsylvania State University Press, 1991), 197–210. On the role of scientific management in the degradation of labor in the 1920s, see Michael E. Parrish, *Anxious Decades: America in Prosperity and Depression, 1920–1941* (New York: Norton, 1992), 89.

31. *LN,* August 8, 1931, 4; September 12, 1931, 4; August 29, 1931, 1 and 4; and September 19, 1931, 4.

32. Frank L. Palmer to FPO, October 27, 1931, FOP and *LN,* October 3, 1931, 4.

33. *LN,* October 31, 1931, 1 and 4; and Harvey O'Connor to FPO, November 3, 1931, and February 15, 1932, and FPO to Dick O'Hare, May 29, 1933, FOP.

34. *LN,* October 31, 1931, 4; FPO to Victor O'Hare, February 18, 1955, and FPO to Sarah Rhue, March 6, 1958, FOP (Pec); Henry Blumberg to FPO, February 14, 1932; FPO to Lancelot Hogben, August 1, 1937; and FPO to Walter Thomas Mills, July 13, 1939, FOP. On Blumberg's career, see "Henry Blumberg," *Who Was Who in America,* vol. 7, *1977–1981* (Chicago: Marquis Who's Who, 1981), 58, and obituary, *School and Society,* July 15, 1950, 46.

35. FPO to Dick O'Hare, October 26, 1938, FOP; FPO, "A Breadline View of New York City," *SLPD,* March 1, 1932; FPO to Clark, January 17, 1932, FOP; Parrish, *Anxious Decades,* 415; Robert S. McElvaine, *The Great Depression: America, 1929–1941* (New York: Times, 1984), 72–94 and Richard H. Pells, *Radical Visions and American Dreams: Culture and Social Thought in the Depression Years* (New York: Harper and Row, 1973), 76.

36. FPO, "The Clerkless Shop," *The Railway Clerk* (June 1932), 215–16; and FPO to Doris, n.d. [1950]; FPO to Dick Bland, April 10, 1932; Harvey O'Connor to FPO, April 27, 1932; FPO to Winfield R. Gaylord, January 24, 1933; FPO to Elwood Street, October 2, 1937; FPO to Gene O'Hare, December 8, 1938; Phil Ziegler to FPO, June 8, 1932; and Anne E. Geddes to FPO, June 10, 1932, FOP.

37. FPO to Dick O'Hare, May 29, 1933; and FPO to Samuel Castleton, April 3, 1945, FOP; and Shannon, *Socialist Party,* 196.

38. Kathleen O'Hare to FPO, June 19, 1935; FPO to Dave, May 5, 1936; FPO, unpublished mss., April 6, 1935; FPO to Irene O'Hare, September 1 [1934]; R. O. Hagerty to FPO, December 27, 1934; and FPO to Bess Goldstein, October 4, 1941, FOP.

39. FPO to Dave, May 5 and 27, 1936; Parrish, *Anxious Decades,* 317–18; and Pells, *Radical Visions,* 86–87.

40. FPO to Dave, May 27, 1936 and FPO, address, April 5, 1937, FOP.

41. FPO to Dick Bland, March 17, 1937; FPO to Dick O'Hare, April 28, 1937; Irene O'Hare to FPO, May 28, 1937; and FPO to Irene O'Hare, June 8, 1937; and FPO to Kathleen O'Hare, June 30, 1937, FOP.

42. FPO to Juan Oliver, October 23, 1937; FPO to Flint Garrison, November 10, 1937; FPO to Victor O'Hare, March 17, 1938; FPO to Irene O'Hare, November 3, 1937; and Memorandum, Caradine Hat Co., n.d. [1938], FOP.

43. FPO to Spurgeon O'Dell, June 12, 1939; FPO to Gene O'Hare, December 6, 1938; FPO to Bess Goldstein, October 4, 1941; FPO to Dick O'Hare, August 29, 1938; and FPO to Dick, Gene, and Victor O'Hare, August 29 and September 12, 1938, FOP.

44. FPO to *SLPD,* n.d. [1939] and William Henry Chamberlin, "Karl Marx, a Dis-

credited Prophet," undated clipping [1939], FOP. See also Chamberlin, "Karl Marx, The False Prophet," *American Mercury* 61 (January 1939): 60–68, and *Collectivism: A False Utopia* (New York: Macmillan, 1938).

45. Pells, *Radical Visions,* 67–69; Pfaff, *Pulitzer,* 210–13; and Markham, *Bovard,* 194–98.

46. *LN,* March 7, 1931, 2; F. W. Rehfeld to Victor Berger, June 7, 1919; Edwin Neudick to Victor Berger, August 16, 1920; John Hegel to Victor Berger, November 23, 1920; and Oscar Ameringer to Victor Berger, November 17, 1921, Berger Papers, Box 13; Victor Berger to Meta Berger, December 3, 1920, *The Family Letters of Victor and Meta Berger, 1894–1929,* Michael Stevens, ed. (Madison: State Historical Society of Wisconsin, 1995), 290–92; Letterbooks, Milwaukee Social Democratic Publishing Company, State Historical Society of Wisconsin, Box 1; and Ameringer, *If You Don't Weaken,* Introduction by James Green, xliii–xliv.

47. FPO, "I Stepped Out Last Night," January 23, 1934, FOP; FPO, "Twenty Years Lopped Off," *AG,* September 21, 1934; "Abundance for All," *AG,* December 30, 1938, 1; and Oscar Ameringer, *Abundance for All* (Oklahoma City: American Foundation for Abundance, 1939), 1.

48. Adam Coaldigger [Oscar Ameringer], "This Cock-Eyed World," *AG,* December 30, 1938, 4; *AG,* January 6, 1939, 4; Greg Mitchell, *The Campaign of the Century: Upton Sinclair's Race for Governor of California and the Birth of Media Politics* (New York: Random House, 1992), 109; Oscar Ameringer, *The Yankee Primer: Continental Congress Edition* (Oklahoma City: American Guardian, 1933); *AG,* January 13, 1939, 4; and Green, *Grass-Roots Socialism,* 413–14. On Shadid's career, see Alana Hughes, "The Road Once Taken: Socialist Medicine in Southwestern Oklahoma," Davis D. Joyce, ed., *An Oklahoma I Had Never Seen Before: Alternative Views of Oklahoma History* (Norman: University of Oklahoma Press, 1994), 145–61.

49. WEZ, *Mexico, 1936: Church, Land, Labor* (New York: Common Sense, 1937).

50. FPO to Ralph Korngold, May 13, 1939, and "Agreement between AFA and Frank O'Hare," April 1939, FOP.

51. FPO to Ralph Korngold, May 13, 1939, FOP; *SLPD,* May 12, 1939; Richard S. Kirkendall, *A History of Missouri,* William E. Parrish, ed., vol. 5, *1919–1953* (Columbia: University of Missouri Press, 1986), 182; and Steven Rosswurm, "Federal Bureau of Investigation," *Encyclopedia of the American Left,* 221–22.

52. FPO to Walter Gelhorn, n.d. [October 1939] and FPO, "A Proposed Solution For the Depression," FOP.

53. FPO to Walter Gelhorn, n.d. [October 1939]; FPO to Walter Thomas Mills, July 13, 1939; FPO to Flint Garrison, August 9, 1939; Ralph Fuchs to FPO, December 4, 1939; and FPO to Ralph Fuchs, n.d. [December 1939], FOP.

54. FPO to Ralph Fuchs, n.d. [December 1939] and FPO to Frank Lynch, July 9, 1939, FOP; "The Townsend Plan and Abundance-for-All," *AG,* June 16, 1939, 1; "O Hear Ye O'Hare!" *AG,* July 7, 1939, 2; George T. Pickett to FPO, July 24, 1939, FOP; and FPO, "Americanism," *AG,* June 30, 1939, 1.

55. WEZ, "The Philosophy of the AFA," *AG,* August 25, 1939, 1; "O Hear Ye O'Hare!" *AG,* September 22, 1939, 2; and "O Hear Ye O'Hare!" *AG,* September 15, 1939, 3.

56. FPO circular, September 5, 1939, FOP and FPO, "NACB Notes," *AG*, December 1, 1939, 3.

57. FPO to Gates, n.d. [November 1939], FOP. On "Ham and Eggs," see *Life Begins at Fifty: $30 a Week for Life* (Hollywood: Petition Campaign Committee, 1938); "Summary and Text of Retirement Life Payments Act" (San Francisco: Ham and Eggs for Californians, 1939); and Luther E. Eggertsen, *The Tragedy of "Ham and Eggs" in 1940* (Los Angeles: California Merchants Council, 1940).

58. Siegfried Ameringer to FPO, December 16, 1939, FOP; *AG*, November 17, 1939, 1; FPO to Upton Sinclair, February 7, 1940; FPO to WEZ, December 11, 1939; and Upton Sinclair to FPO, February 14, 1940, FOP; and "O Hear Ye O'Hare!" January 5, 1940, *AG*, 2.

59. FPO to WEZ, February 7, 1940, and WEZ to FPO, February 9, 1940, FOP.

60. FPO to WEZ, February 12, 1940, and WEZ to FPO, n.d. [February 1940], FOP.

61. FPO to Gene O'Hare, March 20, 1940; John Wall to FPO, April 6, 1940; and Siegfried Ameringer to FPO, February 8, 1940, FOP and *The AFA Organizer,* April 1940.

62. *The AFA Organizer,* May 1940 and "Report of Charles La Grave to the AFA Campaign Committee," April 1940 and FPO, Circular, n.d. [1940], FOP. Charlie McCarthy was the wisecracking dummy of ventriloquist and radio star Edgar Bergen.

63. John Wall to FPO (2), May 9, 1940; John Wall to FPO, April 25, 1940, and FPO to John Wall, May 6, 1940, FOP.

64. FPO to John Wall, May 10 and 11, 1940, FOP.

65. John Wall to FPO, May 21 and 27, 1940, FOP.

66. FPO to Bess Goldstein, October 4, 1941, FOP.

67. "O Hear Ye O'Hare!" *AG*, June 7, 1940.

68. FPO to Bess Goldstein, October 4, 1941, and FPO to Dick O'Hare, May 29, 1940, FOP.

69. FPO to Bess Goldstein, October 4, 1941; FPO to Dick O'Hare, May 29, 1940; and FPO to Upton Sinclair, February 7, 1940, FOP and FPO to Gene O'Hare, March 28, 1947, FOP (Pec).

7. *Gadfly and Sage, 1941–1960*

1. FPO to Bobbie O'Hare, n.d. [1942] and FPO to Margaret Sanger, January 6, 1956, FOP; RB to FPO, n.d., FOP (Pec); and Gene Peciulis to author, February 8, 1990.

2. FPO to the Boys, September 19, 1940; FPO to WEZ, March 25, 1941; FPO to Siegfried Ameringer, September 17, 1940; and FPO to Flint Garrison, November 20, 1940, FOP.

3. Records of the Federal Bureau of Investigation, Freedom of Information Act, File 100–1639 and FPO to Flint Garrison, October 10, 1940, FOP.

4. FPO to Roy Eilers, January 28, 1941 [*sic*, 1942] and FPO to Dick and Bobbie O'Hare, January 27, 1942, FOP.

5. FPO to Flint Garrison, May 17, 1941; FPO to Luther Ely Smith, September 7, 1941; FPO to Brown, November 23, 1942; and FPO to Dick O'Hare, May 12, 1941, FOP.

6. FPO to Luther Ely Smith, September 7, 1941, and FPO to Roy Estes, October 5, 1941, FOP.

7. FPO to Roy Eilers, January 28, 1941 [*sic,* 1942]; Rodney Bedell to Luther Ely Smith, September 24, 1941; Roy Eilers to FPO, January 27, 1942; FPO to Ed Witcoff, n.d. [1942]; and FPO to Dick Mason, June 15, 1943, FOP.

8. FPO to Wiley B. Rutledge, May 8, 1943; FPO to Dick Mason, June 15, 1943; "O'Hare Associates," n.d. [1942]; and "O'Hare and Associates," September 30, 1942, FOP.

9. FPO to Dick Mason, June 15, 1943; FPO to Rodney Bedell et al., January 28, 1944; FPO to Luther Ely Smith et al., March 22, 1945; and U.S. Department of Commerce, Patent Office, Appeal No. 7,723, *Ex parte* Frank P. O'Hare, January 8, 1947, FOP; Gene Peciulis to author, November 1, 1989; and FPO to Luther Ely Smith et al., September 17, 1945, and U.S. Department of Commerce, Patent Office, "In Re Application of Frank P. O'Hare," October 25, 1945, FOP.

10. FPO to C. Wright Mills, November 12, 1956; FPO to Victor O'Hare, January 15, 1955; and W. Stuart Symington to FPO, May 11 and 23, 1944, FOP. In light of O'Hare's experience, it is ironic that Senator Harry S. Truman had been so impressed with the efficiency at Emerson that, when he became president, he brought Symington to Washington for a series of assignments that launched the Missouri businessman's political career. See Ernest Kirschten, *Catfish and Crystal* (Garden City, N.Y.: Doubleday, 1960), 361 and Paul I. Wellman, *Stuart Symington: Portrait of a Man with a Mission* (Garden City, New York: Doubleday, 1960), 95–120.

11. FPO to Wiley B. Rutledge, May 8, 1943, FOP; *SLPD,* December 17, 1941; *SLPD,* December 7, 1941; FPO to H. Allen Smith, December 7, 1941, and FPO to Flint Garrison, December 25, 1941, FOP.

12. FPO to Eleanor Roosevelt, October 12, 1943, Eleanor Roosevelt Papers, Franklin D. Roosevelt Presidential Library, Hyde Park, N.Y., Box 1150; Roosevelt quoted in *SLPD,* October 12, 1943; and FPO to Thais Magrane Prescott, n.d. [1954], FOP.

13. FPO, "How Mass Production Got Its Start," *SLPD,* May 24, 1942, and FPO to Flint Garrison, August 13, 1942, FOP.

14. *SLPD,* August 11 and 22, and September 4, 1942.

15. FPO, "Father Reviews His Son's Book and Learns All About Plumbing," *SLPD,* July 31, 1943; FPO, "Tom Girdler Did Big Things, but Still Feels Frustrated," *SLPD,* September 27, 1943; FPO, "Red Army Both Defends Russia and Helps Educate Its People," *SLPD,* December 13, 1942; FPO, "Russian Tanks Go Into Action: A Superb Eye-Witness Account," *SLPD,* March 15, 1943; William L. O'Neill, *A Better World* (New York: Simon & Schuster, 1982), 59; FPO, "Sketches of the Men of the R.A.F., Glimpses of Anglo-Saxon Spirit," *SLPD,* July 30, 1942; FPO, "Eye-Witness of Dieppe Raid Thinks It Was Worth While, *SLPD,* February 25, 1943; FPO, "Prose Proves to Be Inadequate for Story of Air Super-Heroes," *SLPD,* September 20, 1943;

and Geoffrey Perrett, *Days of Sadness, Years of Triumph: The American People, 1939–1945* (New York: Coward, McCann & Geoghegan, 1973), 421–22.

16. *SLPD,* May 7, 1943, and FPO to editor, n.d. [May 1943], FOP.

17. *SLPD,* June 5 and 28, 1943, and FPO to editor, n.d. [June 1943], FOP.

18. *SLPD,* August 15, September 23, November 10 and 28, 1943. On the Melendes case, see *Time,* August 16, 1943, 22.

19. FPO, letter fragment, n.d. [1942], FOP; *DD,* April 3, 1944; and FPO to Wiley B. Rutledge, May 8, 1943, FOP.

20. *DD,* March 20 and April 3, 1944; Gene Peciulis to author, February 13, 1991; *SLPD,* February 19, 1934; Kirschten, *Catfish and Crystal,* 29; and FPO to Covington Hall, March 16, 1945, FOP.

21. Eugene O'Hare to FPO, March 4, 1944, and FPO to Eugene O'Hare, December 28, 1945, FOP. Eugene O'Hare's books are *How to Make Your Own Furniture* (New York: Harper, 1941) and *The Handbook for Home Mechanics* (New York: New Home Library, 1943).

22. Henry Blumberg to FPO, July 10 [1944], FOP (Pec) FPO to Henry Blumberg, July 1, 1944, FOP.

23. *DD,* May 1 and 29, July 24, and June 19, 1944.

24. *DD,* January 22, 1945; FPO, "Wisdom of an Arctic Explorer," *SLPD,* April 28, 1944; Vilhjalmur Stefansson, *The Standardization of Error* (London: K Paul, Trench, Trubner, 1928); and *DD,* May 1, 1944.

25. *DD,* October 9, 1944; Henry Blumberg to FPO, March 6, 1945, FOP (Pec); *DD,* September 11 and 25 and October 2, 1944; FPO to Henry Blumberg and Irene O'Hare, August 31, 1944, and Kathleen O'Hare to FPO, February 14, 1945, FOP.

26. FPO to Samuel Castleton, April 3, 1945, FOP; Henry Blumberg to FPO, April 4, 1945, FOP (Pec); FPO to Samuel Castleton, April 19, 1945, FOP; Henry Blumberg to FPO, April 21 and May 4 and 21, 1945, FOP (Pec); and *DD,* April 9, 1945.

27. *DD,* July 23 and May 21, 1945, and FPO to RB, n.d. [June 1945], FOP.

28. *SLPD,* May 27 and July 8, 1945; Primm, *Lion of the Valley,* 486–87; and Perrett, *Days of Sadness,* 422–23.

29. *DD,* August 27, September 10, August 6, September 24, and October 15, 1945.

30. *DD,* November 26, 1945, and FPO to A. James MacDonald, February 24, 1947, and April 11, 1948, FOP.

31. FPO, "Atomics," unpublished essay, April 8, 1946, FOP.

32. FPO to Joseph Pulitzer II, April 12, 1947; FPO to WEZ, June 6, 1947; FPO to Thad Snow, July 22, 1947; and FPO to Henry Blumberg, n.d. [1947], FOP.

33. FPO to WEZ, January 15, 1948; FPO to Dick O'Hare, January 13, 1948; and FPO to Lewis Lincoln, January 14, 1948, FOP.

34. FPO to WEZ, January 15, 1948, and WEZ to FPO, January 31, 1948, FOP; FPO to Will and Rose Propper, June 5, 1948, FOP (Pec); FPO to Ray Ginger, August 31, 1948, FOP; Shannon, *Socialist Party,* 192; and Bernard K. Johnpoll, *Pacifist's Progress: Norman Thomas and the Decline of American Socialism* (Chicago: Quadrangle, 1970; reprint, 1987), 290.

35. FPO to Walter Groth, June 1, 1948; FPO to Henry Blumberg, May 5 and 29,

1949; FPO to Margaret Sanger, January 6, 1956; and FPO, Mathematical mss., 1949, FOP.

36. FPO to Henry Blumberg, June 22, June, July 30, and June 23, 1949, FOP.

37. FPO to Luther Ely Smith, May 19, 1949, and FPO to the FBI, March 19, 1948, FOP.

38. FPO, "Kerry Patch—A Vivid Closeup," *SLPD*, February 13, 1949; FPO to Frank J. Swantner, April 17 and June 1, 1950, copies in author's possession; *SLPD*, March 6, 1949; and *DD*, June 20, 1950. The author is indebted to Alice L. Swantner for sharing her father's correspondence with Frank O'Hare.

39. *Saint Louis Argus*, June 16, 1950, and Bonita H. Valien, *The St. Louis Story: A Study of Desegregation* (New York: Anti-Defamation League, 1956), 3, 7–26.

40. FPO to Frank J. Swantner, April 8, 1951, copy in author's possession; *St. Louis Star*, March 22, 1950; *DD*, June 20, 1950; and Irving Dilliard, "The Boy from Kerry Patch," *SLPD*, October 23, 1960.

41. *DD*, June 20, 1950; and FPO to Ed Witcoff, August 9, 1950; FPO to Paul, n.d. [1952]; FPO to Solly Rosenbloom, July 30, 1950; and FPO to A. James McDonald, October 7, 1952, FOP.

42. FPO Mss, 1.

43. FPO Mss, 15 and FPO to A. James McDonald, October 7, 1952, and FPO to Harvey O'Connor, March 17, 1954, FOP.

44. FPO, "Can Mathematics Be Applied to Economics?" January 22, 1933, FOP and FPO, unpublished mss., March 17, 1951, FOP (Pec). For a summary of Marxian analysis of progress, see Tom Bottomore, "Progress," in Bottomore, ed., *Dictionary of Marxist Thought*, 39–40. For a contemporary analysis, written in the wake of the collapse of the Soviet Union and Eurocommunism, see Robert Heilbroner, "Does Socialism Have a Future?" *Nation*, September 27, 1993, 312–16.

45. *DD*, April 24 and May 1, 1951; Gene Peciulis to author, February 13, 1991; RB, unpublished manuscript, FOP (Pec); *DD*, July 3 and October 2, 1951; and U.S. Department of Justice, Federal Bureau of Investigation, St. Louis Office, File 100–1639. Only the index of O'Hare's St. Louis FBI file was released. The file itself was apparently destroyed in 1978.

46. FPO, "When Pigs Died Happy," *SLPD*, January 27, 1951; "Editor O'Hare and the River," *SLPD*, July 24, 1951; and Daniel W. Pfaff, *Pulitzer*, 301–2.

47. FPO to "Brother in X-to Rains," February 17, 1954, and Caroline Nations to Robert J. Blakely, April 27, 1951, FOP.

48. *DD*, October 30, 1951; "Dear Friends and Gentle Hearts," n.d. [April 1952] and FPO to WEZ, December 11, 1952, FOP; Caroline Nations to Gloria Pritchard, July 3, 1957, and FPO to Gloria Pritchard, December 1957, Papers of Gloria Pritchard, Western Historical Manuscript Collection, University of Missouri–St. Louis. On Missouri and the Red Scare in the early 1950s, see Ronald W. Johnson, "The Communist Issue in Missouri, 1946–1956," Ph.D. diss., University of Missouri, 1973, 125–85.

49. FPO to Victor O'Hare, January 24, 1953, and January 15, 1955, and FPO to Gene O'Hare, January 30, 1954, FOP. The financial arrangement with Kathryn

Reynolds lasted until her death in late 1958. See *St. Louis Globe-Democrat*, January 1, 1959.

50. FPO to Victor O'Hare, January 15, 1955, FOP; Telephone interview with Irving Dilliard, November 21, 1991; Irving Dilliard to author, December 2, 1991; Pfaff, *Pulitzer*, 314–20; and *SLPD*, January 16, 1953.

51. Telephone interview with Irving Dilliard, November 21, 1991, and *SLPD*, February 14, September 24 and 28, November 24 and 27, and December 16, 1956; February 21, August 7 and 21, 1957; July 13, 1958; and May 4, 1960.

52. FPO to Bobbie O'Hare, February 12, 1955, FOP.

53. FPO to Arthur Schlesinger, June 7, 1952, and Arthur Schlesinger Jr. to FPO, June 24, 1952, FOP; Max Eastman, "To Keep Our Freedom, Conflicting Interests Must Be Kept in Balance," *Reader's Digest* (June 1952), 133–34; and FPO to Walter Prescott Webb, December 25, 1952, FOP.

54. FPO to Cedric Belfrage, January 4, 1952; FPO to Leo Huberman, October 26, 1954, and January 13, 1955; FPO to Harvey O'Connor, March 17, 1954; and FPO to Leo Huberman, n.d. [1956], FOP.

55. FPO, letter fragment, n.d. [1954], FOP (Pec).

56. FPO to Margaret Sanger, January 6, 1956, and FPO to Theodore Lentz, January 1, 1957, FOP.

57. FPO to Anna Louise Strong, August 8, 1957, and "Extract from PROCEEDINGS OF THE SECOND INSTITUTE ON AGING, April 17, 18, 1953, Washington University, St. Louis, Missouri," FOP.

58. FPO to Anna Louise Strong, August 8, 1957, and FPO to Ralph, January 3, 1957, FOP; Gene Peciulis to author, February 28, 1991; and RB to FPO, January 3, 1956, FOP (Pec).

59. C. Wright Mills, *The Power Elite* (New York: Oxford University Press, 1956), 8–9, 274, 277, 287, 341–42, and 356.

60. FPO to C. Wright Mills, November 12, 1956, FOP and C. Wright Mills, "Comment on Criticism," in G. William Domhoff and Hoyt B. Ballard, eds., *C. Wright Mills and the Power Elite* (Boston: Beacon, 1968), 249.

61. Ralph Milliband, "C. Wright Mills," *Mills and the Power Elite*, 11 and FPO to Ray Ginger, June 24, 1949, FOP.

62. FPO to Irving Dilliard, April 12, 1956, FOP; FPO to Corliss Lamont, November 1956, FOP (Pec); and FPO to Tom Hennings Jr., June 2, 1957, FOP.

63. FPO to John McManus, August 9, 1957, FOP; FPO, "We Didn't Make Much Money but We Had a Lot of Fun," *American Socialist* 5 (March 1958), 17; and FPO, "Kids Know When Their Teachers Are BEGGARS," *Midwest Labor World*, April 15, 1958, 4.

64. FPO to Mrs. Louis Herbst, June 4, 1958; FPO to Dorothy Brockhoff, May 9, 1960; and FPO to "Dear Friend," May 12, 1960, FOP.

65. FPO to Irving Dilliard, November 6, 1959, FOP (Pec) and Telephone interview with Irving Dilliard, November 21, 1991.

66. FPO to Eugene, Berta, and Michael O'Hare, April 28, 1960; FPO to Irving Dilliard, May 5, 1960; and FPO to Wills Propper, n.d. [1959], FOP.

67. FPO to "Dear Friend," May 12, 1960, FOP.

68. Irving Dilliard, "The Boy from Kerry Patch," *SLPD,* October 23, 1960; FPO, Guest Book, FOP (Pec); RB to FPO, March 5 [c. 1950]; Missouri Division of Health, Death Certificate, July 18, 1960; *SLPD,* July 17, 1960, and August 3, 1969; and "Memorial Service for Frank Peter O'Hare," October 30, 1960, FOP.

Bibliographic Essay

While Frank O'Hare burned many of his and Kate's papers in early 1925 as an act of catharsis, he tried to make up for what he later regarded as a moment of madness by saving most everything from the last half of his life, including countless reminiscences of the early days. In the 1940s he began sending copies of his letters and essays to the Missouri Historical Society in St. Louis. After his death in 1960, his wife Irene donated more material to the society and gave other papers to Frank's great friend Gene Peciulis, who planned to edit a volume of O'Hare letters and essays.

Thirty of the forty-four boxes of material in the Frank O'Hare Papers consist of his correspondence files. There is only one box of letters from the period before 1925, which contains material saved by Gertie Petzold, Frank's half sister, and letters to and from the Debs family. The rest of the collection includes one box each of business files, undated correspondence and letter fragments, photographs, newspaper and magazine clippings, miscellaneous publications, the autobiography, and several boxes of essays.

Researchers using the O'Hare collection should proceed with customary caution. In his last few years, Frank's memory and his typing skills declined. His correspondence with immediate family, old comrades, historians of socialism (especially Ray Ginger, David Shannon, and Ira Kipnis), and his close friends (including Henry Blumberg, Roger Baldwin, Irving Dilliard, and William E. Zeuch) is especially remarkable for its candor and veracity, "the 'cream' of what I have to say," as O'Hare once put it. Time and again, this researcher was struck by how accurate Frank's anecdotes proved to be when compared independently with other sources. On the whole, his papers are a remarkable, and largely unappreciated, collection of information and opinions on the American Left during the first half of the twentieth century.

Information on Frank O'Hare was also found in other collections. The Papers of the Socialist Party of America at Duke University contain a few references and are available on microfilm. Especially valuable are Frank's letters to Otto Branstetter, which were part of a lengthy and disapproving report on the Children's Crusade of 1922. The SP collection at the State Historical Society of Wisconsin in Madison provides valuable background on the workings of the NEC. The small SP section in the Western Historical Manuscript Collection in the archives of the University of Missouri–St. Louis has a few references to O'Hare and furnishes useful information on the St. Louis local.

Some, but not all, of the correspondence between Frank O'Hare and the Debs family can be found in *Letters of Eugene V. Debs*, J. Robert Constantine, ed., 3 vols. (Urbana: University of Illinois Press, 1990). There are more letters in *Papers of Eugene V. Debs 1834–1945*, microfilm edition (Glen Rock, N.J.: Microfilming Corporation of America, 1983). The Morris Hillquit Papers (Madison: State Historical Society of Wisconsin, 1969, microfilm), and the Victor L. Berger Papers, Wisconsin State Historical Society, Madison, both have some material on the O'Hares and provide alternative perspectives on the Socialist party. There are letters from both Kate and Frank to their friend Alice Stone Blackwell in the National American Woman Suffrage Association (NAWSA) Papers, Library of Congress, Washington, D.C. There is also relevant material in the J. A. Wayland Collection, Axe Library, Pittsburg State University, Pittsburg, Kansas.

A wealth of material on Frank O'Hare's activities at New Llano Colony can be found in the University of Arkansas Libraries, Fayetteville, Arkansas, including the Richard W. St. John Collection, Newllano Colony Papers and William A. Gilbert Papers. The extensive "Notes" of Frank's good friend Fred Miner Goodhue, written in 1931, in the St. John Collection are particularly insightful.

Of course, there are no Kate O'Hare Papers. Frank O'Hare burned everything that he had, while some years later a young Communist at Commonwealth College incinerated what Kate had managed to save. Her first letters written to Frank and the children during her imprisonment are contained in *Kate O'Hare's Prison Letters* (Girard: Appeal to Reason, 1919). Following her release from prison, Kate, Frank, and Kathleen O'Hare bound up complete runs of the 122 letters for their friends as *"Dear Sweethearts": Letters from Kate Richards O'Hare to Her Family* (St. Louis: Frank O'Hare, 1920). Both the Missouri Historical Society and the State Historical Society of Missouri have copies. Meredith Tax's extensive interview with Kathleen O'Hare (July 4, 1971, New York) contains valuable information on the O'Hares' family life. In 1945, Samuel Castleton, one of Eugene Debs's attorneys, wrote to several old comrades, including both O'Hares, soliciting their memories and memorabilia of Debs for a biography. While the book was never written, the material he collected is in the Samuel Castleton Papers, Eugene V. Debs

Collection, Tamiment Library, New York. Kate's long letter to Castleton of September 16, 1945, is highly autobiographical. Two copies of a much longer autobiographical manuscript (which Frank read and labeled "impossible") are said to exist in the hands of a private individual, but are unavailable to scholars.

Frank O'Hare's first published bylines appeared in *Coming Nation* (Rich Hill, Missouri) in 1902–1903. He wrote for the *Chandler Daily Publicist* (Oklahoma) in 1904–1905. In 1907, O'Hare had printed *Frank P. O'Hare*, a four-page brochure that includes a thumbnail autobiography and favorable comments on his work from newspapers and Socialist comrades. Eager to spread the good news about Oklahoma, he penned "The Oklahoma Vote," *International Socialist Review* 9 (1909): 519–20. From 1911 to 1917, he was de facto editor of the *National Rip-Saw* of St. Louis, where he wrote a regular column, worked with Kate on feature articles, and composed the copy for the various *Rip-Saw* lecture programs. During this time, he developed a special interest in party organization, penning a series of short essays in the *Rip-Saw*; an article, "The Red Card Organization and State Election Law, *International Socialist Review* 12 (1912): 668–69; and a pamphlet, *Putting Socialism Across* (St. Louis: National Ripsaw, 1916). In their fight to keep the country out of the world war, the O'Hares wrote a play together, *World Peace* (St. Louis: National Ripsaw, 1915). While Frank left the *Rip-Saw* in early 1917, he continued to write unsigned articles and ghost-wrote at least one essay under his wife's byline for the *Rip-Saw's* successor, *Social Revolution*. Several institutions have microfilm copies of the *Rip-Saw*.

During Kate's imprisonment, O'Hare wrote almost everything that went into *Frank O'Hare's Bulletin* in 1919–1921, the most complete run of which is held by the New York Public Library. From 1920 to 1924, Frank O'Hare was the publisher of the new *National Rip-Saw* and its successor, *American Vanguard*, and made mostly unsigned contributions.

O'Hare contributed a regular column and wrote some of the copy for *Labor's News*, a weekly publication of Federated Press, in 1930–1931. He performed much the same function for *American Guardian* in 1939–1940 on behalf of "Abundance for All." Both of these weeklies are available on microfilm. In his last stint as a publisher, O'Hare did almost everything for *Dunkerdoings*, including most of the writing. It was published in 1944–1945 and 1950–1952. The O'Hare Papers contain a complete run and the State Historical Society of Missouri has a microfilm copy of most issues. Frank O'Hare's freelance articles include "The Clerkless Shop," *The Railway Clerk* (June 1932): 215–16; "We Didn't Make Much Money but We Had a Lot of Fun," *American Socialist* 5 (March 1958): 17; and "Kids Know When Their Teachers Are BEGGARS," *Midwest Labor World*, April 15, 1958, 4.

From 1929 to 1960, he wrote more than one hundred articles, book reviews, and letters to the editor that appeared in the *St. Louis Post-Dispatch*. The most memorable articles include "James Eads How Seen through Eyes of an Old Friend" (July 27, 1930); "The Rise and Fall of the Soap-Boxer" (August 24, 1930); "Manufacturing without Men" (August 17, 1931); "A Breadline View of New York City" (March 1, 1932); "How Mass Production Got Its Start" (May 24, 1942); "Kerry Patch—A Vivid Closeup" (February 13, 1949); and "When Pigs Died Happy" (January 27, 1951). His obituary appeared in the *Post-Dispatch* on July 17, 1960. Irving Dilliard's masterly tribute to FPO, "The Boy from Kerry Patch," was published on October 23, 1960.

As mentioned in the Introduction, one of the most daunting tasks in researching this book was recreating a fair cross section of Frank O'Hare's scrapbook of newspaper clippings chronicling his early fieldwork. *St. Louis Labor, Appeal to Reason, Coming Nation* (Rich Hill), and the *National Rip-Saw* contain much information on O'Hare's activities, including his speaking itineraries. OCLC, *United States Newspaper Program National Union List*, 4th ed. (Dublin, Ohio: OCLC Online Computer Library Center, 1993) was very useful in tracking down newspapers that might have covered an O'Hare appearance. And many did, especially in small- and medium-sized towns, and the many newspapers sympathetic to labor and the Left. Some newspapers followed an editorial policy of ignoring the activities of Socialist agitators. Others were glad to publish hostile reports.

Another way of tracking the O'Hares' movements, at least in the period from 1917 to 1921, is to examine the files of government agencies charged with spying on critics of American participation in the First World War. *Investigative Case Files of the Bureau of Investigation, 1908–1922*, Record Group 65 (Washington: National Archives and Records Service, 1982) is a valuable guide to the 955 rolls of microfilm available at the National Archives in Washington, D.C., and some research institutions. Reports from agents are listed in the index alphabetically by the name of the person or organization being investigated. There are records of the O'Hares in "Miscellaneous Files," German Aliens ("Old German Files"), and "Bureau Section Files." Material on the O'Hares also appears in U.S. Department of Justice, Record Group 60, Classified Subject Files and U.S. Post Office Department, Records of the Post Office Department, Record Group 28. See also *Surveillance of Radicals in the United States, 1917–1941* (Frederick, Md.: University Publications of America, 1984), microfilm.

If Frank O'Hare has been neglected by scholars in the past, the same cannot be said of his first wife, Kate Richards O'Hare. Begin with the full-fledged biography by Sally M. Miller, *From Prairie to Prison: The Life of Social Activist Kate Richards O'Hare* (Columbia: University of Missouri

Press, 1993). Neil K. Basen, "Kate Richards O'Hare: The 'First Lady' of American Socialism, 1901–1917," *Labor History* 21 (spring 1980): 165–99, gives Frank O'Hare his due as an important force in the Socialist party. There is much material on Frank in Philip S. Foner and Sally M. Miller, eds., *Kate Richards O'Hare: Selected Writings and Speeches* (Baton Rouge: Louisiana State University Press, 1982). FPO's concise biography of Kate appeared in *The Call Magazine* in February 1918 and *Social Revolution* in March 1918. For other articles on Kate O'Hare, see Miller's *From Prairie to Prison,* 241–42.

The biographies and autobiographies of other Socialist luminaries were important both for what they said and sometimes did not say about Frank O'Hare. Oscar Ameringer, *If You Don't Weaken*, Introduction by James Green (Norman: University of Oklahoma Press, 1983) makes no direct mention of Frank, as the two parted company on bad terms after the "Abundance" disaster. On Victor Berger, see Sally M. Miller, *Victor Berger and the Promise of Constructive Socialism, 1910–1920* (Westport, Conn.: Greenwood, 1973). The best biographies of Frank O'Hare's friend and hero, Eugene Debs, are Nick Salvatore, *Eugene V. Debs: Citizen and Socialist* (Urbana: University of Illinois Press, 1982) and Ray Ginger, *The Bending Cross* (New Brunswick: Rutgers University Press, 1949). Ginger found Frank and his Debsiana interesting enough that he spent a week camped out in the O'Hare living room. The work of George Herron, which influenced O'Hare during his early years, is examined in Robert T. Handy, "George D. Herron and the Social Gospel in American Protestantism, 1890–1901," Ph.D. diss., University of Chicago, 1949. On Morris Hillquit, see his autobiography, *Loose Leaves from a Busy Life* (New York: Macmillan, 1934) as well as a biography by Norma Fain Pratt, *Morris Hillquit: A Political History of an American Jewish Socialist* (Westport, Conn.: Greenwood, 1979). The best treatment of Norman Thomas is Bernard K. Johnpoll, *Pacifist's Progress: Norman Thomas and the Decline of American Socialism* (Chicago: Quadrangle, 1970; reprint, 1987).

While Frank and Kate O'Hare had their differences with the IWW, they remained on friendly terms with many Wobblies as individuals. See Ralph Chaplin, *Wobbly: The Rough-and-Tumble Story of an American Radical* (Chicago: University of Chicago Press, 1948); Elizabeth Gurley Flynn, *The Rebel Girl* (New York: International, reprint, 1982); Rosalyn F. Baxandall, ed., *Words on Fire: The Life and Writing of Elizabeth Gurley Flynn* (New Brunswick: Rutgers University Press, 1987); and William D. Haywood, *The Autobiography of Big Bill Haywood* (New York: International, 1983). The O'Hares also forged a bond of friendship with the anarchist Emma Goldman, *Living My Life,* Richard and Anna Maria Drinnon, eds. (New York: Meridian, 1977, reprint). The life of another anarchist that touched the lives of the O'Hares is examined in Roger A. Bruns, *The Damnedest Radical: The Life and World of Ben Reitman* (Urbana: University of Illinois Press, 1987).

Several scholarly treatments of the Socialist party either contain material on Frank O'Hare or provide valuable background. They are James Dombrowski, *The Early Days of Christian Socialism in America* (New York: Columbia University Press, 1936); Donald D. Egbert and Stow Persons, eds., *Socialism and American Life*, 2 vols. (Princeton: Princeton University Press, 1952); Howard H. Quint, *The Forging of American Socialism* (Indianapolis: Bobbs-Merrill, 1953); Ira Kipnis, *The American Socialist Movement, 1897–1912* (New York: Columbia University Press, 1952); David A. Shannon, *The Socialist Party of America* (New York: Macmillan, 1955); Bruce M. Stave, ed., *Socialism and the Cities* (Port Washington, N.Y.: Kennikat, 1975); James Weinstein, *The Decline of Socialism in America, 1912–1925* (New York: Vintage, 1969); Weinstein, *Ambiguous Legacy: The Left in American Politics* (New York: Franklin Watts, 1975); Irving Howe, *Socialism and America* (New York: Harcourt Brace Jovanovich, 1985); and Paul Buhle, *Marxism in the United States* (New York: Verso, 1991). See also Morris Hillquit, *History of Socialism in the United States* (New York: Dover, 1971).

The Socialist press is examined in John Graham, ed., *"Yours for the Revolution": The Appeal to Reason, 1895–1922* (Lincoln: University of Nebraska Press, 1990); Elliott Shore, *Talkin' Socialism: J. A. Wayland and the Role of the Press in American Radicalism, 1890–1912* (Lawrence: University of Kansas Press, 1988); and Joseph R. Conlon, ed., *The American Radical Press*, 2 vols. (Westport, Conn.: Greenwood, 1974). There is material on the O'Hares in Dee Garrison, ed., *Rebel Pen: The Writings of Mary Heaton Vorse* (New York: Monthly Review, 1985) and Emanuel Haldeman-Julius, *My Second 25 Years: Instead of a Footnote, an Autobiography* (Girard, Kans.: Haldeman-Julius, 1949). Federated Press is remembered in Jesse L. O'Connor, Harvey O'Connor, and Susan M. Bowler, *Harvey and Jesse: A Couple of Radicals* (Philadelphia: Temple University Press, 1988). On the mainstream *Post-Dispatch*, see James W. Markham, *Bovard of the Post-Dispatch* (Baton Rouge: Louisiana State University Press, 1954) and Daniel W. Pfaff, *Joseph Pulitzer II and the Post-Dispatch* (University Park: Pennsylvania State University Press, 1991).

Secondary works and documents on St. Louis in the late nineteenth and the twentieth centuries include James N. Primm, *Lion of the Valley: St. Louis, Missouri*, 2d ed. (Boulder: Pruett, 1990); Selwyn K. Troen and Glen E. Holt, eds., *St. Louis* (New York: Franklin Watts, 1977); Ernest Kirschten, *Catfish and Crystal* (Garden City, N.Y.: Doubleday, 1960); "Frank P. O'Hare to Mrs. Margretta Scott Lawler and Miss Mary Porter Scott," *Bulletin of the Missouri Historical Society* 20 (1963): 56–57; Julian S. Rammelkamp, "St. Louis in the Early 'Eighties," *Bulletin of the Missouri Historical Society* 19 (July 1963): 328–39; "When the Boer War Came to St. Louis," *Missouri Historical Review* 61 (April 1967): 285–302; Etan Diamond, "Kerry Patch: Irish Immigrant

Life in St. Louis," *Gateway Heritage* (fall 1989): 23–30; and Bonita H. Valien, *The St. Louis Story: A Study of Desegregation* (New York: Anti-Defamation League, 1956). On Missouri, see Gary M. Fink, "The Evolution of Social and Political Attitudes in the Missouri Labor Movement, 1900–1940," Ph.D. diss., University of Missouri, 1968; Richard S. Kirkendall, *A History of Missouri*, William E. Parrish, ed., vol. 5: *1919–1953* (Columbia: University of Missouri Press, 1986); and Ronald W. Johnson, "The Communist Issue in Missouri, 1946–1956," Ph.D. diss., University of Missouri, 1973.

For an overview of economic events that shaped O'Hare's formative years, see Martin J. Sklar, *The Corporate Reconstruction of American Capitalism, 1890–1916* (New York: Cambridge University Press, 1988). Frank's fascination with dime novels is made understandable by Michael Denning, *Mechanic Accents: Dime Novels and Working-Class Culture in America* (New York: Verso, 1987). On "Tayloring" in business, see Daniel Nelson, *Managers and Workers: Origins of the New Factory System in the United States, 1880–1920* (Madison: University of Wisconsin Press, 1975); Nelson, *Frederick W. Taylor and the Rise of Scientific Management* (Madison: University of Wisconsin Press, 1980); Samuel Haber, *Efficiency and Uplift: Scientific Management in the Progressive Era, 1890–1920* (Chicago: University of Chicago Press, 1964); and Kent Kreuter and Gretchen Kreuter, *An American Dissenter: The Life of Algie Martin Simons, 1870–1950* (Lexington: University of Kentucky Press, 1969). James W. Cortada, *Before the Computer: IBM, NCR, Burroughs, and Remington Rand and the Industry They Created, 1865–1956* (Princeton: Princeton University Press, 1993) put O'Hare's invention of an adding machine with a memory into historical perspective.

Oklahoma radicalism is examined by James R. Green, *Grass-Roots Socialism: Radical Movements in the Southwest, 1895–1943* (Baton Rouge: Louisiana State University Press, 1978); Howard Lynn Meredith, "A History of the Socialist Party in Oklahoma," Ph.D. diss., University of Oklahoma, 1970; James R. Scales and Danny Goble, *Oklahoma Politics: A History* (Norman: University of Oklahoma Press, 1982); Danny Goble, *Progressive Oklahoma: The Making of a New Kind of State* (Norman: University of Oklahoma Press, 1980); and Davis D. Joyce, ed., *An Oklahoma I Had Never Seen Before: Alternative Views of Oklahoma History* (Norman: University of Oklahoma Press, 1994).

The growing intolerance toward Socialists during the period of Preparedness and World War I is addressed in Robert H. Ferrell, *Woodrow Wilson and World War I, 1917–1921* (New York: Harper and Row, 1985); Philip S. Foner, *History of the Labor Movement in the United States*, vol. 6: *On the Eve of America's Entrance into World War I* (New York: International, 1982); Foner, *History of the Labor Movement in the United States*, vol. 7: *Labor and World War I* (New York: International, 1987); Peggy Lamson, *Roger Baldwin:*

Founder of the American Civil Liberties Union (Boston: Houghton Mifflin, 1976); Roger N. Baldwin, *The Reminiscences of Roger Nash Baldwin* (Glen Rock, N.J.: Microfilming Corporation of America, 1972); William Preston Jr., *Aliens and Dissenters: Federal Suppression of Radicals, 1903–1933* (New York: Harper and Row, 1963); H. C. Peterson and Gilbert C. Fite, *Opponents of War, 1917–1918* (Seattle: University of Washington Press, reprint, 1968); and Richard Polenberg, *Fighting Faiths: The Abrams Case, the Supreme Court, and Free Speech* (New York: Viking, 1987). President Wilson's part in the repression is documented in Arthur S. Link et al., eds., *The Papers of Woodrow Wilson*, 69 vols. (Princeton: Princeton University Press, 1967–1994). The Red Scare is analyzed in Robert K. Murray, *Red Scare: A Study in National Hysteria, 1919–1920* (Minneapolis: University of Minnesota Press, 1955); Philip S. Foner, *History of the Labor Movement in the United States*, vol. 8: *Postwar Struggles, 1918–1920* (New York: International, 1988); Burl Noggle, *Into the Twenties: The United States from Armistice to Normalcy* (Urbana: University of Illinois Press, 1974); and Peter H. Buckingham, *America Sees Red: Anticommunism in America, 1870s to 1980s* (Claremont, Calif.: Regina, 1988).

On the Kate O'Hare case, see *United States v. Kate Richards O'Hare*, Records of U.S. Attorney and Marshals, District of North Dakota, Record Group 118, National Archives, Kansas City; William E. Zeuch, *The Truth about the Kate Richards O'Hare Case* (St. Louis: Frank O'Hare, 1919); and J. Louis Engdahl, *Debs and O'Hare in Prison* (Chicago: Socialist Party, 1919), which contains an insightful interview with Frank O'Hare.

New Llano, Commonwealth College, and modern communalism have attracted the attention of a number of scholars and memorialists, including Wilbur S. Shepperson, *Retreat to Nevada: A Socialist Colony of World War I* (Reno: University of Nevada Press, 1966); Ernest S. Wooster, *Communities of the Past and Present* (New York: AMS, 1974, reprint); Henrik Infield, *Cooperative Communities at Work* (New York: Dryden, 1945); Fred Hanover, "Llano Cooperative Colony: An American Rural Community Experiment," MSW thesis, Tulane University, 1936; Paul K. Conkin, *Two Paths to Utopia: The Hutterites and the Llano Colony* (Lincoln: University of Nebraska Press, 1964); Robert V. Hine, *California's Utopian Colonies* (New Haven: Yale University Press, 1966); Edward K. Spann, *Brotherly Tomorrows: Movements for a Cooperative Society in America, 1820–1920* (New York: Columbia University Press, 1989); and William H. Cobb, "Commonwealth College Comes to Arkansas, 1923–1925," *Arkansas Historical Quarterly* 23 (summer 1964): 99–122. The best primary accounts are A. James McDonald, *The Llano Co-operative Colony and What It Taught* (Leesville, La.: privately printed, 1950); Raymond and Charlotte Koch, *Educational Commune: The Story of Commonwealth College* (New York: Schocken, 1972) and Kate Richards O'Hare, *Kuzbasing in Dixie* (New Llano: New Llano Publications, 1926).

The most useful work on the western panaceas of the 1930s is Greg Mitchell, *The Campaign of the Century: Upton Sinclair's Race for Governor of California and the Birth of Media Politics* (New York: Random House, 1992). On "Ham and Eggs," see *Life Begins at Fifty: $30 a Week for Life* (Hollywood: Petition Campaign Committee, 1938); "Summary and Text of Retirement Life Payments Act" (San Francisco: Ham and Eggs for Californians, 1939); and Luther E. Eggertsen, *The Tragedy of "Ham and Eggs" in 1940* (Los Angeles: California Merchants Council, 1940). Regarding "Abundance," see Oscar Ameringer, *The Yankee Primer: Continental Congress Edition* (Oklahoma City: American Guardian, 1933) and Ameringer, *Abundance for All* (Oklahoma City: American Foundation for Abundance, 1939).

Recent scholarly surveys of the Great Depression era include Michael E. Parrish, *Anxious Decades: America in Prosperity and Depression, 1920–1941* (New York: Norton, 1992); Robert S. McElvaine, *The Great Depression: America, 1929–1941* (New York: Times, 1984); and Richard H. Pells, *Radical Visions and American Dreams: Culture and Social Thought in the Depression Years* (New York: Harper and Row, 1973). For the home front during World War II, see, for example, Geoffrey Perrett, *Days of Sadness, Years of Triumph: The American People, 1939–1945* (New York: Coward, McCann & Geoghegan, 1973) and William L. O'Neill, *A Better World* (New York: Simon & Schuster, 1982). The last decade of Frank O'Hare's life is examined by David Halberstam, *The Fifties* (New York: Villard, 1993) and C. Wright Mills, *The Power Elite* (New York: Oxford University Press, 1956). Mills, in turn, is analyzed in G. William Domhoff and Hoyt B. Ballard, eds., *C. Wright Mills and the Power Elite* (Boston: Beacon, 1968).

Index